MW01252767

The Development of Managerial Culture

The Development of Managerial Culture

A Comparative Study of Australia and Canada

Arthur J. Wolak

First published 2015 by
PALGRAVE MACMILLAN

Palgrave Macmillan in the UK is an imprint of Macmillan Publishers Limited, registered in England, company number 785998, of Houndmills, Basingstoke, Hampshire RG21 6XS.

Palgrave Macmillan in the US is a division of St Martin's Press LLC, 175 Fifth Avenue, New York, NY 10010.

Palgrave Macmillan is the global academic imprint of the above companies and has companies and representatives throughout the world.

Palgrave® and Macmillan® are registered trademarks in the United States, the United Kingdom, Europe and other countries

ISBN: 978–1–137–47561–9 hardback

This book is printed on paper suitable for recycling and made from fully managed and sustained forest sources. Logging, pulping and manufacturing processes are expected to conform to the environmental regulations of the country of origin.

A catalogue record for this book is available from the British Library.

A catalog record for this book is available from the Library of Congress.

I dedicate this book to my mother Elizabeth, my brother Richard, and in memory of my father Dr. Edward Wolak. Without their encouragement in all of my endeavors, this book might never have been written.

To my wife Anna for her patience, and to my sons Jacob and Joshua for their inspiration. Though young now, they may one day read this book before traveling to Australia, helping them understand the underlying similarities yet intriguing differences from Canada. .

Contents

Figure and Tables

Figure

Tables

Acknowledgments

Although writing a book represents countless hours of solitary work, this volume would not have been possible without the encouragement of my mother Elizabeth and brother Richard during my years of research, and to my wife, Dr. Anna Wolak, for her personal interest during the completion of my manuscript, despite expecting our second child, Joshua, and the busy months following his birth. I would like to acknowledge my older son Jacob as he often had to wait for me to finish writing, editing, and proofreading before we could play ball or read a book together.

I must express my gratitude to my parents, Elizabeth and Dr. Edward Wolak, because their connection to Australia had sparked my early curiosity about the country, a place that was as far from my native Canada as one could get. Each had separately emigrated from Poland, marrying and residing in Sydney, Australia before migrating to Canada where my brother and I were born and raised. Given my parents' early ties to both Australia and Canada, combined with my subsequent years of study in psychology, history, business, and comparative management, my analysis of these managerial cultures became increasingly fascinating, challenging, and ever more relevant.

Having completed this work, I was intrigued to see my wife's reaction to my book. She had spent nearly a decade in Australia where she graduated from the medical school of the University of Adelaide followed by postgraduate training in Adelaide hospitals before immigrating to Canada. She found the insights contained in these pages highly significant as she reflected on her own experiences in Australian and Canadian work settings, realizing there were indeed discernible differences but without knowing the reasons for them. It had been in pursuit of these very reasons that I spent so many years investigating, which culminated in this book for the benefit of readers with similar curiosity.

I am particularly grateful to: Professor Robert Spillane, my doctoral supervisor at Macquarie University's Graduate School of Management in Sydney, for his enlightening discussions on Australian culture and history, thoughts on cross-cultural issues, and his subsequent advice on the publishing world; Dr. Hartmut J. Will, professor emeritus of the University of Victoria's Graduate School of Public Administration in Canada, and former visiting professor at the University of New

South Wales in Australia, for his helpful suggestions on navigating the complexities of doctoral studies.

I would like to thank the *Australasian Canadian Studies Journal* (ACS) and the *International Journal of Organizational Analysis* (IJOA) for their kind permission to reproduce and/or draw from my articles that were first published in their journals—"Australia's 'Irish Factor' as a Source of Cultural Difference from Canada" in ACS, and "Australian and Canadian Managerial Values: A Review" in IJOA. For the inclusion of Figure 4.1 and the content in Tables 5.1, 6.2 and 6.3, I would like to gratefully acknowledge permission from, respectively, Praeger, publisher of *Burnout Across Thirteen Cultures*; Oxford University Press Canada, publisher of *From Culture to Power: The Sociology of English Canada*; Routledge (Taylor & Francis Group), publisher of the journal, *Australian Historical Studies* (formerly, *Historical Studies of Australia and New Zealand*); and Dr. John Niland, author of *Collective Bargaining and Compulsory Arbitration in Australia*.

Last but not least, many thanks to Kiran Bolla and the team at Palgrave Macmillan for all of their advice and support.

About the Author

Dr. Arthur J. Wolak is president of CMI Chat Media Inc. He received his PhD in Management from Macquarie University, MGSM, Australia, and has published articles in *The International Journal of Organizational Analysis*, *The Australasian Canadian Studies Journal*, and *Reviews in Australian Studies*. He lives in Vancouver, Canada, with his wife Anna and their two sons, Jacob and Joshua.

Introduction

Australia and Canada are two nations poles apart geographically yet share many similarities in their founding and development. Despite their mutual Anglo-Celtic origins, these nations did not evolve into culturally identical societies. Obvious and subtle distinctions separate these two countries from each other. Differences include, though ultimately transcend, diverse geographies and climates, physical and psychological proximities to both the United Kingdom and the United States—reflecting Australia and Canada's unique relationships with these world powers—and the varied cultural influences of populations that settled in Australia and Canada early on in each country's history.

Many of those who arrived to Australia did not arrive by choice. They came as prisoners banished to Australian jails as punishment for various crimes. Many of those who arrived to Canada either fled from the United States out of loyalty to the British Crown, or migrated from Europe, by choice, to settle in a vast "new" land. Largely of Anglo-Celtic origin, these newcomers and their descendants exercised a profound effect on the development of each nation's evolving values and cultures.

In the late nineteenth century, Irish Catholic Australians coined the term "Anglo-Celtic" to assert their identity in Australian society. The term became widely used in Australia since the last quarter of the twentieth century in response to the rise of an official policy of multiculturalism and its focus on ethnic origin.[1] Although Anglo-Celtic collectively refers to people from all parts of the British Isles—English, Irish, Scottish, Welsh, Cornish and Manx—rather than those who emigrated

---

[1] K.S. Inglis, "Multiculturalism and National Identity," in *Australian National Identity*, ed. Charles A. Price (Canberra, ACT: The Academy of the Social Sciences in Australia, 1991), 21.

from continental Europe and elsewhere, Australian historian M.E.R. MacGinley asserts that the term served to incorporate "the Irish within the Celtic context, with its pervasive contribution to the emergence of a recognizable Australianism."[2]

While both Australia and Canada received substantial immigrants of Irish origin in their pre- and post-Federation periods (Confederation in the case of Canada), the Irish impact on Australia proved more powerful and enduring than on Canada, and as such, had a marked effect on Australian values and managerial cultures. In contrast, the influence of British culture, and the existence of a persistent (though diluted) class structure in Canada, exercised a stronger effect on the shape of Canadian values and management behavior. A relic of British cultural influence that endowed Protestants of largely English and Scottish origin with a higher social status, class structure concentrated power in the hands of societal elites.

As the establishment of British colonies and trading posts led to the expansion of the British Empire in the seventeenth century, the English language, along with British customs and methods of governing and managing, proliferated. Canada and Australia are two of the largest nations colonized by the British Empire. Its influence over the establishment and development of these two countries suggests that the impact on each nation would be similar, as would the existence of similar styles of management in the public and private sectors. History does not confirm this view.

Though geographically distant, Australia and Canada have much in common historically. Dependent on primary industries for export income, these small settler economies experienced British colonialism, displacement of aboriginal peoples, and eventual Federation/ Confederation. Since the latter half of the twentieth century, both had grown and developed through substantial immigration, fostering a strong sense of multiculturalism.

Despite these similarities, there are notable differences. Australia is an island continent with English as the dominant and single official language. Canada has English and French as two official languages with the majority of French speakers concentrated in Quebec, the result of French colonization in the sixteenth century. Canada shares a long common border with the United States, a nation of considerable

---

[2] M.E.R. MacGinley, "The Irish in Queensland: An Overview," in *The Irish Emigrant Experience in Australia*, ed. John O'Brien and Pauric Travers (Dublin, Ireland: Poolbeg Press, 1991), 103–4.

influence that also began as a collection of British colonies only to rebel against British rule to forge an independent federation a century and a half before Canada and Australia became freely associated members of the British Commonwealth in 1931. That year represented the first stage in the transformation of the British Empire into the Commonwealth of Nations when the Statute of Westminster officially recognized the independence and equal status under the Crown of these former dominions.[3]

Comparing Australia and Canada not only raises interesting questions concerning two contrasting cultures, but also reveals various influences on management as reflected by those in positions of authority, from community religious, labor and business leaders to political leaders. Considering the powerful influence of British colonial rule imposed on each country, similar administrative styles might be assumed to have prevailed. However, closer examination of the influence of each nation's historical development, sources of immigrants, and management/leadership styles, reveals noticeable differences. While common colonial origins unite these distant nations, contrasting histories, geographical settings, and immigration patterns shaped their experiences, perceptions, and leadership behavior. Cultural values are at the very core of these differences.

Australian and Canadian cultural dimensions

Developing countries dominated by larger powers, Australia and Canada were strongly affected by outside influences yet ultimately cultivated unique homegrown societies. While Australian organizations created and implemented new ideas and practices, no Australian management theory of world significance was derived from them.[4] Nevertheless, Australian psychologist, Elton Mayo, from his academic base at Harvard University, initiated what became the Human Relations Movement in organizational behavior, which transformed organizations in the

---

[3] Although the 1931 Statute of Westminster granted virtual independence to Canada, it was not until 1982 that the "Canada Act" was proclaimed and ratified by Queen Elizabeth II, which made Canada fully independent from Great Britain by giving Canada the right to amend its own constitution. Canada was the first colony given self-governing Dominion status in 1867; Australia was second in 1900; New Zealand, third, in 1907; and South Africa, fourth, in 1910.

[4] Anne McMahon and Nicholas Jans, "Organisation Behavior in Australia" in *Dynamics in Australian Public Management: Selected Essays*, ed. Alexander Kouzmin and Nicholas Scott (South Melbourne, VIC: Macmillan, 1990), 360–62.

United States, Australia, Canada and in many other parts of the world. His thinking derived much from his Australian upbringing. As a whole, however, Australian managers, much like those in Canada, tend to be very conservative. Organizing businesses in "traditional military-style hierarchies" that prevent workers from engaging in ongoing learning opportunities, Australian managers and employees had not changed much over the course of the twentieth century.[5]

Dutch social theorist Geert Hofstede describes Australian and Canadian managers as tolerant of small power distance, weak on uncertainty avoidance, yet individualist and masculine. Australia and Canada fall in the same quadrant of small power difference and high individualism as Ireland, Great Britain, and the United States.[6] These nations occupy a similar quadrant grouping on small power distance and masculine scales, weak uncertainty avoidance and strong masculine measures, and weak uncertainty avoidance-individualist measures.[7] While contemporary Australia asserts a distinct national identity, Australians are ultimately, as Jeremy Davis describes, "very similar to the 'Anglo culture' cluster from which the majority of the Australian population is so far drawn, certainly those working as managers," for, in Australia, it is this very cluster which "has tended to be the controlling influence over cultural transmission."[8]

A similar conclusion applies to Canada. In a study to discern how Canadian managers differ from Irish and Australian managers in Human Resource decision-making, researchers noticed a greater similarity between Australians and Canadians, but concede that Australian, Canadian, and Irish managers share more similarities than differences in their managerial behavior because of their common origins. Indeed, these managers had been immersed in Anglo-Celtic societies.[9] Although

---

[5] Russell D. Lansbury and Robert Spillane, *Organisational Behaviour: The Australian Context*, 2nd ed. (Melbourne, VIC: Longman Cheshire, 1991), 300–1.

[6] Hofstede, *Culture's Consequences: Comparing Values, Behaviors, Institutions, and Organizations Across Nations*, 2nd ed. (Thousand Oaks, CA: Sage, 2001), 217.

[7] Ibid., 299, 334, 249.

[8] J.G. Davis, "Australian Managers: Cultural Myths and Strategic Challenges," in *Australia Can Compete: Towards a Flexible Adaptable Society*, ed. Ian C. Marsh (Melbourne, VIC: Longman Cheshire, 1988), 108.

[9] Sudhir K. Saha, David O'Donnell, Thomas N. Garavan, and Stan Mensik, "An International Comparison of Managerial Values and HR Decision-Making: How are Canadian Managers Different from Irish and Australian Managers?," *Proceedings of the Eastern Academy of Management Conference* (San Jose, Costa Rica, 2001), "Managing in a Global Economy IX," in press, 3.

Table 1 Trompenaars and Hampden-Turner's Cultural Dimensions for Anglo Nations

Country	Percent showing Achieved Status[10]	Percent showing Inner-Directed Control[11]
Australia	60	88
Canada	65	79
USA	75	82
UK	56	77
Ireland	65	77

Source: Adapted from Fons Trompenaars and Charles Hampden-Turner, *Riding the Waves of Culture: Understanding Cultural Diversity in Global Business.* New York, NY: McGraw-Hill, 1998), 108, 148.

research remains inadequate in answering why human resource management practices differ from one country to another, personal values, shaped by discernible historical influences, have played a major role.

Dutch and English cultural theorists Fons Trompenaars and Charles Hampden-Turner collected data measuring the percentages of different national cultures responding to dilemmas to reveal their cultural dimensions. Table 1 shows the results for *achieved status* and *inner directedness* for Australia, Canada, the United States, the United Kingdom, and Ireland.

These scores show that Americans report the strongest attachment to achievement as a priority compared to the other countries. Australia scores below Canada (which tied with Ireland), indicating a lesser cultural focus on achievement in comparison with Canada and the United States. Those in the United Kingdom scored the lowest in this group.

Measurements of the predisposition toward "inner-directedness"—the feeling of control over one's own destiny (power from within) as opposed to the feeling of powerlessness (power from external sources)—also reveals differences among these Anglo nations. Australia scores the highest for inner-directedness, the United States second, with Canada scoring below, suggesting Canadians do not embrace this cultural dimension as strongly as Australians. The United Kingdom and Ireland scored the lowest in this group, but very close to Canada.

---

[10] Fons Trompenaars and Charles Hampden-Turner, *Riding the Waves of Culture: Understanding Cultural Diversity in Global Business* (New York, NY: McGraw-Hill, 1998), 108.
[11] Ibid., 148.

These results underscore subtle cultural distinctions between Australia and Canada, particularly in reference to the United States and UK/Ireland. Achievement appears to be a dominant concern among Americans, a preoccupation that Australians do not share to the same degree. Canadians fall in between, suggesting a measure of concern that could be the result of US geographical proximity. For the UK sample, achievement seems to be much less of a concern. Given Canada's historically close ties to England, it is no surprise that Canada would fall in between the United States and United Kingdom in its views on achievement. Likewise, and not surprisingly, Australians appear to be far more inner-directed than Canadians, who are less inner-directed than Americans. Not only does inner-directedness indicate differences among Australians, Canadians, and Americans—accounting for robust individualism in Australia and the United States—but also a significant difference between Australians and Canadians. In other words, Canadians possess divergent values-based views than Americans despite close geographical location.[12]

How can these differences be explained? Though Australian and Canadian managers share similarities with their British, American and Irish counterparts—representing cultures that Hofstede says are firmly rooted in strong individualism and masculinity, weak power distance between managers and subordinates, and tolerance for uncertainty—these do not explain why Australia's and Canada's respective cultures might have developed as they have. Cultural values are indeed a fundamental element, which the work of Trompenaars and Hampden-Turner attests.

To evaluate the impact of societal values on management/leadership behavior, immigrant groups must be considered for they introduced and helped perpetuate those values in their respective new societies. Historical and political developments, geographical place, climatic conditions, and political, cultural and economic proximity to the United Kingdom and United States are also important to consider for their help in shaping each culture.

Hofstede, Trompenaars and Hampden-Turner, among others, emphasize differences separating national cultures. They also reinforce the importance of culture as a phenomenon that reflects the meanings people attach to various aspects of life, including their worldview, as evident in societal institutions and private organizations. The effect of culture is also evident in management style.

---

[12] According to Hofstede's survey, the Individualism (IDV) index score is 91 for the United States, 90 for Australia, and 80 for Canada. Hofstede, *Culture's Consequences*, 215, Exhibit 5.1.

Personal values are at the very core of each culture. The meaning that individuals give to organizations, their concept of organizations' structures, practices and policies, is culturally defined because, Hofstede asserts, "culture is a shared system of meanings" dictating what people pay attention to, how they act and what they value.[13]

The concept of culture, though highly complex, is a powerful determinant of behavior. "Culture is beneath awareness in the sense that no one bothers to verbalize it, yet it forms the roots of action," affirm Trompenaars and Hampden-Turner who argue that "Culture is manmade, confirmed by others, conventionalized and passed on for younger people or newcomers to learn," while providing individuals with a "meaningful context in which to meet, to think about themselves and face the outer world."[14] However, culture is not a physical object that can be easily probed and tested.

Culture's outer layer of observable products, from language, food choices, to ways of life, are symbolic of a deeper level of culture that reflects norms—the sense among a group of who belongs, what is "right" and "wrong"—and values, a group's ideals which help determine group norms and behavior.[15] According to Trompenaars and Hampden-Turner, culture "is made by people interacting, and at the same time determining further action."[16] These ideas suggest that Australian and Canadian behavior is indeed linked to the respective culture, but also that each culture reflects important underlying and enduring values.

Values refer to pleasures, interests, preferences, likes, duties, moral obligations, wants, needs, desires, aversions and attractions, and many other manners of selective orientation.[17] In other words, values are standards of desirability, and such standards determine social norms. While different kinds and levels of values compose a cultural value system, each culture has a distinctive value system that influences the behavior of its members. Although each society possesses diverse value sets of groups and individuals that vary according to age, gender, personality, and social role, it is still possible to abstract from these diverse sets the general value system of large and complex socio-cultural entities, such

---

[13] Ibid., 13.
[14] Trompenaars and Hampden-Turner, *Riding the Waves of Culture*, 24.
[15] Ibid., 21–22.
[16] Ibid.
[17] Stephen C. Pepper, *The Sources of Value* (Berkeley, CA: University of California Press, 1958), 7.

as a people or a nation. Not only does the behavior of Australian and Canadian managers reflect their cultural values, but their respective values arise from complex influences derived from historical developments. These include the influence of immigrants and their respective geopolitical realities, especially their evolving relationship with the British Crown and the United States, the twentieth century's fastest rising power on the world stage.

While Australia's key geopolitical reality is its remote location far removed from Europe and North America, the most significant geopolitical influence for Canada is its shared border with the United States. Although cultural influences can be transmitted over vast distances, the border that separates Canada from the United States is not only symbolic of Canada's desire for political independence but also its wish for cultural independence. From the mid-nineteenth century through the present, the United States grew and developed into a strong global economic, political, military, and cultural power with the very real potential to consume Canada—a smaller nation in population if not in area—and stifle the development of its own separate cultural identity.

Australia's Irish factor

Cultural evolution brought about by colonial rule, immigration, and the rise of American dominance from the late nineteenth through the twentieth centuries affected Australian and Canadian values and managerial behavior in diverse and subtle ways. While acknowledging the impact of British influence on both Australia and English Canada, the Irish—particularly Irish Catholics—had a strong influence on the development of Australian culture, behavior and values, an influence far less pronounced in Canada. While English Canada—regions historically governed by British colonists, as opposed to the unique cultural identity in French Canada concentrated in the province of Quebec—tended to cling more strongly to British colonial values to assert a "Canadian identity" in reaction to the increasing dominance of its powerful neighbor to the south, French Canada appears to have remained more closely aligned with the values of France and other Latin-influenced cultures.[18]

---

[18] Quebec's cultural and value ties to France and the Latin world, and Quebec's unique position as a cultural intermediary between Anglo and Latin worlds, is discussed extensively in Carolyn P. Egri, David A. Ralson, Cheryl S. Murray, and Joel D. Nicholson, "Managers in the NAFTA Countries: A Cross-Cultural

Studies suggest that Australians and Canadians are distinguishable from one another.[19] Canadians are more deferential to authority and relatively more concerned with achievement than Australians, while Australians are more cynical about authority, emphasize social egalitarianism more, and are more "inner directed" than Canadians.

Trompenaars and Hampden-Turner's relative measures of inner-directedness and achievement (Table 1) suggest that Canadians' greater deference to authority could reflect a relative lack of inner-directedness compared to Australians, whose interest in individual achievement is less valued but may be more survival-oriented due to the oppressive heat of Australia. Although Canadians are relatively more concerned with achievement than Australians—evident in Canadians' desire to fit into an existing social hierarchy—this concern is not shared by Australians who prefer to achieve on their own terms. In the Canadian context, a person is marginalized if he or she does not fit in somewhere along the established social milieu or dominant sociopolitical hierarchy.

Why such differences exist and what contributed to the development of such cultural values are important questions that require answers. American and British influences, whether geographical, cultural, economic, or political, have had a practical impact on each culture. However, the key source differentiating Australia from Canada is the "Irish factor."

* * *

Although Australian and Canadian history is similar in many respects, common British colonial origins suggest that Australia and Canada should be more similar than they actually are. Differences in underlying values confirm cultural distinctions. While Australia and Canada both received substantial immigrants of English, Scottish, and Irish origin in their pre- and post-federation periods, the Irish impact on Australia appears to have been more powerful and enduring than on Canada, and consequently had a marked effect on shaping Australian values and management behavior.

Comparison of Attitudes Toward Upward Influence Strategies," *Journal of International Management* 6, no. 2 (2000): 154–55.

[19] For an analysis and comparison of several research studies, *see* Arthur Wolak, "Australian and Canadian Managerial Values: a Review," *International Journal of Organizational Analysis* 17, no. 2 (2009): 139–59.

Unlike Australia, the Irish were not a prominent factor in Canada since Irish Catholic migration to Canada was not merely less than in Australia, but was less spread out geographically. For instance, while many Irish settled in Newfoundland and Labrador on the Atlantic coast, the British colony did not become a province of Canada until 1949. Although Irish-Catholic immigration to the United States was substantial for ideological, economic and social reasons, the impact was not as pervasive as in Australia because Irish immigration to the United States was less concentrated than to Australia. Irish migration to America occurred in large waves that included other European immigrants. Australia, unlike Canada, saw substantial Irish immigration relative to other European settlers, which left a distinctive cultural mark.

Lacking Australia's powerful Irish factor for its cultural and sociopolitical development, Canada derived its values and business culture primarily from the British mercantile and colonial tradition, perpetuated by subsequent British migration and retention of British values. This pattern proved influential and enduring, and had a pronounced effect on Canadian values and management behavior. First, a strong Irish Catholic influence, associated anti-English sentiments, and a robust working class ethos had a profound impact on Australia's cultural development. Second, a strong British influence, subtle anti-American sentiments (sociologically, politically, militarily and economically) led English-speaking Canada—more intensely influenced by the mores of English, Scottish, and Irish Protestants—to embrace a greater pro-British position, thereby also asserting an independent Canadian identity. Differing cultural values helped shape each society and, therefore, had an important impact on the development of managerial practice and professionalism in Australia and Canada.

Differences stem from Australia's more vigorous cultural opposition to English rule and traditions compared to Canada, especially due to Irish influence on the development of Australian culture during its formative period in the nineteenth century. English Canada was more embracing of English colonialism, likely intended as a means to preserve its distinctiveness against the growth of American cultural, political, and economic power, thus clinging tightly to its English colonial heritage in support of its independent identity. Australian and Canadian managerial culture therefore experienced a different evolution based on different cultural circumstances.

1
Culture and Values

When considering national characteristics, individual idiosyncrasies should never be confused as representative of the society or its general culture as a whole.[1] While societies reflect different personalities at the individual level, the most common in a particular nation tends to approximate its national character. Dimensions of culture advanced by Hofstede, Trompenaars, and Hampden-Turner, among others, prove helpful in making assessments among different cultures at the macro level—for example, comparing Australia and Canada—more so than analyzing trends at the micro level, such as cities like Sydney and Melbourne or Toronto and Vancouver, though geographical distinctions are often evident even at this level.

Values are arguably at the root of national character. But in order to discern which values, cultural differences that separate Australia from Canada are crucial to consider because the large cohesive Irish population in Australia and the achievements and influence of leaders of Irish descent represent powerful influences on Australian managerial culture, more so than in Canada.

Discerning the Irish from the British

Non-British European immigrants represented a very small minority in nineteenth-century Australia and Canada. Among colonists, the English were the largest in number, and, therefore, English ideas and

---

[1] Dean Peabody, "Nationality Characteristics: Dimensions for Comparison," in *Personality and Person Perception Across Cultures*, ed. Yueh-Ting Lee, Clark R. McCauley, and Juris G. Draguns (Mahwah, NJ and London, UK: Lawrence Erlbaum, 1999), 65.

customs provided these new and developing nations their primary characteristics. Excluding the unique position of the French province of Quebec, it was English—not any of the Celtic languages of the British Isles—that became the dominant language of Australia and Canada. Likewise, it was English Common Law, not the separate and distinctive law of Scotland, that formed the basis of Australian and Canadian law (with Quebec, once more the singular exception, favoring the Civil Law tradition). However, in Australia, observes English-born Australian academic Geoffrey Partington, "The English majority dissolved into unhyphenated Australians even more quickly than the minorities."[2]

Others from the British Isles found their way to Australia and influenced the country, but not in the same manner as the English and Irish. While the Welsh contributed to Australian culture, the impact did not vary significantly from the contributions made by those from London, Cornwall, and North or East Anglia, whereas the Scots, asserts Partington, "typically took a little longer to dissolve and were highly prominent, especially in business and the professions, in all of the Australian colonies, but they had no distinctive political or ideological program."[3] However, due to the events taking place in Ireland and the domestic issues in Australia, such as the lack of funding of Roman Catholic schools, a substantial number of Roman Catholic Irish in Australia retained their identity as "Irish-Australians" and held on to a distinctive program to a much greater extent than the other settler populations.[4]

The Irish dynamic differed in Canada. While the Irish represented the single largest immigrant group in nineteenth-century Canada, most came prior to the Great Potato Famine. Fewer than half of the 450,000 Irish emigrants who arrived in British North America between 1825 and 1845 were Catholic, and among the Protestant majority most were Anglican.[5] Moreover, the Irish who came to Canada in the nineteenth century, much like the English and Scottish immigrants of that era, did not find a fully developed society, and, therefore,

---

[2] Geoffrey Partington, *The Australian Nation: Its British and Irish Roots* (New Brunswick, NJ: Transaction Publishers, 1997), xviii.

[3] Ibid.

[4] Ibid.

[5] Franca Iacovetta, "The Irish in Nineteenth-Century Canada: Class, Culture, and Conflict," in *A Nation of Immigrants: Women, Workers, and Communities in Canadian History, 1840s–1860s*, ed. Franca Iacovetta, Paula Draper, and Robert Ventresca (Toronto, ON: University of Toronto Press, 1998), 3.

observes Canadian historian David Wilson, "In the half-century before Confederation, English Canada was a highly malleable cultural entity, within which the Irish, English, and Scottish shared the basic assumptions that English was the language of everyday life and that some form of the British tradition of representative government was desirable."[6] The Irish, English, Welsh, and Scottish "worked out a kind of mutual cultural accommodation, with each group contributing to and drawing from the economic, social and cultural characteristics of the others," asserts Wilson, and helped found the greater society into which subsequent immigrant groups would acculturate during the twentieth century.[7]

Before considering the Irish contribution to national identity and culture in greater depth, the Irish need to be discerned from others who left the British Isles to settle in Australia and Canada, in order to account for their impact on managerial culture and values. While there is no single proper definition of "Irishness," Irish psychoanalyst Bea Gavin observes that the word embodies a "shared sense of history, a common language, music, humour and the experience of large-scale emigration."[8]

Despite the multilayered complexity, Irish Catholic influence is apparent in the Australian setting. While Irish Catholics perceived themselves to be the original dwellers of Ireland, Protestants represented the English and Scottish colonists who came to Ireland when it was under the rule of the British; hence, in the words of Canadian historian Peter Toner, it has become "common practice to refer to Irish people as either Catholic or Protestant," even though "religion itself has never been much more than the easiest determinant of a group affiliation that consists of many factors."[9]

While Irish Protestants blended more easily into Australia's ruling British society, Irish Catholic assimilation was less prevalent, leading to a strong, independent voice in Australia. "Whereas much Irish national culture may be assimilated, this cannot be the case with Catholicism, as no one would seriously argue that Catholicism can be assimilated

---

[6] David A. Wilson, *The Irish in Canada* (Ottawa, ON: Canadian Historical Association, 1989), 14.

[7] Ibid.

[8] Bea Gavin, "A Sense of Irishness," *Psychodynamic Counselling* 7, no. 1 (2001): 87.

[9] Peter M. Toner, "Irish," in *The Canadian Encyclopedia: Year 2000 Edition*, ed. James H. Marsh (Toronto, ON: McClelland & Stewart, 1999), 1,190.

into Protestantism," explains Australian Irish historian Colm Kiernan. "If Catholicism in Australia is ethnicity, that opens the way to a significant ethnic presence, in that from early times there have been Catholic churches and Catholic schools in Australia."[10] Irish Catholics did indeed retain a strong identity that had a profound impact on Australia's cultural identity.

In Canada, Irish Protestants stressed the importance of the "British connection" to facilitate distance between them and their "Catholic compatriots," asserts Toner, since "both groups were rich in cultural traditions, but with significant differences," notably the Irish Catholic tendency to "keep alive traditions of being Irish," whereas the Protestants generally glorified "their contributions to British civilization."[11] This was not limited to Irish Protestants or the English in Canada's evolving society, since the significant Scottish population also proved a powerful force in helping forge a strong and enduring connection to Britain as a distinctive source of Canadian identity.

In large part, it was the Presbyterianism spread by Scottish Protestant clergyman John Knox that helped create the character of the disciplined Scot who contributed so greatly to the corporate life of Canada. In comparisons made between the composition of the Canadian "elite" and the general Canadian population, Canadian sociologist John Porter observed that of the various "Protestant groups the Anglican church had the greatest representation," but the Scottish "Presbyterian church was also over-represented."[12] The Canadian elite, largely comprising of Canadians of English and Scottish descent, reflected and helped perpetuate Canada's national character, which owed so much to preserving some of the most important aspects of the British cultural identity.

As the analysis of such notable Australian historians as Russel Ward and Patrick O'Farrell suggests, Australia's national character appears to have been the product of a plethora of influences including Irish, Roman Catholic, convict, and British working class that melded into a collective Australian identity. Even the trade unions and the Australian

---

[10] Colm Kiernan, "Introduction," in *Ireland and Australia*, ed. Colm Kiernan (Dublin, Ireland: Mercier Press, 1984), 5.

[11] Toner, "Irish," 1,190.

[12] John Porter, *The Vertical Mosaic: An Analysis of Social Class and Power in Canada* (Toronto, ON: University of Toronto Press, 1965), 290.

Labor Party (ALP) played a critical role.[13] However, Irish Catholics were always prominent in the ALP, and labor factionalism had a sectarian aspect to it.

The antagonism between Catholics and Protestants was a regular feature of social and political life from at least the 1860s through the 1920s, with its effects felt well into the 1960s. "A predisposition to sectarianism came to Australia in the mental baggage of many migrants," observes Australian historian Mark Lyons. "For Protestants of fundamentalist or evangelical faith, particularly those from the north of Ireland, Catholicism was not only an erroneous and superstitious creed, but one whose adherents actively sought to force Protestant nations back under the rule of Rome."[14] However, given that attitudes of many Catholics had been shaped by the popular movement for Irish independence since the mid-nineteenth century, combining religion and nationalism into a unified identity, clashes with Protestants were inevitable, with the consequence being the preservation of a distinct Irish Catholic identity that helped shape Australia's character. By the early twentieth century, a significant number of Catholics turned to the ALP, thus forging an important political–cultural link that endured for decades.[15]

Proposing that the Irish played a huge role in the development of the Australian identity does not minimize the impact of other ethnic communities to the development of Australia or Australian culture. Rather it reflects the predominant character of Australia, pointing to a strong Irish influence that makes this observation appropriate. For instance, the Scots, notes Australian historian Malcolm Prentis, certainly made a significant contribution to Australia, having "been prominent in pastoral pursuits, politics, poetry and education."[16] However, their influence on the Australian personality is less pronounced.

Although settler societies in both Australia and North America were primarily Protestant, strong Roman Catholic minorities, particularly Irish, were present. Thus, the Irish, especially Irish Catholics, exercised a robust influence on Australia as it grew and developed under English rule. The Irish in Australia proved to be extremely successful. "From

---

[13] Malcolm D. Prentis, *The Scots in Australia: A Study of New South Wales, Victoria and Queensland, 1788 to 1900* (Sydney, NSW: Sydney University Press, 1983), 1.

[14] Mark Lyons, "Sectarianism," in *The Oxford Companion to Australian History*, ed. Graeme Davison, John Hirst, and Stuart Macintyre, rev.ed. (South Melbourne: Oxford University Press, 2001), 583.

[15] Prentis, *The Scots in Australia*, 1.

[16] Ibid., 2.

poor beginnings as transported convicts, many of them have risen to achieve the highest positions in Australia," observes Kiernan, with the primary reason for their success being that in Australia, "those who might have blocked their way were disorganized."[17] In contrast, while the French remain the largest Catholic "minority" in Canada, their influence appears to have been mostly confined to the province of Quebec and neighboring regions where their population centers have remained historically the largest.

Quebec's uniqueness was the consequence of a sequence of intentional government actions. In 1763, following the Seven Years' War with France, Great Britain issued a *Royal Proclamation* that, among other things, established government in the former French colonies, Quebec among them; in 1774, Great Britain passed the *Quebec Act* guaranteeing Quebec residents the freedom to practice Catholicism, restoring French Civil Law for private legal matters while English common law remained in force for such public matters as criminal law; in 1791, the *Constitution Act* divided Quebec into two political entities—a primarily French-speaking Lower Canada and English-speaking Upper Canada. In 1840, the *Act of Union* combined Upper and Lower Canada into a singular "Province of Canada," until the *British North America Act* of 1867 established Canadian Confederation, expanding the number of provinces and calling the result, the "Dominion of Canada."[18]

However, many among the *Québécois* argued that Quebec was not merely a province like any other but, as a unique culture typified by the use of a language other than English, Quebec was more like a nation unto itself. As a result, notes Canadian historian John Saywell, "it was argued that within the federal system, Quebec should have 'special status,' with vastly increased powers over the economy and social policy and a much larger slice of the tax pie to pay for them. Some nationalists went further and argued that the only solution to Quebec's place in the Canadian federal state was, in fact, to separate and form an independent state."[19]

The Quebec independence movement has proven highly contentious in Canada, with the need for secession to preserve unique French cultural attributes deemed unnecessary by many Canadians, including a

---

[17] Kiernan, 7.

[18] For a review of key dates in Canadian constitutional history, *see* Adam Dodek, *The Canadian Constitution* (Toronto, ON: Dundurn, 2013), 145–47.

[19] John Saywell, *Canada: Pathways to the Present* (Toronto, ON: Stoddart Publishing, 1999), 89–90.

substantial number of French-speaking residents of Quebec. Yet, in many ways, English Canada is as distinct from French Canada as Australia is distinct from Canada despite common origins. However, in the latter case, the Irish are the major source of differentiation between Australia and Canada.

While Great Britain exported to many of its colonies some of the better ideals and institutions, such as justice, freedom of inquiry, and a free press from which Americans and Canadians prospered, and which the Anglo-Celts could proudly praise, the first settlement of Australia served primarily as a jail for convicts. Instead of freedom, Kiernan notes, "its opposite, autocracy and its institutions," such as jails, "the lash, chains and bars, were exported to Australia, the unattractive side of British culture," leaving Anglo-Celtic Australians "with nothing to defend." Whether the Irish came as convicts or as free immigrants later on, the Irish were not likely to be impressed by Britain's empire in Australia.[20]

Since the Irish in Canada tended not to oppose close ties to Britain, the word "Irish" acquired a Catholic connotation from the mid-eighteenth century onward. The reason, Toner observes, is because the Catholic Church, "the institutional bedrock of the Catholic Irish community in Canada, laboured to gain acceptance for its people, which meant that Irish priests and bishops were often opposed to any manifestations of sympathy for nationalism in Ireland."[21] However, for the Irish in the United States—and Australia for that matter—there was no such predicament, asserts Toner, "because there it was possible to be a good Irishman, a good Catholic and a good American"—as it was to be a good Australian—but within Canada, "where citizenship remained British for so long, it was extremely difficult to be Irish politically and a good citizen as well."[22] Consequently, Australia and Canada gave rise to dissimilar environments where the Irish influence was felt in a different way.

Discerning English from French Canada

Although Australia and Canada are situated within the "Anglo cluster" of countries, the nation of Canada—as opposed to Australia which was

---

[20] Kiernan, 6–7.
[21] Toner, 1,191.
[22] Ibid.

founded by the English—was established by two distinct geographically based cultural groups, the English and the French.[23]

Modern remnants of the British Empire, the Anglo cluster, consists of Australia, Canada, England, Ireland, New Zealand, (White) South Africa, and the United States. Since the cultural values of the English have spread across the globe, today the Anglo cluster includes some of the most progressive and strong democratic economies in the developed world. "Central to this development has been Judeo-Christian values, the sense of secular tolerance introduced by Oliver Cromwell in the seventeenth century, a strong legal infrastructure, and naval control of the high seas," the researchers, Ashkanasy *et al.* assert, and "these values underlie all the countries of the Anglo Cluster, giving them a sense of confidence and power hitherto unknown in history."[24]

Hence, while Australia maintains English as its single *de facto* language, Canada includes both English and French as official languages, enshrined in law by the *Official Languages Act, 1969*, amended in 1988 to protect official language minority rights even further.

Unlike the rest of Canada, the province of Quebec was established as a French colony, in which French remains the language used by the majority of Quebec residents, and where cultural differences remain important, reflecting the dominant religious affiliation of the population, its writers, musicians, and legal system. The October 1995 provincial referendum on the question of Quebec separation from the rest of Canada typifies the significant cultural differences between Quebec's French speakers and English speakers. Although the result of the 1995 Quebec referendum was (by a very small margin) in favor of remaining part of Canada, similar to the outcome of the 1980 Quebec

---

[23] The Global Leadership and Organizational Behavior Effectiveness (GLOBE) international research program divides more than sixty countries around the world into one of ten clusters intended to describe, understand, and predict the impact of particular cultural variables on organizational processes, leadership, and the effectiveness of each. These countries are grouped according to various geographical or linguistic headings, such as South Asia, Anglo, Arab, Germanic Europe, Latin Europe, Eastern Europe, Confucian Asia, Latin America, Sub-Sahara Africa, and Nordic Europe. GLOBE examines national cultures in terms of nine dimensions. *See* Robert House, Mansour Javidan, Paul Hanges, and Peter Dorfman, "Understanding Cultures and Implicit Leadership Theories Across the Globe: An Introduction to Project GLOBE," *Journal of World Business* 37, no. 1 (2002): 5–6.

[24] Neal M. Ashkanasy, Edwin Trevor-Roberts, and Louise Earnshaw, "The Anglo Cluster: Legacy of the British Empire," *Journal of World Business* 37, no. 1 (2002): 33.

referendum, there is little doubt that Quebec is a distinct society within Canada from cultural, linguistic, political, and legal perspectives, but that does not require Quebec's secession from Canada. It remains a political issue.

Given Quebec's distinct society, however, there is little surprise that research shows that the managerial style of French Canadians in the province of Quebec differs from the style of the majority of English Canadians.[25] Therefore, English Canada's geography and population—which represents the greater share of Canada—is the aspect of the Canadian cultural and geographical mosaic that is of particular interest in making meaningful, and often subtle, comparisons with Australia. French Canada shows more obvious differences from Anglo cultures.

But what is culture? The word itself is intangible and needs defining because culture is a crucial motivating force behind human behavior. Not only is culture "a distinctly human means of adapting to circumstances and transmitting this coping skill and knowledge to subsequent generations," but culture gives individuals "a sense of who they are, of belonging, of how they should behave, and of what they should be doing," with the effect of impacting morale, behavior, and even work productivity, including "values and patterns that influence company attitudes and actions."[26]

Dutch theorist Geert Hofstede distinguishes culture between two types. The first type or level of culture he refers to as "civilization" or "refinement of the mind," particularly the results of those refinements as revealed by education, art, and literature. For Hofstede, however, this definition of culture is the "narrow sense" of the term because Hofstede prefers a broader definition of culture which he shares with social anthropologists; that is, a definition of culture which not only includes all patterns of thinking, feeling, and acting that refine the mind but also the "ordinary and menial things in life" from greeting, eating, and showing (or not showing) feelings, to keeping physical distance from other people.[27] According to Hofstede and other theorists, "culture

---

[25] A. Chanlat and R. Bedard, "Managing in the Quebec Style: Originality and Vulnerability," *International Studies of Management and Organization* 21, no. 3 (1991): 10–37.

[26] Philip R. Harris, Robert T. Moran, and Sarah V. Moran, *Managing Cultural Differences: Global Leadership Strategies for the Twenty-First Century*, 6th ed. (Amsterdam, The Netherlands: Elsevier/Butterworth-Heinemann, 2004), 4.

[27] Hofstede, *Cultures and Organizations: Intercultural Cooperation and its Importance for Survival* (London, UK: McGraw-Hill, 1991), 5.

is learned, not inherited. It derives from one's social environment, not from one's genes."[28] Given this view, "history" is indeed among the most profound, powerful, and fundamental of all environmental influences.

History's effect on culture transcends the mere passage of time. History shapes culture through the impact of human habitation, and the corresponding culture-building values, beliefs, and habits people come to share. According to cultural theorists Charles Hampden-Turner and Fons Trompenaars, "Members of a culture are likely to share common attitudes because they share a common history."[29] While *symbols, heroes, rituals,* and *values* all help describe the complex manifestations of culture, Hofstede says that symbols—like words, gestures, or pictures that hold a certain meaning recognized by members of the same culture—represent the most superficial manifestations due to their frequent transformation over time. In contrast, *values* reflect the deepest aspects of culture because of their strength and endurance over time. *Heroes* and *rituals* fall somewhere in between these two extremes.[30] In light of these distinctions, cultural values are extremely significant.

The role of values in differing cultures

Just as culture requires a definition so do personal values. While values have been defined in a number of ways, there is reasonable consistency among definitions. Kluckhohn defined values as "a conception, explicit or implicit . . . of the desirable which influences the selection from available modes, means, and ends of action."[31] According to Milton Rokeach, values are global beliefs that "transcendentally guide actions and judgments across specific objects and situations."[32] Building on Kluckhohn's ideas, Rokeach emphasizes that values are best viewed as "abstract ideals, not tied to any specific object or situation, representing a person's belief about modes of conduct and ideal terminal modes."[33] George England

---

[28] Ibid.

[29] Charles Hampden-Turner and Fons Trompenaars, *The Seven Cultures of Capitalism: Value Systems for Creating Wealth in the United States, Japan, Germany, France, Britain, Sweden, and the Netherlands* (London, UK: Judy Piatkus, 1993), 13.

[30] Hofstede, *Cultures and Organizations.* 7–9.

[31] C. Kluckhohn, *Values and Value Orientations in the Theory of Action* (Cambridge, MA: Harvard University Press, 1951), 389.

[32] M. Rokeach, *Beliefs, Attitudes and Values* (San Francisco, CA: Jossey-Bass, 1968), 160.

[33] Ibid., 124.

considers values to comprise "a relatively permanent perceptual framework which shapes and influences the general nature of an individual's
behavior."[34] These descriptions indicate that values are strong, persistent,
and guiding beliefs that influence behavior.
Although related, *attitudes* are not the same as values. Attitudes are
cognitive and emotional positions concerning particular situations and
objects, whereas behavior itself is the expression of a person's primary
values and matching attitudes.[35] This distinction is important. Values
have been conceptualized as "global beliefs" about desirable modes of
behavior or "desirable end-states" that "underlie attitudinal processes."[36]
Values are therefore the precursors of attitude formation.

Persistence of values

Values are essential for differentiating one society from another.
Influencing a society over time, values reveal themselves through
action and behavior, which contribute to the development of culture.
Comparing cultures reveals underlying values that are persistent, strong,
and highly influential. Hence, leaders emulate prevailing values, but
how do values perpetuate? In the case of Australia and Canada, history
reveals processes that have led these two ostensibly similar nations to
retain or emphasize certain values within their respective cultures that
contribute to the uniqueness of each culture. However, *values* lie at the
core of culture. They are learned by children at a subconscious level from
a very early age.
Developmental psychologists say most children have already developed a strong fundamental value system by age ten, and after that age
value-change is difficult. The reason is that values are acquired so early in
our lives that many values remain unconscious; therefore, they cannot
be easily discussed, nor can outsiders directly observe them. Rather,

---

[34] G.W. England, "Personal Value Systems of American Managers," *Academy of Management Journal* 10, no. 1 (1967): 54.

[35] For a more comprehensive treatment of attitudes, *see* I. Ajzen, and M. Fishbein, *Understanding Attitudes and Predicting Social Behavior* (Englewood Cliffs, NJ: Prentice-Hall, 1980); and R.H. Fazio, "How Do Attitudes Guide Behavior?" in *Handbook of Motivation and Cognition: Foundation of Social Behavior*, ed. R.M. Sorrentino and E.T. Higgens (New York, NY: Guilford, 1986).

[36] Patrick E. Conner, Boris W. Becker, Takashi Kakuyama, and Larry F. Moore, "A Cross-National Comparative Study of Managerial Values: United States, Canada and Japan," in *Advances in International Comparative Management*, ed. S. Benjamin Prasad and Richard B. Peterson, Vol. 8 (Greenwich, CT: JAI Press, 1993), 4.

maintains Hofstede, values "can only be inferred from the way people act under various circumstances."[37] Taking into account how people behave, what they say, and how they think, helps reveal what values they hold and determine their significance on cultural development.

Nearly everyone belongs to different groups concurrently. As a consequence, people carry different layers of culture simultaneously, reflecting national, regional, ethnic, religious, linguistic, gender, generational, social class affiliations, and those reflecting the workforce within organizations.[38] Regarding national characteristics of culture, however, whereas nations as "political units into which the entire world is divided and to one of which every human being is supposed to belong," is a relatively recent phenomenon in history, Hofstede asserts they often "form historically developed wholes even if they consist of clearly different groups and even if they contain less integrated minorities."[39] This is an especially powerful process given strong forces that encourage further integration, such as a dominant national language, common mass media, national educational system, and political system, which help foster common cultural sentiments among citizens.[40] Core societal values help shape prevailing national cultures.

If the environment in which people reside plays a strong role in their internalization of principal group values, then a nation's established culture has an influential role in shaping the behavior of those steeped in that culture. This process helps perpetuate those values. When comparing Australian and Canadian cultures, therefore, whether managerial aspects or general qualities of leadership style, an examination of values in each culture is crucial to identify similarities and subtle differences between them. Since values are not only taught by parents to children but are instilled through cultural immersion, they are a powerful influence on behavior.

Australian and Canadian values

Given their common origins as British colonies and prominence among the Anglo group of world cultures, should Australia and Canada be expected to exhibit *identical* values? No. Values, being an intangible feature of prevailing cultural contexts are therefore necessary to

---

[37] Hofstede. *Cultures and Organizations.* 8.
[38] Ibid., 10.
[39] Ibid., 12.
[40] Ibid.

consider, because of the influence they have on behavior and the influential role they play in helping create and preserve often subtle cultural differences.

Research has shown that, while common values certainly exist, each nation's dominant values are neither identical for all values nor are specific common values necessarily shared to the same degree. Children best reveal the existence of differing values among superficially "identical" cultures. Comparing group values of children from five English-speaking countries—Australia, New Zealand, Canada, England, and the United States—Russell and Mollie Smart showed that values are not universally shared by children in each nation despite their shared Anglo cultural origins.[41] The unique cultural environment of each nation was highly influential on the values to which they adhered. Representing similar ethnic background, samples of children of preadolescent boys and girls drawn from each nation were compared, therefore, attributing variations to environmental influences rather than genetic influences. Comparing the samples on levels of cooperation, competition, and humor among other value indicators, the researchers found significant differences.

Cooperation, competition, and humor

While Canadians showed a high degree of cooperation and work ethic, Australians ranked highest in humor. American children differed more from the English than did either Canadians or Australians.[42] By studying children who have not yet been immersed and socialized in years of formal educational or employment settings—who therefore have not yet experienced the full power of environmental conditioning—the results revealed just how early children internalize societal values which reinforce the notion that culture is indeed a reflection of values perpetuated throughout society by its inhabitants.

The findings confirm that Anglo cultures are not identical to each other because, however subtle they may be, certain values—or the relative attachment to a common value—differ among nations within this group. Moreover, the study suggests that despite being geographical neighbors, Canadians differ from Americans notwithstanding popular

---

[41] Russell C. Smart and Mollie S. Smart, "Group Values Shown in Preadolescents' Drawings in Five English-Speaking Countries," *The Journal of Social Psychology* 97, no. 1 (1975): 23–37.

[42] Ibid., 23.

opinion to the contrary. Likewise, the study indicates that Australian children do not behave exactly like their fellow Anglo cluster members. Australian boys and girls ranked first in observed levels of humor. In fact, Canadians scored the lowest rating of humor compared to the other samples.[43] This is not to say Canadians have no sense of humor. Not only is Canada the source of many popular "American" comedians, but Canadians, having chosen colonial status and carefully cultivated a close affiliation with Britain, notes Canadian comedy critic Andrew Clark, "We absorbed British rule and culture and by osmosis absorbed British comedic forms."[44]

Yet the relative dourness of Canadians appears to reflect British deference and geographical position north of the US border compared to Australian humor that evokes an Irish sensibility. "The Irish are a happy people," observes British literary critic Terry Eagleton, who "have a tendency to put a good face on things, [often] smirking cheerily."[45] Canadians, suggests Canadian comedy writer Rosie Shuster, "are more neutral and critical of each other." They prefer to "be nice" because, unlike the United States where fervent outspoken achievement is the norm, in Canada "it's rude to have a big personality."[46]

Canadian Prime Minister Pierre Elliott Trudeau once commented that residing next to America is comparable to sleeping next to an elephant since every twitch is felt. In Clark's view, however, "Living next to America is like living next to the wildest party ever held" because, from the outside, "Canadians have seen revolution, a slave economy, a civil war, rampant individualism, capitalism beyond comprehension, and creativity and industriousness beyond anyone's dreams." Hence, Clark perceptively contends that Canadians "see sublime achievement and extreme failure. Although we observe, we do not feel the sting of defeat or the exhilaration of success inevitable in the myth of the American dream." Despite what Canadians see, he asserts, Canadians are not envious of the United States. An insightful interpreter of popular culture, Clark argues that "We do not covet the Americans' crime, guns, imperialism, racism. We don't even covet their nationalism. Americans are proud to be American. Canadians

---

[43] Ibid.

[44] Andrew Clark, *Stand and Deliver: Inside Canadian Comedy* (Toronto, ON: Doubleday, 1997), 2, 14.

[45] Terry Eagleton, *The Truth About The Irish* (New York, NY: St. Martin's, 1999), 93.

[46] Quoted in Clark, *Stand and Deliver*, 15–16.

are relieved to be Canadian."[47] While Americans might be surprised at such observations, and as much as most Canadians like their neighbors to the south, his sentiments ring true. Hence, just as value differences separate Australians from Canadians, subtle yet significant value differences separate Canadians from Americans.

Fairness, egalitarianism, and tolerance of status

Numerous implications spring from such observed differences. Another study on children showed that they frequently ask riddles in countries where high authority rests in adults and where ridicule is used.[48] This link between Australian children's use of riddles with the practice of "ridicule" is revealing since it evokes the Australian tendency toward egalitarianism, or fairness, among social classes and the cultural practice of "knocking," which is the custom of "disparaging the ideas, suggestions, actions, and achievements of others."[49] This is culturally, historically, and sociologically insightful.

In contrast, English Canadians, recipients of more vigorous British influences, are more conscious of status differences and emulate a reserved English nature. Canadians from all backgrounds tend to favor stability and security in society. They have a national passion for the more modest and restrained "peace, order and good government" rather than the American constitutionally protected quest for "life, liberty, and the pursuit of happiness." Such American priorities have been deemed "lesser Canadian ideals" because "liberty" is perceived as too strong a word for Canadians, who prefer the more passive term "freedom"; "liberty" suggests escape whereas "taking leave," a more historically acceptable Canadian phrase, implies permission.[50] In contrast, Australians' fervent egalitarianism is apparent in their national sentiment to "live, let live and allow a fair go."[51]

---

[47] Ibid., 15.
[48] B. Sutton-Smith, "A Development Structural Account of Riddles," paper presented to meetings of the Society for Research in Child Development, Philadelphia, PA, March 31, 1973, cited in Smart and Smart, 33.
[49] Gwenda Beed Davey and Graham Seal, *A Guide to Australian Folklore* (Sydney, NSW: Simon & Schuster, 2003), 170.
[50] Pierre Berton, *Why We Act Like Canadians* (Toronto, ON: McClelland & Stewart, 1982), 16.
[51] Henry S. Albinski, "Australia and the United States," in *Australia: The Daedalus Symposium*, ed. Stephen R. Graubard (North Ryde, NSW: Angus & Robertson, 1985), 404.

A "fair go" reflects the firmly ingrained Australian value of equality and a rigorous resistance to any obstruction that might arise. While Australians may not have equal property or wealth, having a "fair go" underscores a sense of equality of opportunity without facing societal obstacles that come from class distinctions. Each society's different expectations are revealed in the respective national slogans, relying on culturally determined assumptions about human nature and the appropriate role of the state.

Considering the differences separating Canadians from Americans, popular Canadian historian Pierre Berton writes that Canadians "were never a community of rebels, escaping from the clutches of a foreign monarch." For many years, while Americans were establishing "often through violence, the liberty of the individual to do his own thing, [Canada] remained a society of colonials." Berton asserts, Canadians basked "in the security and paternalism that [its] constitutional phraseology suggests." Canadians sought to achieve their "own form of independence" in a gradual and nonviolent manner.[52]

As Canadians tend to embrace quiet determination rather than boldly assert themselves over others, it is no surprise that Canadians view their culture as different from American culture largely because of underlying distinctions in values. Value differences, as Smart and Smart's study of children's values suggested, indicate dissimilarities between Canadians and Americans from an early age. Likewise, the Australian tendency toward social equality and knocking distinguishes Australians from both Canadians and Americans.

Regarding Australians and Americans, more noteworthy distinctions exist. In his cross-cultural analysis on interactions, George Renwick observes that Americans tend to view their lives as ruled by the ideals of "justice, freedom, equality, the sanctity of the individual and of private property." According to Renwick, Americans acquire these principles from a very young age, enshrined as they are in the nation's historical documents that constitute the outline according to which national, social, and political debates take place. However, in Australia, he argues, ideals appear to fit within the sphere of "preachers, labor union leaders, and mothers," because "for the men, fairness is the simple, all-pervasive norm. 'Come on, give us a fair shake!' is usually enough to gain compliance . . . in situations where disagreement is strong, though little attention is given to the relative apportionments needed to ensure fairness."

---

[52] Berton, *Why We Act Like Canadians*, 16.

Renwick maintains that this results in a blend of acceptance that achieves feasible cooperation without any need for further debate. In contrast, he argues, "Americans are more complex. They depend upon quite explicit norms, frequently couched in absolute terms, but at the same time they are very pragmatic and are ready to resolve differences and disagreements over principle in a practical process of negotiation and compromise."[53]

The Australian tendency for fairness, therefore, relates to the much lamented though persistent Australian custom of "cutting down tall poppies," which describes the Australian tendency to criticize, undercut, or bring down to earth individuals perceived as being too highly elevated above others by reason of ability, wit, or luck.[54] This contrasts significantly with American cultural acceptance of individual achievement.

Quest for achievement

The Australian cultural phenomenon of "cutting down tall poppies," or "leveling," intended to prevent people from getting an inflated sense of their own status, arguably stems from an Irish and British working-class background shared by many Australians. Therefore, they also share a correspondingly lesser tolerance for large status differences. This is markedly different from Americans who tend to glorify those who succeed and tend to favor "achievement" above all else.

Though Americans like to think that they resist authority, Americans accept authority quite readily when compared to Australians. In the organizational context, "title and position are important," relates Renwick, "even though the manager or executive may slip quite naturally into a first-name basis with workers and 'roll up one's sleeves,' make no mistake about who is in charge; informal friendliness can metamorphose into stern directives when the situation calls for decisiveness." Reflecting cultural differences, Renwick asserts, while Americans are considered to be "respectful within limitations," "respectful of superiors," and "like to be in control," Australians in comparison are "disrespectful," "resent superiors," and "resist control."[55]

While Canadians share an interest in achievement, they tend to be more modest than Americans and more deferential when it comes to

[53] George W. Renwick, *A Fair Go For All: Australian/American Interactions* (Yarmouth, ME: Intercultural Press, 1991), 27–28.

[54] Davey and Seal, *A Guide to Australian Folklore*, 82.

[55] Renwick, *A Fair Go For All*, 64.

exercising their bragging rights. Given that the United States began through revolution, and fought battles to conquer more land, as was proven by the disastrous War of 1812 and subsequent policy of Manifest Destiny—America's ambition to extend its borders northward to the Arctic which, following the US Civil War, prompted several British colonies toward Canadian Confederation by 1867—it is not difficult to understand why self-glorification, extreme competition, and high achievement would be widely admired values in American culture. From a Canadian perspective, Berton observes, "The only way to fight American values was to make them appear vulgar and vaguely comic," with numerous popular journals from the turn of the nineteenth century featuring such depictions, appealing to Canada's "pro-British, pro-Loyalist upper classes."[56]

Identifying value differences between Australians and Canadians

Despite variances among countries and unquestioned diversity among individuals, there exists a unique pattern in the personal values of Australian and Canadian national cultures, visible in managerial and leadership behavior. Various studies have indicated the strength and influence of values, and reveal their impact on forging an equally strong national culture solidified by historical and ethnic influences.[57] Do values differentiate Australians from Canadians? The results from cross-cultural studies strongly suggest the answer is yes. Their respective values, including the intensity of some common values, are not identical. Variations in Australian, Canadian, and American cultural values are discernible.

Among the most clear differences is that Canadians show greater deference—respect for the opinions and ideas—to those in positions of authority compared to Australians.[58] This conclusion appears to be supported by Ashkanasy *et al.* who describes Canadians as less "assertive" and more embracing of a "humane orientation" than Australians

---

[56] Berton, *Why We Act Like Canadians*, 55–59.

[57] For an analysis and comparison of several research studies, *see* Arthur Wolak, "Australian and Canadian Managerial Values: a Review," *International Journal of Organizational Analysis*, 17, no. 2 (2009): 139–59.

[58] Helen Peters and Robert Kabacoff, *Shared Beginnings and Diverse Histories: A Comparison of Leadership Behavior in Five Countries with Anglo-Saxon Based Cultures* (Portland, ME: Management Research Group, 1999).

and Americans.[59] Humane orientation is defined as the degree to which individuals in organizations or societies encourage and reward people for being altruistic, fair, generous, friendly, caring, and kind to other people.[60] This combination of attributes adds credibility and support to the observed Canadian tendency toward deferential behavior.

George England asserts that Australian managers are less obsessed with profit maximization than Americans, and place a corresponding lower perceived value on high achievement and individual success. England categorizes Australian managers' orientation as primarily moralistic and humanistic whereas American managers tend to be oriented more toward pragmatism, achievement, and competence, leading Australians and Americans to respond differently to their environments.[61]

Since England argues that a personal value system is "a relatively permanent perceptual framework, likely to shape and influence the general nature of an individual's behavior," and that values are related to attitudes, he claims that values "are more deeply embedded in the personality and more permanent." As noted earlier, values are not synonymous with attitudes. However, England asserts, an individual's personal value system can be thought of as an "integrated group of attitudes and beliefs" that reflects the interaction of biological and environmental factors.[62]

As personal value systems of managers are quite stable and do not change rapidly, even during periods of major environmental and social change, there is a common pattern across countries in translating values to behavior.[63] This is important in showing that, for cultures, values are powerful and durable. Table 1.1 reveals distinct differences between the value patterns of Australian and American managers.[64]

England asserts that United States managers are more pragmatic and focused on high achievement whereas Australian managers have greater moralistic and humanistic orientations with less focus on profit maximization, and not possessing strong values that favor the glorification

---

[59] Ashkanasy, Trevor-Roberts, and Earnshaw, "The Anglo Cluster," 28–39.

[60] House, Javidan, Hanges, and Dorfman, "Understanding Cultures and Implicit Leadership Theories Across the Globe," 5–6.

[61] George W. England, "Managers and Their Value Systems: A Five-Country Comparative Study," *Columbia Journal of World Business* 13, no. 2 (1978): 33–44.

[62] Ibid., 35.

[63] Ibid., 39, 41.

[64] Ibid., 40–41. *See also* George W. England, *The Manager and His Values: An International Perspective from The United States, Japan, Korea, India, and Australia* (Cambridge, MA: Ballinger Publishing Company, 1975), 10.

Table 1.1   George England's Value Patterns of US and Australian Managers

US Managers	Australian Managers
• Large element of pragmatism • Have a high achievement and competence orientation • Emphasize traditional organizational goals such as profit maximization, organizational efficiency and high productivity • Place high value on most employee groups as significant reference groups	• High degree of moralistic orientation • High level of humanistic orientation • Place low value on organizational growth and profit maximization • Place low value on such concepts as achievement, success, competition, and risk • Major regional (geographical) differences in values of managers

Source: Adapted from George W. England, "Managers and Their Value Systems: A Five-Country Comparative Study," *Columbia Journal of World Business* 13, no. 2 (1978): 40–41.

of achievement, success, competition, and risk. Australians' lesser desire for achievement seems to be supported by historical factors, namely a particularly influential immigrant group such as the Irish. In other words, culturally based values are not identical just because two countries might fall within the same cluster, in this case the Anglo cluster of nations.

Though dissimilar views on achievement distinguish Australians from Americans, managers with pragmatic orientations (Americans) and moralist orientations (Australians) also reveal significant differences. According to England, "Pragmatists have an economic and organizational competence orientation as opposed to a humanistic and bureaucratic orientation for moralists."[65] While moralists are more likely to be influenced by philosophical or moral justification, pragmatists are more likely to be influenced by persuasion, training, and leadership styles that focus on the potentially successful outcome of an idea or an action. Above all, these two groups tend to explain or rationalize the reasons behind their behavior in different ways.[66]

Australian managers' relatively high behavioral relevance scores on "Tolerance, Compassion, Trust, Loyalty, Honor, Employee Welfare and Social Welfare" suggest that Australian managers are more embracing of "organizational egalitarianism" as an essential part of their value structure

---

[65] Ibid., 41.
[66] Ibid.

than American managers who reject organizational egalitarianism.[67] England concludes that personal values of managers are "measurable and important to measure" because values are connected to such practical "concerns as decision making, managerial success and organizational context differences."[68]

Consistent with England's views, Westwood and Posner reveal that, contrary to Australians, Americans are socialized to be highly achievement-oriented and to express openly and forthrightly their personal ambitions for power and success. In contrast, Australians are said to possess a relatively greater concern for community over individual interests, a focus supported by such cultural phenomena as "mateship" and the common practice of cutting down "tall poppies," or high achievers. In a management context, the greater concern for community over individual interests is revealed by the Australian propensity to strive for organizational effectiveness, high morale, service to the public, and to achieve value for society.[69] These findings fit with England's description of Australians being more "moralistic" and Americans more "pragmatic" in their respective value sets.

American managers value ability, co-operation, job satisfaction, skill, flexibility, and creativity, while Australian managers value ability, job satisfaction, skill, achievement, success, and co-operation (though to a lesser degree than Americans).[70] However, given that Australian managers are alone in rating the goals of "service to the public" and "value to the community" as more important than "organizational growth" and "organizational stability," the observed Australian concern for people, or their "humanistic orientation" described by England, is further supported.

Given that Australian and American managers differ on so many factors only confirms that Anglo cultures differ in their value orientations from one another, which is consistent with Renwick's observation, described earlier, concerning the Australian tendency relative to Americans to resist authority, resent superiors, and resist control. These differences help confirm Westwood and Posner's contention, that "Values shape both individual and organizational decisions and are, in turn, shaped by

---

[67] England, *The Manager and His Values*, 91.

[68] Ibid., 11.

[69] Robert I. Westwood and Barry Z. Posner, "Managerial Values Across Cultures: Australia, Hong Kong and the United States," *Asia Pacific Journal of Management* 14, no. 1 (1997): 31–66.

[70] Ibid., 57.

cultural, geo-political and socio-economic factors as well as managerial role responsibilities."[71]

While England describes American managers as pragmatic individuals who value achievement and competence, he asserts that successful American managers have a specific orientation toward profit maximization, ability, aggressiveness, influence, power, success, change, and risk.[72] In contrast, a Canadian investigation produced a profile of Canadian managers as valuing achievement, accomplishment, ambition, and intellectual stimulation in their work.[73] Although these are general observations, another study showed Canadian business students to strongly emphasize happiness, a comfortable life, true friendship, and self-respect, combined with honesty, responsibility, and ambitiousness.[74] The conclusion was that Canadians give "a higher importance to the family-oriented values . . . which are necessary for social success."[75] This observation is comparable to an earlier result that Canadian business students emphasize values that reflect their "pragmatic approach to taking care of oneself and one's immediate family."[76]

Similarities between Americans and English-speaking Canadians certainly exist. For instance, such values as family security (taking care of loved ones), delayed gratification, and a personal rather than social orientation have been shown as almost identical for English-speaking Canadian managers and American managers, while French-speaking Canadian managers do not show a shared trend of similar values.[77] Not only do these results indicate different cultural values between French Canadians and Americans, but also between French-speaking Canadians and English-speaking Canadians. However, just because there appears

---

[71] Ibid., 60.

[72] England, "Managers and Their Value Systems," 33–44.

[73] M.W. McCarrey, S. Ahmed, Y. Gasse, G. Conrad, S. Seguin, M. Major, and P. Mercier, "The Subjective Culture of Public Sector Women and Men Managers: A Common Instrumental/Expressive Value Orientation, or Two Different Worlds?" *Canadian Journal of Administrative Sciences* 6, no. 2 (1989): 54–61.

[74] S.A. Ahmed, "Impact of Social Change on Job Values: A Longitudinal Study of Quebec Business Students," *Canadian Journal of Administrative Science* 7, no. 2 (1990): 12–24.

[75] Ibid., 20.

[76] S.A. Ahmed and J. Jabes. "A Comparative Study of Job Values of Business Students in France and English Canada," *Canadian Journal of Administrative Sciences* 5, no. 2 (1988): 55.

[77] N.J. Adler and J.L. Graham, "Business Negotiations: Canadians Are Not Just Like Americans," *Canadian Journal of Administrative Sciences* 4, no. 3 (1987): 222.

to be some identical values shared between English Canada and the United States, it does not mean to imply that there is unanimity among all values. Differences between Canada and the United States exist—differences which flow from complex historical developments, population settlement patterns, and distinct culture.

It is not surprising, therefore, that Conner *et al.* would conclude that, while there are value differences between Canadians and Americans, similarities include a shared preference for values of "Delayed Gratification, Competence, Self-Expansion, a Personal Orientation, Family, Security, Love, and Inner-Directedness."[78] Differences in values between Canadians and Americans may be in degree rather than of value type. For instance, Americans place greater importance on the value of "competence" relative to Canadians,[79] which underscores the American tendency to favor individual achievement. Whether different values exist or there are merely different degrees of acceptance of common values, differences between Canadian and American values underscore different cultures.

Since personal values of those in managerial positions differ across countries, as Westwood and Posner note, "Sometimes such differences are subtle, but nonetheless significant and potentially important."[80] Even if similarities between Canadian and United States values appear to more closely unite the cultures than separate them, there is little doubt that there are significant differences between Australian values and US values, and by implication, therefore, between Australian and Canadian values.

The intensity of some Canadian values appears to be positioned between Australia and America. For instance, compared to Canadians, Australians show less importance to values of conformity and more importance to social equality, or egalitarianism.[81] The Australian penchant for showing less importance to values of conformity and more importance to social

---

[78] Patrick E. Conner, Boris W. Becker, Takashi Kakuyama, and Larry F. Moore, "A Cross-National Comparative Study of Managerial Values: United States, Canada and Japan," in *Advances in International Comparative Management*, ed. S. Benjamin Prasad and Richard B. Peterson, Vol. 8 (Greenwich, CT: JAI Press, 1993), 14.

[79] Ibid., 22.

[80] Westwood and Posner, 59.

[81] Norman T. Feather and John G. Adair, "National Identity, National Favoritism, Global Self-Esteem, Tall Poppy Attitudes, and Value Priorities in Australian and Canadian Samples," in *Latest Contributions to Cross-Cultural Psychology*, ed. J.-C. Lasry, J. Adair, and K. Dion (Lisse, The Netherlands: Swets & Zeitlinger, 1999): 57–58.

equality compared to Canadians is consistent with the stereotype that views Australians as "egalitarian in outlook" and possessing the tendency to "react against restrictive forms of authority and rules of conduct," dispositions that are associated with "superior social class, higher status, and pretentiousness." In comparison with Australians, Canadians more strongly endorse values that relate to "control, conformity, salvation, ambition, and recognition."[82] These Canadian values seem to point to British cultural leanings, and consistent with cultural differences, namely, that Canadians tend to be more deferential and conforming than the more independent-minded, less pro-English, more egalitarian Australians.

While Australians appear less conformist relative to Canada, Australian political scientist Ian McAllister believes that conformism is among the five themes—along with utilitarianism, egalitarianism, collectivism, and materialism—that characterize Australian political culture.[83] McAllister argues that conformism, like egalitarianism, developed in reaction to the feeling among unskilled early settlers that they must rely on one another for their survival in the harsh conditions of the country. According to McAllister, "Conformism ensured that the prevailing values of mateship and egalitarianism were maintained and that collective survival was made more likely." Such values were perceived as "central to the security and ultimate prosperity of outback settler communities."[84]

McAllister asserts that the presence of conformism in Australian society continued into the twentieth century as part of the widespread application of "legalism," a principle best illustrated by the Australian system of industrial arbitration. According to this system, "award wages are laid down for particular categories of workers and then applied uniformly, regardless of the often very different market conditions that apply to various sectors of the economy."[85] Furthermore, McAllister argues that conformism is an important feature of the " 'tall-poppy syndrome,' by which those who are seen to have been successful often attract opposition and cynicism from their peers, and receive little additional material or non-material reward for their efforts." Lastly, McAllister sees conformism in "the suburban sprawl of many Australian cities, where blocks of land and the houses that are built on them differ little in size, character or style."[86]

---

[82] Ibid., 56–57.

[83] Ian McAllister, *Political Behaviour: Citizens, Parties and Elites in Australia* (Melbourne, VIC: Longman Cheshire, 1992), 23–27.

[84] Ibid., 25–26.

[85] Ibid., 26.

[86] Ibid.

According to McAllister's application of the term, it is not clear if Australians actually favor conformity, or instead find little interest in asserting particular individualist values compared to the United States. However, perhaps conformity is an accurate feature of Australia's political culture? As McAllister concedes, it is difficult to directly link patterns of political behavior with political culture because the latter is just one of several variables that interact with political behavior.[87] Hence, perhaps Australia, viewed on its own rather than compared to other cultures such as Canada, appears to show conformity that, compared with Canada, is of lesser degree.

Australians' greater tendency to embrace the value of equality and lesser tendency to embrace conformity values in comparison with Canadians, are likely linked to both Australia's humble historic beginnings as a place where convicts and the working class formed the majority early on, and the Irish ethos that not only exercised a powerful impact on Australian cultural values but represented a dominant group among Australia's inhabitants, which helped form Australia's national culture. Given their historically stronger affinity for British culture, it is not surprising that Canadians would demonstrate a greater tendency toward values of conformity.

The above helps account for the greater acceptance among Canadians of the existence of broad social hierarchies and the greater deference exhibited by Canadians toward authority, relative to Australian society's tendency to embrace flatter hierarchies and greater social equality among classes. Americans emphasize achievement and competence more highly than Canadians and Australians.[88]

Countries typically described as "individualist" in orientation, such as Australia, Canada, and the United States might be assumed to favor "tall poppies," or high achievers, given their respective individualist orientation as opposed to nations with collectivist orientations, particularly those of Asia. However, Australian social psychologist Norman Feather asserts that it may not be accurate to state that a culture is either "individualist" or "collectivist" since there may be differences relating to the extent to which the individualism in each nation tends to be more horizontal (the emphasis that people should be similar, particularly with

---

[87] Ibid., 48.

[88] N.T. Feather, "Attitudes Toward High Achievers, Self-Esteem, and Value Priorities for Australian, American, and Canadian Students," *Journal of Cross-Cultural Psychology* 29, no. 6 (1998): 749–59.

regard to status) or more vertical (the emphasis of inequality and differences in status).[89]

According to American cross-cultural psychologist Harry Triandis, though all individualistic cultures tend to be horizontal, some individualistic countries, such as Australia, are more horizontal than other individualistic cultures, while other countries, such as the United States, are more vertical.[90] The implication of this vertical component, therefore, is that Americans might be more willing to reward "tall poppies" due to greater tolerance of power distance while Australians are less willing. This suggests a relative desire for Australians to want to cut them down, indicating a subtle collectivist nature that reveals itself in a disdain for excessive distinction for the individual.

Feather believes that Americans are prone to favor the rewarding of "tall poppies" because of their culture's more vigorous emphasis on success and achievement, compared to the notion that Australians are more prone to favor the fall of "tall poppies" in light of their stronger views on equality and equal status.[91] Again, this points to the Australian cultural tendency toward equality, mateship, and a dislike for singling out high achievers for admiration, which is the accepted norm in the American cultural environment. Why such a difference? Historical developments and settlement patterns are key influences.

The word "mate" is a very common form of address derived from British usage, which has become almost uniquely Australian having been in use since the earliest years of settlement. "Mateship" is a kind of "code of male bonding and camaraderie often said to lie at the core of Australian national identity," observe Davey and Seal, "endemic in the folklore of the strongly male-oriented bush tradition and also implicit in the traditions of the digger, though rarely explicit in the folk expressions of that group."[92] Therefore, immigrants and settlement patterns helped foster such personal values that became a central feature of Australian culture.

Feather observes, the Australian concern with mateship, friendship, and relaxed and positive relationships with others has been noted in

---

[89] Ibid., 750.

[90] Harry C. Triandis, *Individualism & Collectivism* (Boulder, CO: Westview, 1995), 46.

[91] Feather, "Attitudes Toward High Achievers, Self-Esteem, and Value Priorities for Australian, American, and Canadian Students," 750.

[92] Davey and Seal, 186.

numerous studies.[93] However, Feather found Canadians were unique in rating these values as less important when compared with the Australians and Americans,[94] suggesting differences in their respective cultures. The implication is that Canada's reserved British roots have left a lasting impact on Canadian culture, whereas the United States and Australian cultures both had considerable influence from the Irish, who traditionally favor strong affiliative inclinations.

Australian and American cultures' differing views on "tall poppy" attitudes is consistent with the observation that, despite Australia and the United States sharing similarities among most culture-level value dimensions, the United States shows more emphasis on "mastery," whereas Australia gives more importance to "harmony."[95] Again, historical factors cannot be ignored when accounting for these value differences.

Americans appear to be much more in favor of rewarding tall poppies. They also appear to have higher levels of self-esteem, and rate values connected to competence, accomplishment, and conformity as more important than they are to Australians and Canadians, results which strengthen the view that American culture is distinctive in emphasizing individual achievement and recognizing and rewarding success.[96] An individual's attitudes toward tall poppies are related to that individual's values, particularly values that relate to achievement, power, equality, and conformity.[97] Those who place high value on achievement and power are more in favor of rewarding tall poppies, and those who place a high value on equality are more in favor of seeing tall poppies fall.[98] Such are significant marks of difference between Australian and American culture.

---

[93] N.T. Feather, *Values in Education and Society* (New York, NY: Free Press, 1975), 212–14.

[94] Feather, "Attitudes Toward High Achievers, Self-Esteem, and Value Priorities for Australian, American, and Canadian Students," 757.

[95] S.H. Schwartz, "Beyond Individualism/Collectivism: New Cultural Dimensions of Values," in *Individualism and Collectivism: Theory, Method, and Applications*, ed. U. Kim, H.C. Triandis, C. Kagitcibasi, S.-C. Choi, and G. Yoon (Thousand Oaks, CA: Sage, 1994), 85–119.

[96] Feather, "Attitudes Toward High Achievers, Self-Esteem, and Value Priorities for Australian, American, and Canadian Students," 756–57.

[97] N.T. Feather, "Attitudes Toward High Achievers and Reactions to Their Fall: Theory and Research Concerning Tall Poppies," in *Advances in Experimental Social Psychology*, Vol. 26, ed. Mark Zanna (New York, NY: Academic Press, 1993), 66.

[98] Ibid.

Moreover, Australian culture was shown to possess collectivist concerns for equality, friendship, and group solidarity.[99] Related to these concerns are a distrust of status seekers, a dislike of rank and privilege—especially if not earned—and a rejection of the notion of self-importance. Hence, Australian attitudes toward authority reflect a combination of respect, suspicion, and cynicism.[100] According to Feather, "Australian individualism may often be reflected in following one's own path without necessarily conforming to the dictates of others."[101] This appears to be an intrinsic form of rebelliousness closely aligned with the Irish of Australia.

The Australia Irish have historically been viewed in a negative light due to the large number of convicts from Ireland and vocal Irish discontent evident from the 1790s onward. However, Australian historian Geoffrey Bolton notes, "it is instructive to see the ingredients of many later complaints against the Irish and against the Australian working class, who are so often alleged to have absorbed many of the characteristics of their Irish ancestors: they are turbulent; they object to social control; they are dissatisfied with the status quo; they will not work. This reputation was reinforced during the first half of the nineteenth century."[102] In other words, the Irish of Australia reflected their ancestors' characteristic Irish rebelliousness. Bolton's views are echoed by Australian historian Miriam Dixson who asserts, "It is scarcely possible to underrate Irish influence in shaping Australian identity."[103]

* * *

Given their greater emphasis on pro-social values and social equality, therefore, Australians appear less compliant, more rebellious, and less status-oriented than Canadians or Americans. The implication is to view Australia as a less conformist society that does not favor individual

[99] N.T. Feather and I.R. McKee, "Global Self-Esteem and Attitudes Toward the High Achiever for Australian and Japanese Students," *Social Psychology Quarterly* 56, no. 1 (1993): 65–76.

[100] Ibid.

[101] Feather, "Attitudes Toward High Achievers, Self-Esteem, and Value Priorities for Australian, American, and Canadian Students," 757.

[102] Geoffrey Bolton, "The Irish in Australian Historiography," in *Australia and Ireland, 1788–1988: Bicentenary Essays*, ed. Colm Kiernan (Dublin, Ireland: Gill and Macmillan, 1986), 5.

[103] Miriam Dixson, *The Imaginary Australian: Anglo-Celts and Identity—1788 to the present* (Sydney, NSW: University of New South Wales Press, 1999), 94.

achievement to the same extent as other cultures within the Anglo group of nations, an enduring sentiment within Australian culture that is reflected in the expression of attitudes of suspicion and cynicism toward those who occupy positions of authority.

The relative lack of conformity among Australians has helped foster a society more "inner directed" than Canadian society. Conformity and deference to authority evident in Canadian society contributes to a relatively greater propensity for "external direction." Such a relative external locus of control not only supports Canada's traditionally closer ties to Australia and Canada's mutual colonial power but Canada's enduring fondness for the British monarchy.

Adherence to significant "British" traditions and behaviors helped Canada assert an identity separate from the United States. Hence, despite being under the imposing shadow of its American neighbor, Canada's values did not embrace America's focus on dominance—a cultural, political, and economic position that striving toward individual achievement, competence, accomplishment, and personal ambition tends to support.

Australia, Canada, and the United States, despite sharing similar characteristics ranging from common language to similar European origins, have not evolved into identical societies. Clear differences in cultural values support this observation. In the chapter that follows, Australia's and Canada's national characters are compared and analyzed for historical insights that contributed to the development of these cultural value differences. In probing the distinctions, the Irish of Australia emerge as a critical difference from Canada. Dixson maintains, "With a self-conscious identity more potent than most other groups, with a literature and institutions stronger than those of the Scots or others from Britain, the Irish exerted a 'galvanic' influence on Australian identity," helping forge the Australian identity in relation to authority and work ethic.[104] During Australia's culturally formative period, asserts Dixson, "ethnicity as represented by the Irish, inscribed in Australian life a complex and potent cultural tension."[105]

---

[104] Ibid., 94.
[105] Ibid.

2
National Character

Despite how culturally similar contemporary Australia and Canada are on the surface—both multicultural nations with common colonial roots where English is the predominant language—their cultural values, as reflected by Australia's and Canada's contrasting personalities, are not identical. How each society evolved seems linked to the disproportionate effect culturally influential Anglo-Celtic groups had in each society. Although Australia and Canada received immigrants from throughout the British Isles in their formative periods, their proportion was not the same. Contrary to the Canadian experience, the Irish of Australia appear to have profoundly influenced the Australian national character. The question that needs to be answered is how.

Cultural difference and national character

International travelers familiar with Australia, Canada, and the United States recognize that subtle dissimilarities among these superficially similar nations transcend mere variations in accent. Though particular characteristics are shared among the Anglo group of national populations, the total profile of each respective culture is unique. It was pointed out in the prior chapter that Canadians tend to be more deferential to authority than Australians and that, along the spectrum of achievement orientation, Australians tend to be less focused on high achievement and individual success compared to Americans. Likewise, it was observed that Canadians are less driven by a need for individual distinction in comparison with Americans and, while Australians are more concerned with community interests than individual power and success, Canadians tend to take the middle ground by exhibiting a Canadian penchant for "compromise"—showing concern for social welfare on the one hand, balanced by a tolerance of vertical hierarchy on the other. In between Australians' moralistic orientation and Americans' pragmatism, one finds in Canadians a sense of "moral pragmatism," a balance between old world values and US-style modern competitiveness, with greater pro-social sentiments than in the United States, but less workplace egalitarianism than in Australia. As these observations suggest, each nation's character is distinctive.

Considering the significance of such cultural features, sociologist Alex Inkeles defines *national character* as the "relatively enduring personality characteristics and patterns that are modal among the adult members of . . . society."[1] Given that societies are comprised of individuals, and conditions of life yield distinguishing patterns in the personalities of their members, national character reflects the set of psychological and social characteristics embraced by a particular national population. Indeed, each society has a "national character" that differentiates one from another, making this concept a subtle but unmistakable marker of culture and values.

The formation of national character therefore depends on the influence of predominant groups whose customs and social views impact the greater society over time. Through an ongoing process of socialization, subsequent generations and succeeding waves of immigrants acculturate to the prevailing environment, making national character an enduring and powerful expression of national culture.

Contemporary Australia and Canada are multicultural nations where minority ethnic groups have largely become successfully integrated into society without becoming totally assimilated and losing all of their own distinctive cultural characteristics. While maintaining significant ethnic values and customs, immigrants to Australia and Canada also absorb core cultural values of their host nations, helping perpetuate and preserve the established national character.

From a demographic perspective the Canadian population, much like the Australian population, has experienced significant cultural assimilation among recent immigrants. This has occurred through a variety of means, including ethnic and religious intermarriage between members of minority ethnic origins and, in the Canadian environment, between members of the two primary categories of culturally dominant groups, British and French. It has also stemmed from acculturation pressures of peer groups and schools in subsequent generations of original

---

[1] Alex Inkeles, *National Character* (New Brunswick, NJ: Transaction Publishers, 1997), 17.

immigrant families.[2] But into what dominant culture have immigrants acculturated? For Australia and English Canada, they entered dissimilar Anglo-Celtic cultures shaped over many generations.

Amid the various influences that contributed to each nation's character development, Anglo-Celtic society dominated because of the significant representation those from the British Isles had among the overall population and among positions of cultural influence. Underlying Anglo-Celtic differences proved instrumental in helping Australia and Canada form their separate identities, and once formed, they were kept alive by the native-born inhabitants and later waves of immigrants. As a consequence of these early influences, Australia and Canada formed stable identities possessing national characteristics that, once established, led to the acculturation of future settlers.

The new national identities that emerged became just as strong as their European antecedents. Researchers examining Canadian ethnicity have looked into the degree of attachment to Canada over attachment to nations of ethnic origin. Survey results show that although Canadians remain proud of their ethnic roots, an overwhelming majority of Canadians from most backgrounds show similar attachment to Canada, suggesting an implicit acceptance of Canadian values and identity. Those of French origin also identify themselves as Canadian but at a lower percentage reflecting their closer identification with the province of Quebec for reasons of language and culture.[3] Those with some ethnic self-identity still have a relatively strong Canadian personality indicating that a Canadian identity is compatible with a self-identity connected to ethnic origin.[4] Hence, researchers looking into what it means to be "Canadian" have done so because the predominant values that help mark Canada's cultural identity are strengthened by diverse immigrant cultures that came to identify themselves as Canadian.

A study considering immigration and cultural influence shows that Canadian cultural identity encourages newcomers to conform, indicating that instead of immigrants changing the prevailing national character, an established national character influences the newcomers to adapt to it.

[2] Warren E. Kalbach, "Ethnic Diversity: Canada's Changing Cultural Mosaic," in *Perspectives on Ethnicity in Canada: A Reader*, ed. Madeline A. Kalbach and Warren E. Kalbach (Toronto, ON: Harcourt Canada, 2000), 70–71.
[3] Rudolf Kalin and John W. Berry, "Ethnic and Civic Self-Identity in Canada," in Kalbach and Kalbach, *Perspectives on Ethnicity in Canada*, 94–95.
[4] Ibid., 97.

Researchers compared three groups of people in terms of five personality factors: (a) Chinese immigrants to Canada, (b) Canadian-born citizens of Chinese descent, and (c) Canadian-born citizens of European descent.[5] Fewer differences between Canadian-born of Chinese origin and Canadian-born of European origin were found than there were between Chinese Canadians and ethnic Chinese in China. This underscores the strength and durability of a distinct national character once it has been shaped.

National culture has proven to be a strong, enduring cohesive force in society. Considering whether personality differences are the result of country of birth and/or ethnic background, other researchers found that differences between those who were Canadian-born and raised, whether of Chinese or European descent, were smaller than differences between Chinese immigrants and Canadian-born people of either European or Chinese descent. For contemporary Canada, these results indicate that, regardless of one's ethnic origins, being raised in Canadian culture, rather than in another culture like China, tends to make Canadians relatively more *extraverted*, *open to experience*, and *agreeable*—in other words, typically Canadian—which supports the view that culture and socialization are powerful forces shaping personality development as reflected by national character.[6]

These two studies strongly suggest that having an ethnic identity is compatible not only with having a strong Canadian identity but also with having a strong commitment and attachment to Canada.[7] The same observation also applies to Australia where having a strong attachment to Ireland, for example, may not preclude having a similarly strong attachment to Australia. However, Norman Feather maintains that "National identification with Australia has been shown to differ according to whether subjects identify themselves as Australian or as

----

[5] When personality scales measuring a broad array of traits are properly translated and administered to members of other cultures, they tend to show results similar to the five-factor structure of personality, that is, the five basic dimensions of extraversion, agreeableness, conscientiousness, neuroticism, and openness to experience, familiar to contemporary psychologists. Robert R. McCrae and Oliver P. John, "An Introduction to the Five-Factor Model and Its Applications," *Journal of Personality* 60, no. 2 (1992): 175–215.

[6] Robert R. McCrae, Michelle S.M. Yik, Paul D. Trapnell, Michael Bond, and Delroy Paulhus, "Interpreting Personality Profiles Across Cultures: Bilingual, Acculturation, and Peer Rating Studies of Chinese Undergraduates," *Journal of Personality and Social Psychology* 74, no. 4 (1998): 1041–55.

[7] Kalin and Berry, "Ethnic and Civic Self-Identity in Canada," 101.

belonging to some other national group."[8] Yet Feather concedes that it could very well be "that there are both similarities and differences in the values that predict to national identification for different segments of Australian society." He qualifies, "While there may be certain core values that relate to national identification, there may be other values that vary from group to group in the way they relate to identification with Australia, depending on the degree to which a particular group's values are satisfied or obstructed with the nation."[9]

Nonetheless, Feather reveals that strong national identification with Australia is positively related to the importance assigned to such non-abstract value types as hedonism and security. In other words, Australians who assign greater importance to values related to enjoyment and pleasure, to order and security tended to identify more strongly with Australia.[10]

Egalitarianism, as mentioned in the prior chapter, also appears to be a strong Australian national value. The Australian social phenomenon best described as the "tall-poppy syndrome"—the tendency of people to disparage or criticize high achievers in society—confirms a type of egalitarianism, notes Trevor-Roberts *et al.*, "associated with a strong element of equality pervading Australian leadership culture."[11] The role of values related to "power and authority" was more difficult to determine in connection with national identification, because, notes Feather, "Australians tend to have ambivalent attitudes toward authority and high status," sometimes exhibiting "conformity and dependence" but other times "irreverence and anger."[12]

* * *

[8] N.T. Feather, "Devaluing Achievement Within a Culture: Measuring the Cultural Cringe," *Australian Journal of Psychology* 45, no. 3 (1993): 182–88.

[9] N.T. Feather, "Values and National Identification: Australian Evidence," *Australian Journal of Psychology* 46, no. 1 (1994): 39.

[10] Feather, "Values and National Identification: Australian Evidence," 36, 38.

[11] Edwin Trevor-Roberts, Neal M. Ashkanasy, and Jeffrey C. Kennedy, "The Egalitarian Leader: A Comparison of Leadership in Australia and New Zealand," *Asia Pacific Journal of Management* 20, no. 4 (2003): 523.

[12] Australian ambivalence toward authority and high status is explored in N.T. Feather, "Authoritarianism and Attitudes towards High Achievers," *Journal of Personality and Social Psychology* 65 (1993): 152–64; N.T. Feather, "Attitudes toward High Achievers and Reactions to Their Fall: Theory and Research Concerning Tall Poppies," in *Advances in Experimental Social Psychology*, Vol. 26, ed. Mark Zanna, 1–73 (New York, NY: Academic Press, 1993); and R. Taft and K.F. Walker, "Australia," in *The Institutions of Advanced Societies*, ed. A.M. Rose, 131–91 (Minneapolis, MN: University of Minnesota Press, 1958).

Canadians are famous for being a highly deferential and modest people. According to Canadian journalist and historian, Peter C. Newman, Canadians have traditionally preferred to remain "deferential and blindly obedient to the powers-that-be" instead of seeking out glory for its own sake.[13] With humor and eloquence, Newman describes Canada's national character as embracing "a national affinity for discomfort and self-denial," a state where "winners were frowned upon unless, like Terry Fox," the Canadian runner who traversed Canada on one leg to raise money for cancer research, "or Dr. Norman Bethune," the Canadian surgeon who established hospitals for modern Westernized medicine in China, "they placed themselves in heroic circumstances that guaranteed their deaths." Newman notes, "Winners in any endeavour found themselves having to mumble excuses about how winning had really been an accident that would—with any luck—never happen again." Where else, he asks, would a tennis star on the rise like Margorie Blackwood in 1980 firmly set her long-term goals "on being among 'the top forty tennis players,' " instead of aiming for gold?[14] Such is the Canadian temperament.

Rather than assert their identity or challenge authority, therefore, Canadians have traditionally remained content to avoid American-style high achievement and the self-glorification it evokes. Although Australians do not place high regard for individual eminence and distinction—perhaps with sport being a singular exception[15]—Australia's typical irreverence for things authoritative or institutional is in stark contrast to Canada's deferential behavior.[16] British understatement and

---

[13] Peter C. Newman, *The Canadian Revolution: From Deference to Defiance* (Toronto, ON: Penguin, 1995), xiii.

[14] Ibid., xiii.

[15] From his linguistic analysis, Bert Peeters observes that Australians tend to set sports heroes apart from high achievers by the use of phrases such as "except (in) sport," "with the exception of sport," or "except for sporting legends." Another common Australian linguistic procedure is to use conjunctions such as "despite" or "in spite of" followed by a reference to the tall poppy syndrome. According to Peeters, "Australians *love* their sporting heroes, but only—broadly speaking—as long as modesty and unpretentiousness (especially in victory) prevail." Bert Peeters, " 'Thou Shalt Not Be a Tall Poppy': Describing an Australian Communicative (and Behavioral) Norm," *Intercultural Pragmatics* 1, no. 1 (2004): 79–80.

[16] It should be noted, however, that even in Australia there are limits to the behavior of sport figures. According to Peeters, "even sports stars, irrespective of the discipline in which they excel, should not appear 'uppity' (Australian English for 'self-assertive, arrogant, affectedly superior') to the general public.

reserve made a lasting imprint on the Canadian psyche as opposed to Irish-infused Australia, where the use of wit, humor, and informality is far more accepted.

Sport, the Irish, and the roots of Australian irreverence

An obsession with sport seems to contradict Australia's "leveling tendency," which Australian historian Geoffrey Blainey characterizes as "a suspicion of the powerful, a mistrust of excellence, and an ambivalence towards training and education."[17] In Blainey's view, Australia's favorable bargaining position for labor and success in spectator sports are causally linked. The Australian infatuation with sport took root at about the same time as the strong trade unions arose, Blainey asserts, with the result being that "Of all the advantages that Australia in the period 1860 to 1890 offered to sport, the favorable outdoor climate and the provision of free government land for sporting fields—vital as they were—were not as important as the ample leisure of workingmen." Laborers had long relied upon their solid bargaining positions to push for shorter working hours.[18]

Shorter hours in the form of the "eight-hour day" or "forty-eight-hour week" was won largely because governments were significant employers of labor, particularly in the construction and operation of railways, and governments were swayed by populist politicians who advocated what their laboring constituents demanded.[19] Thus, while Australians' penchant for knocking, leveling, and cutting down tall poppies are

---

Those who occasionally overstep the mark to underscore their prowess, either during a sporting event or in media coverage afterwards, will be forgiven, provided they do not hoist themselves on too high a pedestal. There is a clear perception that ability and hard work, drive and determination earned them the well-deserved distinction of outperforming their opponent(s). Those who lose any sense of perspective and indulge in ego-trips that are either too frequent or simply over the top soon meet with public wrath. In other words, sports people are *not* immune against the tall poppy threat; at the very most, for reasons to do with merit, they are perhaps less likely to be tall poppies and more likely to be celebrated than high achievers in other areas." Peeters, " 'Thou Shalt Not Be a Tall Poppy'," 82.

[17] Geoffrey Blainey, "Australia: A Bird's-Eye View," in *Australia: The Daedalus Symposium,* ed. Stephen R. Graubard (North Ryde, NSW: Angus & Robertson, 1985), 23.

[18] Ibid., 22.

[19] Ibid.

Australian national characteristics, achievement in sport appears to be an exception to the rule. According to Blainey, "As Australia was so isolated, the best sportsmen did not have much chance to compete internationally, but their skills blossomed in an environment with such a fine climate, numerous sports grounds, ample leisure, and [relative] prosperity."[20]

Another aspect of the Australian tolerance of distinction in sport points to the Irish. Irish Australian historian Richard Davis recognizes an Irish influence on Australia, but instead of focusing on politics as the realm of cultural impact—though he concedes the Australian Labor Party's (ALP's) long succession of Irish-descended leaders from Prime Ministers John Curtin and Ben Chifley to Paul Keating, among others—he identifies sport as its primary channel of expression. "Australia, unlike Ireland, never fought Britain for its independence and sport against the Mother Country became an important focus of national identity," asserts Davis, "the importance of sport was heightened by the need to demonstrate that the English race was not degenerating in the hot southerly sun and could hold its own with the sporting champions of the Motherland."[21]

The prototypical English game of cricket, for example, emerged as critical to the establishment of the nation's self-confidence and an abundant source for Australian national sentiments.[22] While cricket may not have been the most appealing game to the Irish because of its pro-English connections, beyond cricket, a glance at a list of top Australian Rules Football players reveals many names of Irish origin, confirming that an association between Australian Rules Football and Ireland has always been strong.[23] "Sport, rather than revolution, has been a strong source of Australian identity," Davis asserts. "The Irish have made their contribution to this identity, carrying with them diverse intellectual baggage from the homeland." The 1880s' attempt to separate Irish sport from overseas' sport was matched by the advance of Australian Rules football, "a game which, while attracting many expatriate Irish, preferred an imperialist to an Irish lineage." Davis notes, however, that in the 1880s "Test cricket developed as a means to identify by successful

---

[20] Ibid., 22–23.

[21] Richard Davis, "Irish and Australian Nationalism: The Sporting Connection: Football & Cricket," *Centre for Tasmanian Historical Studies Bulletin* 3, no. 2 (1991–1992): 48.

[22] W.F. Mandle, *Winners Can Laugh: Sport and Society* (Ringwood, VIC: Penguin, 1974), 5, quoted in Davis, "Irish and Australian Nationalism," 48.

[23] Davis, "Irish and Australian Nationalism," 50.

competition with the mother country. This process culminated in the bodyline series of 1932–3. While in Australia individuals could move easily between Australian Rules football and cricket in Ireland, the link between the new GAA [Gaelic Athletic Association] and the revolutionaries marginalised cricket, a game increasingly portrayed to the unreflecting Irish as an unpatriotic agent of de-nationalisation. Unlike India, where nationalist antagonism to cricket finally gave way to direct, and immense, competition with the occupying power, in both north and south, Irish cricket has remained in limbo."[24]

Addressing the question whether Ireland had influenced Australian nationalism through sport, Davis concedes, "not perhaps negatively in an excessively anti-British direction, but positively through the Celtic dash and flair of performers" like C.G. Macartney, Stan McCabe, Bill O'Reilly and Jim Stynes.[25] Even a former ALP leader and prime minister like Bob Hawke, not of Irish origin but Cornish, famously loves the sport of cricket. Same is true for former Liberal leader and prime minister, John Howard, of English, Scottish, and Irish descent.

Sport, therefore, reveals underlying cultural influences that had an effect on the national consciousness. While individual distinction is not generally the Australian norm, its tolerance in sport reflects an assertion of independence from the British colonial powers, a feeling that the Irish had in Ireland and imparted on Australia. Australian irreverence, therefore, has at least some tangential connection to the Australian Irish community.

Why cricket proved more popular in places like Australia and India but not Canada is likely because, in these countries, people excelled in the sport in order to demonstrate their superiority despite being politically subservient to the colonial power. In other words, to show that they could beat the English at their own game. Perhaps due to the close historic alignment with the British, English Canadians have not generally felt this way. When it came to sport, this difference might be one of the reasons that focus and energy was not on cricket, because proving that Canadians were superior to the colonizer was not a strong motivation.

Another reason of some significance could be climatic differences, helping Canadians excel much greater at winter sports such as ice hockey instead of field games like cricket. Ice hockey became so immensely popular throughout Canada that even Canada's prime minister since 2006, Stephen

---

[24] Ibid., 58.
[25] Ibid., 59.

Harper—an economist by training but also an amateur hockey historian and a member of the Society of International Hockey Research—has written a serious book on the early years of the sport in Toronto.[26]

Indeed, while the sport of choice might differ, Canadians praise their sports heroes for similar reasons as Australians. "As in many other countries," suggest Jackson and Ponic, "sports heroes in Canada are viewed as representatives of the nation state and play an important role in the social construction of national identity."[27] Just as Edward "Ned" Hanlin was celebrated as a Canadian hero for his international rowing prowess in the 1880s, so was Wayne Gretzky for his achievements in ice hockey over a century later.[28] In both cases, their achievements provided a means by which Canadians could differentiate themselves from the Americans and British in order to cultivate and maintain an independent and respected identity. While Canadians might admire their champions in sport, their praise rarely exceeds the level of admiration Americans show for theirs. This reflects cultural differences in both achievement aspiration and recognition, as well as a relatively reserved Canadian personality influenced by the British. Such Canadian deference traces itself to British origins, unlike Australian irreverence that links more to the Irish.

Agreeableness, the British, and the origins of Canadian deference

Unlike Australian irreverence, the personality dimension of "agreeableness"—reflecting a readiness to consent or submit to authority figures in an attempt to achieve harmonious interaction—is quite compatible with Canada's propensity toward deference, identified in the prior chapter as a feature of Canadian culture.[29] "Deference" was linked to less assertiveness compared to cultures such as the United States and Australia. However, just as "less assertiveness" does not equate with "weakness," being deferential, a mode of behavior Canada appears to

---

[26] *See* Stephen J. Harper, *A Great Game: The Forgotten Leafs & the Rise of Professional Hockey* (Toronto, ON: Simon & Schuster Canada, 2013).

[27] Steven J. Jackson and Pam Ponic, "Pride and Prejudice: Reflecting on Sport Heroes, National Identity, and Crisis in Canada," *Culture, Sport, Society* 4, no. 2 (2001): 44.

[28] Ibid.

[29] "Agreeableness" is one of the five broad personality dimensions of the Five-Factor Model, the others being openness to experience, conscientiousness, extraversion, and neuroticism. This model is popular among psychologists for studying personality traits or temporally stable, cross-situational individual differences.

have inherited from the British, does not imply total compliance with perceived authority figures. As the history of relations with the United States indicates, Canada has tended to articulate its own positions on critical matters in accordance with its distinct national values.

Though significantly smaller than the United States in terms of population and military and economic power, Canada has not shown a tendency to bow to the whims of its American neighbor but rather has revealed a remarkable tendency to resist attempts at intimidation. For example, willingly participating in antiterrorist efforts in Afghanistan, Canada risked cold relations with the United States by refusing to join the 2003 American-led war in Iraq despite pressure to do so. Contrary to the position taken by the Canadian government, the Australian government chose to participate in the Iraqi conflict.

Canada's opposition to certain aspects of American foreign policy is neither a new development nor is it contradictory to the Canadian deferential character. In the 1960s, Canada, under the leadership of Prime Ministers Lester B. Pearson and Pierre Elliott Trudeau, opposed America's active involvement in the Vietnam War, not just precluding Canadian participation in the conflict, but even permitting American conscientious objectors to enter Canada to the dismay of US government officials.[30]

Into the early twenty-first century, a similar independent foreign policy stand has been taken by Canadian Prime Minister Stephen Harper, particularly in connection with the ongoing Israeli–Palestinian conflict on which Harper has shown unwavering principled support for Israel. Former Canadian Prime Minister Joe Clark writes, "Canada's support has become more adamant than that of other countries who are clearly 'friends of Israel,' including the United States of America," but he adds, "beyond the Middle East, that fierce commitment to Israel also guides Canadian policy on much broader international issues." Clark explains, "the Harper government's hostility towards the United Nations is framed regularly in the context of solidarity with Israel, boycotting UN

---

[30] In 1972, however, the Trudeau government changed immigration legislation to make it illegal to apply for landed immigrant status from within Canada or at the border. This new policy was practically the same as closing Canada as a haven for most military war resisters and deserters, serving to limit the virtually unimpeded continuous flow into Canada of American citizens opposed to their government's war and draft policies. Despite President Ford's amnesty and President Carter's pardon, many of these American exiles in Canada never returned to the United States, preferring Canada as their nation of residence.

conferences on racism because they would include extremist rhetoric that is anti-Semitic, leading the opposition to Palestinian observer status and describing nations who voted overwhelmingly for that observer status as 'abandon[ing] policy and principle.'"[31]

Indeed, adhering to "principle" is a subtle Canadian characteristic. Even the controversial former Canadian global newspaper mogul, Conrad Black, would entitle his second memoir, *A Matter of Principle*—to share his account of the trials and tribulations that dragged him through the US legal system, accused of contentious white-collar crimes, and his eventual incarceration despite his protestations of innocence.[32] Harper reveals this characteristic in a pronounced stereotypically Canadian fashion without apparent concern if it meant opposing US wishes. Principles matter to Canadians. Clark relates, "When [President] Obama sought support for his proposal at the 2011 G8 economic summit at Deauville, France, Prime Minister Harper was the only G8 leader to deny a consensus. The White House is not likely to forget."[33] Despite risking potential icy relations with the United States, Harper's manner is generally consistent with the Canadian temperament.

Canada has never been opposed to military intervention because of pacifism. Instead, Canada has pursued military action when it was independently deemed to be an appropriate course of action, not because of American foreign policy dictates. As minister of external affairs, future Prime Minister Lester Pearson had helped lead Canada into the Korean War as a contributor to the UN army and, in 1952, became president of the UN General Assembly where he tried to find a solution to the Korean conflict. Canadian historian Robert Bothwell notes, "His efforts displeased the Americans, who considered him too inclined to compromise on difficult points of principle."[34] However, adhering to principle while demonstrating the ability to compromise—much like agreeableness—are stereotypical Canadian characteristics exemplified by Pearson's efforts.

---

[31] Joe Clark, *How We Lead: Canada in a Century of Change* (Toronto, ON: Random House Canada, 2013), 84.

[32] *See* Conrad Black, *A Matter of Principle* (Toronto, ON: McClelland & Stewart, 2011).

[33] Clark, *How We Lead*, 146.

[34] Robert Bothwell, "Lester Bowles Pearson," in *The Canadian Encyclopedia: Year 2000 Edition*, ed. James H. Marsh (Toronto, ON: McClelland & Stewart, 1999), 1,777.

Pearson's greatest diplomatic achievement came during the Suez Crisis of 1956, when he proposed the creation of a UN peacekeeping force as a means of withdrawing the British and French out of Egypt, a successful plan for which he was awarded the Nobel Peace Prize in 1957. His efforts demonstrated that Canada is not a pacifist state opposed to military intervention but rather a nation that prefers to define its own policies without succumbing to obvious pressure from foreign governments, most notably the United States but also the United Kingdom.

As much as Canada owes its present form to British colonization, Canada has pursued and achieved political sovereignty. Thus, *agreeableness* and *deference* cannot be confused with weakness or pacifism. Rather, such signs of Canada's national character reflect values and cultural differences rooted in history, brought in by immigrants, and cultivated by succeeding generations of Canadians.

Australia's close military alliance with the United States did not begin with 2003's war in Iraq, but reflected many years of close military cooperation throughout the twentieth century. Although Australian support for South Vietnam in the early 1960s was consistent with the policies of other nations, most notably the United States, to curtail the spread of communism in Europe and Asia, Australia's participation accelerated as US involvement grew. By the mid-1960s, when it became evident that South Vietnam could not successfully resist being overcome by communist insurgents and their North Vietnamese comrades, the United States commenced a major escalation of the war, committing two hundred thousand troops to the conflict. As part of the buildup, the US government requested further support from friendly countries in the region, including Australia. The Australian government complied and dispatched tens of thousands of troops to the region during its decadelong involvement in the Vietnam War.

Notwithstanding the highly contentious politics surrounding the Southeast Asian dispute, Australian participation was an important contribution to the resolution of global conflict, a tradition that goes back to Australia's involvement in the First World War and the Boer War in South Africa. However, the formation of such a strong alliance with the United States might seem to contradict Australia's national character, given the Australian dislike for American-style individualism. Still, because of complex strategic and geopolitical reasons behind most military conflicts, there is no significant contradiction on this point. Australia's geographic distance from

America made Australia less fearful of American cultural and political encroachment, which has concerned Canada from the time of the Revolutionary War.

The cultivation of a distinct Canadian identity

Despite common features, Canada and the United States are not identical societies. Fundamental value differences separate the two nations. Although friendly relations outweigh historic differences, there is little doubt that the Canadian national character was formed, at least in part, by the belief that the United States represented a threat to the development and maintenance of an independent Canadian identity, a view that persisted among many Canadians in response to the contentious issue of cultural, political, and economic sovereignty.

Although a Canadian will occasionally, but very rarely, assert the argument for unification between the nations—most recently by journalist Diane Francis, touting the economic benefits in her book *Merger of the Century: Why Canada and America Should Become One Country* (2013)—this is not remotely a popular Canadian view. Canadian–US cultural convergence is a myth. From the earliest period to the present, Canadians have cherished their differences from the United States in order to preserve their separate national identity.

Despite a pattern of increased economic integration and strategic interdependence, therefore, Canadians have not aspired toward a greater political and philosophical alliance with the United States. Far from it, suggests public opinion researcher Michael Adams. The reason Canada's cultural integrity and political sovereignty are well secured is because "Canada's founding values, historical experiences, and political institutions are very different from those in the United States and have a greater influence on Canadians' contemporary values than the much vaunted forces of globalization."[35]

Values of Canada and the United States are different, and continue to diverge in significant ways. Yet distinguishing Canada from the United States, Adams points out, is no simple exercise, "Because the cultural differences between Canada and United States tend to exist beneath the consciousness of our daily lives, it is sometimes possible to imagine

---

[35] Michael Adams, *Fire and Ice: The United States, Canada and the Myth of Converging Values* (Toronto, ON: Penguin, 2003), 143.

that those differences do not exist. . . . But differences—both subtle and marked—do exist, and do endure." Adams argues, "Some are external (gun control, bilingualism, health care), but many exist only inside the minds of Canadians and Americans—in how they see the world, how they engage with it, and how they hope to shape it."[36]

From the vehicles Canadians purchase to the deference they pay to authority, Canadians are distinctive in their attitudes and opinions. Consequently, Canada cannot be viewed as an identical northern satellite of the United States as some outside of Canada might mistakenly conclude based solely on close geographic proximity and common language. During the height of the Vietnam War era, for instance, Canada emerged as the most logical destination for American war resisters, not just because of relative ease of access—the United States and Canada share the longest nonmilitarized border in the world—but rather because Canadians, reflecting Canada's values, were largely sympathetic to their plight. This attitude underscored Canada's conscious cultivation of an identity and national character distinct from its larger and more powerful American neighbor.

The Canadian tradition of welcoming dissenters began with the United Empire Loyalists, who were loyal to England during the American Revolution, and extended through the Civil War with the admission to Canada of runaway slaves. In contrast with the United States, the policy of slavery, which led the United States into Civil War in the mid-nineteenth century, had been formally abolished by a 1793 enactment in Upper Canada (today the province of Ontario), and all slaves in the British colonies were emancipated by Imperial legislation in 1833. As a result, many slaves who escaped from the United States sought refuge in Canada because African Americans felt safer in British territory.[37] Lacking a fugitive slave law, Canada followed the common law doctrine that slaves became free upon arriving on free soil.

Hence, Canada's national character has proven distinct from the United States, thereby confirming that North America does not consist of culturally identical nations possessing an identical set of values or, at the very least, not sharing similar values to the same degree. Their differences are largely attributable to divergent histories and national characters derived from values disseminated by early waves of immigrants interacting within local environments.

---

[36] Ibid., 49.

[37] Charles L. Blockson, *The Underground Railroad* (New York, NY: Prentice-Hall, 1987), 62.

Transmigration of British values

American political philosopher Louis Hartz asserted in his "fragment theory" that such new societies as Canada, the United States, and Australia were initially established by incomplete fragments of culture and diverse values brought by emigrants from Europe to their new societies, which ultimately became solidified as part of the founding cultures of the "new world."[38] Therefore, because the United States and Canada were settled and developed by different immigrant populations, the respective cultures within Australia, Canada, and even the United States differ as a result.[39] Consistent with Hartz's theories, Patrick O'Farrell observes that, arguably, "many of the evident distinctions between the character of the American and Australian Irish spring from their being established, in the main bulk, by different generations of Irish: America absorbed the Famine; Australia's Irish population was mainly post-Famine, those whose families had come through that period and who were better educated, less traumatised, with more 'English' ways."[40]

While more recent Australian Irish may have had more "English ways," they remained understandably unsympathetic to British rule. Nonetheless, given that nearly four million Irish went to North America and just over one-third of a million migrated to Australia and New Zealand in the post-Famine period of 1851–1921, the contrast between Australia and the United States is quite evident. However, there was a discernible difference between the typical Irish immigrant who went to Australia and one who chose to go to the United States.

O'Farrell points out that the typical Irish who went to Australia in the post-Famine period—unlike the convict era—did so by a "sense of adventure, and by those moved by enterprise and calculation," notably the economic incentive of the Australian gold rushes which brought 101,000 Irish immigrants to Australia in the decade of 1851–60. For many, the lure of gold was sufficient enough of an attraction to migrate by one's own financial means rather than seek government assistance for the voyage. For instance, of the 6,200 Irish who came to Australia

---

[38] Louis Hartz, *The Founding of New Societies: Studies in the History of the United States, Latin America, South Africa, Canada, and Australia* (New York, NY: Harcourt, Brace Jovanovich, 1964), 3–23.

[39] Mebs Kanji and Neil Nevitte, "Who are the Most Deferential—Canadians or Americans?" in *Canada and the United States: Differences that Count*, ed. David M. Thomas, 2nd ed. (Orchard Park, NY: Broadview Press, 2000), 121.

[40] Patrick O'Farrell, *The Irish in Australia: 1788 to the Present* (Notre Dame, IN: Indiana University Press, 2000), 63.

in 1854, a significant 1,200 who arrived in Victoria arrived without any government assistance even though the journey to Australia was more expensive than the voyage to the United States.[41]

Furthermore, O'Farrell notes, the relatively large number of Irish immigrants to Australia in the mid-to-late nineteenth century suggests other important factors. "To these later immigrants, the Famine was history, not direct experience, nor was it subject to its embittered American interpretation." O'Farrell argues, these Irish "came from a rapidly changing Ireland in which the arbiters of the quality of life—education, health, prosperity, religion—were all improving in character, becoming more 'English'—whatever nationalists might think, easing the integration of Irish immigrants into the Australian colonies."[42]

The immigration experience may have eased in this way, but total assimilation was neither expected nor achieved. After all, while the Irish who came to Australia might have been less militantly nationalistic compared to many of the Irish who were attracted to America, they still possessed cultural characteristics that precluded them from embracing the British characteristics of the ruling elites. As Australia's national character developed, therefore, it appears to have absorbed cultural characteristics from the growing Australian Irish Catholic community.

American sociologist Seymour Martin Lipset has argued that differences between Canadian and American culture are the result of distinct formative experiences. Unlike Canada, the United States began out of a *revolutionary* past, and, besides Iceland, was "the first new nation, the first colony . . . to become independent."[43] Thus, instead of maintaining the tradition of social hierarchy and status differences typical of post-feudal and monarchical cultures, the new American society embraced and institutionalized what Lipset calls the "American Creed," the five values of egalitarianism, individualism, liberty, populism, and free-market capitalism.[44]

In contrast to these developments in the United States, the founding fragments of Canada have been described by Lipset as being "*counter-revolutionary*" because rather than go along with the Americans, Canadians

---

[41]   Ibid., 63–65.

[42]   Ibid., 65.

[43]   Seymour Martin Lipset, *American Exceptionalism: A Double-Edged Sword* (New York, NY: W.W. Norton & Company, 1996), 18.

[44]   Ibid., 19.

chose instead to maintain their ties to England.[45] One important reason was the legitimate fear of US invasion that would eventually prompt the need for the British North America Act of 1867—renamed in 1982 as the *Constitution Act, 1867*—by which the British Parliament (Westminster) transformed a British colony into the semi-independent Dominion of Canada, a nation that directed its own domestic interests while England controlled its foreign policies.[46]

If, as Lipset asserts, the United States formed as a result of revolution to create a new kind of government, and Canada formed as the result of counterrevolution through its extended struggle to maintain a historical source of legitimacy, Canada's government derived its right to rule from a monarchy linked to church establishment as opposed to the US government's adherence to sacrosanct provisions and ideals set out in its revolutionary constitution. Hence, both the Canadian government and Canada's immigrants enjoyed the maintenance of links to England's monarchy and government, in part out of respect for the traditions of English rule but also to preserve its distinctiveness from its much larger and powerful neighbor to the south.

The divergence that separates Canada from the United States began with the impact of their respective founders and continued as a result of the perpetuation of different values and frames of reference. According to Lipset, "The very organizing principles that framed these nations, the central cores around which institutions and events were to accommodate, were different." Lipset asserts that the United States "was Whig and classically liberal or libertarian—doctrines that emphasize distrust of state, egalitarianism, and populism—reinforced by a voluntaristic and congregational religious tradition." At the same time, Canada "was tory and conservative in the British and European sense—accepting of the need for a strong state, for respect for authority, for deference—and endorsed by hierarchically organized religions that supported and were supported by the state."[47]

Indeed, not unlike the Roman Catholic Church from which King Henry VIII parted ways in the early sixteenth century, the traditional structure of the Church of England remained very hierarchical. As a result, many of its adherents were accustomed to social stratification,

---

[45] Seymour Martin Lipset, *Continental Divide: The Values and Institutions of the United States and Canada* (New York, NY: Routledge, 1990), 1–2.

[46] Kanji and Nevitte, "Who are the Most Deferential—Canadians or Americans?," 122.

[47] Lipset, *Continental Divide*, 2.

whether communal or ecclesiastical. People implicitly accepted the notion that some individuals had privilege based on their position in society, a practice sanctioned by the dominant culture for centuries. This familiarity would be expected to encourage deference among English Canadians.

In the Australian context, acceptance of social disparity was likely limited to local communities of cultural affiliation—such as among Australian Irish Catholics—rather than garner broad approval of the legitimacy of hierarchy that was embraced by the governing British establishment. Thus, deference to those of higher rank was more widely accepted across Canadian society given relative tolerance of British tradition, class differences, and power disparity—a feature of Canadian culture particularly noticeable when compared with the more vocal and assertive behavior of United States organized labor relative to Canada.

However, besides religious influence, there was the impact of practical political thought on people, preserving beliefs about how individuals ought to behave in the new societies. Canada's different outlook from the United States is clear when key phrases in the formal documents that founded each nation are compared. In the US Constitution, the objectives of the "good society" are described as "life, liberty, and the pursuit of happiness." In contrast, the founding fathers of Canada defined their guiding rationale as "peace, order, and good government," underscoring deference to British parliamentary tradition and social ideals. Hence, while the authority for the former is "the people"—as stated in the preamble to the US Constitution and ratified by state legislatures— Canada, observes Lipset, "saw its new government as a continuation of the ancient English monarchy and sent its constitution to London to be enacted by the British Parliament and proclaimed by the Queen."[48]

In Australia, where "to live, let live and allow a fair go" is a guiding national sentiment,[49] the dual Anglo-Celtic identity was implicitly recognized early on, which highlights the powerful influence the Irish exerted over the course of the nineteenth century. According to Australian political scientist Alastair Davidson, Australia's Nationality

---

[48] Ibid., xiii.
[49] Henry S. Albinski, "Australia and the United States," in *Australia: The Daedalus Symposium*, ed. Stephen R. Graubard, 395–420 (North Ryde, NSW: Angus & Robertson, 1985), 404.

and Citizenship Act (1948) "defines an 'alien' as a 'person who is not a British subject, an Irish citizen, or a protected person,' "[50] reinforcing the image of Australians as that of an Anglo-Celtic people.

Although in law there was no such thing as an "Australian citizen" until 1948 as all Australian nationals were considered British subjects, Davidson notes, "The citizen rights which they enjoyed—the vote which through its equal exercise by all reasoning beings makes the people sovereign and establishes a democracy, and what is needed to exercise that vote properly: freedom of conscience, speech, organization and freedom from economic and social constraints—were all remarkably restricted in Australia," at least until the 1972 reelection of the ALP government.[51] That the ALP had considerable Australian Irish support from the outset appears to be a profound indication of the significant power the Australian Irish community exerted on the Australian national consciousness.

Like their Australian counterparts, Canadians were classified as British subjects until the 1947 *Canadian Citizenship Act* officially changed the label of national identification to Canadian citizen. While citizenship acknowledged Canada's rising stature as an independent nation, Canada's cultural, political, and emotional pro-British stance remained in force. This is particularly evident in Canadian views of Americans. The Canadian propensity for anti-American sentiment has become as much a part of the national character as value differences. Although resentments have risen and fallen over the centuries, they have not been extinguished and therefore lie beneath the surface of Canadian identity and values, contributing to a Canadian sense of independence.

Although much farther away from the United States than Canada, Australia has also developed a reserved view of the United States. According to Australian historian David Mosler, "Historically, the Anglo-Australian elite had a traditional Tory disdain for everything American, especially the products of its popular culture and education system; all things British were superior. In the 1970s, the left opposition to the Vietnam War hardened antagonism to the American behemoth, and this antagonism spread into the arts, literature, film, and popular culture. Australians feel swamped and threatened by the global

[50] Alastair Davidson, *From Subject to Citizen: Australian Citizenship in the Twentieth Century* (Cambridge, UK: Cambridge University Press, 1997), 144–45.
[51] Ibid., 145.

homogenization of culture emanating from the United States."[52] This opposition, one might argue, also reflects Irish rebellious influences. For Canada, however, anti-American sentiments exist in a more subtle manner perhaps because of such close proximity to the United States as well as the Canadian tendency toward deference.

"Anti-Americanism" as a unifying force in Canadian culture

Canada's relatively small population yet enormous geography has always caused Canadians some concern, if not qualified suspicion, of the potential for American political and military expansionist interests to encroach into Canada, and thereby cause Canadians legitimate fear of the potential loss of their independent cultural identity. Once culture is lost, political autonomy is not far behind. Given the threat of Manifest Destiny—the popular early nineteenth-century American desire to expand its borders throughout the North American continent—such a fear was not irrational. Dealing with the challenge, however, Canadians derived a greater sense of national identity and strengthened their separate national character.

In contrast, Australia lacked the political and cultural pressures that geographic proximity to a large power like the United States entailed. Yet, the vast distance from Europe meant that any voluntary migration to Australia had to be made with considerable seriousness. "The fact of distance and the time patterns of Irish migration suggest that the Irish emigrant to Australia was a thoughtful one," observes O'Farrell, "not necessarily well informed . . . but thoughtful in the sense that it represented a forward commitment and investment of life."[53] Unlike Australia's experience being far removed from Europe and the United States, therefore, Canada's close proximity to the United States posed some unique challenges. Among the earliest and most pivotal was the War of 1812.[54]

---

[52] David Mosler, *Australia, The Recreational Society* (Westport, CT: Praeger, 2002), 89.

[53] O'Farrell, *The Irish in Australia*, 65.

[54] The War of 1812 was instigated by the British Navy's boarding of American ships to forcibly enlist sailors of British origin and the attempts to prevent the United States from trading with France. In addition, the Americans, who were encountering strong resistance from Indians in their push westward, believed that Great Britain was encouraging Indian opposition. However, the War of 1812 was not a fight among equals since 7.5 million Americans were at war

The War, declared on Great Britain by US President James Madison on June 18, 1812, remains a source of pride especially for English-speaking Canadians. Many inhabitants, primarily of Upper Canada (present-day Ontario) but also of Lower Canada (Quebec), fought alongside the Regular British Army and Indian allies to thwart American plans to capture what were then the British colonies on their northern border. Since the invasion and conquest of Canada was a major objective of the United States, the War of 1812 remains of considerable historical significance for Canada and marked the intensification of an enduring trend of Canadian suspicion toward the United States.

Given the failure of the United States to conquer Canadian lands, the war was of enormous existential importance to Canadians. If the United States had been successful, Canada would not have evolved into the independent country it is today. Hence, the War of 1812, Canadian military historian Desmond Morton asserts, "was reshaped to suit local mythology," with the Battle of Chateauguay and the Battle of Queenston Heights "reflecting the French–English duality and the American-born Laura Secord," who had warned a British officer of America's planned attack on his outpost, "symbolizing heroic Canadian womanhood."[55] While the War of 1812 did not arouse the same level of interest in Great Britain, Canadian diplomat and historian Hugh Keenleyside observes, "in Canada it aroused the provinces of British North America to a consciousness of nationhood."[56] Although Canada owes its present shape to negotiations that grew out of the peace, "the war itself—or the myths created by the war," observes Pierre Berton, "gave Canadians their first sense of community."[57]

Formative experiences that led to the development of the Australian and Canadian national characters reveal the influence of the dominant ethnic populations who settled there. In turn, their influences helped perpetuate local culture. "The modern Canadian," observes historian F. George Kay, "is as much a national individual as the Briton of the

---

with a neighboring region populated by a mere 500,000. Nonetheless, on June 18, 1812, at the height of the Napoleonic conflict in Europe, the United States declared war on Great Britain and struck at the only British possession on the continent—Canada.

[55] Desmond Morton, *A Military History of Canada: From Champlain to Kosovo,* 4th ed. (Toronto, ON: McClelland & Stewart, 1999), 70.

[56] Hugh Keenleyside, *Canada and the United States: Some Aspects of the History of the Republic and the Dominion* (Port Washington, NY: Kennikat Press, 1929), 56.

[57] Pierre Berton, "The War of 1812," in *The Canadian Encyclopedia: Year 2000 Edition,* ed. James H. Marsh (Toronto, ON: McClelland & Stewart, 1999), 2,475.

late Middle Ages—and can be of quite as mixed an ancestry. The young Canadian may have descended from half a dozen nationals who have migrated to Canada in the past two centuries, and the girl he marries may have family links with another half-dozen countries. With this mixed ancestry this typical young Canadian couple will not be of French origin, and so they will speak English. Perhaps unconsciously they will observe British customs, and certainly they will be conscious that their rights as citizens are based on British traditions."[58] Kay's observation underscores Canada's traditionally close ties to Britain and British influences, and its resistance to acceptance of an American identity.

*   *   *

English-speaking Canadians share an identity heavily nuanced by a mixture of British values, beliefs, and customs, but they embrace a unique national character that has been maintained and perpetuated by immigrants who may not have reflected Anglo-Celtic backgrounds, yet, because of socialization and acculturation, took on cultural features of the predominant groups that helped shape Canadian values, character, and identity. With regard to core values, Australia is similar to Canada in having a unique national character that persons of varied ethnicity within the Australian mosaic come to share.

As waves of immigrants from diverse lands settled alongside indigenous peoples, many ethnic cultures had an impact on Australia and Canada in one form or another. Yet settlers from the British Isles— English, Scots, and Irish—set the dominant cultural course because they represented the majority of immigrants in the nineteenth and early twentieth centuries. Just because Australia and Canada share in common a particular source of migrants, however, does not imply their respective Anglo-Celtic–based cultures should be identical. They are not because settlers came from a region in Europe that was itself not culturally or geographically uniform. Hence, the different sensibilities the English, Scottish, and Irish brought to Australia and Canada did not produce culturally identical societies. The subtle disparities gave rise to unique nations.

Given stable contemporary national identities and well-articulated independent voices on the international stage, Australian and

---

[58] F. George Kay, *The British: From Pre-History to the Present Day* (London, UK: Frederick Muller, 1969), 165.

Canadian cultural differences can therefore be traced to the influence of the primary source of immigrants during their early years as British colonies, a time when national identity and culture began to form. For Australia, the Irish Catholic factor exercised a decisive role, whereas for English Canada, British and American influences proved most influential.

The Irish Catholic factor in Australian culture

For a half-century following the arrival of the First Fleet in 1788, Australia served primarily as a jail where the vast majority of initial immigrants from the British Isles did not arrive by choice. Canada, lacking Australia's convict history, attracted a substantial number of voluntary immigrants from a similar region of Europe. Though convicts and majority of nineteenth-century free settlers to Australia—from all socioeconomic classes—originated in England, Ireland, Scotland, and Wales, the convicts were significantly represented by the Irish and their influence proved particularly strong on the Australian working class. In contrast, the influence of the Scots on Australia was disproportionately weak, and the impact of the Welsh, negligible. In the early nineteenth century, there were few Welsh convicts and immigrants. In the census of 1841, for example, of 51,680 persons in New South Wales only 558 gave Wales as their birthplace.[59]

Therefore, convicts in Australia—an overwhelming number being of Irish extraction—represented a different stratum of Anglo-Celtic society. Population statistics for New South Wales reveal that in 1828 convicts comprised 43 percent of the population and free immigrants just 13 percent. The geographic reference to New South Wales includes present-day Queensland, an area that was part of New South Wales until 1859 when it became a separate British colony (and later federated as a state of the Commonwealth of Australia in 1901). This area is emphasized because New South Wales contained most of the population in the early period of Australia's modern history. It is also the location from which the "Old Australian," up-country ethos described by Australian historian Russel Ward began and subsequently spread to the rest of the continent.[60] By 1851, however, the numbers had notably reversed with about 1.5 percent convicts and 41 percent free

[59] Russel Ward, *The Australian Legend* (Melbourne, VIC: Oxford University Press, 1958), 47.

[60] Ward, *The Australian Legend*, 68, fn. 2.

Table 2.1   Composition of the Australian Population

Year	Roman Catholic	Presbyterian	Church of England plus remainder of population	Total	Roman Catholic	Presbyterian
					Percentage of Total Population	
1841	33,249	11,109	72,630	116,988	28.4	9.5
1851	56,899	18,156	112,188	187,243	30.4	9.7
1947	1,569,726	743,540	5,266,091	7,579,357	20.7	9.8

Source: Adapted from Russel Ward, *The Australian Legend* (Melbourne, VIC: Oxford University Press, 1958), 47, Table IV.

immigrants.[61] Hence, the substantial population of Irish who came to the country was indeed a dominant cultural force. In Australia, as in most other nations, convicts were viewed as members of a lower social class, yet given their overrepresentation in early Australian society—and subsequent transition into organized labor and politics—held enormous influence on the development of Australia's national character.

Numbers help reveal how significant the Irish community was in Australia. Since Australian census returns ask about religion, this helps discern place of origin, or the ethnicity of the population. Although there were Scots who were Catholics, and Irish who were Presbyterian—not to mention English who were Catholic and Presbyterian—Russel Ward asserts in *The Australian Legend* that these were rare cases that offset each other. The implication is that the number of professing Catholics in Australia, until the significant immigration following the Second World War, reasonably represented the size of the population of Irish descent. Similarly, the Presbyterian presence served as an estimate of the number of Australians of Scottish ancestry. Table 2.1 provides a picture of the population from Ward's perspective, using census data from 1841, 1851, and 1947.[62]

---

[61] *See* Ward, 15, Table 1.

[62] *See* Ibid., 47, Table IV. Figures for 1841 and 1851 refer to New South Wales, except for the Port Phillip District and Van Diemen's Land, from where so many of the colony of Victoria's population came. The figures for 1947 refer to Australia as a whole.

The greater number of Catholics relative to Presbyterians—roughly 3:1 in the nineteenth century and 2:1 in the twentieth—indicates just how large the Irish population was relative to the Scottish population in Australia. Significantly, this ethnic composition did not mirror the same composition in Britain and Ireland combined. The numbers reveal, asserts Ward, that "in the formative period of the 1840s, there were proportionately not twice but about three times as many people of Irish descent in New South Wales as there were in the British Isles," a numerical fact that underscores just how significant a presence the Irish was in early Australian society.[63] Prior to 1851 about half of the assisted immigrants arriving in New South Wales were Irish.[64]

Even more revealing of Irish influence on Australia's developing culture and national character was the uneven distribution of those of Irish and Scottish descent throughout colonial society. In Australia, most Irish convicts and immigrants were unskilled laborers—a large segment of the overall population—while a very high proportion of Scots, "even of those who landed with little or no capital," observes Ward, "became rich or at least 'successful.' "[65] Research by historian Bill Rubenstein has found that, among the wealthy of New South Wales in the middle of the nineteenth century, almost none were Irish Catholics.[66]

The reason why the Irish comprised such a substantial number of early convicts is largely because the majority of Scottish convicts were kept in jails in Great Britain rather than shipped off to the Australian colonies. Due to differences between the English and Scottish legal systems, the relatively fewer Scottish convicts who were sent to Australia were likely to have been very serious criminals. As for why Scots did better financially in Australia, Ward cites three reasons. First, a high proportion of Scottish migrants were of middle class, tenant–farmer stock. Second, the Scots' Presbyterian faith, at least in practice, "often came near to equating virtue with material success," and instilled in the minds of Scottish immigrants "the habits of hard work and frugality," the origins Max Weber discussed persuasively in his *Protestant Ethic*. Third, the average standard of education was "as much above that of England as England's was above

---

[63] Ibid., 46–48.

[64] R.B. Madgwick, *Immigration into Eastern Australia, 1788–1851* (Sydney, NSW: Sydney University Press, 1969), 234.

[65] Ward, 48.

[66] Bill Rubenstein, "The Top Wealth-holders of New South Wales in 1830–44," *The Push from the Bush* 8 (December 1980): 34–35.

Ireland's," which helped give the Scottish immigrants to Australia a clear
lead in the race for material and social success in the colonies.[67]

Regarding the financial success of many Scottish immigrants, in *The
Protestant Ethic and the Spirit of Capitalism*, Max Weber argued that the
Protestant ethic encouraged people to apply themselves rationally to
their work. His analysis concluded that the Calvinist beliefs around
the concept of predestination were critical. Followers of Calvin believe
that one could not do good works or perform acts of faith to assure
one's place in heaven. Rather, one is either among the "elected" or
one was not. However, wealth was deemed to be a sign by the populace whether or not one was among God's elect, thereby serving to
encourage people to acquire wealth. In this way, the Protestant ethic
provided religious sanctions that fostered a spirit of rigorous discipline that encouraged people to apply themselves rationally toward
the acquisition of wealth.

Given their desire to establish economic and professional roots,
therefore, the Scots were more accepting of British rule, and many Scots
assumed leadership positions in Australia as part of a large contingent
of patriotic British overseers. In New South Wales, three of the first six
governors were Scottish born: John Hunter was from Leith, Lachlan
Macquarie from Ulva, and Thomas Brisbane from Larges in Ayrshire.
Moreover, the first governor of Western Australia, Sir James Stirling of
Lanarkshire, governor of Victoria, Sir Henry Barkly, and governor of
South Australia, Sir James Fergusson of Edinburgh, were all of Scottish
origin. As the Scots rose in prominence, their ties to the British ruling
culture grew stronger, whereas the Irish, whose Catholic religious
identity was a unifying and cohesive force, were able to preserve their
distinctiveness in Australian society in which they represented a large
proportion of the working class, and therefore held a powerful advantage over other ethnic groups.

Unlike the Scots, many Irish Catholics tended to disapprove of
British rule given resentment of continued British control over Ireland.
Without a doubt, Irish Catholics presented a great challenge to the
established Protestant/Anglican colonial society in Australia because
of the Irish culture's natural antagonism toward England, with its
different religious traditions, values, and colonial hold on Australia.
This strong Irish Catholic influence has prompted O'Farrell to assert
that "the Irish have been the dynamic factor in Australian history"

---
[67] Ward, 48–49.

and therefore "the galvanizing force at the centre of the evolution of [Australia's] national character."[68]

Indeed, Roman Catholic belief and Irish nationality had been intimately associated in colonial Australia.[69] As mentioned, the first Catholics in Australia were convicts, almost entirely of Irish origin, as well as some of the members of the military. Up until 1868, among the convicts transported to Australia, roughly one quarter, or nearly 30,000 men and slightly more than 9,000 women, arrived directly from Ireland. "Of these a significant group were not ordinary criminals," O'Farrell observes, "Even in their felonry the Irish tended to stand apart, particularly in the early years of the penal colony. Whereas the English and Scots were mostly thieves, nearly a third of the 2,086 offenders transported from Ireland up to 1803 had been convicted of riot or sedition, crimes of political or social protest." O'Farrell asserts, "Among the Irish convicts were a considerable number whose personal characters were incorrupt, men of principle, spirit and integrity whose crime was some form of rebellion against British rule. Heinous and dreadful though that crime might be to English eyes, it was of a kind radically different from that which sprang from personal depravity."[70]

These are strong words, but O'Farrell provides a vivid picture of the European population of the early Australian era. While Australia has few reasons to celebrate its origins as a prison or a colony of exported criminals, Australian Catholicism has little reason to delight in many of those who shared the faith in the early years of colonization. O'Farrell points out, however, that Australian Catholicism "had less taint, for some of its convict members were men of piety, far from common criminals"; nonetheless, true criminals did comprise two-thirds of the Irish transportees.[71] Although a high number of Irish convicts to Australia were genuine criminals, O'Farrell stresses that all research suggests that they were "a better type of convict, less criminally inclined . . . less likely to turn to crime in Australia," and most of the Irish convicts were peasants, one-third of whom possessed skills of one sort or another.[72]

Given their composition, therefore, the majority of the Irish convicts were able to join the urban and rural working class in Australia.

[68] O'Farrell, *The Irish in Australia*, 10.
[69] Geoffrey Partington, *The Australian Nation: Its British and Irish Roots* (New Brunswick, NJ: Transaction Publishers, 1997), 59.
[70] Patrick O'Farrell, *The Catholic Church and Community: An Australian History*, 3rd rev. ed. (Kensington, NSW: New South Wales University Press, 1992), 2.
[71] O'Farrell, *The Catholic Church and Community*, 3.
[72] O'Farrell, *The Irish in Australia*, 24–25.

"Political rebels" who were imprisoned for nationalist activities, comprised fewer than 600 in the entire history of transportation, which represented about 1.5 percent, with the vast majority arriving prior to 1806. "Social rebels," comprised of those convicted of crimes related to violent protest against poverty and landlords, represented 20 percent. Thus, the record indicates that 80 percent of Irish convicts during the penal colony period were "ordinary criminals," about a third of them having prior convictions.[73] As mentioned, among convicts the Irish were nearly all Catholic while the English and Scottish convicts were virtually all Protestants. This made "Irish" and "Catholic" for all intents and purposes synonymous in early Australia.[74]

Whether the Irish arrived to Australia as convicts or as free immigrants, they were not likely to embrace the values of the British rulers of Australia. One overriding reason for this is that in Australia an embittered rift existed between the Irish Catholic convicts and their English and Scottish overseers who held power and authority. From his keen insights in both Irish and Australian Irish history, O'Farrell writes:

> To the Protestant ascendancy of penal Australia—comprising the governors, the officers, the administrators, the leading churchmen and citizens—there were two essential conditions of civilisation: the Protestant religion and British political and social institutions. On both counts the Irish were barbarians. Irish history offered the British ample evidence of this. Since the sixteenth century Ireland had constantly resisted British rule, resistance met with repression. From the misery and ignorance of eighteenth-century Ireland, burdened in defeat with confiscation, saddled with an expropriating colonialism, and constricted by penal laws, sprang something of noble nationalism, but mostly an anarchy of brutality, drunkenness, irresponsibility, malevolence, breaking out, in 1798, in bloody rebellion.[75]

The result of this assertion of fierce Irish rebelliousness was ever increasing condemnation by non-Irish rulers. According to O'Farrell,

---

[73] O'Farrell, *The Catholic Church and Community*, 3.
[74] Ibid., and O'Farrell, *The Irish in Australia*, 25.
[75] O'Farrell, *The Catholic Church and Community*, 3–4.

The righteous English Protestant (and even more so the Presbyterian Scot) regarded the Catholic Irish with dark suspicion and short contempt. And fear. English rule in Ireland bred rebellions, and seemed, to hostile eyes, to enshrine the power of the priesthood as leaders of disloyalty and discontent. Popery and priestcraft, expressed in resistance to English rule, were seen as sinister menaces to that higher order of civilisation which the English so resolutely assumed they represented. As in Ireland, so in Australia: there, planted with the colony itself, grew local forms of the Irish social relationships, composed of ignorance and misunderstanding, myths and prejudice, fear and hatred. This obsessive antagonism between Anglo-Scots Protestant ascendancy and Irish convict Catholicism, established with the foundation of Australia, has been a central and persistent theme in the history of Catholicism's relations with its Australian environment. Its influence has been tragically corrosive.[76]

As O'Farrell's description vividly details, the deep-rooted divide between Irish Catholic and British Protestant came over from the shores of the British Isles to the shores of Australia. However, this divide was not as significant in Canada where Protestant Irish outnumbered Catholic, and Catholic Irish appeared more content with pro-British rule in Canada.

Canada's Irish community

While the Irish were fewer in Canada due to a preference for the United States when settling in North America, Colm Kiernan observes, "From the beginning there was always the impression that emigrants from Ireland were different from those of other lands." The primary distinction was their religion since "Irish Protestants assimilated so easily into the Australian community."[77]

They assimilated without difficulty in Canada as well. Between 1825 and 1845, about 450,000 Irish left Ireland for Canada. Most settled in Quebec, New Brunswick, and Upper Canada (Ontario), with the number of Irish migrants arriving in Newfoundland, Nova Scotia, and Prince Edward Island declining by the 1830s. Since passage to British North America (as Canada was known prior to 1867) was cheaper than

---

[76] Ibid., 4.
[77] Colm Kiernan, "Introduction," in *Ireland and Australia*, ed. Colm Kiernan (Dublin, Ireland: Mercier Press, 1984), 7.

traveling directly to the United States, about a half of these migrants ultimately made their way to the United States; however, given that 80 percent of Ireland's population was Catholic, the vast majority of migrants who came to Canada and traveled onto the United States were Irish Catholic.[78]

Unlike the dominant Catholicism among Australia's Irish settlers, the majority of Canadians of Irish ancestry was Protestant. In total, close to 900,000 Irish arrived to Canada between the years 1825 and 1870, a figure which outnumbered English and Scots two to one and therefore changed the nature of British North America, especially Ontario and New Brunswick where United Empire Loyalists had formerly been the majority. The Irish, by the time of Confederation in 1867, had become the largest ethnic group in Canada after the French, comprising about 25 percent of the population.[79]

According to population statistics, however, the Irish in Canada fell from nearly a quarter of the general population in 1871 to less than one-tenth in 1961, a dramatic decline that occurred primarily because Irish migrants tended to select the United States in which to settle rather than Canada.[80] As a consequence, English Canada's passive resistance to American influence, and lack of a resilient, domestic Irish Catholic factor, led to the retention of English colonial values and stronger emotional attachment to England. Australia's significant Irish Catholic population's opposition to English colonial traditions helped shape Australian values, which led this fervently independent nation to be more receptive to American anticolonial sentiments and culture.[81]

While Australia experienced a more profound and enduring cultural influence from the Irish, Ireland itself did have an impact on Canada by providing important models of social control. For instance, as David Wilson points out, the dominant form of law enforcement in Canada—the Royal Canadian Mounted Police, or RCMP—followed the Irish precedent of the Royal Irish Constabulary, which had been established in Ireland in the 1830s and organized along military lines, supplied with weapons and housed in barracks, in order to deal with

[78] Donald Mackay, *Flight from Famine: The Coming of the Irish to Canada* (Toronto, ON: McClelland & Stewart, 1990), 13.

[79] Ibid., 14.

[80] David A. Wilson, *The Irish in Canada* (Ottawa, ON: Canadian Historical Association, 1989), 11–12.

[81] Partington, viii–xi.

the special circumstances of widespread agrarian violence in Ireland that required a special type of policing, as opposed to England and Scotland, where local municipalities dealt with disorder within their own boundaries and satisfied by a centrally controlled police.[82] Ireland created its own type of force, just as was subsequently established in Canada.

The Irish system of education also became extremely influential in early Canada. For instance, the Irish system of strong central control over what was instructed in school was employed in Ontario, as was the Irish pattern of providing local school boards daily control of the schools and of teacher employment policy. Just like in Ireland, therefore, Ontario's structure of education combined a strong central educational authority with considerable local control without a "middle management."[83] This system, introduced into Ontario during the 1840s by educational reformer Egerton Ryerson, was incorporated into British Columbia by John Jessop, who had studied in Ryerson's teacher-training school in Toronto in the 1850s—a school operated by masters who came from the central Irish normal school in Dublin—and as a result British Columbia's Public School Act of 1872 was based on Ryerson's Ontario legislation of 1846–71. In fact, Ryerson's system was followed in Manitoba and the Northwest Territories, giving the Irish educational model considerable indirect influence in Canada.[84]

The content of the Ontario school curriculum was brought in directly from Ireland. Since 1831, Ireland had created a system of mass education built around a set of schoolbooks called the "Irish National Readers," which, notes Wilson, "have been described as the best series of elementary school texts in the nineteenth century English-speaking world."[85] During the 1840s, when Ryerson took charge of the Ontario school system, he introduced these Irish texts into Ontario's schools; thus, by the time of Confederation in 1867, asserts Wilson, "virtually all young people of English, Scottish and Irish ethnicity in that province," as well as many individual schools in Quebec and the Atlantic provinces, "acquired their ideas of political loyalty and were taught moral values through a curriculum that had been designated specifically for Ireland."[86]

---

[82] Wilson, 18.
[83] Ibid., 19.
[84] Ibid.
[85] Ibid., 18.
[86] Ibid., 18–19.

It must be stressed, however, that these Irish books *did not* contain Irish history, language or folklore, but rather served to "reflect and reinforce British cultural and political values."[87] Therefore, these "Irish" influences were more "Anglo-Irish" since English ideas were perpetuated in these books. Likewise, since fewer Irish settled in Canada in favor of the United States, those who remained in Canada were "quickly and easily assimilated into the Canadian mainstream." Their knowledge of English, and familiarity with British political, social, and cultural traditions ensured quick assimilation.[88] Irish influence over other aspects of Canadian life, such as in the areas of organized labor and politics, was therefore less powerful than in Australia where notably the Irish Catholics, given their strong hold on Irish identity, exercised a profound influence on Australian society.

Religion also helped Irish assimilation in Canada. Canadian historian Donald Akenson asserts that "the Irish immigrant of Anglican persuasion entered easily into a religious system in which Irishmen were the largest single power bloc and the liturgy and theology very close to those of his old parish church in Ireland."[89] Especially in Upper Canada (Ontario), Akenson maintains, "one should look behind the pretensions of the 'Church of England' and recognize four facts: the Irish were the largest nineteenth-century immigrant group; most Protestants in Ireland were Anglicans; this numerical dominance was heightened by the Anglicans in Ireland almost certainly being overrepresented among the emigration-prone lower and lower-middle classes as compared to the Presbyterians; and the Anglican Church in Upper Canada had a strong Irish bias in its clergy."[90]

While an overwhelming majority of the Irish who remained in Canada was Protestant Anglo-Irish—half of the Irish who stayed in Canada had settled in Ontario where Protestants outnumbered Catholics of all ethnicities two to one—there was still a significant number of Catholic Irish among them.[91] But the Irish Catholics of Canada were very different from those in the eastern United States. As the majority of Irish Catholics who settled in Canada took up

---

[87] Ibid., 19.

[88] Ibid.

[89] Donald Harman Akenson, *The Irish in Ontario: A Study in Rural History*, 2nd ed. (Montreal, QC & Kingston, ON: McGill-Queen's University Press, 1999), 266.

[90] Ibid., 267.

[91] Partington, 329.

farming, Canadian historian Donald Mackay observes, there were "few Irish ghettoes and the raw Irish politics of cities such as Boston and New York were foreign to the Canadian experience."[92] One of the reasons the strongly Irish Catholic-influenced Atlantic-bordering colony of Newfoundland had declined to join the Canadian Confederation, notes Mackay, "was the fear that Confederation would mean domination by the Protestant Irish of Ontario," thus underscoring the substantial British Protestant influence over Canadian culture.[93] The former UK colony and dominion of Newfoundland—known officially as Newfoundland and Labrador since a 2001 Canadian constitutional amendment—did not join Canada as a province until 1949.

Thomas D'Arcy McGee, a journalist and lawyer who "became the leading Irish-Catholic politician in Canada," perhaps best exemplified the different attitude of the Irish Catholic who chose to settle in Canada instead of the United States. Disillusioned with Irish American nationalism and his impression of the marginal treatment the Irish received in the United States, Irish-born McGee changed his views about English rule and left Boston for Montreal in 1859 where over the next nine years, Mackay notes, "he had become a surprisingly ardent Canadian."[94] However, his contentious opposition to the Fenians—an American-based Irish militant organization that aimed to topple English rule in Ireland—led to his demise.[95] In 1868, after leaving a parliamentary session in Ottawa, a Fenian sympathizer assassinated him.

---

[92] Mackay, *Flight from Famine*, 15.

[93] Ibid., 329. The question of whether Newfoundland and Labrador should remain as an independent political entity or join the federation of the other British North American colonies was a contentious issue between 1864 and 1949. In 1864, Newfoundland delegates attended the Quebec Conference and signed the resolutions, which led to the 1867 British North America Act. But it was not until over eighty years later, in 1949, that Newfoundland finally chose to become a Canadian province.

[94] Mackay, 323–25.

[95] During the US Civil War, a number of Irish Americans began to organize themselves under the banner of Fenianism—the name given to the Irish Republican Brotherhood formed in 1858 in Ireland to establish a free and independent Ireland—with the intention to invade Canada and overthrow English rule. Threats of invasion turned to action during the "Fenian Raids" of 1866 and 1870, when bands of Fenians crossed into Canada but were ultimately repelled by the Canadian militia.

Comparing the Irish of Australia and Canada

An aggressive, even violent, opposition to English rule was supported by a significant number of Irish Catholics abroad who wanted an Ireland free of British control. This political objective differentiated Irish Catholics from Irish Protestants, and represents an indirect yet fundamental difference between Australia and Canada. While a preponderance of Irish Catholics who came to Canada moved on to the United States, the vast majority of the Irish who arrived in Australia remained in Australia and therefore had a greater and more enduring impact on Australian culture than on Canadian culture. Australians who trace their origins to Ireland form a substantial portion of contemporary society even though the number of Australians actually born in Ireland reached their height in 1891 with a population of 228,000, falling to a mere 44,813 by 1947 due to the twentieth-century's considerable drop in Irish immigration.[96]

In Australian historian Geoffrey Bolton's assessment of the Irish in Australian historiography, throughout the course of modern Australian history, writers of history have viewed the Irish and their influence through different lenses. Some writers have valued Irish Australians because they won acceptance among the ruling and wealthy classes and cultivated prominent positions for themselves in politics and the professions, while other historians "valued the Irish precisely because they represent dissent and rebellion, though there has been disagreement about the cause for which the Irish stood, whether religious freedom, democracy, nationalism, the right of small property-owners, or the advance towards Marxism."[97]

Yet, rebelliousness was a characteristic of Irishness in early Australia that was epitomized in some ways by the late-nineteenth century uprising at the Eureka Stockade, and the actions of outlaw Ned Kelly and his gang in Victoria. Whether or not their rebellious sentiment of dissent associated with anti-British convict-era settlers was reflective of their Irish ethnicity is difficult to determine since social conditions of

---

[96] Eric Richards, "Irish in Australia," in *The Oxford Companion to Australian History*, rev. ed., ed. Graeme Davison, John Hirst, and Stuart Macintyre (South Melbourne, VIC: Oxford University Press, 2001), 353.

[97] Geoffrey Bolton, "The Irish in Australian Historiography," in *Australia and Ireland, 1788–1988: Bicentenary Essays*, ed. Colm Kiernan (Dublin, Ireland: Gill and Macmillan, 1986), 6–7.

the time could have also contributed to such actions.[98] Nonetheless, the stereotype of the rebellious Irish Catholic who opposes authority and embraces egalitarianism, or social equality, is a feature of the Australian national character that persists to this day.

For Australia, suggests Australian writer Simon Caterson, the Irish rebels of the Castle Hill and the Eureka Stockade signify "an Irish-Australian, if not plain Australian, taste for gestures of defiance, a reflexive anti-authoritarianism which is paradoxically central to [Australian] culture." He notes, "One of the topsy-turvy things about Australia is the way people rush to identify themselves as an underdog or a battler, the way in which being an outsider, a misfit, is the conservative, established position."[99]

The Australian Irish sensibility is also found in poetry and song. Australian folk singer John Dengate illustrates this well in his popular poem, "The Answer's Ireland" (sung to a tune by Roddy McCorley).[100] Dengate's poem starts and ends with the verse, "Who gave Australia the tunes to sing, the tunes of songs so grand. Songs to inspire, full of beauty and Fire? The answer's Ireland."[101] This sentiment underscores the depth and breadth of Australia's Irish sensibilities. In light of different Anglo-Celtic cultural influences, however, Australia's Irish Catholic "rebellious" stereotype is completely foreign to the English Canadian personality.

British cultural dominance in Canada

Early in Canada's history, from the settlements in New France and subsequently in British North America, the national origin of residents was clear-cut. French settlements reflected the ethnic and religious dominance of the Roman Catholic Church. The settlements established by immigrants from Britain, and later increased by the arrival of United Empire Loyalists following the Peace of Paris in 1783, were characteristically Protestant. Hence, the British played a particularly important role in shaping Canadian culture and Canadian values in which later immigrant groups would become socialized. Indeed, Canadian sociologist Warren Kalbach notes, "those of English origin and Anglican

---

[98] Ibid., 15.

[99] Simon Caterson, "Irish-Australian Attitudes," *Quadrant* 48, no. 11 (2004): 12.

[100] Colleen Z. Burke and Vincent Woods, ed., *The Turning Point: Poems and Songs of Irish Australia* (Armidale, NSW: Kardoorair Press, 2001), 2.

[101] John Dengate, "The Answer's Ireland," in Burke and Woods, 12.

faith, while not always the majority, represented the dominant social, economic, political, and cultural power base, and thus gave early Canada its distinctive" British character.[102] However, the Scots, too, proved fundamentally important in the success of this effort.

Considering the inverse relationship between population and geography—Canada always being larger but less populous than the United States—the articulation and preservation of an independent Canadian identity rested on maintaining metaphorical distance from the United States through political and cultural emulation of British traditions and values. Maintaining a close connection with Great Britain—close enough to assert distinction from the United States, but not too close to deny Canadian political and cultural independence—was the best means available to achieve and maintain Canadian sovereignty from what was regarded by many Canadians as a territorially ambitious US neighbor. Canadian nationalism is therefore among the critical reasons for traditional Canadian caution toward the United States and American influences.

According to Canadian economist Henry Angus, Canada's distinctive character required maintaining bonds with Britain and resisting "any political vassalage to the United States." Social and economic relationships with the United States, though considered desirable by most pragmatic Canadians, "appeared as a danger the moment they involved the prospect of loss of identity."[103] Maintaining a barrier between Canada and the United States—via a strong cultural bond with Great Britain and corresponding deference to the British—was, therefore, as important to ensuring the preservation of a unique "Canadian" international identity as it was maintaining language and cultural barriers between English and French Canada to preserve each as inherent aspects of a single domestic Canadian identity. Outside the French province of Quebec, the alliance with "British" values and customs proved critical for Canada's successful resistance against US encroachment. Striking this alliance was not difficult considering the ethnic composition of English Canada's elites and general populace was mostly British.

From the nineteenth century onward, Canada grew as Canadian territory expanded from the center toward new borders along both the Atlantic and Pacific coasts. Within this vast territory, settlement

---

[102] Kalbach, "Ethnic Diversity: Canada's Changing Cultural Mosaic," 62.

[103] H.F. Angus, "Canadian Nationalism," in *Canada and Her Great Neighbor: Sociological Surveys of Opinions and Attitudes in Canada Concerning the United States*, ed. H. F. Angus (New Haven, CT: Yale University Press, 1938), 3–4.

patterns differed and British influence was stronger in some areas than others, which impacted regional opinions and attitudes toward Great Britain and the United States. The Maritime Provinces along Canada's eastern coastline are often described as "more British than the rest," observes Canadian philosopher H.L. Stewart, and therefore have proven strong supporters of " 'old country' institutions and usages," and were "less susceptible to influence from their great southern neighbor."[104] According to 1931 census records, about 72 percent of the population of Nova Scotia, New Brunswick, and Prince Edward Island could trace their ethnic origins to the British Isles, either through direct immigration by their ancestors or indirectly through United Empire Loyalists who escaped political persecution in the United States by settling in Canadian territory.[105] Other regions of Canada experienced a similarly large percentage of settlers who originated from the British Isles, the most from England but significant numbers from Scotland and Protestant Ireland.

Despite southern Ontario's close proximity to large, densely populated American cities, such as New York, Detroit, and Chicago, cultural development on each side of the border was not identical. By the early twentieth century, the ethnic composition of the urban population in the northern US states and the cities of Ontario had significantly diverged. While the large urban population centers of the United States received a huge number of immigrants from continental Europe in the latter half of the nineteenth century, the towns of Ontario continued to attract mainly British settlers, with the majority of continental European migrants to Canada moving west to the prairies.[106] According to the 1931 census, of the 3.4 million inhabitants of Ontario about 75 percent indicated British as their ethnic origin, with the English population greater than Irish and Scottish combined.[107]

Although United Empire Loyalists in Ontario fostered anti-American sentiments in the early part of the nineteenth century, their force gradually declined. Nonetheless, Canadian economist Alexander Brady points out, the substantial population in Ontario of British birth or extraction still feared "that the ever present American influence might destroy sympathies for things British," and thus proved extremely loud

[104] H.L. Stewart, "The Maritime Provinces," in Angus, *Canada and Her Great Neighbor*, 27.
[105] Ibid.
[106] A. Brady, "The Province of Ontario," in Angus, 43.
[107] Ibid., 43–44.

in defense of the British connection. In the 1890s, for instance, when news was released that the University of Toronto planned to confer upon English-born Canadian writer and academic Goldwin Smith an honorary degree, descendants of United Empire Loyalists carried out a vocal campaign objecting to the award given Smith's outspoken bias favoring the United States over Great Britain and Canada, a determined reaction which led Smith to decline the honor.[108]

Goldwin Smith had formerly been a Canadian nationalist. In the 1870s, he supported "Canada First," a nationalist movement founded in 1868 partly in response to the assassination of Thomas D'Arcy McGee, which sought to cultivate a strong sense of Canadian national identity. The organizers of the nationalist movement were committed to Canadian independence from the United States and to a strong British connection; however, following the conclusion of the 1871 *Treaty of Washington* between Britain and the United States—which among other provisions allowed US access to Canadian and Newfoundland inshore fisheries and the transfer of ownership of San Juan Island in British Columbia's Strait of Georgia to the United States—Canada First focused its energies on strengthening Canadian self-reliance and autonomy. But the aim, notes Canadian historian Bernard Vigod, "was some form of imperial federation, not separation from Britain."[109]

Although Canada First soon left the national stage as its leaders' interests moved into Ontario political action, which was not consistent with Canada First's original intentions, the "heirs were the later imperialists," asserts Vigod, who called for even greater ties to the British Empire as a means of protecting and advancing British values and institutions that they believed superior to others and the best route to defining and asserting a strong Canadian identity.[110]

Similar to nationalist groups in other parts of the world, the Canada First movement held some extreme discriminatory views—in the case of Canada, it was blatantly anti-Catholic and anti-French—but the general pro-British, anti-American sentiment resonated in many corners of Canada. Nonetheless, because of the demise of the Canada First movement, Goldwin Smith had arrived at the controversial opinion by the 1880s that Canada should join the United States, a widely criticized view

---

[108] Ibid., 49.

[109] B.L. Vigod, "Canada First," in *The Canadian Encyclopedia: Year 2000 Edition*, ed. James H. Marsh (Toronto, ON: McClelland & Stewart, 1999), 359.

[110] Ibid.

he published in his controversial 1891 book, *Canada and the Canadian Question*.[111]

Toronto's deference to British culture was less the result of continuing United Empire Loyalist tradition than a reflection of the dominant population's ethnic presence. Indeed, well into the twentieth century, Canada's biggest and most populous city had the largest population reflecting British origin in Canada. This community maintained strong cultural organizations, including the Orange Order and the Sons of England, which vigorously upheld this proud population's interpretation of British traditions.[112]

The Orange Order, named after England's William III, formerly William of Orange in Holland, the Protestant king who defeated the Catholic king, James II, at the Battle of the Boyne in Ireland on July 12, 1690, is a society formed by Irish Protestants in Northern Ireland in 1795. A Canadian branch was organized by Ogle Gowan, an Irish immigrant, who formed the Grand Lodge of British North America in 1830 at Brockville, Ontario. By 1870 there were more than a thousand Orange lodges in Canada. In Canada, as in Northern Ireland, Orangemen commemorate this victory each year because most Orangemen are fiercely loyal to Britain and wanted British culture and Protestantism to dominate throughout Canada. Historically, they opposed Catholic schools and use of the French language outside Quebec.

According to Akenson, the key to grasping how useful the Orange Order—comprised of about one hundred thousand members by

---

[111] Smith's work was written during a pessimistic era in late-nineteenth-century Canada when regions from east to west were isolated and the perception that English Canada would eventually assimilate with US social and cultural life was rising. Canadian Confederation was seen by Smith as artificially held together by corrupt politicians and commercial interests. Carl Berger, introduction to *Canada and the Canadian Question*, by Goldwin Smith, vi–vii. Smith's views were highly controversial. He postulated, "How much does an ordinary Canadian know or care about Australia, an ordinary Australian about Canada, or an ordinary Englishman, Scotchman, or Irishman about either? The feeling of all the Colonists towards the mother country, when you appeal to it, is thoroughly kind, as is that of the mother country towards the Colonies. But Canadian notions of British politics are hazy, and still more hazy are British notions of the politics of Canada . . . . A grand idea may be at the same time practical. The idea of a United Continent of North America, securing free trade and intercourse over a vast area, with external safety and internal peace, is no less practical than it is grand." Goldwin Smith, *Canada and the Canadian Question* (Toronto, ON: University of Toronto Press, 1971).

[112] Brady, "The Province of Ontario," 49.

1860—"was to the Protestant Irish is to recognize that in Canada West it was not an Irish society." Akenson asserts, "Unlike the St George's Society, the St Andrew's Society, and the (Catholic) St Patrick's Society, the Orange Order was not an ethnic or national association, and this was the key to its strength. Although Irish in origin, the Order attracted non-British Protestants of all denominations to its membership," serving as both a fortress of Protestantism and Britishness, and a fortification of colonial Protestantism.[113]

Anglo-Protestant ties to the British tradition, primarily through identification with history and monarchy, was therefore a formidable force preventing Canadian culture from becoming too close to the United States, a prospect that many feared could lead to Canada's political absorption into the United States.

This identification with Britishness was not confined to the Maritimes and Ontario, Canada's most populous province. Despite significant immigration from Central and Eastern Europe to Canada's largely agricultural Prairie Provinces, British dominance continued into the twentieth century. In Manitoba, Saskatchewan, and Alberta, the proportion of British-born in 1931 was 76.3 percent in Saskatchewan, 73 percent in Alberta, and about 52 percent in Manitoba.[114] British Columbia's population was then about 70 percent British in origin, of which roughly 56 percent was English.[115]

Even though the population in the West was not as uniformly British as in Ontario and the Maritimes, British elites achieved cultural dominance. By the twentieth century, British settlement had clearly dominated the Canadian landscape outside of the French province of Quebec. However, the strength of Canada's British character depended on earlier waves of Loyalists whose defense of British values provided a strong base of support for subsequent immigrants.

Canadians of English origin are by far the largest group whose ethnic origin was recorded as "British," which includes Scots, Welsh, and Irish, as well as English.[116] People of English descent came to Canada either

---

[113] Akenson, *The Irish in Ontario*, 277.

[114] G.M. Smith, "The Prairie Provinces," in Angus, *Canada and Her Great Neighbor*, 50–51.

[115] H.F. Angus, "British Columbia," in Angus, *Canada and Her Great Neighbor*, 55.

[116] The term British—referring to the inhabitants of, or whose ancestors inhabited, the British Isles—is controversial. According to Kay, "To be able to

directly from England or indirectly through the American colonies. While economic motives led migrants from England to Canada, for those of English descent who emigrated from the United States, motivation was largely political since most of them were United Empire Loyalists, who exercised a critical contribution to the establishment of Canada's national character.

The British Loyalist tradition

The American Revolution drove nearly one hundred thousand colonial Americans into exile due to their preference for British authority as a means of preserving their security and identity. The majority of these refugees came to Canada where they assimilated into local societies while preserving Loyalist traditions. In New Brunswick and Nova Scotia, in parts of Quebec, and in most of early settled Ontario, many towns and communities founded as a result of the Loyalist migration grew into large developed cities whereas others have remained quietly in the rural areas of the country. Canadian historian Christopher Moore asserts, "by numbers alone the loyalists command attention: conscious of it or not, many thousands of Canadians in every part of the country have loyalists in their family tree or loyalist communities in their background."[117]

The Loyalists are a key element in the development of Canada's national character because they "created a critical mass for Protestantism in Canada," notes Canadian religious historian Robert Choquette, "a tradition whose small numbers had formerly led to marginalization."[118] Their effective defeat during the American War of Independence, and their mistreatment under a new anti-British regime, drove the United Empire Loyalists northward into Canada where they were attracted as

---

dub oneself British is a statement of one's citizenship, hardly of race." The term Briton was not meaningful until 1603 when James I became the King of Britain, but not a significant description for most inhabitants until the 1707 Act of Union brought the Scottish and English Parliaments into one political entity. Even then, not everyone regarded themselves as "British." Kay asserts, "The Irish, the Channel Islanders and the Manxmen, not to mention thousands of Scotsmen and Orcadians, were neither British by culture nor political outlook." Kay, *The British*, 198–99.

[117] Christopher Moore, *The Loyalists: Revolution, Exile, Settlement* (Toronto, ON: McClelland & Stewart, 1994), 9.

[118] Robert Choquette, *Canada's Religions: An Historical Introduction* (Ottawa, ON: University of Ottawa Press, 2004), 160.

much by close political and emotional ties to Great Britain as they were to the free land made available to loyal British subjects leaving the new republic. A varied group, the Loyalists were tradesmen, farmers, soldiers, and frontiersmen of various religious traditions. Choquette notes, "the majority was Protestant, but some Catholics, Amerindians, and Jews were . . . among them."[119]

Following the Treaty of Paris in 1763 that formally ended the Seven Years War with Britain's victory, the French colonies in North America had been transferred to the British Crown. On July 4, 1776, the United States declared their independence from Great Britain and then fought the American Revolutionary War against their former English colonizers until 1783. England and France were at war with each other from 1792 to 1814, an era when Napoleonic France controlled most of Europe, and England ruled the oceans with its ships. Despite its victories in 1763, England's authority over North America had been limited to Upper and Lower Canada (Ontario and Quebec) and other northern colonies as a consequence of the American Revolution. With the influx of the Loyalists and subsequent British immigrants, Canada's national character was swiftly shaped.

The American Revolution had given the British an opportunity to maintain a North American stronghold by ensuring its cultural values and traditions would be preserved in Canada. There was a powerful conservative feeling underlying this activity. The kind of society the British wanted to create in Canada would be very different than what was created in the United States because that society would be a more conservative society that supported British institutions and the legitimacy of monarchy. The British government's policies for the new colonies of British North America proved very effective in ensuring that both the political institutions and the landholding structure not only were more conservative but also reinforced to help lay the foundations for the type of society that the Loyalists had desired in the American colonies.[120]

Loyalist conservatism in Canada was strengthened by two elements. First, those who preferred Canada over the United States—particularly the Highland Scots and the English gentry—were inherently conservative. Second, the general reaction of the conservatives, especially in England,

---

[119] Ibid., 160–61.

[120] Canadian Broadcasting Corporation, "The Loyalists," *Ideas* (Montreal, QC: CBC Enterprises and CBC Transcripts, 1983), 17.

regarding the French Revolution and the ensuing Napoleonic Wars made the Loyalists indispensable in firmly establishing conservatism on Canadian soil. The Loyalists proved to be the crucial link in helping solidify British conservatism with a prevailing American sense of pragmatism.[121]

The arrival of the Loyalists significantly enhanced the "Britishness" of Canada. Situated next to a revolutionary American nation, therefore, a solidly pro-British community in Canada prevailed, one which possessed an outlook that appealed to various immigrant groups, including those Irish who chose to reside in Canada rather than elsewhere. However, the Scottish impact on Canada was also very significant in the retention of Canada's British nature.

The Scottish aspect of English Canada's "Britishness"

Censuses reveal a relatively consistent picture of ethnic settlement and influence throughout Canadian history. Just as French cultural dominance of the Roman Catholic Church has been a consistent feature of Quebec, the ethnic picture of Nova Scotia, for example, has not changed dramatically from the census in 1767 that showed 85 percent of the population as Protestant, followed by a more detailed census in the mid-nineteenth century revealing Presbyterians as the largest Protestant denomination with 30 percent, followed by the Church of England's 23 percent, Baptists' 16 percent, Methodists' 8 percent, dissenters' 4 percent, and Lutherans' 2 percent.[122]

Although censuses show that between 1871 and 1971 Canada's population of British origin declined from 60 percent to 45 percent, and those of French origin from 31 percent to 29 percent, in actual numbers the population of Canadians with British origins increased by 356 percent from 2.1 million to 9.6 million, whereas the population of French origin rose by 464 percent from 1.1 million to 6.2 million. However, this proportionate decline of the founding populations, notes Kalbach, "was primarily due to the faster-growing populations of other European origins, fed by the heavy immigration to Canada in response to its efforts to settle the West, develop its natural resources and transportation networks, and industrialize and expand its economy, all

---

[121] Ibid.
[122] Kalbach, 62.

without significantly changing the basic nature of Canada's bicultural and bilingual society."[123] By the middle of the twentieth century, therefore, Canada's national character had been set. As important as the English were to this process, the Scots proved particularly vital.

The impact of the Scots in binding Canadian society to British sensibilities cannot be understated. While the English represented the most influential group in Canada's history outside of Quebec—thus imparting on Canadians a degree of cultural acceptance of social hierarchy and inequity—according to the census figures of 1971, Canadians of Scottish origin formed the third largest ethnic group, representing 10.43 percent of the Canadian population. Their impact on Canadian cultural development outweighed their numbers. In Canada, Scots have been very prominent in politics and business. While the first two Canadian prime ministers, John A. MacDonald and Alexander Mackenzie, were born in Scotland, many subsequent prime ministers had Scottish ancestry, such as William Lyon Mackenzie King, leader of Liberal Party and prime minister for 21 years between the 1920s and 1940s, Pierre Elliot Trudeau—the son of a French father and Scottish mother—who led Liberal governments for nearly 16 years from the late 1960s through the early 1980s, and Kim Campbell, Canada's first (and only) female prime minister, who led the Progressive Conservative government in 1993.

Indicative of how significant the Scottish community has been in Canada, Scottish-born Tommy Douglas—former Saskatchewan premier, former leader of the federal New Democratic Party and father of Canadian Medicare, the universal publicly funded health insurance system—was declared in 2004, by extensive viewer polling, as *The Greatest Canadian*, a CBC Television program of the same name.[124] Beyond politics, however, Scots dominated the fur and timber trade, banking, and railway management. Half of the nation's industrial leaders in the 1880s had Scottish family backgrounds.[125]

---

[123] Ibid., 63.

[124] Proclaimed the *The Greatest Canadian* on a CBC Television program of this same name, Tommy Douglas joined Konrad Adenauer, Winston Churchill, and Nelson Mandela as the "Greatest" of their respective nations in similar popular television polls. Alex Strachan, "And the Winner is . . . Tommy Douglas," *The Vancouver Sun*, November 30, 2004, C6.

[125] J.M. Bumsted, "Scots," in *The Canadian Encyclopedia: Year 2000 Edition*, ed. James H. Marsh (Toronto, ON: McClelland & Stewart, 1999), 2,120.

In assessing the impact of the Scots on the development of Canada, Canadian historian W. Stanford Reid asserts that "The traits of character, the ways of thinking, the prejudices and the biases with which the Scottish immigrants came to this country and which they passed on to their descendants even to the third and fourth generations, found their origins in the homeland which they had left."[126] The Scots, both in Scotland and in Canada, savored their independent identity and have always considered themselves distinct from the English.

In some respects, Canada's position alongside the United States can be likened to Scotland's position next to England. Both Scotland and Canada have independent histories and distinct identities. Both have populations smaller than their respective neighbors to the south—England and the United States. Both have distinguishing characteristics and values shaped by years of cultural and national developments separate but alongside their larger next-door neighbors. Despite Scotland and England sharing a political connection since the early eighteenth century, Scotland can still be distinguished from England just as Canada is distinguished from the United States, even though some outsiders view Canada and the United States as superficially identical based on close proximity.

The Scots' position as a critical part of Canada's dominant British culture was balanced by their equally fierce struggle to maintain their own identity. However, notes Reid, "While cherishing their Scottish heritage they have transferred their primary loyalty to Canada."[127] Relating to Scotland's experience beside a more dominant England, Scottish Canadians have tended to insist upon Canada's individuality and independence from its powerful US neighbor and the United Kingdom, its mother country on the other side of the Atlantic.

Like the Irish, the Scots are a diverse people. They possess traits according to their geographic origins in Scotland. Regarding the Scottish character, Scottish author Iain Finlayson observes:

The Scot abroad is assumed to be one of two types: either he is a Lowlander and thought to be "dour, unimaginative, cautious, reliable and, if not exactly dull, good company only in a dry sardonic fashion, a master of understatement and in his general character to be compounded of the austere grey colours of the North." If his

---

[126] W. Stanford Reid, "The Scottish Background," in *The Scottish Tradition in Canada,* ed. W. Stanford Reid (Toronto, ON: McClelland and Stewart, 1976), 1.

[127] W. Stanford Reid, "The Scot and Canadian Identity," in *The Scottish Tradition in Canada,* ed. Reid, 310.

origin is Highland, he is expected to conform to type that is "high-spirited, gay, and melancholy by turns, something of a savage and something of a poet; and any moments of quietness or extraction in his behaviour will be put down to a touch of feyness."[128]

Such distinctions in Scottish regional character have been intensified by the Scots' religious differences. Many Highlanders were Roman Catholic while Lowlanders were typically Protestant. Although both are proud Scots, there are "definite differences among those of Scottish background and that such distinctions have in part determined their attitudes and roles in Canada," observes MacLean. "In effect, they have helped to mould views concerning man and his role in Canadian society."[129]

Although the Scottish Lowland Protestant is considered to have exercised a greater impact on Canadian character development, the Roman Catholic Highlanders are famous for their distinctive mobility, and therefore impacted Canada while they traversed the land as fur traders, soldiers, and explorers, including such well-known names as David Thompson, Alexander MacKenzie, and Simon Fraser, each with Canadian rivers named after them. But the Highland Catholics did not generally stay together within a specific geographic area for extended periods of time and, therefore, observes MacLean, they became "less Scottish and more Canadian or Nova Scotian, or Islanders" and were increasingly Anglicized.[130] Yet, although many Highland cultural traits and traditions have survived to the present day—from traditional bagpipes to participation in the Highland Games—the Catholics shared many basic traditions with the Presbyterian Scots: "their loyalty to the Crown, their repugnance toward certain aspects of society to the south, and, for many, their common Scottish inheritance." Asserts MacLean, in Canada "the religious hatreds which had kept them apart in Scotland were largely ignored or sublimated; pioneer conditions and common political problems helped in forcing a greater tolerance."[131]

"The [Scottish] nation's philosophically defined 'psychology of improvement' impelled many Scots to take advantage of the opportunities

---

[128] Iain Finlayson, *The Scots* (London, UK: Constable, 1987), 42.

[129] R. MacLean, "The Highland Catholic Tradition in Canada," in *The Scottish Tradition in Canada*, ed. Reid, 93.

[130] Ibid., 94.

[131] Ibid., 95.

their British identity afforded them in the Empire," observes Canadian historian Sarah Katherine Gibson. As a result, "The Scots' political identity appears 'paradoxical' and 'ironic' because Scots moved so easily between positions as colonized Scots and British imperialists."[132]

Given the significant number of Scots who settled in Canada, the Scottish character exercised a strong mark on Canada's sense of Britishness. Among Scottish Protestants, a significant number were brought up in the Calvinistic-Presbyterian tradition, an outlook on life which, according to historian W. Stanford Reid, "formed one of the basic drives in the Scottish character. It has meant an emphasis upon personal responsibility which manifests itself in what has often been labeled 'the Protestant work ethic.' " According to Reid, "This has meant, however, not only a sense of divine calling to work, but a God-given responsibility to show initiative, foresight and risk-taking." However, this did not mean simply a focus on accumulating "worldly goods." Reid asserts,

> A concept of "stewardship" has gone along with it. The individual is responsible to use his gifts, talents and the wealth which they may bring for the benefit of others. The outcome of such an outlook on life has often been the formation of an individual who is hard-working, frugal sometimes to penuriousness, but also capable of acts of considerable generosity when the occasion requires. And all of this bred a race of people who were inclined to be independent, sometimes irascible, argumentative and often very sure of their own correctness of vision and action. Thus the Protestant Scot, although by no means always a "lovable" character, has very often been a person possessing the necessary drive and self-assurance to make a good colonist.[133]

British immigrants who arrived after 1763—the pivotal year the French colonies in North America were transferred to the British Crown—brought these salient characteristics of the Scottish

[132] Sarah Katherine Gibson, "Self-Reflection in the Consolidation of Scottish Identity: A Case Study in Family Correspondence 1805–50," in *Canada and the British World: Culture, Migration, and Identity*, ed. Phillip Buckner and R. Douglas Francis (Vancouver, BC: UBC Press, 2006), 31.
[133] W. Stanford Reid, "The Scottish Protestant Tradition," in *The Scottish Tradition in Canada*, ed. Reid, 120.

Protestant tradition to Canada. Addressing what part the Scottish Protestant tradition played in the development of Canada, therefore, Reid stresses that

> The Protestants, like their Roman Catholic fellow-countrymen, if they settled on farms usually congregated in family and kinship groups. But the many artisans, businessmen or professional men tended to put down their roots in the burgeoning cities and towns. Moreover, not infrequently after two or three generations on the land, the Scottish Protestants began to move into the urban areas, breaking with their rural and agricultural background. This meant that the Protestant tradition, while often losing much of its specifically Scottish character, e.g. [church] services in Gaelic, has exercised a wider influence than has the Scottish Roman Catholic tradition which tended to keep the people [farming] on the land.[134]

Though Canadians of Scottish origin found themselves in an ambivalent position, both part of the dominant British culture and yet insistent on maintaining some semblance of their own identity, Canadian historian B.M. Bumsted notes, "it was largely because of their influence that the preponderant culture in Canada was British, rather than English."[135]

* * *

Contrary to Australia's strong Irish Catholic influence and less deferential response to British rule, English Canada, with the help of its large and powerful population of Loyalist, English, Scottish, and Irish Protestant immigrants, clung more strongly to a British identity because of their origins and also out of concern of being in such close proximity to a politically, economically, and culturally assertive United States. While Canada and the United States share many common aspects, from language to geographic setting, Canadians retain a distinct national character. Consequently, the deep-rooted British conservative attitude of deference to authority became more pronounced in Canada as opposed to Australia or the United

---

[134] Ibid., 131.
[135] Bumsted, "Scots."

States. This trait especially reflects Canada's historical and cultural experiences.[136]

For English Canada, British power and cultural identity were accepted aspects of Canadian life that fostered a culture emulating British values and traditions. By protecting a developing independent Canadian identity, however, Canadian nationalism often reflected subtle anti-American sentiments. Yet, concurrent with restrained anti-Americanism has been the strengthening of power by dominant groups in Canadian society. Patricia Wood observes that the patriotic rhetoric that marked the Canadian general election of 1891 was used by English Canadian, middle-class males "to further entrench their positions of social, cultural and political power," rhetoric that was not only well-received at that time but "echoed far into the twentieth century."[137] Their dominant cultural values helped differentiate Canadians from Americans and Australians.

In Australia during the nineteenth century, with about a quarter of Australia's Irish population settled in New South Wales, the number of Irish was substantial.[138] Given Ireland's status as a nation ruled by England, many proud Irish were opposed to English rule both in Ireland and in Australia. In fact, the majority of the working-class Irish of Australia were firmly anti-imperialist.[139] Australian Catholic theologian and historian Edmund Campion notes, "By the end of the [nineteenth] century republicanism was a popular alternative to imperial loyalty."[140] The very presence of the Irish in Australia helped foster this substitution. Hence, the Irish were a disproportionate influence in shaping the national character of Australia, which differed from both the Canadian and American experience. Canada lacked a large formidable Irish Catholic community—thus lacking an "Irish factor" compared to Australia—while the Irish in the United States, though significant in size, were not dominant nationally or in the population relative to society as a whole.

---

[136] Lipset, *Continental Divide*, 1.

[137] Patricia K. Wood, "Defining 'Canadian': Anti-Americanism and Identity in Sir John A. MacDonald's Nationalism," *Journal of Canadian Studies* 36, no. 2 (2001): 49.

[138] Luke Trainor, *British Imperialism and Australian Nationalism: Manipulation, Conflict and Compromise in the Late Nineteenth Century* (Cambridge, UK: Cambridge University Press, 1994), 96.

[139] Ibid.

[140] Edmund Campion, *Australian Catholics: The Contribution of Catholics to the Development of Australian Society* (Ringwood, VIC: Penguin, 1987), 61.

In subsequent chapters, focus shifts to the means of value retention following culture formation. Among the key sources are class distinction and consequent ethnocultural differences among holders of power. Another is religion and the powerful impact it has on encouraging group cohesiveness and solidarity, particularly among a minority such as the Irish that feels oppressed. The next chapter, therefore, turns to the elites of both Australia and Canada in order to see how Australia's Irish Catholic community interacted with the ruling Protestant cultural elite, revealing how group cohesion strengthened, perpetuated, and transferred cultural values to the national culture. As will be seen later in the study of management and labor, this impact spread through the working classes into labor politics and trade unions, thereby indirectly affecting Australian management trends. In the case of Australia, the Irish appear to have played an instrumental role.

3
Class and Identity

Given their overwhelming presence in colonial Australia and Canada, the most pervasive impact on national cultural values appears to have come from the Anglo-Celtic Catholic and Protestant communities, whose impact on the evolution of national values, culture, and national character was profound. As the contribution of the Irish Catholic sensibility to Australian irreverence, rebelliousness, and egalitarianism—or desire for flatter hierarchies—is evident in such Australian practices as "knocking," "cutting down tall poppies," and even the social phenomenon of "mateship"—features of Australian culture absent in Canada—the significant number of Irish Catholics in Australia is the critical factor that guided Australian culture in a different direction compared to Canada where Irish Catholics, as a percentage of the Canadian population, did not possess the same cultural force.

A distinct Irish Catholic subculture, combined with unequal power between elites and working class, underlies Australia's distinctiveness from Canada despite both countries' shared membership in the Anglo cluster. While the previous chapter considered the general Anglo-Celtic influences on the formation of Australian and Canadian national character, how Anglo-Celtic ethnoreligious origins, intertwined with class membership, helped retain and foster cultural values that became dominant in Australia's and Canada's respective societies are now the focus.

Although similar geographical origin contributes to community solidarity, a shared religious tradition and membership in a common social class are particularly powerful means by which people band together into culturally strong social groups. Common religious affiliation and socioeconomic class—both separately and in combination—help retain and perpetuate values. They have therefore proven essential to the establishment and maintenance of cohesive communities.

Religion and community leadership proved a cohesive force in Australia's and Canada's cultural development. Catholicism provided the Irish with a different identity, a sense of second-class citizenship within a nation ruled by a British Protestant elite. Yet this dynamic also helped the Irish keep a strong identity that impacted the general Australian culture. In contrast, English-speaking Canada—the largest part of Canada which excludes most of the French-speaking province of Quebec—was largely a product of the British Protestant tradition and lacked Australia's dominant "Irish factor."

Characteristics of the ruling elites

Australia's and Canada's upper ruling/governing class—the "elites"—share similar ethnic and religious origins attributable to a common historical and social cause—the shared colonial experience that witnessed political and economic power was maintained by a strong elite comprised largely of British Protestants. Since strong ethnic and religious loyalties tend to reinforce each other as adaptations to lower economic status, the Irish Catholics who were more numerous in Australia than Canada proved to be an assertive group that vied for a powerful role in society. Before considering the nuances of Australia's and Canada's working class, the similar ethnoreligious identities of their respective elites are necessary to understand.

Ever since the colonial era, the composition of the socioeconomic and political elites in Australia and English Canada has largely been British in origin. Their religious tradition, and therefore their values and general outlook, tended to reflect their ethnoreligious heritage, which meant that the elites typically shared a British Protestant background. In *Elites in Australia*, a study of Australia's business, trade union, political, public service, media, and academic elites, John Higley *et al.* observed that, in 1975, 83 percent of national leaders were born in Australia, 67 percent of whom were at least in the second generation, and that they were particularly dominant among political, academic, business, and trade union leaders.[1] Moreover, of the Australian-born leaders, 75 percent could trace their paternal origins to Great Britain which, according to Higley *et al.*, "meant that approximately three-quarters of all leaders were 'brought up' in one of the Protestant religions," the most

---

[1] John Higley, Desley Deacon, and Don Smart, *Elites in Australia* (London, UK: Routledge, 1979), 77.

common being Anglicanism (44 percent), Presbyterianism (15 percent) and Methodism (10 percent).[2]

According to the data, while individuals of Protestant backgrounds tended to dominate all elites, there was some variation among them. Business leaders generally came from Anglican and Presbyterian backgrounds whereas trade union and academic leaders often had a Methodist and Congregationalist background. But, among the largest non-Protestant groups to have substantial membership among certain elites were individuals from Catholic backgrounds, found most frequently among Australian Labor Party (ALP) leaders and media editors.[3] Although it is not possible to determine whether the irregular distribution of leaders from different religious backgrounds was the result of discrimination or from independent selection, Australian sociologist Solomon Encel, in his analysis of the recruitment of Catholics to the business, political, and public service elites, asserts that the Catholic Church's traditional influence in the labor movement—and the lengthy history of "discrimination against Catholics in employment, especially in commerce and industry"—are the primary reasons.[4] Hence, there was legitimate cause for the large Irish Catholic minority to assert itself in Australian society.

The ethnoreligious background of the Australian elite was not substantially different from English Canada. In his seminal book, *Vertical Mosaic: An Analysis of Social Class and Power in Canada*, Canadian sociologist John Porter analyzed seven specific institutional elites in society, encompassing business, labor, political, public service, mass media, religious, and intellectual elites. Porter learned that "Canadians of British origin have retained, within the elite structure of the society, the charter group status with which they started out, and that in some institutional settings the French have been admitted as a co-charter group whereas in others they have not."[5] Porter made an important contribution to the understanding of Canada's obsession with class distinctions. Born in Vancouver and educated at the London School of Economics, Porter's personal and professional concerns were for greater comprehension of inequality in Canada and the exercise of power by bureaucratic, economic and political elites.

[2] Ibid., 78.
[3] Ibid.
[4] S. Encel, *Equality and Authority: A Study of Class, Status and Power in Australia* (Melbourne, VIC: Cheshire, 1970), 178–79.
[5] John Porter, *The Vertical Mosaic: An Analysis of Social Class and Power in Canada* (Toronto, ON: University of Toronto Press, 1965), xii–xiii.

Central to his research was an explanation of social class and power in Canada, two crucial themes he analyzed in *Vertical Mosaic*, a creative and lasting contribution to scholarship that established Porter as a veritable pioneer in the field of Canadian sociology.[6]

Porter's analysis reveals that in a social environment comprised of diverse cultural groups there tends to be a connection between membership in the elites and shared ethnoreligious background, and, therefore, the opportunity of achieving positions of power and cultural influence.

A "charter group" is defined as the first ethnic group to enter into a previously unpopulated (or underpopulated) region, perhaps including the conquering of an indigenous group in the process to establish its claim, and emerge as the effective possessor of the territory thereby establishing a position of dominant influence in society.[7] In this way, the charter group's authority is retained, at least initially, through the exercise of administrative power and transmission of cultural values.

In composition and number, Canada and Australia differ since Australia has one charter group comprised of the British who colonized it whereas Canada has two, the English and the French. In Canada, the dominance of the English charter group never faced a serious challenge since the French population's strength remained largely confined to the French province of Quebec, whereas English Canada's position expanded due to significant levels of British immigration in the rest of Canada. According to Porter, this shows that "the ethnic structure of a community in terms of its charter and noncharter groups is determined early and tends to be self-perpetuating."[8] In light of their significant cultural influence, however, Australia's substantial population of Irish Catholics behaved much like a charter group.

Whereas the French participated in Confederation in 1867, Canada's economic and political leaders were British and, understandably, were interested in creating a decisively "British" enclave in North America. Not only was this the kind of society with which these British Canadians were most familiar, but also one they were most interested in replicating. Therefore, as Porter points out, it is no surprise that "as a source of immigrants, Britain should have been preferred by those in power."[9] Over the course of the nineteenth century, immigrants' social class was, on the

---

[6] Wallace Clement, "John Porter and the Development of Sociology in Canada," *Canadian Review of Sociology and Anthropology* 18, no. 5 (1981): 584.

[7] Porter, *The Vertical Mosaic*, 60.

[8] Ibid., 60–61.

[9] Ibid., 62.

whole, defined by what it had been in Great Britain. "Within the cities and larger towns the upper class English as officials, administrators, professionals, and clergy attempted to reconstruct an aristocratic way of life, while the bottom layer was made up of large numbers of destitute immigrants from the factory cities," Porter asserts, with the result that "in the rural areas class differences tended to break down under hardships that were felt by 'gentry' and destitute alike, despite attempts to create a landed gentry patterned on the English style."[10]

Indeed, given Canada's large population with British family origins, it is not unexpected to find their dominance among the elites in the urban centers. Canadian sociologist Wallace Clement argues that the most powerful elites in Canada, those who command the greatest resources in the country today, are the business ("corporate") and political ("state") elites. According to Clement, admission to these elites is powerfully affected by social-class origins, ethnic origins, gender, and region of birth and residence. Clement asserts, "The most powerful decision-making positions in Canada are therefore held by people who do not represent a cross-section of Canadians."[11] Whereas only 1 percent of Canadian society is classified as "upper class," in the year 1972, for example, 61 percent of these elites had upper class origins, 33 percent came from the middle class (compared to roughly 15 percent of the general population), and 6 percent came from the working class, which constitutes about 85 percent of the Canadian population.[12] Since the ethnic composition of the general population of English Canada has been strongly British Protestant, the masses were reflected in the ethnic composition of the Canadian elite. This was the situation until immigration in the latter half of the twentieth century resulted in a more diverse ethnic population. By then, however, Canada's national character had already been established with the elites embracing a "Canadian" outlook forged by generations of British dominance.

Australia's and Canada's elites were largely united by a common British Protestant cultural affiliation, exercising influence equivalent to members of the traditional British upper classes.[13] Peter C. Newman

---

[10] Ibid., 62–63.

[11] Wallace Clement, "Elites," in *The Canadian Encyclopedia: Year 2000 Edition*, ed. James H. Marsh (Toronto, ON: McClelland & Stewart, 1999), 755–56.

[12] Ibid.

[13] It is useful to note that, in Australia, the definition and requirements of social status had changed from England. The social distinction most accessible to the would-be colonist was that of developing into a "gentleman." As Australian

observes that those in positions of power in Canada "have always lived with a colonial mentality which deems that *real* power" is situated elsewhere, whether across the pond in Great Britain or beneath the border with the United States. A sense of supremacy, Newman asserts, that remained "among the imperial interest groups who must be viewed with awe, emulated with care, but on no account challenged lest they withdraw their dollars and their moxie."[14]

Since the Establishment was not reinforced by an aristocracy like in Britain or based on generations of inherited wealth as in the United States, elite membership appears to have been rooted largely in their ethnoreligious affiliation. This became particularly clear in 1965 when Porter's examination of Canada's power structure, *The Vertical Mosaic*, was published. Porter's monumental work, Newman asserts, "banished forever from the Canadian psyche the comfortable notion that this is a classless (or at any rate an entirely middle class) country."[15] Hence, the *Canadian Establishment*, as Newman refers to this social stratum, reveals an underlying undemocratic class structure that surprises many Canadians given Canada's history as a democratic nation. The reason for surprise, according to Newman, is not just because it denies "the populist belief in the wide open spaces, the notion of Canada as a land of freely accessible opportunities." It is also due to the fact that the *Establishment* in Canada was never "reinforced by an aristocracy (as it

---

historian John Hirst notes, gentlemen wore distinctive dress of "frockcoat, top hat, kid gloves" and were publicly recognized by other gentlemen; they were saluted by policemen, addressed by the title "Esquire" in formal correspondence, and workers were expected to address them as "Sir." While the traditional English standard of a "gentleman" reflected one's connections to a good family and ownership of lands, in Australia, observes Hirst, "the balance changed. The core of true gentlemen was small and not self-sustaining; the claimants at the edges numerous. There were enough true gentlemen to retain the rank's traditional prestige, but too few, owning too few resources, for the traditional criteria to maintain a commanding influence." Hirst points out, "Everyone in the colonies—including those with the best claims to be gentlemen—was closely involved in money-making. This was traditionally forbidden to the English gentleman, who could invest his fortune to advantage but was essentially a man of leisure, not preoccupied with money matters." Hence, the status of a "gentleman" was held by anyone in a certain position of the occupational hierarchy or who possessed independent means. John Hirst, "Egalitarianism," in *Australian Cultural History*, ed. S.L. Goldberg and F.B. Smith (Cambridge, UK: Cambridge University Press, 1988), 61–62.

[14] Peter C. Newman, *The Canadian Establishment: Volume One* (Toronto, ON: Penguin, 1999), 386.

[15] Ibid.

is in Britain) or based on several generations of wealth (as it is in the U.S.)." The majority of Canadians generally regard the designations upper, middle, and lower class "as referring mainly to life styles and levels of sophistication," maintains Newman, but even if the existing Canadian Establishment is viewed as fleeting, Canada has social classes that are considerably more than "temporary way-stations." Newman asserts, "Paradoxically, this does not mean that all members of the Canadian Establishment necessarily belong to or come out of the upper strata. Many if not most of them are part of what George Orwell once described as 'the lower upper middle class'—a class that could give its offspring the advantages of education and the right entree but not necessarily inherited wealth."[16]

Porter's assumptions, methodology, and conclusions have not gone without criticism. Prefacing his searing attack by praising *The Vertical Mosaic* as "the most important contribution to Canadian scholarship on social class and power to date," with "richness of insight and detail" that make it "relevant without question to any analysis or dialogue on the subject," Canadian sociologist James Heap faulted Porter's definition of "classes" as inadequate. His claim that social classes, defined as "social groups within which members have a sense of identity with one another, share common values and traditions, and have an awareness of unity and common purpose," is somehow misguided or patently false. Heap also criticized Porter's discernment between power and authority as inadequate.[17]

With regard to the first critique, Porter vigorously defended himself by showing how Heap had misrepresented Porter's argument. Porter stated unequivocally that he did not define classes in the manner mentioned above. Rather, he refers to a passage in *The Vertical Mosaic*, where he writes, "Clearly then classes arrived at in such a way are not more than artificially constructed statistical groups. They are not social groups because in social groups members have a sense of identity with one another, share common values and traditions, and have an awareness of unity and common purpose."[18] In his own defense against Heap's allegations, Porter remarks, "Why [Heap] should take my statement about social groups as my definition of classes when I make the particular point that groups are what classes are not, escapes me. Since I never did make class consciousness the basis of my definition of class it is difficult to see how

---

[16] Ibid., 387.

[17] James L. Heap, "Conceptual and Theoretical Problems in the Vertical Mosaic," *Canadian Review of Sociology & Anthropology* 9, no. 2 (1972): 176–87.

[18] Porter, *The Vertical Mosaic*, 10.

I could have shifted my definition from that basis."[19] Despite such inevitable criticism, Porter's ideas have stood the test of time.

While the notion that social elites tended to have wielded control in English Canada—and that their typical ethnicity was British Protestant—might seem undemocratic, it reflects reality. Indeed, Porter's work revealed that power was maintained by a predominantly British Protestant elite, an insight Newman suggests confirms that "ethnic origin was virtually as significant in determining membership in the elite in 1951 as it had been in 1885 and 1910."[20] The *Canadian Establishment* that encompasses the economic, business, and corporate elite, represents a loosely knit group of contenders for economic, political, and cultural power. While its sources of authority and structure has fluctuated over time, the elites' members have effectively controlled the country's decision-making processes, and therefore influenced the nation's character, through the perpetuation of values via political, economic, and cultural dominance.[21] This concentration of power in Canadian society persisted well into the twentieth century and still exerts a strong impact on the Canadian consciousness.

Although the ethnoreligious background of the elites in both countries was largely British Protestant, the origin of Australia's and Canada's working classes was not the same precisely because of the presence of a large Irish Catholic community within the Australian working class. However, with power primarily in the hands of a privileged British Protestant elite, the rest of society—comprised of various ethnicities and religious affiliations—had the choice to fully assimilate and emulate the values and traditions of the elites, or attempt to assert their own identities and aspirations for influence. Contrary to the experience in Canada, the Irish Catholics of Australia, due to the relatively large size of their community, represented the strongest contester of power.

The ethnoreligious identity of the emerging working class

Considering that the upper echelon of Australian colonial society had been firmly British Protestant, and the lower socioeconomic levels of

---

[19] John Porter, "Conceptual and Theoretical Problems in the Vertical Mosaic: A Rejoinder," *Canadian Review of Sociology & Anthropology* 9, no. 2 (1972): 188.

[20] Peter C. Newman, "Business Elites," in *The Canadian Encyclopedia: Year 2000 Edition*, ed. James H. Marsh (Toronto, ON: McClelland & Stewart, 1999), 334.

[21] Ibid.

society—convict and working class—strongly Irish Catholic in composition, their respective identities remained potent and nonconforming
from early on. Whereas the upper/governing class in English Canada
was also largely comprised of British Protestant stock, the Canadian
lower/working class was not as contrary to the upper/ruling class as
their counterparts were in Australia. In terms of predominant cultural
values, therefore, the divergent societies that emerged appear to
reflect the different composition, background, and motivations of the
working class—for Australia, significantly Irish Catholic; in Canada,
either British Protestant or sympathetic to British tradition and
outlook. If British colonial society can be characterized as a struggle
between holders of power—the British elite—and the lower classes,
then in Australia the Irish, a potent and sizeable force among the
masses, provided enough counterweight to stretch power more evenly
in comparison with Canada where the British Protestant elite largely
won the struggle for political, economic, and cultural power.

Despite the Australian colonies' great advancements in democracy,
it would be false to view Australia as a "classless" society. Australian
political scientist Graham Maddox observes that "radical attitudes
and ideas were transplanted from Britain and were allowed to blossom
into democracy unimpeded by the thorns of a defensive traditional
ruling aristocracy, or by the rocks of ancient political institutions." He
maintains that, at least in some respects, this understanding is correct.
While Australia "never had a hereditary nobility with entrenched political privileges," he notes, "there were, nevertheless, divisions between
those who ruled and those who were ruled, divisions so sharp and
deep as to leave wounds that would not quickly heal without leaving
permanent scars."[22]

While class divisions in early nineteenth-century Britain were more
rigidly delineated, the divergent interests and dissimilar ethnocultural
composition of the upper and lower classes had a powerful impact on
Australian culture. Russel Ward remarks that "The fact that, initially,
practically all 'lower-class' Australians were also convicted criminals
strongly underlined the dividing line between them and their masters
and intensified mutual hostility."[23] Due to penal policies of the era,

[22] Graham Maddox, "The Australian Labor Party," in *Political Parties in
Australia*, ed. Graeme Starr, Keith Richmond, and Graham Maddox (Richmond,
VIC: Heinemann Educational Australia, 1978), 168–69.
[23] Russel Ward, *The Australian Legend* (Melbourne, VIC: Oxford University
Press, 1958), 38–39.

a significant percentage of convicts were of Irish Catholic origin, and later, many Irish free immigrants settled in Australia. Hence, the upper/lower class divide reveals a significant contrast in ethnic membership with more Irish Catholics among the working class than upper/ruling class.

Canada lacked this composition among its lower/working class since Irish Catholics were fewer in relation to the overall working class population, and the Irish Catholics who chose to reside in Canada tended to emulate Canada's prevailing pro-British and subtly anti-American outlook. Significantly, therefore, whereas the socioeconomic and ethnic composition of Australian and Canadian upper/ruling/governing classes was not so different from each other, working class cultural and social ties were more varied and, as a consequence, are of considerable interest since in Australia the latter is where the Irish factor made its greatest impact.

In Canada, the working class reflected a large proportion of different ethnic groups, but lacked a strongly assertive underlying ethnoreligious motivation to successfully contest the dominant British Protestant elites who controlled society. As a result, the working classes tended to tolerate, if not actively support British colonial rule. Even in places where the working class may not have entirely matched the elite's British origins, the elite's hold on power prevailed. As part of the British Empire, the Canada's West Coast city of Vancouver offers an example of this trend.

In *Making Vancouver: Class, Status, and Social Boundaries*, Canadian historian Robert A.J. McDonald observes that, whereas the British Protestant population dominated the powerful elites, the working classes reflected a diversity of Native and immigrant populations over whom the elites ruled. According to McDonald, it was no surprise

> given the city's economic structure, class leadership among Vancouver's working people came from the most privileged sector of the working class: White men of British heritage whose skills provided them with employment security, solid wages, and the ability to develop a sense of community with fellow workers off the job. Such privileged workers tended to see class interests in narrow terms and to limit their empathy for wage earners who were less skilled, less settled, and often not part of the ethnic and racial majority. The fact that many workers—most of whom were men without families in Vancouver—considered themselves to be sojourners and had

no desire to participate in local institutions such as trade unions intensified fragmentation.[24]

Vancouver's British Protestant upper class, defined by McDonald as "those who owned or managed the means of production and those whose interests or outlook link them to owners," therefore possessed the advantageous social position of "ideological consensus and ethnic coherence."[25] Their ideology provided a firm commitment to capitalism and its corresponding private property rights, and their ethnoreligious heritage was the foundation of their respect of British institutions. Indeed, British background itself was a primary source of prestige clearly visible along Vancouver's busy waterfront commercial center at Burrard Inlet where, in the 1870s observes McDonald, "The mill-centred elite successfully cloaked itself in the mantle of respectability by linking economic power to British ethnicity," thus enabling the British elite to separate itself from "the ethnically and racially heterogeneous majority of residents on the Inlet."[26] Hence, with the onset of urbanization during the 1880s, the ethnic composition was rapidly redefined as society was increasingly controlled by British Protestant elites.

As investment opportunities and work opportunities attracted more settlers to Vancouver, notes McDonald,

the workforce that emerged was overwhelmingly White, Protestant, and of British heritage. The Inlet's Native and Mixed-Blood population did not disappear from the south shore but declined rapidly as a proportion of the whole ... In the new city of Vancouver, however, to be of Native heritage or from a non-British background was to be marginalized, to be cast outside the mainstream. Rather than divide the elite from the majority, as it did in the 1870s, British ethnicity now functioned as an instrument that linked the majority across class lines. The attack by White workers on Chinese labourers and the effort of government and police to clear away the Indian rancherie to the east of Hastings Mill, both in 1887, marked the apex of this early movement by the new anglophone [English speaking] majority to establish its cultural dominance. The racial category of "whiteness"

---

[24] Robert A.J. McDonald, *Making Vancouver: Class, Status, and Social Boundaries, 1863–1913* (Vancouver, BC: UBC Press, 1996), 233.
[25] Ibid.
[26] Ibid., 234.

illustrates as well the importance of status as an instrument of social differentiation.[27]

An immigration policy favoring "Whites," maintained by the governments of Canada and Australia, was not abandoned until 1962 and 1973, respectively. The development of these policies occurred during a key era from the mid-nineteenth century onward when the Australian and Canadian nations were being built and their constitutions formed. Canadian political scientist Freda Hawkins observes:

> In Canada, in a national sense, these early origins and indeed the whole lengthy episode of White Canada is often downplayed, or clothed in discreet silence, or simply not extrapolated from its historical context. In Australia, however, this is not the case. There, White Australia has been a *public* policy in the plainest sense of the term. Hostility against non-white immigrants plus a determination to keep them out or reduce their numbers began in both Canada and Australia during the early gold rushes. It was generated first by the migration of considerable numbers of Chinese to California after the discovery of gold there in 1848, then by similar movements to Britain's growing Pacific colonies, as gold was discovered in Australia in 1851, in British Columbia in 1858, and in New Zealand in 1861.[28]

As a consequence of these ethnic-based immigration policies, Australia's Irish Catholic population grew substantially whereas Canada attracted fewer Irish Catholic immigrants relative to those from the British Isles. Not unlike other Canadian and Australian cities, the situation in Vancouver reveals that "whiteness" had emerged as a tool by which those of British heritage established their status as citizens of "high esteem." McDonald argues that "The extent to which the city's British majority constructed a language of race to serve this status-defining function was revealed during the [pre-Second World War] boom, when an influx of Italian workers challenged the majority's cultural and social identity." McDonald asserts that as a response, the British majority "defined Italians as 'non-White,' and thus as outsiders." In this situation, Vancouver's dominant ethnic group marginalized

---

[27] Ibid., 235.
[28] Freda Hawkins, *Critical Years in Immigration: Canada and Australia Compared*, 2nd ed. (Montreal, QC & Kingston, ON: McGill-Queen's University Press, 1991), 8.

Italians as "immigrants" in a similar way as it did the Chinese, Japanese, and Sikhs.[29]

Although the "Vancouver Establishment" would, by the late twentieth century, become divided between what Peter C. Newman describes as "the new Acquisitors and the more sedate group that belongs to the older Establishment strain," the ethnic composition of either camp was not dramatically different from McDonald's description.[30] The older Establishment still featured members of the same social, ethnocultural strain that dominated in the earlier period throughout English Canada.[31] From the late nineteenth century through most of the twentieth, therefore, the ethnoreligious context of power was clear. British Protestant elites held it in both Australia and Canada, but among the working classes of Canada, non-Whites were effectively marginalized, whereas among Australia's working classes there existed a growing Irish Catholic population which, although "white" in appearance, did not share the British Protestant tradition and strong attachment shown by the British-dominant governing elite. At this time, suggests Russel Ward, "Australian patriotic sentiment was usually more or less deeply tinged with 'disloyalty,' with radical notions of complete republican independence."[32] The reasons, revealing class and ethnoreligious alliances, were not unexpected. Ward asserts that "Prisoners and assisted immigrants had less reason to love Britain than did more prosperous persons and were less able to maintain their connections with 'home' however much, in many instances, they may have wished to do so." Ward adds, "Still, to love the new land more seemed often to mean loving the old one less, in so far as Australian national sentiment was felt to weaken the attachment to Crown and Empire."[33] Ward's description evokes the Australian Irish who were more likely to oppose colonial rule given a long history of Irish–British conflict, if not through active rebellion then symbolically through their disdain of, or conflicts with, colonial administrators.

---

[29] McDonald, *Making Vancouver*, 235.

[30] Peter C. Newman, *The Canadian Establishment, Volume Two: The Acquisitors* (Toronto, ON: Penguin, 1999), 50–55.

[31] Although the Vancouver Establishment retained much of its earlier ethnic composition, with the transfer of Hong Kong to Chinese rule in 1997, and substantial immigration to Western Canada, Vancouver's elite did change considerably by the new millennium.

[32] Ward, 56.

[33] Ibid.

104 The Development of Managerial Culture

Given their natural preference to be rid of British rule, Australian patriotism was appealing to many Irish Catholics. "The Irish-nationalist sentiments of the Irish-Catholic community, and their concomitant dislike of Britain, remained strong until the establishment of the Irish Free State in 1922," observes Encel, "but their major political interest had been guided into other channels long since."[34] Indeed, labor and politics became their vehicles but not always in opposition. In some respects, asserting a sense of independence from colonial rule seemed to underscore the depth of pro-Australian sentiments. Hence, as the presence of Irish Catholics rose among the working class, so did their patriotism. In light of the significant presence of Irish Catholics in this large segment of the population, Australian culture could not help but be profoundly impacted. Historical sources agree that in the decades of Australia's formative development, Catholics, dominated by the Irish, were overrepresented among the lower classes and seldom rose above them. This was as true in the Australian states of Victoria and New South Wales as it was in Western Australia and South Australia where they occupied modest positions in society and experienced considerable poverty.

In *The Faith of Australians*, historian Hans Mol cites many observers of Australian history who have noted the overrepresentation of Catholics among the lower classes, which has given Australian Irish workers a distinct cultural voice. Speaking in reference to the last half of the nineteenth century in Victoria, Henderson says, "Irish Roman Catholics seldom rise above the lower levels, and never as a class represent the mercantile, banking and squatting interests." In Western Australia the situation was similar. Reilly reports Catholics as occupying "the humblest positions in society." Pike stressed their poverty in South Australia. In Queensland, relates Phillips, Brisbane's Bishop Dunne observed in a letter to Cardinal Moran in 1884 that Catholics represented only a small proportion of the skilled labor force and that too many of them were to be found in the socially, morally, and physically undesirable occupations, such as tavern workers, policemen, cab drivers, wharf laborers, and pick-and-shovel men.[35]

---

[34] Encel, *Equality and Authority*, 179.
[35] R. Henderson, *Ninety Years in the Master's Service* (Edinburgh, UK: Andrew Elliott, 1911), 222; J.T. Reilly, *Fifty Years in Western Australia* (Perth, WA: Sands and McDougall, 1908), 31; Douglas Pike, *Paradise of Dissent* (London, UK: Longmans Green, 1957), 492; Walter W. Phillips, *Defending "A Christian Country": Churchmen and Society in New South Wales in the 1880s and After* (St. Lucia, QLD: University

Even by the 1960s, the relative proportion of Catholics among the business elite, not unlike the Canadian experience, was particularly small. However, the Irish Catholic presence was highly concentrated among the lower occupational categories where their greater representation relative to others was as notable as their lesser representation in the upper occupational categories. According to Spann, the number of Catholics among business executives has been particularly small relative to British Protestants in Australia. In academia, Catholics were considerably underrepresented as Tien showed in a study of academic staff from Sydney and Melbourne Universities, revealing that just 8 percent was Catholic compared to the 1966 census which showed a Catholic representation of 26 percent of the general Australian population.[36]

As mentioned, positions of influence and power in government and business were held by those of similar ethnoreligious origins. Given the dominance of English and Scots among the elites, Anglicans and Presbyterians were in the majority. According to historical sources, these denominations were certainly overrepresented in the upper occupational categories of Australia, just as they have been in Canada. The Church of England, as the largest denomination in Australia, was always well represented in every category. Writing in the late nineteenth century, Twopenny observed that the Anglicans had the least strength among the middle class and that Anglicanism was mostly the religion of the upper class, which is understandable given the circumstances of British colonialism.[37]

The high concentration of Irish Catholics among the lower classes in Australia, as opposed to the upper class or elite, reinforced their resolve to look after their interests, which coincided with their primary working class position. This is consistent with the implications of shared status. According to Seymour Martin Lipset, "Those in a similar status position tend to see themselves as located in a comparable position on the social hierarchy."[38] From the nineteenth through early twentieth centuries, the

---

of Queensland, 1981), 17; quoted in Hans Mol, *The Faith of Australians* (Sydney, NSW: Allen & Unwin, 1985), 165.

[36] Richard N. Spann, "The Catholic Vote in Australia," in *Catholics and the Free Society: An Australian Symposium*, ed. H. Mayer (Melbourne, VIC: Cheshire, 1961), 123; H.Y. Tien, *Social Mobility and Controlled Fertility* (New Haven, CT: College and University Press, 1965), 65; quoted in Mol, *Faith of Australians*, 166.

[37] R.E.N. Twopenny, *Town Life in Australia* (London, UK: Elliott Stock, 1883), 116–17, quoted in Mol, *Faith of Australians*, 166.

[38] Seymour Martin Lipset, "Social Class" in *Social Stratification: Canada*, ed. James E. Curtis and William G. Scott (Scarborough, ON: Prentice-Hall, 1973), 26.

relative lack of university-educated Australians of Catholic background is indicative of their lack of upper class power and social mobility, an imbalance that could be overcome by dominance in other social positions. Hence, power was achieved in other areas, notably by the Irish Catholic movement into organized labor and politics. These are very powerful arenas in society, and education has not been a formal prerequisite compared to the traditional professions. But substantial community support was crucial.

The Australian context reveals that the Protestants and Catholics were divided by their respective positions. Observes Encel, "Roman Catholics are disproportionately strong in Labor politics and disproportionately weak in the higher levels of business, the professions, and the public services; the Catholic educational system, moreover, ensures a lifetime form of social segregation and group-consciousness."[39] As the influence of the working-class Irish Catholics spread into unions and politics, therefore, their impact on Australia's national character became increasingly apparent. But how did the working-class Irish Catholics retain their cultural force to exert such profound effects on Australia's national culture? While the Irish impact on labor radicalism—as will be considered later—was influential, initially it was religious leadership that played an instrumental role in the formation and retention of community identity, culture, and values.

The role of Irish Catholic leadership in solidifying group identity

Although contemporary Australia appears more secular in comparison with other Anglo nations, religion has played an enormous role in shaping Australia's character, particularly with regard to Irish Catholics. Not only did a common religious, cultural identity help Irish Catholics remain a relatively cohesive and, therefore, influential group in Australia, the interactions between religious leaders and the dominant culture in Australia were significant ever since European settlement of Australia first began. English settlement brought with it the Anglican Church, or the established Church of England headed by the British monarch. Many Scots brought with them their Presbyterian faith. However, the Irish brought with them Catholicism. This made the sizeable Irish community distinct from the dominant Protestant overseers—which

---

[39] Encel, 104.

included a large number of pro-British Irish Protestants—who governed Australia since its early era as a burgeoning colony.

Catholics, particularly the Irish before mid-twentieth century immigration policies attracted Catholic immigrants from other lands, formed a cohesive group in large part due to their religious identity. In Australia, church attendance among Catholics in particular has always remained strong. Speculating why Australian Catholics were such active worshipers, Australian historian Ken Inglis asserts that anti-Catholics have a ready answer that

> the priests, who dominate their flock, make the sheep go to Mass. It is indeed true that presence at Mass is spiritually necessary to Catholics in a sense more precise than is attendance at a religious service for Protestants. But as this is true of Catholics everywhere, it cannot explain why the proportion of Catholics attending worship in some European countries is so far below the proportion in Australia. There must, it seems, be social as well as spiritual reasons for the Australian pattern. What are they? A short answer is that the ancestors of most Catholics came from Ireland, where a solidarity between the priest and the plain man had grown up under alien Protestant rule; that a sense of community persisted among the descendants of Irish immigrants; and that the Catholic Church set up a system of schools which became both popular and efficient.[40]

Just as in Ireland, therefore, in Australia Irish Catholics were a cohesive group and had practical reasons to remain so. While most leaders among the ranks of government, police, and penal administrators were Anglican or members of other Protestant denominations, among convicts—at least those identified as Catholic—the majority were Irish.

Ever since King Henry VIII's sixteenth-century split from the Church of Rome, many Anglicans took a dim view of Catholicism and the Irish who embraced the faith. In the case of Australia, given that convicts were looked down upon in society, convicts who happened to be of Catholic background were likely viewed with even greater disdain. Even with subsequent waves of free immigrants from Ireland, therefore, religious prejudice persisted, helping foster a strong sense of separateness instilled by the Protestant dominant leadership and felt by the Irish

---

[40] K.S. Inglis, "Religious Behaviour," in *Australian Society: A Sociological Introduction*, ed. A.F. Davies, and S. Encel, 2nd ed. (Melbourne, VIC: F.W. Cheshire, 1970), 440.

Catholics. Hence, the Irish community clung together to preserve its common religious/cultural identity and support of its members. This was a strongly egalitarian movement born, at least in part, by having been viewed with scorn or contempt by those in the ruling or upper classes. While this is certainly common among people from diverse backgrounds, in Australia the large number of Irish Catholics as a percentage of the general population made their presence and cultural influence that much more powerful.

From the early nineteenth century, conflict characterized the relationship between Irish Catholics and the Protestant officials who ruled Australia. Against many Anglican clergy who were largely Evangelical in their beliefs—that is, emphasizing the place of the Bible and preaching more than the sacramental aspects embraced by Catholicism[41]—perhaps what made the Irish even more likely to cling together was that in the first years of the colony, Irish convicts—most of whom being Catholic—had no clergy of their own to serve their spiritual needs. They, like others who were not members of the Church of England, had little choice but to attend Anglican religious services. Hence, among Irish Catholics in Australia, resentment of British rule and its different religious traditions became ingrained. While this resentment seemed to strengthen Irish Catholic disaffection for the British and made Irish Catholics more cohesive in their cultural identity, their lack of clergy made them much more casual than their brethren in Ireland in the practice of the tenets of their faith. Therefore, as Irish Catholic clergy arrived in Australia in the early nineteenth century, they began to play an important role in the development and character of the Australian Catholic Church and its adherents.

In fairness to the British Protestant rulers, Catholics did take a long time "to take advantage of the British government's willingness to accept a suitable Catholic chaplain," observes Patrick O'Farrell, and "Catholicism took a long time to recognize the necessity for an Australian mission."[42] It was not until 1820—30 years after the arrival of the first Catholic convicts—that the first Catholic chaplains arrived in Sydney.

---

[41] The overall feature that most distinguishes Protantism from Catholicism is its emphasis on scriptural readings and preaching. Protestant Evangelicals focus their study on the Bible, whereas Catholics tend to rely on the *missal*, a book containing all the prayers and responses necessary for celebrating the Mass throughout the year. These distinct religious practices reinforced different customs.

[42] Patrick O'Farrell, *The Catholic Church and Community: An Australian History*, 3rd rev. ed. (Kensington, NSW: New South Wales University Press, 1992), 17–18.

The experience of Irish priest, Father John Joseph Therry, who dominated Australian Catholicism between 1820 and 1833, reveals the significance of clerical leadership in the Irish Catholic community's development in Australia. As Therry's interaction with Governor Lachlan Macquarie suggests, while the Australian political leadership appeared accepting of religious toleration of Catholics, notes O'Farrell, "continuance of this 'benign spirit' largely depended on their conforming to Protestant expectations that their role in the community would be subordinate, inferior and passive."[43]

The underlying sentiments of the time were quite clear on this point. Provided that Catholics limited their influence to religion, O'Farrell quotes from the Sydney *Atlas* of May 1848, "We shall do not more than smile at their nonsensical mummeries, or pity their senseless superstition," but if they set their gaze on "politics" then they would be subject to resistance or even outright attack.[44] " 'Politics' was construed in the most general as well as the precise sense," O'Farrell explains, and "meant any attempt to change or challenge the colonial *status quo.*"[45] The seeds of Irish rebelliousness were planted early in Australian culture, which only increased Australian disdain for those in positions of power.

A strong sense of Irish resilience and cohesion was further ensured by Governor Macquarie's policies regarding education and interreligious marriage. Macquarie forbade Catholic clergy from interfering with the religious education of orphans in the government's charitable institutions, ensuring Anglican dominance, and forbade the priests from officiating at marriages between Protestants or between a Catholic and a Protestant. With regard to nuptials, Macquarie's main concern was "social harmony," suggests O'Farrell, "and particularly the fact that such prohibited marriages would raise, in law, questions of legitimacy, property and inheritance." As for education, retaining Anglican control over religious education served to ensure that Catholicism did not spread beyond the Catholic community.[46] While there may have been legitimate religious reasons on which to limit Catholic priests' involvement in marriages, the effect was to keep Protestants and Catholics separate, which served to strengthen each community's sense of difference. However, the Irish Catholic community grew and its influence did

---

43 Ibid., 20.
44 Quoted in Ibid.
45 Ibid.
46 Ibid., 22.

indeed spread into the political realm, precisely what the governing elite seemed inclined to avoid.

Therry exemplified the kind of proud Irishness that would become characteristically Australian. In response to the pressing demands of individual situations, he occasionally broke Governor Macquarie's regulations. After Governor Darling came to power in 1825, the animosity between Therry and the administration only grew more intense. Whereas for Therry the interests of religion and individuals were of fundamental importance, for officials, as in any bureaucracy whether in Australia or elsewhere, the law had to be enforced. Perhaps inevitably, Therry's actions further pit the demands of Irish Catholic Australians against that of the British administration. Faced with the prospect of Anglicanism securing a privileged and domineering place within the colony, Therry was particularly incensed at Macquarie's regulation placing the Orphan Schools squarely under the jurisdiction of the Anglican religion. "Therry regarded this as naked proselytism," O'Farrell relates, "designed to rob Catholic children of their faith."[47] While Therry held many Protestant clergymen in high esteem, he vigorously argued for the establishment of a Catholic Education Society in order to prevent the Catholic poor in Australia from having to choose between two equally undesirable outcomes, at least from the perspective of the Irish Catholic community—having their children educated in the Anglican Orphan Schools at the expense of their Catholic religion, or depriving their children of an education.

Due to rising concerns among Australia's Protestant clergymen, Therry was removed from his position as official Catholic chaplain and told to leave Australia. However, Therry refused to leave the colony and built up a popular reputation among the Irish for his feverish criticisms of the government. Ultimately reinstated in 1837—long after the *British Act* of 1829 had emancipated Catholics and allowed them to hold government positions— Father Therry and his leadership retains a strong position in the history of Australian civil liberties. Therry's unwavering and tenacious assertion of the fundamental rights of religion made him both a popular and significant figure among many, which gave Australia's burgeoning Irish Catholic community a platform from which to become even more assertive.

This assertiveness would be expressed among the ranks of labor— represented by significant numbers of Irish Australians—in the form

---

[47] Ibid., 25.

of unions and development of the national Labor Party. Tracing this cultural power to ethnoreligious origins is legitimate because if not for the perception of oppression or lack of equal consideration relative to Protestants in Australia, the Irish Catholic community may not have remained as strong a force as it did.

Although the influence of Therry was a significant early example of leadership among the Irish Catholic community in Australia, particularly among Irish Catholic religious leaders, Australian historian Michael Hogan argues, "for most of the nineteenth century the social message of the clergy was in accord with that of the Protestants." While there were examples of Irish patriots who endeavored to sustain a critical view of British political authority, he asserts, "the hierarchy and clergy reinforced law and order both in their sermons and in their actions" without much encouragement from Australia's bishops "to think of themselves as an oppressed working class or to organise as a class."[48] Nonetheless, this conformity to prevailing societal norms certainly changed under the ecclesiastical leadership of Patrick Francis Moran, who became Archbishop of Sydney in 1884.

Faced with an economic crisis during the 1890s and conscious of a strong grassroots support among Catholics for trade unions in the most important strikes of the era, Moran made a public statement in 1891 that provided moral support to the strikers at the same time as he carefully avoided any condemnation of the employers. However, when the strike tactic failed, Moran encouraged Catholic union leaders to also seek representation in Parliament. Indeed, Moran was the "principle agent of this change," observes Encel, since "it was Moran who persuaded Catholics to see in the Labor movement their chosen instrument of political redemption."[49]

Moran's encouragement of the Irish working class toward significantly more culturally assertive behavior was strengthened by the publication of an encyclical by Pope Leo XIII (1878–1903), *Rerum Novarum*, an important papal document on social justice. While the Pope encouraged Catholic leaders to criticize many of capitalism's excesses, *Rerum Novarum* also negatively affected the working-class movement due to its strong disapproval of socialism. Since the leaders of the labor movement in Australia and of the developing ALP were socialists, causing difficulties for Catholic leaders for many ensuing years, Hogan asserts

---

[48] Michael Hogan, *The Sectarian Strand: Religion in Australian History* (Ringwood, VIC: Penguin, 1987), 138–39.
[49] Encel, 174.

that "Moran was able to defuse the issue for the time being by making the point that socialism meant many different things, and that most Australian variants were acceptable."[50]

Cardinal Moran defended the socialism of the ALP on the basis that it was not like the "doctrinaire socialism" of Europeans. Focusing on what served the interests of Australian Catholics, Moran initially believed that ALP was as acceptable as any other party, with exception of the Australian Socialist League since its socialism was not acceptable in light of papal teachings. However, given the rise of socialism among workers over the course of the 1890s Moran focused more intently on the implications of the movement. However, when Labor began to express a close affinity for socialist ideas, particularly between 1893 and 1897, Moran became a vocal opponent of Labor because, according to Moran's biographer Patrick Ford, Moran "presumably sought to free the Party of Socialist influence, as it originally had been free of it, when it did not alienate Catholic workers." Between 1898 and 1901, when the Labor Party broke its alliance with socialism in favor of a more moderate path, Moran was satisfied in playing the quiet role of observer. Nonetheless, in the first decade of the twentieth century, Moran seems to have implicitly defended the Party, suggests Ford, "presumably on the grounds that it was moderate and could provide one of several political habitats for Catholic workers." Ford maintains that Moran's silence in the years between 1898 and 1901 probably helped Labor in the elections since the 1901 ballot reflected "a considerable influx of Catholic support."[51]

At the time, Australian Catholicism was viewed as radical by world standards, so Moran's defense only reasserted this already well-known stereotype. As the socialism associated with Continental Europeans was rejected by the Catholic Church as being too revolutionary, doctrinaire, devoid of practicality, and antireligious, the socialism of the ALP was deemed acceptable because, observes Australian social policy specialist, Paul Smyth, it was characterized "in terms of practical social reformism."[52] In an interview with *L'Univers*, a Paris newspaper, Moran stated, "Our Labor Party does not cherish any vague theories, any ambitious and high sounding formulae. Its object is precise reforms and

---

[50] Hogan, *The Sectarian Strand*, 139.
[51] Patrick Ford, *Cardinal Moran and the A.L.P.* (Melbourne, VIC: Melbourne University Press, 1966), 280–81.
[52] Paul Smyth, "Reclaiming Community? From Welfare Society to Welfare State in Australian Catholic Social Thought," *Australian Journal of Politics and History* 49, no. 1 (2003): 19.

concrete measures in favour of the toiling masses. It is a clan movement if you like, in the sense that these self-trusting men feel that they are able to look after their own affairs."[53]

This "clan movement" was especially strong among members of the working class, or, as Moran described them, the "toiling masses." As the earlier discussion of class and ethnoreligious identity stressed, "status" is a culturally defined position in society, which reflects a set of shared ideas about how people are expected to respond toward the individual, and how the individual should behave when in a given position. However, as the composition and actions of the Australian working class suggest, perceptions of status are not the same everywhere. In contrast to Canadian and American views, Australians are not as accepting of broad status differences since glorification of individual achievement is not part of Australian culture. Compared to Canadians, Australians reflect a strong Irish sensibility. Hence, this phenomenon, linked to Australians' lower tolerance for power distance and greater acceptance of egalitarianism, strongly points to the Irish as a fundamental influence.

* * *

If the Irish did indeed exert a profound influence on Australia, the source of their power was their presence among the working class. A significant proportion of the Australian working class—and their leaders—were of Irish origin. The Australian Irish Catholics tended to cling to their independent identity as separate from British. Thus, the Irish contribution was not only significant but may have been essential to the process of Australia's cultural development. How did the Irish remain a cohesive and therefore culturally influential group? Religious leadership was initially essential, but labor and political leadership proved vital later. Hence, in the chapter that follows key cultural dimensions are reviewed to help identify where and how Canada differs from Australia and why these differences point to Australia's unique and powerful Irish factor.

---

[53] A.E. Cahill, "Cardinal Moran's Politics," *The Journal of Religious History* 15, no. 4 (1989): 525–31. Quoted in Smyth, "Reclaiming Community?" 19.

4
Australia's Irish Factor

The contribution of an Irish sensibility to Australian irreverence, rebelliousness, and egalitarianism—or desire for flatter hierarchies—is evident in such Australian practices as "knocking," "cutting down tall poppies," and the social phenomenon of "mateship." These Australian cultural features distinguish Australia from Canada and point to a historically significant "Irish factor" that Canada does not share. In contrast, while the Scots also represented a sizeable immigrant community in Australia and Canada, there does not appear to have been an equivalent "Scottish factor" despite their cultural significance. For economic and ethnocultural reasons, the Scots in both countries tended to align with the British establishment far more than did the Irish, whose numbers in Australia were particularly large. As Hofstede's cultural dimensions are useful indicators of national variation,[1] this chapter explores power distance and individualism–collectivism to attribute Australia and Canada's salient cultural characteristics to particular regions of Anglo-Celtic origin.

Power distance and ethnocultural distinctions

According to American psychologist Victor Savicki's study of English-speaking cultures, important differences exist in Hofstede's cultural work value dimensions of power distance and individualism–collectivism but

---

A version of this chapter originally appeared as an article by the author as, Arthur J. Wolak, "Australia's 'Irish Factor' as a Source of Cultural Difference from Canada," *Australasian Canadian Studies* 25, no. 1 (2007): 85–116. It is included here, with kind permission from the *Australasian Canadian Studies Journal*.

[1] Geert Hofstede, *Culture's Consequences: Comparing Values, Behaviors, Institutions, and Organizations Across Nations*, 2nd ed. (Thousand Oaks, CA: Sage, 2001), 29.

not on uncertainty avoidance or masculinity–femininity measures.[2] While Hofstede's dimensions of culture compared dozens of nations, including Australia, Canada, Ireland, the United States, and the United Kingdom, Savicki segregated Scotland from England, and English Canada from French Canada, which helps ascribe Australia and Canada's salient cultural characteristics to the regions of Anglo-Celtic origin.

The British who came to Australia and Canada—and their descendants who assumed powerful roles in each society—arrived with a cultural background immersed in the rigidly formal English class system. Although not overtly replicated in Australia or Canada, notions of class were sufficiently familiar to the dominant British Protestant population of English Canada to encourage tolerance of social hierarchy. Thus, contrary to the "melting pot" of the contemporary United States where different ethnic cultures are expected to subordinate their identities to a singular "American" culture,[3] Canadians have been encouraged since the 1960s to retain their multicultural identities as part of a "Canadian" identity cultivated by a founding population largely sympathetic to British cultural tradition as distinct from American.[4] Like Canada, Australia since the 1970s has also transformed from a settler country to a multicultural nation.[5] However, as the Irish comprised a large percentage of Australia's colonial and later migrant population,[6] the Australian national character was disproportionately influenced by them.

In *The Irish in Australia*, historian Patrick O'Farrell asserts that the very presence of a "substantial and insubordinate Irish minority deflated and confused the English majority." According to O'Farrell, "Their refusal to act out a deferential role discomfited the elite, eroded their superior certainties, provided a constant liberalising creative irritant, and gave notice that the old-world social order could not be reproduced in Australia."[7] Irish Catholics, therefore, presented a great challenge to Australia's established Protestant/Anglican colonial society because

---

[2] Victor Savicki, *Burnout Across Thirteen Cultures: Stress and Coping in Child and Youth Care Workers* (Westport, CT: Praeger, 2002), 160–61.

[3] Peter Kivisto, *Multiculturalism in a Global Society* (Malden, MA: Blackwell Publishers, 2002), 46–50.

[4] Ibid., 90–91.

[5] Ibid., 101, 109–112.

[6] Prior to 1851, about half of the assisted immigrants arriving to New South Wales were Irish. R.B. Madgwick, *Immigration into Eastern Australia, 1788–1851* (Sydney, NSW: Sydney University Press, 1969), 234.

[7] Patrick O'Farrell, *The Irish in Australia: 1788 to the Present* (Sydney, NSW: New South Wales University Press, 1987), 11.

of the Irish culture's different religious traditions, values, and natural antagonism toward England.

The significance of this Irish Catholic force in nineteenth-century Australian culture prompted O'Farrell to conclude that the powerful Irish minority represented the "key dynamic factor" in Australia:

> Whereas the smaller minorities—Germans, Italians—tended to be content with tolerance within a dominant British system, the Irish rejected or questioned the system, or at least demanded that it be adjusted to meet their requirements, with the effect of creating a new, modified system, a unique Australian blend and compromise which fitted the character of a mixed and interacting group of people, on the basis of equity.[8]

According to Donald Akenson's review of the composition of Australia's Irish population, the Irish—from the mid-nineteenth century onward—were indeed Australia's second largest ethnic group.[9] As for how the Australian Irish broke down between Catholics and Protestants, he concludes from the available data that, first, "Irish Catholics were a very significant group in the general population and, second, that among the overall Irish ethnic group the Protestants were a very noticeable minority."[10] Akenson estimates that, by 1891, Irish Catholics comprised 18.6 percent of the total population of Australia relative to 7.1 percent Irish Protestant. This compared to 48.8 percent English, 14.0 Scottish, and 1.5 percent Welsh.[11] Hence, Catholicism provided the Irish with a different identity, a sense of second-class citizenship in a land ruled by a powerful British Protestant elite. In contrast, English-speaking Canada, largely a product of the British Protestant tradition, lacked Australia's culturally dominant Irish Catholic presence.[12]

---

[8] Ibid., 10–11.

[9] Donald Harmon Akenson, *Small Differences: Irish Catholics and Irish Protestants, 1815–1922* (Montreal, QC & Kingston, ON: McGill-Queen's University Press, 1988), 61.

[10] Akenson, *Small Differences*, 62.

[11] Ibid.

[12] It is interesting to note for comparison that the Irish population, as a proportion of the total population, was less in both the United States and New Zealand compared to Australia. Akenson notes that, "The Irish-born reached their demographic apogee in the United States in 1860 when they comprised 5.12% of the total population, whereas in 1867, their top year in New Zealand, they were proportionately more than twice as many: 12.8%." Donald Harman Akenson,

John Porter's classic study of Canadian power structures, *The Vertical Mosaic*, described a vertical or hierarchical relationship among Canada's cultural groups with elite membership and ethnoreligious affiliation determining who has power in society. Russel Ward's classic study of Australian culture, *The Australian Legend*, asserted that the Australian elites, although largely comprised a similar ethnic composition as the Anglophone Canadian elites—that is, English, Scottish, and Irish Protestants—effectively ruled over a society where Irish Catholics comprised a significant proportion of the influential working-class population.[13] Hence, the significant Irish Catholic impact on Australia has long been emphasized over that of other Celts. As Malcolm Prentis asserts,

> Russel Ward wrote the Scots out of the working class, yet the general image of Scottish success should not blind us to the fact that Scots were in fact found in all parts of the social spectrum. Perhaps the difference was that most Scots did not necessarily regard a lowly position as permanent, and did not see themselves as class-bound.[14]

Indeed, the cohesive nature of the Irish Catholic community among the working class strengthened their collective impact. In Canada, there were fewer Irish Catholics (as a percentage of the Canadian population) over whom to dominate.[15] In fact, according to Akenson, "it is true that there were proportionately fewer Catholics than Protestants among the Irish in Canada—in the case of Ontario, roughly one-third of the Irish cohort was Catholic."[16] Moreover, Akenson suggests, "the Irish who migrated to Canada were, in some vague way, too Protestant."[17] Hofstede's relative measures of power distance support these influences.

"Immigration and Ethnicity in New Zealand and the USA—the Irish Example," in *New Worlds? The Comparative History of New Zealand and the United States*, ed. Jock Phillips (Wellington, NZ: Stout Research Centre, 1989), 29.

[13] Russel Ward, *The Australian Legend* (Melbourne, VIC: Oxford University Press, 1958), 47–53.

[14] Malcolm D. Prentis, *The Scots in Australia: A Study of New South Wales, Victoria and Queensland, 1788–1900* (Sydney, NSW: Sydney University Press, 1983), 275.

[15] Donald Mackay, *Flight from Famine: The Coming of the Irish to Canada* (Toronto, ON: McClelland & Stewart, 1990), 12–15.

[16] Donald H. Akenson, "Data: What is Known about the Irish in North America?" in *Ireland and Irish-Australia: Studies in Cultural and Political History*, ed. Oliver MacDonagh and W.F. Mandle (London, UK: Croom Helm, 1986), 5.

[17] Akenson, *Small Differences*, 100.

Hofstede defines power distance as "the *extent to which the less powerful members of institutions*"—such basic elements of society as the family, school, and the community—"*and organizations within a country expect and accept that power is distributed unequally.*"[18] In other words, this cultural dimension is concerned with the issue of human inequality, which occurs in diverse areas such as wealth, prestige, and power. According to Hofstede, the significance of the power distance measure is that "different societies put different weights on status consistency among these areas."[19] Since inequality in power within organizations is a common and practical means by which work productivity and accountability are achieved, inequality of this type is typically found in relationships between managers and subordinates.

Societies with relatively low power distance—such as Ireland and Australia that rank 28 and 36, respectively—are characterized by decentralized authority and decision-making responsibility, consultative or participative management style, flat organizational structures, small proportion of supervisory staff, lack of acceptance and questioning of authority, greater consciousness of rights, and tendency toward egalitarianism.[20] In contrast, higher power distance cultures like Canada, with a power index score of 39, are generally marked by centralized decision structures, greater concentration of authority, more supervisors, managers who rely on formal rules, and tall organizational pyramids featuring hierarchies that highlight inequality between those higher up and those lower down.[21]

Although religion does not account for all differences in power distance, the shared identity and values that are built up and retained by religious communities provide an important source for relative tolerance of power distance. Hofstede suggests that the earlier Roman Empire may have been more decisive than the later Church because Catholic non-Latin Ireland scores were similar to largely Protestant non-Latin Britain compared to Latin-based Catholic nations.[22] However, since scores are not identical between Ireland and Britain, differences appear strongly linked to culture and dominant religious affiliation.

---

[18] Geert Hofstede, *Cultures and Organizations: Intercultural Cooperation and its Importance for Survival* (London, UK: HarperCollins, 1994), 28.
[19] Hofstede, *Culture's Consequences*, 79.
[20] Ibid., 87, 107–8.
[21] Ibid.
[22] Ibid., 114.

Hofstede asserts that "once a religion has been established in a country, it will reinforce the values that led to its adoption."[23] This statement is reasonable for both Australia and Canada where British Protestant rule, and the values associated with it, was imposed from the top down. Yet in Australia where Irish Catholics were widely dispersed, it also appears reasonable that their communities would reinforce their shared values. "Catholicism, with the supreme authority of the pope and the intermediate authority of the priest," Hofstede argues, is a better fit than Protestantism with its greater tolerance of power distance.[24] Although logical, the assertion is contrary to the Australian experience.

Hofstede's generalization that Catholicism in and of itself suggests greater compliance with high tolerance of power distance may not apply when unique cultural circumstances are considered. Irish Catholics in Australia, despite their Catholicism, were opposed to social hierarchy endemic in British colonial rule. However, among European countries with Catholic majorities, Ireland and Poland are the only ones that lack a Latin past, and both nations, Hofstede asserts, "used their Catholicism as a source of identity to protect them against powerful non-Catholic occupants."[25] Indeed, this source of identity proved powerful. For the Poles, their strong Catholicism helped bring down communism in the late twentieth century since they shared more in common with members of their own culture than with the former nieghboring Union of Soviet Socialist Republics and its contrary values. The Soviet opposition to religion could not suffuse Poland's culturally cohesive religious tradition.

Similarly, though on a less dramatic scale, the Irish Catholics of Australia did not share an identical culture with the British. Irish Catholicism was a strong reason. According to Lovejoy's *The Great Chain of Being*, European religious and social tradition fostered deference by lower links to those deemed higher.[26] Everyone knew their place and did not question their position. After the Reformation, the reigning English monarch could expect deference since the pope was no longer a viable rival along the links of the Great Chain. Catholics, however, tended to defer to papal authority before the reigning monarch in matters of religion. Irish Catholics could, therefore, feel justified in showing less deference to British rule because they were not in defiance of their view of legitimate

---

[23] Ibid.

[24] Ibid.

[25] Ibid.

[26] *See* Arthur O. Lovejoy, *The Great Chain of Being*, new ed. (Cambridge, MA: Harvard University Press, 2005).

hierarchy. Since the English were obsessed with order, and the Great Chain accomplished order by ensuring that every person and object had its place within the hierarchy, the Irish were, therefore, a constant thorn in the sides of British rulers who feared the breakdown of social order.

Irish objection to the lack of self-determined authority and independent political power in Ireland remained a strong force among the Irish Catholics of Australia. While tolerance of power distance exists within the Church and Catholic community, this does not equate with having a tolerance of power distance in society in general. While Australia's relatively lower power distance is arguably more Irish than English, Canada's comparatively higher power distance evokes its English cultural heritage where disparity among classes—in social circles and work environments—was the accepted norm.

Social class and the relative tolerance of power distance

The Canadian elite, comprising individuals of predominantly British Protestant parentage, effectively ruled over a substantial working class of similar ethnicity, who were implicitly respectful of differences in rank because of their familial understanding of the British cultural practice. The result was the cultivation of a social atmosphere that gave elites even greater power. This broad acceptance of social hierarchy is an important yet subtle factor that distinguishes Canadian from Australian society. While Australia's elite was similarly dominated by a powerful group of British Protestants, the significant Irish working class was not as receptive to the largely Protestant elite's authority.

While a respect for class distinction and privilege was transmitted to Canada—though without England's upper class preoccupation with nomenclature—acceptance of formal hereditary distinctions and British honors was not. Although Canada inherited a respect for deference associated with English social hierarchy and stratification—in other words, people knew their place in society and accepted it—this acceptance was not absolute when it came to Canadians and royal peerages. Indeed, Canada enacted legislation in 1919 that precludes Canadian citizens from accepting title, or even being knighted by the Queen.[27] In the

---

[27] The Nickle Resolution, passed by the Canadian House of Commons in 1919, established the policy of not granting knighthoods and peerages to Canadians, and set the precedent for later policies, forbidding Canadians from accepting or holding titles of honor from foreign countries.

1950s, this provision was cited to veto the award of the Garter to Vincent Massey—Canada's first native-born Governor General, an Anglophile whose disappointment was lessened after receiving the Royal Victorian Chain, which provides no accompanying title—and used again in the 1990s to deny a British peerage for media baron Conrad Black.[28]

Acceptance of title represented a challenge to Canada's sovereignty as Canadian citizenship—symbolic of political and cultural independence—is held in higher esteem. The alternative would imply that Canada remains a colony of the British crown, an important distinction given Canada's proximity to the United States and the desire to avoid any implication of Canada being less independent, less sovereign than the United States. Nonetheless, the British Protestant elite remains enamored with ties to England as a means of retaining a sense of cultural superiority and maintenance of a grand tradition that goes back to the early colonial era.

While Massey could only mask his disappointment given his privileged political position in Canadian society, Conrad Black, among whose global collection of newspapers once included Canada's *National Post* and London's *Daily Telegraph*, was not held back by any patriotic or political obligations. An extreme example of the monarchy-supporting Canadian elite's fondness for British tradition, Black's desire for title, rank, and privilege led him to renounce his Canadian citizenship in 2001 to become a British citizen, accept a peerage as Lord Black of Crossharbour, and take his seat in the House of Lords.[29]

Black's fondness for British tradition was cultivated early. Educated at the elite, Anglo-Protestant Upper Canada College, which, like most of Canada's institutions, emulated English progenitors, Black's British cultural indoctrination included reverence for British tradition and education which helped foster his infatuation with Europe and social hierarchy. Raised in Toronto, an environment Black described in his first autobiography, *A Life in Progress*, as "dour, dreary earnest and envy

---

[28] David Cannadine, *Ornamentalism: How the British Saw Their Empire* (Oxford, UK: Oxford University Press, 2001), 145.

[29] A recent application of the Nickle Resolution occurred when Canada's Prime Minister Jean Chrétien invoked the measure to prevent Canadian publishing mogul Conrad Black from becoming a British life peer. Black appealed to the courts, which upheld the government's interpretation of the Resolution. This prompted Black to renounce his Canadian citizenship to become Lord Black of Crossharbour on October 31, 2001. Crossharbour is both a London neighborhood as well as a subway stop on the Docklands light railway, near the Daily Telegraph building.

of low-church Protestant Ontario," his brewery executive father, took young Conrad and his brother to London "in a fine monarchist gesture" to see the 1953 coronation of Queen Elizabeth II, an experience that helped shape his outlook.[30]

Black's awe for England and British tradition reflects Porter's view that elite membership in Canada—largely the domain of British Protestants—has proven highly conducive to the acquisition of wealth and power.[31] Private schools, universities, and other locations of cultural interaction provided common exposure to an instrumental and normative socialization process.[32] The ethnoreligious heritage of the Canadian elite served as a form of class distinction that Canadians have not typically opposed. Such subtle notions of class have been tolerated in Canada where steep vertical social hierarchy is a significant cultural element linked to Canada's British tradition. Hence, Australia's lack of tolerance for genuine or perceived social inequality reflects a major difference from Canada that exists precisely because of Australia's significant Irish Catholic presence.

In Australia, Irish Catholics and radical labor had a preference for St. Patrick's Day and, following the First World War, Anzac Day. They were far less impressed by the British hierarchical festival of Empire Day.[33] However, in the nineteenth century, there had been other less subtle displays of anti-British sentiment by rebellious Irish Catholics. For instance, during the Australian visit of the Duke of Edinburgh in 1868, an Irishman tried to assassinate him. Although violence was rare, there were instances that reflected considerable animosity across the Catholic–Protestant divide.[34] Well into the middle of the twentieth century, St. Patrick's Day and the anniversary of the Battle of the Boyne, notes Australian historian Michael Hogan, served "as occasions for at least symbolic saber-rattling by each side," and Catholic churches and schools fostered a "sense of Irishness and isolation in a Protestant society which helped to maintain divisions."[35] Legitimate fear among Catholics and Protestants was at the root of social disharmony.

[30] Conrad Black, *A Life in Progress* (Toronto, ON: Key Porter Books, 1993), 6–8.
[31] John Porter, *The Vertical Mosaic, The Vertical Mosaic: An Analysis of Social Class and Power in Canada* (Toronto, ON: University of Toronto Press, 1965), 98–103.
[32] Ibid., 304.
[33] Cannadine, 145.
[34] Michael Hogan, *The Sectarian Strand: Religion in Australian History* (Ringwood, VIC: Penguin, 1987), 65–67.
[35] Ibid., 69.

The importation of the contentious Irish political question into Australian society, combined with institutions such as the Orange Order helping to perpetuate sectarian and ethnic disharmony, ensured that a growing Australian Irish Catholic community would maintain anti-British sentiments. This outlook spread to others whose Australian nationalism precluded a desire for British political connections. Thus, the result was that Australians have been less enamored than Canadians with their nation's British ties. "Even Queen Elizabeth II's tour of Australia in 1953/4," notes British historian David Cannadine, "was sceptically greeted by radicals who thought it was all an upper-class racket, and by Catholic-Irish-Australians who found Menzies's snobbish sycophancy nauseating."[36] Although not every Australian would share these sentiments, they expressed the mood of many, whether Irish Catholics or those influenced by them.

Indeed, Canada's tolerance of greater power distance relative to Australia appears indicative of English cultural acceptance that has persisted despite the development of a more culturally varied contemporary society. In contrast, Australia's lesser tolerance of power distance compared to Canada and the United States seems to reflect Australians' lesser acceptance of hierarchy, or the blatant power difference that often accompanies social inequality, particularly in work environments.[37] Australia's Irish factor helps account for this cultural difference.

Hofstede classifies Ireland as very low on power distance,[38] and Feather observes that the Australian inclination to "cut down tall poppies" is consistent with Australia's low power distance culture.[39] Hence, the Australian disdain for high individual achievement seems largely attributable to the Irish since Australia, like Ireland per Hofstede, is a low power distance culture, and Australia received an enormous influx of Irish immigrants in its formative period during the nineteenth century. Just as the Irish did not want to be dominated by the British but treated as an equal power, Australians do not favor those who seek attention or adulation for their accomplishments, particularly in the workplace.

---

[36] Cannadine, 146.

[37] Australia scores below Canada and the United States on Hofstede's power distance index, revealing a lower tolerance for social hierarchy. Ireland scores even lower than Australia. Hofstede, *Culture's Consequences*, 87.

[38] Ibid.

[39] N.T. Feather, "Attitudes Toward High Achievers, Self-Esteem, and Value Priorities for Australian, American, and Canadian Students," *Journal of Cross-Cultural Psychology* 29, no. 6 (1998): 749–59.

Cultural difference at work

Few examples are more revealing of Australia's cultural difference from North America as Telecom Australia and Westpac Banking Corporation. In the early 1990s, they imported two American executives to transform, lead, and reverse the companies' downward spiral. Frank Blount became chief executive officer (CEO) of Telecom Australia (known as Telstra since the mid-1990s); Bob Joss became CEO of Westpac, Australia's oldest bank and among the largest Australian banking corporations. In contrast with North American management cultures, Blount and Joss found in their respective Australian corporations a reluctance to take on leadership roles. When Blount arrived to Telstra he found *"an unwillingness to put up the hand to take on challenging tasks. There was a fear of risk of failure."*[40] Joss expressed a similar sentiment at Westpac:

> *We used to have these relief managers who would go from branch to branch and fill in for managers who were away on vacation or leave even though they didn't know anything about the customers. . . . When I asked why the assistant managers in each of the branches didn't fill in, why they didn't jump at the chance to show us what they were made of, I was told that that would be taking advantage of them.*[41]

Rather than reflecting a fear of failure, the reticence to take on leadership roles exposed a key Australian cultural trait. Blount and Joss came from America where individual distinction is a culturally accepted and widely desired goal to which many managers aspire.[42] As a result, these American-born and -bred executives failed to recognize—at least initially—that what they interpreted as avoidance of leadership or fear of failure was an expression of the Australian cultural reluctance to stand out from the crowd and assert individual authority. Individual distinction appears less prized in the workplace despite a strong individualist side to Australian society. While cultural instincts of Australian workers reveal evidence of Australian egalitarianism, a desire for equality among colleagues was not the sole reason for this behavior.

---

[40] Frank Blount, Bob Joss, and David Mair, *Managing in Australia* (Sydney, NSW: Landsdowne Publishing, 1999), 162.

[41] Ibid., 163.

[42] George W. England, "Managers and Their Value Systems: A Five-Country Comparative Study," *Columbia Journal of World Business* 13 (Summer 1978): 40–41.

Experience prevents many Australians from seeking out individual distinction, especially at work. Although achievement is consistent with the strong Australian propensity for individualism, the process of socialization in the Australian environment teaches that individual distinction also means risking social humiliation by being, in the inimitable words of the oft-heard Australian expression, "cut down like tall poppies." Because of this culturally conditioned fear, Telstra and Westpac were wise to bring in leaders from a culture far removed from Australia, a culture where aspirations toward achievement were not considered culturally undesirable. Indeed, Blount and Joss, executives whose experiences were obtained primarily within an American setting, were not encumbered by Australia's prevailing cultural norm.

A conditioned fear response seems plausible since individualism is strong in Australian culture. In a study of Australian and Canadian work supervisors' recollections of their attributional and evaluative responses to high and low levels of subordinate performance, Ashkanasy found that Australians endorse more "internal attributions" for subordinate performance than Canadians, and that they focus more on "individual characteristics" in evaluating performance.[43] However, while an individualist trait would include a desire for social distinction and a powerful position, the egalitarian impulse favoring group cooperation likely results in a culturally conditioned fear of being cut down. Consequently, although Australians are capable of demonstrating similar leadership abilities—after all, since the 1960s many modern business schools emerged in Australia where the principles of management are taught—it would have proven difficult for those steeped in Australian culture to go against the grain and take on the challenge required to effectively transform each organization. Australia's prevailing cultural norm that discourages individuals from wanting to rise to the top and achieve individual distinction simply proved too strong. Compared to Canada, the Australian egalitarian impulse diminishes Australian tolerance of hierarchy.

Despite many similarities among members of the "Anglo Cluster" of nations with common British colonial roots,[44] Australia is not a mirror image of America. Relative to the United States and Canada, Australia

---

[43] N.M. Ashkanasy, "A Cross-National Comparison of Australian and Canadian Supervisors' Attributional and Evaluative Responses to Subordinate Performance," *Australian Psychologist* 32, no. 1 (1997): 29–36.
[44] A strong argument for an "Anglo Cluster" of nations sharing similar values is made in N.M. Ashkanasy, Edwin Trevor-Roberts, and Louise Earnshaw, "The

is lower in power distance. According to Hofstede, in countries where small power distance is the norm, "there is limited dependence of subordinates on bosses, and a preference for consultation, that is, *interdependence* between boss and subordinate." As Hofstede's research suggests, subordinates will approach and contradict their superiors because the "emotional distance" between them is relatively small.[45] As a result, it appears that for the successful implementation of organizational change in an Australian setting, a leadership approach that is less hierarchical and dictatorial encourages acceptance by subordinates, and provides an atmosphere in which managerial workers feel less reluctance to take on a leadership role for fear of being cut down to size. This is the kind of organizational environment that Telstra and Westpac successfully implemented. Australian employees do not want autocratic or paternalistic bosses. Hence, American-style high achievement and competence orientation represent a stark contrast from Australia's moralistic and humanistic orientation's preference for social equality and lower value on individual achievement, competition, risk, and success.[46]

At Telstra and Westpac the "tall poppy" effect was circumvented by the application of basic psychological principles to encourage behavioral modification. Conditioning and feedback to reward desired behavior and extinguish undesired behavior were emphasized. As a result, managers were inspired to take greater initiative in seeking out higher levels of responsibility.[47] Although behavior can change given appropriate and effective conditioning, cultural norms still exist on the outside and, therefore, likely persist at some level within the organization. While people can readily change their behavior, reason the CEOs, "individuals can rarely change their personality traits or characteristics."[48]

According to Blount, "*Australians broadly view leadership as something rather uncomfortable, the job for the masochist, the insanely ambitious, the workaholic, or the outsider.*"[49] Such reticence to stand out is understandable, given the prevailing tendency to be cut down to size. Hence, the lack of aspiration to leadership that Blount and Joss witnessed was hardly incompatible with Australian cultural norms. It reflected them.

Anglo Cluster: Legacy of the British Empire," *Journal of World Business* 37 (2002): 28–39.
[45] Hofstede, *Cultures and Organizations*, 27.
[46] England, "Managers and Their Value Systems," 40–41.
[47] Blount, Joss, and Mair, *Managing in Australia*, 165.
[48] Ibid., 168.
[49] Ibid., 183.

While the "tall poppy syndrome" may account for this behavior, which dictates that those who stand up for prominent roles in Australian society face the distinct possibility of being cut down by their compatriots—a feature of unfettered egalitarianism—there is also another point of view expressed by Blount: *"perhaps the solitary, self-reliant heroes of Australian myth and fiction—like Ned Kelly or even Mad Max—represent a distrust of tribes and teams and their leaders."*[50] Egalitarianism and individualism need not be mutually exclusive.

Trompenaars and Hampden-Turner suggest that evaluations of obligation—that is, whether universalism (concerned with societal rules) or particularism (focused on personal relationships) take precedence—are an important dimension of culture.[51] Considering that egalitarianism appears stronger in Australia than in Canada or the United States, and universalism—especially among workers—is weaker in Australia, the particularistic and equalitarian value of "mateship" is considered by many Australians as contradictory to the value of "achievement" so highly regarded in America's strongly individualist culture, and, to a lesser degree, in Canada.[52] Individualism, though common among the Anglo cluster of nations, is expressed differently in Australia, Canada, and the United States.

Individualism–Collectivism and Anglo-Celtic distinctions

In cultural psychology, individualism reflects a social pattern comprised of individuals motivated primarily by their own needs, preferences, and rights, who give priority to personal rather than to group goals. Collectivism, by contrast, refers to a social pattern wherein people who are closely linked to one another consider themselves as parts of a whole, whether represented by a family, a tribe, a nation, or a network of coworkers. They are motivated in large part by the norms of, and duties imposed by, the collective entity, whose goals they are willing to give priority over their own personal goals.[53] Put simply, individualistic

---

[50] Ibid., 177.

[51] Fons Trompenaars and Charles Hampden-Turner, *Riding the Waves of Culture: Understanding Cultural Diversity in Global Business*, 2nd ed. (New York, NY: McGraw-Hill, 1998), 29–38.

[52] Seymour Martin Lipset, *The First New Nation: The United States in Historical Perspective* (New York, NY: Basic Books, 1963), 252.

[53] H.C. Triandis, *Individualism & Collectivism* (Boulder, CO: Westview, 1995), 2.

cultures stress "personal action and responsibility" while collectivist cultures stress "interpersonal relatedness and group action."[54]

In other words, for individuals in individualist cultures, their self-identity and personal goals are considered independent of the larger social group, whereas in collectivist cultures self-concept and personal goals are inseparable from the larger social group. This difference points to "ingroups" as a source of distinction. While individualistic societies are distinguished by loose ties among individuals who focus on the core family, collectivist societies are distinguished by strong ties among individuals who focus on larger extended families and ingroups. According to Triandis, "Ingroups are usually characterized by similarities among the members, and individuals have a sense of 'common fate' with members of the ingroup."[55] Since each culture has its own significant ingroups, emphasis varies among family, friends, political parties, social classes, religious groups, or tribal, ethnic, linguistic or territorial collectives.[56] Cultural differences are most apparent when people from a strongly individualist culture, such as the United States, interact with people from a solidly collectivist culture, like Japan.[57] However, among such cultures as Australia and Canada, closer together along the spectrum, differences are less obvious but still discernible.

According to Triandis, cultures that are more homogeneous with less division of labor are more likely to be collectivist, and cultures that are more heterogeneous, or those that share strong historical ties to the United Kingdom, such as Australia, Canada, and the United States, tend to be individualist. However, within societies where individualistic orientations dominate, ethnically based minority groups may be more collectivist than the dominant culture. Members of the Asian and Latino subcultures in the United States rate higher on the collectivist dimension than the majority culture.[58] French Canadians rate higher on collectivism than English Canadians who rate higher on individualism.[59] Likewise, Hofstede's research indicates the Republic of Ireland scores significantly lower on the individualism dimension than

---

[54] Savicki, *Burnout Across Thirteen Cultures*, 39.

[55] Triandis, *Individualism & Collectivism*, 9.

[56] Ibid.

[57] Ibid., 12–13.

[58] H.C. Triandis, G. Marin, C. H. Hui, J. Lisansky, and V. Ottati, "Role Perceptions of Hispanic Young Adults," *Journal of Cross-Cultural Psychology* 15, no. 3 (1984): 297–320.

[59] Savicki, 44.

Australia, Canada, the United States, and Great Britain.[60] Hence, the impact of Irish Catholics in Australia, comprising a large percentage of the working class, may indeed have modulated the effects of individualism by their ingroup collectivism's focus on community concerns, which, in turn, grew outward to reflect such collectivist interests as social egalitarianism.

How did the Irish have this effect? First, as noted, Irish Catholics were significantly represented among the Australian urban work force since the nineteenth century. Second, as Hofstede showed, Ireland scores lower on individualism compared to Great Britain, the United States, or Canada.[61] In other words, while Australia scores second highest after the United States on individualism, the nature of this individualism differs since Australian egalitarianism, seemingly rooted in an Irish Catholic collectivist cultural tradition, appears to have exerted a strong influence. Although Australia, Canada, and the United States are considered to be strong examples of individualist nations,[62] there is significant dissimilarity among them because of the diverse influences immigrants had on each culture. This complexity is reflected in what Triandis labels horizontal and vertical aspects of the individualism–collectivism social pattern.[63]

Horizontal and vertical dimensions of individualism–collectivism

Adding hierarchy, Triandis subdivided individualism and collectivism into two different types based on how much inequality is accepted. The vertical dimension accepts inequality and considers rank and stratification as beneficial. In contrast, the horizontal dimension emphasizes that individuals should be similar on most attributes and considers status differences less desirable. Hence, there are four possible dimensions: horizontal individualism, vertical individualism, horizontal collectivism, and vertical collectivism.[64] Triandis's broader

---

[60] Hofstede, *Cultures and Organizations*, 53.
[61] Ireland scored 70 on Hofstede's Individualism Index compared to 91 for the United States, 89 for Great Britain, and 80 for Canada. Hofstede, *Culture's Consequences*, 215.
[62] Hofstede, *Cultures and Organizations*, 53.
[63] Triandis, *Individualism & Collectivism*, 44–52.
[64] H.C. Triandis and M. Gelfand, "Converging Measurement of Horizontal and Vertical Individualism and Collectivism," *Journal of Personality and Social Psychology* 74, no. 1 (1998): 118–28.

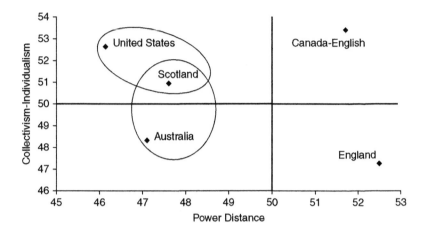

Figure 4.1   Comparison of Anglo Cultures on Power Distance and Individualism–Collectivism

Source: Victor Savicki, *Burnout Across Thirteen Cultures: Stress and Coping in Child and Youth Care Workers* (Westport, CT: Praeger, 2002), 161, Fig. 13.1.

view of individualism–collectivism offers an intriguing lens to observe Australian–Canadian differences.

Triandis asserts that Australia favors horizontal individualism and the United States vertical individualism.[65] For Australia, horizontal individualism prizes self-reliance with a diminished desire for high status, as reflected in a disdain of individuals who stick out from the crowd. For America, vertical individualism celebrates significant individual achievement. In contrast, horizontal collectivism emphasizes social cohesion, egalitarianism, and agreement with ingroup, whereas vertical collectivism emphasizes a sense of supporting the ingroup and sacrifices made on its behalf.[66] Given the distinctive social patterns of cultural dimensions, is it possible to identify a particular culture's disproportionate influence? Savicki's study suggests cultural trends.

Employing Triandis's categories, Savicki asserts that England falls in the vertical collectivism quadrant, English Canada in the vertical individualism quadrant, Australia in the horizontal collectivism quadrant, and the United States and Scotland together in the horizontal individualism

---

[65] Triandis, *Individualism & Collectivism*, 46.

[66] Ibid., 44–46.

quadrant.[67] Although there appears to be a conflict between Savicki's claim that Australia is marked by horizontal collectivism and Triandis's view that Australia reflects horizontal individualism, the difference relates to Anglo nations included in his comparison rather than an absolute difference in relation to a greater diversity of cultures.

Though broadly considered individualistic cultures, those Savicki included in his study are identified as individualist or collectivist, horizontal or vertical, based on a much narrower range of scores than would have resulted had collectivist Asian and South American cultures been included. While theorists may argue with Savicki's labels, his results are useful because they show differences within Canada and the United Kingdom, differences that suggest British influences on English Canada and Australia. Savicki observes, "When restricting one's consideration of cultural differences to the cultures in the current sample, the differences described in Triandis's categories can be helpful in capturing important contrasts and comparisons."[68] Indeed, Savicki's results are consistent with Triandis's identification of Australia's horizontal aspect, which emphasizes equality, and English Canada's vertical aspect, which emphasizes hierarchy.

Patterns in Savicki's data suggest that Australia shares its relatively low power distance with Scotland and its lower individualism (which Savicki labels as "collectivism" relative to the other cultures in his study) with England.[69] Likewise, English Canada's relatively higher power distance appears to be close to, but not quite as high, as England, but shows a level of individualism closer to Scotland. Given that the formal class system is an English tradition that is practically absent from Scottish culture, it is a reasonable conclusion that English Canada would have derived its greater acceptance of class differences from the English, while Australia was less inclined to accept notions of social hierarchy due to its significant Irish population. Similarly, English Canada's cultural acceptance of individualism could be attributed to the influence of Scottish industriousness and the Scottish Protestant Work Ethic. If individualism is closely tied to the Protestant work ethic, then the strand of collectivism in Australian culture could relate to the Catholicism of the Irish community.

Although Savicki's data suggests that English Canada clearly benefited from diverse influences attributed to England and Scotland,

[67] Savicki, 160–61.
[68] Ibid., 50.
[69] Ibid., 161.

Australia may not be so clear-cut, given the significant Irish impact on the culture. Rather than Scots being the key influence for the observed trend of lower power distance in Australia, it is just as likely to have been a result of the Irish. While Savicki did not include Irish data in his study, results from other studies, such as Hofstede described earlier, support Ireland's dimensions.

According to a GLOBE study by Keating and Martin, Irish society is more collectivist than even Hofstede suggested. Irish collectivism points to a strong feeling of belonging to a parish and of interdependence at the community level, and is reflected in a high level of indigenous Irish sports being team based, and statistics indicating trade union density at 53 percent and membership in the Catholic Church at 92 percent.[70] Hence, collectivism and the historic rebelliousness of the Irish can be reconciled with the seemingly antithetical placidity in Ireland that emerged following 1922's achievement of the Irish Free State.

This euphoric moment was of immense psychological importance for both the Irish in Ireland and abroad. After being a subjected people for so long, their collective focus necessarily shifted from active rebellion to nation building, requiring skills of conciliation and diplomacy. During the balance of the twentieth century, however, active rebellion did not cease as the turmoil in Northern Ireland proved. In contrast with the Irish Republic, Northern Ireland emerged as a place of considerable agitation as the traditional Irish antagonism between Protestant and Catholic became increasingly violent. For the larger numbers of Irish in an independent Ireland, some degree of rebelliousness was understandably placated by other important features of an emerging sovereign nation. Irish historian Thomas E. Hachey describes the reasons for this shift of focus:

> Against the backdrop of political uncertainty, life in the Irish Free State was anything but the utopia some revolutionary idealists might have expected. The country was without any important natural resources, or at least none that were known or could be easily retrieved during the 1920s. Partition had deprived the Free State of the only industrially developed portion of the island, and the Civil War had squandered funds that might otherwise have been used to

---

[70] Mary A. Keating and Gillian S. Martin, "Leadership and Culture in the Republic of Ireland," in *Culture and Leadership Across the World: The GLOBE Book of In-Depth Studies of 25 Societies*, ed. J.S. Chhokar, F.C. Brodbeck, and R.J. House (New York, NY: Lawrence Erlbaum, 2008), 375.

help build the economy . . . . Free State politicians, however, soon realized the necessity of making theories conform to reality, given the reciprocal responsibilities and trade concessions that Dominion status implied.[71]

With the achievement of independence, therefore, rebelliousness was joined by a strong sense of purpose and responsibility. This new situation enhanced the Irish collective impulse that had served to build Irish Catholic solidarity over the centuries, a sentiment that continued among the Irish of Australia. Like other newly independent states that emerged in continental Europe following the First World War, Ireland now had to prove that it had not won its self-determination in vain. Thus, in the Republic of Ireland a sense of relative placidity grew alongside the characteristic rebelliousness that had been a distinctive Irish trait for centuries, but it did not eradicate rebellion as demonstrated by subsequent decades of tragic violence in Northern Ireland. Therefore, contrary to Australia's relative collectivism/individualism, which points to Ireland as a strong influence given Australia's large and influential population of Irish, Canada's individualism appears to stem from its significantly British—strongly Scottish nuanced—heritage.

In English Canada, the Scots held a cultural position as strong as the Irish Catholics of Australia, but blended in due to an affinity for Canada's British ties. Indeed, among the Loyalists who came to Canada after the American Revolution—whose allegiance to Britain was, therefore, maintained north of the border—were many Highlanders. There was good reason for this. Between 1768 and 1775, 60 percent of the Scottish emigrants to the American colonies were Highlanders, and, between 1776 and 1815, Highlanders continued emigrating from Scotland in significant numbers, only their destination changed from the United States to Canada and the Maritime colonies.[72] According to Prentis, until the 1880s, the higher proportion of Scots migrating to Canada over the United States can be "attributed to the chain-reaction effect stemming from a long tradition of Scots emigration there from

---

[71] Thomas E. Hachey, "From Free State to Republic, 1922–1996," in Thomas E. Hachey, Joseph M. Hernon, Jr., and Lawrence J. McCaffrey, *The Irish Experience: A Concise History*, rev. ed. (Armonk, NY: M.E. Sharpe, 1996), 178.

[72] Marianne McLean, *The People of Glengarry: Highlanders in Transition, 1745–1820* (Montreal, QC & Kingston, ON: McGill-Queen's University Press, 1991), 79.

the eighteenth century."[73] Hence, while Presbyterians had become, by 1851, the second largest Protestant denomination in Canada,[74] a small but strong community of Scottish Catholics thrived, particularly among the Highlanders. Nonetheless, there did not appear to be fervent sectarianism between them and the British Protestants. The Highland Catholics accepted the prevailing political situation because of self-interest and from deference to those in authority. There was little, if any, evidence showing they thought along radical lines.[75] According to MacLean, Catholic Highland influence was epitomized by Reverend Alexander Macdonell, the first Roman Catholic bishop of Upper Canada [Ontario]—not just for Scots but all Catholics in the territory—whose shrewd cultivation of civil and ecclesiastical power advanced the welfare of his religious followers through aligning their interests with British culture.[76] In these efforts, Macdonell was helped by Scotland-born priest, William Peter MacDonald, who Macdonell had personally invited to immigrate to Canada. In the late 1820s, MacDonald became vicar-general in Kingston, and a couple of years later began, together with Macdonell, a Catholic newspaper (*The Catholic*) in order to ward off attacks against the Church.[77]

Macdonell assumed a similar role for Scottish Catholics of Canada as Australia's Father Therry and Cardinal Moran did for the Irish Catholics of Australia, but with an important difference. In the absence of a deep cultural cleavage between Catholic and Protestant, the Scots in Canada acted more out of collective interest. Thus, just like the Scottish Presbyterian Lowlanders, Macdonell sought to align the Scottish Catholics with the British rulers in Canada. Macdonell was a fierce patriot and Conservative, who defended Catholicism and British interests with equal determination during an era when Catholics had not yet been given access to full citizenship in the British Empire.[78]

---

[73] Prentis, *The Scots in Australia*, 28.

[74] W. Stanford Reid, "The Scottish Protestant Tradition," in *The Scottish Tradition in Canada*, ed. W. Stanford Reid (Toronto, ON: McClelland & Stewart, 1976), 124–25.

[75] R. MacLean, "The Highland Catholic Tradition in Canada," in *The Scottish Tradition in Canada*, ed. Reid, 98.

[76] Ibid., 96.

[77] Stewart D. Gill, " 'The Sword in the Bishop's Hand': Father William Peter MacDonald, A Scottish Defender of the Catholic Faith in Upper Canada," *Canadian Catholic Historical Association, Study Sessions* 50 (1983): 438, 442.

[78] Franklin A. Walker, *Catholic Education and Politics in Upper Canada* (Toronto, ON: Nelson, 1955), 18, quoted in MacLean, 96.

After becoming bishop in 1819, Macdonell was made a legislative councilor in 1831 and effectively combined these roles to help the Catholic cause. With a population large enough to compel government response, Macdonell succeeded in obtaining aid for Catholic schools and teachers in return for providing the government of the time consistent political support.[79] Bishop Macdonell's loyalty to established authority was evident when he encouraged his followers to support Lieutenant-Governor Bond Head instead of the Reformers of the era, for which he received praise by the Orange Order despite his longstanding differences with its members.[80] Macdonell's pro-British leanings could have also been intensified by his alleged anti-Irish views that may have been cultivated in Scotland where Scottish Catholicism had become dominated by Irish Catholics in the early nineteenth century, and as a result of his stint as a military chaplain during the 1798 quashing of the Irish Rebellion. "Scottish priests in Canada merely reflected the views of their brothers in Scotland with regard to the Irish," suggests Stewart Gill, and "Macdonell carried with him to Canada ideas of the Irish that were prejudicial to a harmonious relationship with them."[81]

While Scottish Catholic and Protestant religious differences were replaced by a common sense of Scottish ancestry and tradition, the Scots became accepted members of the Canadian elite. The Scots were less rebellious toward British Protestant rule compared to the Irish Catholics of Australia. This innate rebelliousness is perhaps among the reasons the emigrating Irish had an overwhelming preference for the independent and revolutionary United States. As Prentis observes, "First, the Irish were poorer and passage to North America fitted their meagre pockets best. Secondly, they had no love of the Crown and Canada was still British."[82] Indeed, Akenson asserts, "it is almost certainly true that, over the entire history of Irish migration to the United States, more individual Catholics than Protestants arrived."[83] Although Scottish Catholic tradition remains stronger in Nova Scotia than in other parts of Canada, their loyalty to the state and its institutions and leaders, combined with their view of the importance of maintaining their religious traditions, folk culture, and attachment to their native Scotland, were reinforced

---

[79] Walker, *Catholic Education and Politics in Upper Canada*, 97.
[80] Ibid., 98.
[81] Gill, " 'The Sword in the Bishop's Hand' ", 445–46
[82] Prentis, 28.
[83] Donald Harman Akenson, "Irish Migration to North America, 1800–1920," in *The Irish Diaspora*, ed. Andy Bielenberg (New York, NY: Longman, 2000), 117.

and perpetuated over the generations.[84] Scottish patterns of settlement were well established throughout Canada. However, Scottish Catholics remained a minority since the Highlanders, not all of whom were Catholic, were increasingly dominated by Lowlanders whose influence in medicine, law, journalism, education, politics, and the ministry helped assert their Protestantism in Canada.[85]

Protestants represented a significant community among Scottish Canadians and were not confined to the Presbyterianism for which they are best known. The Scottish Protestant tradition, with Scots from various Protestant denominations besides Presbyterian, significantly influenced the development of Canada.[86] A considerable number of Scots who came to Canada as Presbyterians, for one reason or another, joined other denominations including Anglican, Baptist, and Methodist. According to Reid, "some of the most vigorous supporters of the Anglican Establishment came from this group," such as Anglican Bishop John Strachan who joined the Church of England upon arrival to Canada when no Presbyterian congregation had called him to serve.[87] In 1839, he became bishop of Toronto, ruling the Anglican Church of Upper Canada.

Indeed, in Canada there appeared to be no contradiction between Scottish identity and British loyalty. As Gillian Leitch observes, "the distinct identity of the Scot was integrated into the more general one of a loyal Briton," a process evidenced by the formation of St. Andrew's Societies that, similar to the formation of other national societies like St. Patrick's, St. George's and German Societies, asserted its identity in Canadian society, helping forge a persistent Scottish–British identity that was accepted across Canada. Even in Montreal, suggests Leitch, "It is clear that those who did not support the British [Tory] Party did not join the Saint Andrew's, Saint George's, Saint Patrick's, or German Societies but chose instead to be members of the [French] *Société Saint-Jean Baptiste* or the [Irish] Hibernian Benevolent Society."[88]

---

84 Walker, 102.

85 T.M. Devine, *Scotland's Empire: 1600–1815* (London, UK: Penguin, 2003), 191.

86 Reid, "The Scottish Protestant Tradition," 131.

87 Ibid., 128.

88 Gillian I. Leitch, "Scottish Identity and British Loyalty in Early-Nineteenth-Century Montreal," in *A Kingdom of the Mind: How the Scots Helped Make Canada*, ed. Peter E. Rider and Heather McNabb (Montreal, QC & Kingston, ON: McGill-Queen's University Press, 2006), 211–14.

Despite the significant impact of the Scots on Canada, there was no "Scottish factor" that equates with the Australian "Irish factor." While the Irish represented a distinctive, noncompliant element that helped influence the national Australian culture, the Scots of Canada fostered acceptance of the prevailing British culture. Hence, Scottish membership in the Canadian elite was more closely connected to their deference and connection to British Protestant rule than class differences. In Montreal, for example, "Many of the same men who held power in business and government also held high office in the Saint Andrew's Society," a situation, Leitch argues, that indicates how "the society reflected not only their identity as Scots but their aspirations to power in Lower Canada [Quebec]."[89] The Saint Andrew's Society, founded to express dual Scottish identity and British loyalty, was the result of "a group of conservative, or Tory, men who resorted to unifying along common lines of ethnic heritage," and who "remained strongly linked to British political institutions with its support of the British Party during the Rebellions" of 1837–1838. As Leitch observes, "The Saint Andrew's Society aligned the Scottish identity of its members under the umbrella of loyalty."[90] As the case of Montreal demonstrates, "being Scottish meant not only identifying with the heroes of the land, its poets, and its culture and celebrating Saint Andrew's Day but also identifying with the British institutions in British North America, the Crown, and the government."[91]

As Bishop Macdonell and Father MacDonald's influence on the Catholic Church in Canada demonstrates, "Macdonell, portrayed as the archetype Scottish priest, was by the 1830s trying to maintain control on the basis of Scottish ethnicity with the appointment of priests like MacDonald, when the majority of Catholic adherents were Irish."[92] Relying on ethnoreligious data from census records, Akenson has shown that, during the nineteenth century, an overwhelming two-thirds of the Irish of Ontario—contemporary Canada's largest province—were Protestant. The greater preponderance of Irish Protestants in Canada suggests the Catholics' general preference to migrate to the United States,[93] leaving a significant population of Irish more likely to

---

[89] Leitch, "Scottish Identity," 213.
[90] Ibid., 224.
[91] Ibid.
[92] Gill, 452.
[93] Bruce S. Elliott, *Irish Migrants in the Canadas: A New Approach* (Montreal, QC & Kingston, ON: McGill-Queen's University Press, 1988), 102–106.

share English Canada's pro-British sentiments as opposed to the large Irish Catholic population of Australia. Concerning the Irish Protestants, Akenson notes, "Neither their hunger for land nor their commercial assertiveness was apt to cause the Irish Protestants difficulty in British North America. Indeed, these were adaptive traits for migrants to a new world and would seem to lead them directly and efficiently to economic success."[94]

While the Scottish period in Upper Canada's Roman Catholic Church was short lived, it was nonetheless "at the very base of the heritage of Catholicism in Canada."[95] As Marianne McLean observes, "The Highlanders who emigrated to [Ontario's] Glengarry County were a remarkably homogeneous group who came to Canada by choice."[96] Yet the Protestant element among the Scots was arguably even more signifi-cant. As Jenni Calder observes, "a Canadian Presbyterian church emerged on an equal footing with the Anglicans, Catholics and Methodists, but it was Scottish enough to keep alive the divisions that characterised Presbyterianism in Scotland."[97]

Thus, according to Reid, "Whether the Scots came as farmers, fish-ermen, labourers, merchants or professional men they all seem to have had very much the same point of view."[98] The primary reason for this unanimity was religious, however, for "Scottish Protestants did not accept any rigid class structure," Reid asserts, "but stressed the importance of every man developing his God-given gifts to the best of his ability in this life. Class divisions, therefore, were to be ignored."[99] However, the significant presence of the Lowland Scots in Canada could explain why Canadians, though respectful and deferential to British tradition and cultural values, frowned upon formal titles of the British peerage system. As an acquired Canadian cultural character-istic, therefore, this may account for why Conrad Black derived little sympathy from Canadians in his quest for a British peerage. Despite the Scottish Protestant disinterest in hierarchy, Scottish deference to

---

[94] Donald H. Akenson, "Ontario: Whatever Happened to the Irish?" in *Immigration in Canada: Historical Perspectives,* ed. Gerald Tulchinsky (Toronto, ON: Copp Clark Longman, 1994), 119.

[95] Gill, 452.

[96] Marianne McLean, "Peopling Glengarry County: The Scottish Origins of a Canadian Community," in *Immigration in Canada: Historical Perspectives,* ed. Gerald Tulchinsky, 74.

[97] Jenni Calder, *Scots in Canada* (Edinburgh, UK: Luath Press, 2003), 115.

[98] Reid, "The Scottish Protestant Tradition," 131.

[99] Ibid.

British rule in Canada enabled English toleration of distinctions in rank and privilege to become part of the accepted Canadian tradition.

* * *

Whereas Australian culture evolved in fierce opposition to the inequality inherent in the European notion of class distinction, a strong sense of social hierarchy was transmitted to Canada from England where, if not as overtly as in England, it thrived. This is not to say that social stratification does not exist in Australia. Rather, Australians have proven to be more vocal in their abhorrence of the idea of hierarchy and the pretentiousness it evokes. Those who seek achievement for its own sake—either out of a desire for personal accolade or out of a desire for higher status—are generally disappointed since Australian society tends to greet tall poppies with unequivocal disdain, bringing big heads down to size via a less vertically oriented culture. As Russel Ward, Patrick O'Farrell, and other historians suggest, a significant Irish working-class ethos appears to have contributed to this Australian cultural pattern, aspects of which help account for the growth in republican views in a society that frowns on steep social stratification, notions of class distinction, and the perceived subservience it implies.

Considering power distance and individualism–collectivism, influences become more apparent. Anglo-Celtic migrants not only helped establish the cultural direction of Australia and Canada but implicitly defined for subsequent immigrants and their descendants the characteristics that an Australian and Canadian should possess. However, their collective impact was not uniform. It is possible to see a differential influence among Anglo-Celtic groups in shaping these diverse and distinct new cultures. The impact of historical patterns of migration appears to support the observation that English Canada owes its high power distance largely to the English and its individualism to the industrial Lowland Scot, while Australia's lower power distance relative to Canada, and collectivism per Savicki—or horizontal individualism per Triandis—can be seen in its Irish heritage.

The cultural dimensions of power distance and individualism–collectivism suggest that the Irish factor was particularly important for Australia compared to Canada where British influences have proven more powerful shapers of cultural values, norms, and attitudes. Many of the cultural features of Australia—prevalence of wit, humor, informality, rebelliousness, hedonism, and social egalitarianism—evoke characteristics of the Irish, whereas descriptions of Canadians—deference, modesty, and compromise—are more typically British in origin. The powerful differentiating effect Anglo-Celtic immigrant groups had on the development of Australian and Canadian culture is evident in their respective national characters.

5
Australian versus Canadian Managerial Styles

Although Australian and Canadian industrial relations have been influenced by such issues as global economic change and increased competition, domestic factors are just as important to help account for dominant styles of management and workplace behavior. The primary domestic aspect is the Anglo-Celtic cultural influence and its divergent impact on Australia and Canada. Management positions in both countries tended to be held, at least until recent decades, by middle- and upper-class English and Scottish immigrants and their descendants who were accustomed to a privileged status in British colonial society. Reflecting the assertive liberal spirit of the nineteenth century, managers therefore retained a strong element of individualism.

While collectivism is less evident among the ranks of Australian managers, the Australian working class absorbed the Irish collectivist impulse, given the dominant Irish Catholic presence among the masses. But British radicalism also shaped their characters. Canadian workers, in comparison, were generally less radical, lacked the Australian Irish factor, and appear to have been influenced more by British Toryism and British socialist trends. As a result, there was tension in Australia and Canada between a more individualist management layer versus a workforce and assertive labor parties that were more accepting of collectivism.

Besides Australian and Canadian managerial style, how management responded to the culturally dominant values of the respective working classes reveal significant cultural differences. The divergent expression of egalitarianism in Australia and Canada helps account for the historic ideological influences that affected not only the Anglo-Celtic character of managers and workers but also their interactions and behavior.

The rise of modern management

Since Scottish economist Adam Smith published *The Wealth of Nations* in 1776, arguing the importance of the division of labor and launching the era of specialization, a formal managing role—initially personified by the owner of the enterprise—became necessary to coordinate the diverse tasks and operations of machines and workers.

As a modern profession, management is relatively new. It rose in importance during the twentieth century as formerly unskilled preindustrial workers transformed into skilled workers, and their increasingly specialized knowledge and skills needed coordinators and supervisors to ensure the attainment of organizational objectives. Although the managerial role subsequently shifted from owners to professional managers, the latter tended to pursue similar goals as the wealthy elite who retained corporate ownership interest.[1]

Comparing business owners in two of the largest English-speaking nations, the United States and the United Kingdom, suggests they were quite distinct from each other. The American business leader was typified by Horatio Alger-type stories of rising from the depths of poverty to the height of financial success. The rapid economic growth of the Gilded Age in the decades that followed the Civil War contributed to a stereotype of achievement, suggesting the existence of "equality of Opportunity."[2] This American cultural striving for—and adulation of—achievement reflects the strength of individualism in American society. In contrast, the role of the businessman in Britain and Canada was different. Australian sociologist Sol Encel suggests that the typical representative during the eighteenth and nineteenth centuries was not just a male who owned a small business but one who was capable of seizing the opportunities provided by technological change to increase the size of his plant or create a completely new enterprise revealing "a tradition of hard work, self-denial, the ploughing back of profits and the gradual building up of small firms into large ones." There was less ruthless competition and vicious battles with trade unions compared to the United States, but similar to the US tradition, British leaders of industry were viewed as "self-made men," typified by a Scotsman like Samuel Smiles.[3]

---

[1] T. Nichols, *Ownership, Control and Ideology: An Enquiry into Certain Aspects of Modern Business Ideology* (London, UK: Allen and Unwin, 1969), 112–20.

[2] S. Encel, *Equality and Authority: A Study of Class, Status and Power in Australia* (Melbourne, VIC: Cheshire, 1970), 376.

[3] Ibid., 377.

Encel rightfully alludes to Alger and Smiles for they provided flattering images of individuals who successfully built up their enterprises ostensibly on their own initiatives whose achievements were admired by their peers and workers alike. There is a notable absence of such images in Australia where, in contrast with these other cultures, Encel observes, "Businessmen, apart from isolated individuals, are not generally regarded as having contributed prominently to the 'development' of Australia."[4] Credit for this largely belongs to members of the working class who championed egalitarianism and preferred flatter hierarchies, often to the chagrin of the more individualist managerial class.

As the managerial role evolved following the Second World War, it was no longer seen exclusively in the context of business. In the words of American management guru Peter Drucker, management "pertains to every human effort that brings together in one organization people of diverse knowledge and skills."[5] In a modern sense, "management" applies as much to the functioning of nonprofit organizations—from religious institutions, charities, social service agencies, and public academic institutions—to the world of business and government. The term "manager" therefore signifies a role known by various titles, from supervisor, director, and department head, to team leader, and coordinator among numerous other possibilities. Regardless of the title, contemporary managers focus their efforts on controlling, directing, or coordinating the work of others.

Although the activities of managers have evolved to include a more supportive role to help the work efforts of people by coaching and otherwise supporting their labors,[6] whether first-line, middle, or top managers, they have customarily been defined as people to whom other people directly report. This arrangement suggests vertical hierarchy with management above workers, so the term manager applies to holders of positions of authority who not only possess the ability to influence how people work or behave but also indirectly impact their quality of life. Hence, the origins and implications of differences between Australian and Canadian egalitarianism and the role of political ideology in the development of the managerial outlook expose subtle variances in managerial culture. Management models also provide a window to

---

[4] Ibid.

[5] Peter F. Drucker, *The Essential Drucker: The Best of Sixty Years of Peter Drucker's Essential Writings on Management* (New York, NY: HarperCollins, 2001), 7–8.

[6] John R. Schermerhorn, James G. Hunt, and Richard N. Osborn, *Basic Organizational Behavior*, 2nd ed. (New York, NY: John Wiley & Sons, 1998), 4.

identify salient Anglo-Celtic cultural features in managerial style. How workers organized is also revealing.

Unions in Australia and Canada emerged in the late nineteenth century as powerful representatives of workers in their dealings with management. In the last quarter of the twentieth century, however, there was a rise in employment arrangements with individual employees rather than the workforce as a collective entity, a development that reflects a largely Anglo-Protestant management's preference to reduce as much as possible union involvement in employment policy matters. Even in instances when union involvement could not be excluded from the bargaining process, the heightened focus on the individualization of employment has been evident in the increased use of performance-based pay systems over job- or grade-based pay, and with greater reliance on individual goal-setting procedures and appraisal, and more direct communication with individuals instead of unions as an intermediary.[7] Prior to the rise of this individualist trend, however, collectivism strongly affected employment policies due to the strength of unions and the ideological and ethnic influences that helped shape Australian and Canadian society. The ideological influences on each culture were not identical. But what do the terms individualism and collectivism mean when applied specifically to the context of management? Above all, they provide a useful way to see influences on labor–management relations.

Individualism and collectivism in the managerial context

Industrial relations and work organization are important to distinguish. Whereas *industrial relations* involve union–management relations and the process of negotiation and bargaining, *work organization* reflects both the nature of work tasks and job design. Although individualism and collectivism are big, expressive terms, they can also be overly theoretical and vague. Because of the potential for different meanings in the industrial relations, work organization and human resources fields, the terms need to be applied with care to be understood and properly applied.[8]

In the language of industrial relations, "collectivism" is generally synonymous with trade unionism and "individualism" with nonun-

---

[7] Stephen Deery, David Plowman, and Janet Walsh, *Industrial Relations: A Contemporary Analysis* (Sydney, NSW: McGraw-Hill, 1997), 2.6.

[8] John Storey and Nicolas Bacon, "Individualism and Collectivism: Into the 1990s," *The International Journal of Human Resource Management* 4, no. 3 (1993): 670, 683.

ionism.[9] In the area of work organization and labor process analysis, however, the term individualism reflects scientific management ideas, specifically the Taylorist strategy of fragmenting and deskilling work, while collectivism is more suggestive of work teams and participative group methods of work. These are not alternative uses of the terms as much as a particular way of using them. In other words, work organization and labor process analysts would not propose these meanings in place of those used by industrial relations specialists but rather would tend to ignore in their use of the terms any presence of trade unions. Likewise, industrial relations specialists would tend to neglect the collective aspects of jobs that do not relate to trade unionism.[10]

An organization assuming new human resource management policies could therefore be taking on both an individualistic and collectivist character at the very same time. For instance, an organizational change toward greater teamwork could be interpreted as increased collectivism due to the more participative nature of group interaction as opposed to the more individualist approach that is reflected by Taylorist fragmentation and deskilling of jobs. While this is a valid interpretation, if such a form of work organization is initiated without the involvement of relevant trade unions, the implication could be greater individualism because of the industrial relations view that individualism reflects the lack of trade union participation and the inevitable decline of the collective voice of workers.[11] Depending on what aspects are under consideration, both individualism and collectivism may coexist, especially in Australia and Canada in view of the particular historic influences that shaped their respective characters.

Given the collective orientation of trade unions, one would expect to see less individualism where union strength is high. While trade union membership has proven very strong in Australia, particularly in comparison with the United States, Canadian union membership has been lower than Australia but higher than in the United States. In 1977, for example, 58 percent of Australia's workers were registered union members.[12] A reason suggested for Australia's high level of union membership is the prevalence of the "closed shop," restricting employment of workers to those who possess a union card, and the "union

---

[9] Ibid., 670.

[10] Ibid.

[11] Deery, Plowman, and Walsh, *Industrial Relations*, 2.7.

[12] David Wright, *Australians At Work: Harmony and Conflict in Industrial Relations* (Carlton, VIC: Pitman, 1980), 26.

shop," which precludes employment of workers who are not willing to join a union after employment. In both cases, union members are given preferential treatment in filling positions or retaining them over nonunionists during layoffs. In this sense, an atmosphere of "compulsory unionism" may be fostered because employers who operate as closed shops or union shops act as "recruiting agents for unions." They do so to conform to clauses in Federal and State awards or just to preserve labor harmony through an informal arrangement with unions.[13]

Nonetheless, compulsory unionism is not the only cause and may not even be the primary cause of Australia's historically high level of union membership. Solidarity among works is fostered by trade unionism, and membership can offer advantages to workers that transcend better pay and working conditions that unions have battled to achieve, but also include other financial and nonfinancial benefits including discounts at retailers, insurance plans, and access to recreational facilities.[14] Above all, there is a sense of "solidarity" associated with collectivism that preserves camaraderie among the membership ranks. Hence, Australia's high union membership also reflects Australian labors' collectivist impulse.

Indeed, trade unions have successfully prevented management from introducing such individualistic work practices and employment arrangements as profit-sharing plans and individual performance-appraisal and incentive pay systems. Moreover, trade unions have not typically opposed group-level pay systems or gainsharing plans, indicative of organized labor's opposition to rewarding the individual over the collective entity of workers.[15] Trade unions are not philosophically opposed to the connection between pay and performance but unions are against such a connection when an atmosphere of rivalry is created and increased pay differentials arise among individual employees.[16]

Not only does a strong trade union membership suggest the existence and acceptance of a certain level of collectivism in a particular culture but a successful corporate policy fostering greater teamwork, flatter hierarchies, and more equitable distribution of corporate gains could also be viewed as hints of collectivist policies that, when positively received within an organization, suggests a fit with the mood of

---

[13] Ibid., 27.
[14] Ibid.
[15] Ignace Ng and Dennis Maki, "Trade Union Influence on Human Resource Practices," *Industrial Relations* 33, no. 1 (1994): 121–35.
[16] Ibid., 134.

the prevailing culture. Due to positive results in the application of such policies, therefore, Australian work culture could be viewed within a collectivist framework.

With the aim of protecting employment, Australia's collectivist mood is clearly evident. For instance, when Australia's second largest cargo handling company, Patrick Corporation, fired dock workers in the 1990s after reporting that the subsidiary companies that employed them had gone bankrupt, Patrick replaced these dockers with nonunion workers who had been secretly trained and hired on short-term contracts. Although the federal government was strongly supportive of Patrick's rationalistic, coercive strategy, Australia's unfair dismissal law assisted the fired dock workers and their union. The union sued Patrick in the Federal Court, which ordered Patrick to reinstate the workers and not to replace them with others hired on short-term contracts. Patrick may also have broken the law against dismissing workers merely on the grounds of union membership. After Patrick appealed the decision, it was upheld by the High Court. Hence, Patrick's human resource management strategy—which, from a managerial point of view, fostered flexibility and deregulation—had been thwarted by a regulation represented by individual employment protection law. Moreover, despite the individual nature of the employment contract, it ultimately could not be segregated from the collective characteristics of the employment relationship.[17]

In other words, collective and individual employment rights are interconnected, which in this Patrick case appear to have protected Australian workers from sub-contracting. Beyond employment law, there are other features of Australian work culture that appear to emphasize particular aspects of its collectivist nature.[18]

---

[17] Jack Eaton, *Comparative Employment Relations* (Cambridge, UK: Polity Press, 2000), 121–22.

[18] In a comparative study of the contents of corporate codes of ethics, Greg Wood found that Australian codes tend to emphasize community involvement, environment issues, and product quality, which are examples of collective concerns. Furthermore, he found that Australian codes tend to highlight more than Canadian or American codes, both employee health and safety and product safety. Overall, while Australian codes are not so different in content and form compared to Canadian and American codes, they do tend to concentrate more on the social perspective of corporate relations. Greg Wood, "A Cross Cultural Comparison of the Contents of Codes of Ethics: USA, Canada and Australia," *Journal of Business Ethics* 25, no. 4 (2000).

In *Catching the Wave: Workplace Reform in Australia*, Australian international business specialist, John Mathews, describes how an innovative group of Australian service and manufacturing organizations transformed their operations in the 1980s and 1990s by breaking with the traditionally segmented, hierarchical organizational structures—structures that were inconsistent with the Australian collectivist impulse. They were replaced with more focused and flexible organizational networks of self-managing teams, the implementation of which he calls "new production systems."[19]

According to Mathews, *"Rather than reforming the management of inefficient work procedures, the new production systems represent a reform of the work structures themselves,"* stimulating a transformation in how management is carried out, such as by replacing the "command and control structures designed to enforce rigidity and compliance" with practices that "call for management that offers facilitation, guidance and coordination between self-managing groups of employees who are capable of looking after the details of production for themselves."[20]

These new production systems differ significantly from the quality of working life (QWL) and various job redesign initiatives of the 1970s, including job enlargement and job rotation. While QWL programs dealt with the symptoms, they did not grapple with what Mathews refers to as the "cause of workplace inefficiencies," nor did they deal with the basics of "enhancing the responsibility carried by employees for achieving better results, which is the issue that underpins all the new production systems."[21]

Mathews describes a variety of organizational and technical innovations consistent with new production systems that have occurred at a number of service and manufacturing organizations in Australia. An example of the former occurred at Australia Post, where Mathews relates how the corporation successfully negotiated technological change in the early 1990s during the implementation of optical character recognition (OCR) in its mail-sorting operation. While the successful implementation of OCR required cooperation between management and unions—due to common concerns over rising industry threats, such as increased competition private mail carriers and potential loss of the

---

[19] John Mathews, *Catching the Wave: Workplace Reform in Australia* (Ithaca, NY: ILR Press, 1994), 1.

[20] Ibid., 10.

[21] Ibid., 10–11.

public monopoly over mail services—each had to modify their traditional positions.

The role of supervisors changed to allow for a more participative workplace as there is no room in a participative environment for dictators hired to keep the workers in line. As a result, cooperative supervisors were offered inducements to stay while those who remained unaccommodating were marginalized. Mathews argues, "There is no role for the sergeant in the participative workplace, and the new team leaders are expected to be working members of the team, not arm's-length superiors."[22] Similarly, the Australian Postal and Telecommunications Union changed from a confrontationist approach to one of cooperation as its leaders followed and monitored the various issues derived from the OCR Project, and had to convey their observations to their membership while encouraging member involvement and minimizing resistance.[23]

Beyond the realm of services, Mathews described a successful change at an Australian manufacturing concern. The implementation of team-based performance pay and gainsharing proved a positive development at CIG Gas Cylinders. As a workplace motivator, money has always proven to be a primary tool. However, according to Mathews, money can act as a negative influence when used as an individual incentive payment system because Taylorist "individual incentive payments are incompatible with group-based performance measurement."[24]

Although pay is an intrinsic motivator that tends to signal an employer's view of an employee's worth, changing from the traditional practice of paying a particular rate for a particular job—the common form of remuneration throughout the industrialized world—is a challenge. Nonetheless, CIG Gas Cylinders successfully introduced a gainsharing system to link employee remuneration with measured organizational performance at both the team level and the plant level. In this way, it linked its payment system to overall employee skills and performance instead of wage rates to individual job performance. Distributing the gains attributable to superior performance is different from profit-sharing because the latter is affected by other factors including exchange rates, interest, and sales efforts, which have a profound influence on total profits. Gainsharing is more closely tied to people's efforts.[25]

---

[22] Ibid., 216.
[23] Ibid., 216–17.
[24] Ibid., 219.
[25] Ibid., 220.

Gainsharing schemes were pioneered in Australia by using Common Interest Programs which combined employee participation in the improvement of productivity—defined by controllable costs per unit of production, such as cost per kilogram of product, as opposed to uncontrollable costs like fuel. Improving controllable costs per unit of production over a particular baseline gave rise to a pool of funds each month that was to be shared equally between staff and the organization.

As CIG Gas Cylinders effectively introduced this equitable program, the firm recognized that its traditional organizational structure prevented further improvements. The company dismantled "the previous hierarchical supervisory structure" and moved in favor of "self-managing shop floor teams," which was successfully accomplished.[26] With full support of the union, teamwork, flexible hours, multi-skilling, annualized salaries, and team-based performance measures were introduced. This transformation appealed to workers and managers who accommodated the new policy which saw marked improvements. For instance, the acetylene plant team produced 10 percent more each week in a five-day period than was formerly produced in six.[27]

The successful implementation of such new production techniques in these Australian firms and others that Mathews describes—including Ford Plastics, Bendix Mintex, and Colonial Mutual—signals their cultural acceptance and general fit with the Australian character. Although Mathews' examples provide compelling evidence for the collective predisposition in the Australian workplace, Australian organizational studies specialist Christopher Wright, in *The Management of Labour: A History of Australian Employers*, argues that the overall implementation of such new techniques has been limited to a relatively small number of employers, particularly subsidiaries of foreign multinationals. While Wright does not disagree that such techniques are being used by Australian firms, he argues that any assertion that the nature of work and employment practices only recently transformed "from traditional conflictual relations towards increased management and labour consensus" is too simplistic. Wright argues for a more complex interpretation "in which both low and high trust forms of labour management have co-existed over time."[28]

[26] Ibid., 227.
[27] Ibid., 228.
[28] Christopher Wright, *The Management of Labour: A History of Australian Employers* (Melbourne, VIC: Oxford University Press, 1995), 215.

While Wright's view represents a different perspective from Mathews, it is still supportive of Australian cultural patterns as all firms would not be expected to apply techniques that are more consistent with the Australian collectivist impulse. Those who have not either owed their ethnocultural allegiance to British approaches or they followed a more strict reliance on American mechanistic trends, particularly in the early twentieth century when industries were expanding. However, those who transformed their work practices appear more in line with Australian cultural preference for smaller hierarchies, teamwork, and nonauthoritarian leadership.

This more consensual approach to Australian management appears to succeed for two essential reasons. First, it meets the expectations of a working class culturally attuned to a greater sense of egalitarianism, significantly influenced by the Irish character and personality. Second, it reflects historic cultural and ideological patterns in the context of managerial models.

The individualist scientific management model

American engineer Frederick Winslow Taylor's scientific management model gained prominence between the late 1800s and early 1900s. Taylor's method of scientific analysis of manufacturing processes, reduction in production costs, and payment of employees based on performance, led to an emphasis on task simplification and performance-based pay to achieve increased profits for organizations and higher wages for workers.[29] As significant as the organizational movement was, scientific management—also known as Taylorism—was troubling for many cultures, particularly those marked by less individualism and greater collectivism. Although scientific management had its detractors in the United States, overall it persisted longer there than in Britain where it failed to gain a foothold.[30]

The American railroad industry of the mid-nineteenth century had pioneered management techniques of large-scale enterprises and was the first to have a force of salaried managers whose local managerial

---

[29] F.W. Taylor, "The Principles of Scientific Management," in *Classics of Organization Theory*, 2nd ed., ed. J.M. Sharfritz and J.S. Ott (Chicago, IL: The Dorsey Press, 1987), 66–81.

[30] Mauro F. Guillen, *Models of Management: Work, Authority, and Organization in a Comparative Perspective* (London, UK, and Chicago, IL: The University of Chicago Press, 1994), 43.

authority was coordinated by a central office via the use of the tele-graph. This was followed in the early 1900s by the introduction to large industrial and commercial enterprises of various cost-controlling and output-expanding measures, such as the Ford assembly lines that allowed mass production. Germany saw a similar rise of large-scale enterprises that absorbed comparable processes of managerial rationalization and integration. Such processes had not taken hold as swiftly in Great Britain because British family-owned companies and individual proprietorships tended to remain small and independent, especially in such areas as textiles.[31]

British managers tended to reject American scientific management as a paradigm primarily because Britain lacked two elements prominent in the United States: the rising influence of engineers and a positive view among the public and business elite—the key decision makers—favoring scientific management and Fordism, despite opposition by laborers and their unions.[32] However, the greater acceptance of scientific management in the United States compared to Britain reflected more than these two elements. There were also important ideological reasons.

Whereas management refers to the technical job of organization—and, therefore, management models represent a collection of technical knowledge that applies to practical situations—management also serves as a significant method of hierarchical authority. In the latter use of the term, American management theorist Mauro Guillen suggests, a model of management serves as "an ideology aimed at establishing legitimacy and reinforcing credibility."[33] As much as it was a managerial method of achieving particular production goals, scientific management reflected ideological views that certain societies, such as the United States and Germany, accepted more than others. Discussed later in more depth, Canada, occupying an ideological position in between British Toryism and American liberalism, stood similarly in between British rejection and American acceptance of scientific management.

Despite Canada's small size relative to the United States, big business also emerged in Canada. By 1930, there were roughly 600 companies producing in excess of two billion dollars' worth of goods, which accounted for nearly 60 percent of total manufacturing output by value. Moreover, about 25 percent of all employees worked in companies

---

[31] Graham D. Taylor and Peter A. Baskerville, *A Concise History of Business in Canada* (Toronto, ON: Oxford University Press, 1994), 309–10.

[32] Guillen, *Models of Management*, 208, 267.

[33] Ibid., 3.

with more than 500 people, of which 68 percent represented eleven industries.[34]

"Big business" is a relative term. For example, in 1909, the total assets of the 30 largest nonfinancial corporations in Canada did not reach the asset value of the American industrial powerhouse, United States Steel Corporation.[35] Nonetheless, corporate capitalism was firmly entrenched in Canada by the 1920s as manufacturing investment and service industries, including transportation, communications, retail, finance and government, grew steadily along with the emergence of a new industrial society.

In the first three decades of the twentieth century, however, manufacturing was the primary driving force behind the economic revolution. During this period manufacturing production grew tenfold, a development that is attributable to the increasing number of American branch plants dominating the Canadian economy.[36] As confirmed in the census of 1930, about 50 percent of Canadian businesses were carried out by corporations.[37] These corporations required layers of managers to keep track of business activity and to keep office and plant-floor workers satisfied and productive. Hence, Canadian business historian Michael Bliss observes, "Office managers organized and reorganized their armies of clerks along functional, increasingly specialized lines and tried to develop "scientific" standards to govern pay and promotion."[38]

Concurrent with this rise in production was the introduction of scientific management. Canada's adoption of this approach was due to American influence. Ever since the 1880s when Taylor advocated his scientific analysis of work functions, the "science" of management emerged as a popular trend that enabled Americans to develop precise methods for describing and classifying work positions. In the public service, while Canada, prior to 1918, had followed British tradition of a less precise classification system based on rank as opposed to task, the Canadian Civil Service Commission drew upon the new American model to overcome the corruption inherent in patronage. According to Dwivedi and Gow, "When the qualifications for a job are very

[34] Taylor and Baskerville, *A Concise History of Business in Canada*, 311.

[35] Ibid.

[36] Graham S. Lowe, "The Rise of Modern Management in Canada," *Canadian Dimension* 14 (December 1979): 32.

[37] Michael Bliss, *Northern Enterprise: Five Centuries of Canadian Business* (Toronto, ON: McClelland & Stewart, 1987), 407.

[38] Ibid., 407–8.

precisely defined, it is much easier to determine which candidate is best qualified."[39]

In industry, scientific management had come to Canada primarily through branch plants and hired consultants, but also through the broad thinking of enthusiastic managers.[40] For example, H.C. McLeod, the general manager of the Bank of Nova Scotia, introduced in 1901 a unit system of work based on complex cost analyses of all positions in a bank branch expressed as units of labor. Whereas the most efficient employees were awarded with special bonuses, Bliss concedes, "We do not know enough about innovations like these to be able to generalize about the passion for productivity."[41] However, considering the numerous cases of objections to scientific management tools, it is a fair conclusion that, as in Australia, scientific management was not very popular in Canada.

In fact, the taking up of scientific management practices was far from consistent across Australian industry, and tended to represent significant exceptions to the general industry rule. According to Christopher Wright, "even within the larger manufacturing establishments that applied such techniques, it was mostly semi-skilled workers employed in routine assembly and packing jobs that faced the full brunt of time study and wage incentives." Wright asserts, "In contrast, maintenance, service, administrative and managerial employees within the same establishment were often able to avoid these forms of strict labour control."[42]

Such variations in managerial practice continued into the 1970s and 1980s when managers adopted techniques such as job redesign, employee participation, Just-in-Time (JIT), and quality management in a gradual yet pragmatic way.[43] The response of trade unions to scientific management practices similarly varied. From the perspective of workers, their opposition to scientific management was strongest among metaltrade laborers, who "viewed such practices as part of a broader effort to 'speedup' production and undermine their craft skills."[44] Likewise, trade union officials from such unions as the Amalgamated Engineering

---

[39] O.P. Dwivedi and James Iain Gow, *From Bureaucracy to Public Management: The Administrative Culture of the Government of Canada* (Peterborough, ON: Broadview Press, 1999), 69.

[40] Bliss, *Northern Enterprise*, 354.

[41] Ibid.

[42] Wright, *The Management of Labour*, 215.

[43] Ibid.

[44] Ibid., 85.

Union (AEU), Moulders' Union and Boilermakers' Society completely rejected scientific management techniques. Those in the metal trades often refused to work if they saw a stopwatch, putting down their tools until the time-study analyst left the premises. "Where outright rejection of work study failed, workers instituted other forms of shopfloor resistance," Wright relates, including " 'go-slow' campaigns, refusals to fill out job cards, general non-cooperation, as well as more extreme reactions."[45]

There were similar sentiments in Canada where some workers chose to rebel against the new requirement to punch the time clock each day. Prior to the First World War, there were at least three significant—though unsuccessful—strikes waged over the use of such time clocks. The first was fought in 1902 in Toronto involving three hundred carpet weavers, the second in 1905, also in Toronto, involving fifty garment workers, and a third in 1913 in Hamilton, Ontario's Canadian Westinghouse plant. Individual battles were more common, such as the 1905 example of Flora MacDonald Denison, who quit her job at Simpson's department store to protest the installation of a time clock.[46] Indeed, the scientific management model did not seem to appeal to Canadian workers any more than Australian workers.

The time clock—a benchmarking tool of scientific management—had launched the arrival of the industrial age throughout the Western world. Canadian labor historian Craig Heron observes, it quickly became "one of the tools of the new efficiency-conscious managers, a reflection of their renewed concern to reduce production costs by a more rigorous exploitation of their workers' labor power."[47] The result may have been improved managerial and cost control but such scientific management tools made the workplace far more impersonal as numbers increasingly replaced workers' names. Throughout the nineteenth century, employers had tried to control lateness, laziness, and absenteeism; hence, notes Heron, the time clock served as "a device to isolate more 'scientifically' this counter-productive behaviour."[48]

The use of such time measurement equipment was part of a long struggle between owners/managers and workers over the amount of value derived from a worker's labor over the course of a given day. For

---

[45] Ibid., 85–6.
[46] Craig Heron, "Punching the Clock," *Canadian Dimension* 14, no. 3 (1979): 29.
[47] Ibid., 26.
[48] Ibid., 28.

the business owner a time clock was part of a set of innovations deemed helpful to increase the pace of production. In turn, workers retaliated not only through passive resistance as described above but also with public demands for shorter hours. Thus, by the end of the First World War, the "eight-hour day" emerged at the top of the list of the Canadian labor movement's demands.[49]

While Canadian workers disliked management's application of scientific management techniques, they were downright passive compared to Australian workers' more vocal expression of displeasure at the introduction of this management model. For instance, members of the AEU were at the forefront of a number of battles in the metal engineering industry, including a fourteen-week strike in 1945 fought to protest the introduction of time study. Their opposition transcended metal engineering, however, when the union opposed GM-H Woodville's attempt to extend time study from production areas into the tooling and maintenance sections, resulting in a strike that led to the closure of the entire factory. There were similarly successful AEU-led disputes against time study at De Havilland Aircraft and Commonwealth Engineering, among other places. After many years of such resistance, management ultimately gave up trying to study workers, and agreed to pay a general efficiency allowance instead of a direct bonus.[50]

Although the opposition of metal tradesmen successfully stopped employers from attempting to introduce scientific management techniques, other Australian unions had less success because, for many semi-skilled workers, the attraction of bonus payments was a powerful motivator in their acceptance of management's reform proposals. Unions therefore took various approaches, including attempts to regulate incentive schemes. For example, whereas the Sheetmetal Workers' Union (SMWU) had engaged in fierce strikes against the introduction of time and motion studies and incentive plans during the Second World War years, their policy of strict opposition had to be softened in the postwar era when workers were more willing to accept bonus payments. As a consequence, the SMWU, despite strong opposition to these techniques, worked to protect the interests of its members who accepted such incentives.[51] While worker resistance to the scientific management trend was strong in Australia, it was undermined by right-wing unions which tended to accept scientific management practices.

[49] Ibid.
[50] Wright, *The Management of Labour*, 86.
[51] Ibid., 87.

The popularity of such work incentives led trade unions like the Australian Workers' Union (AWU), Brushmakers' Union, the Federated Tobacco and Cigarette Workers' Union, the Rubber and Allied Workers' Union, the Artificial Fertilisers and Chemical Workers Union, and the Shop Assistants' Association, to accept scientific management practices. In defense of their position, leaders of these unions cited worker receptivity to workplace incentives and the rise in employment from the resulting increased productivity.[52] Not only did the AWU General Secretary argue, in 1950, for more incentives and work study to increase efficiency in industry but during the late 1950s the right-wing leadership of the Federated Ironworkers Association (FIA) advocated the benefits of these individualist scientific management practices in light of the higher wages, better workshop organization, and reduction in physical labor that benefited union members.[53]

Notwithstanding the successful advocacy of scientific management by some unions, the overwhelming majority of unions and workers were not in favor of Taylor's model. The subsequent human relations movement, which rose to prominence between the 1920s and 1940s, proved far more appealing because it emphasized a humane approach that many felt was lacking in scientific management. Chief among its founders was George Elton Mayo, pioneer in the field of industrial human relations, who, as a native Australian, reflected Australian cultural values in his approach to management.

The collectivist impulse of the human relations movement

Although the challenges that accompanied the rise of large-scale industry found solutions in the technically focused scientific management model, managers in America, Britain, Canada, Australia, and elsewhere, had to confront not only technical obstacles but also ideological problems unique to their culture. While productivity and profits certainly remained relevant to business and industry, it was increasingly recognized that ignoring employee and managerial morale, their emotions and sentiments, would limit company productivity and profits.[54] Beyond industrial self-interest, however, there were genuine

---

[52] Ibid., 87–88.
[53] Ibid.
[54] Guillen, 58.

cultural differences that made particular managerial models more effective, or accepted, than others.

While the main center of human relations research was in America, the most influential theorist among Harvard University's human relations group was Elton Mayo. According to Guillen, "Mayo's thought included two crucial elements: hostility to the idea of progress understood as technological and material advance (i.e., against the Progressives), and nostalgia for a better (preindustrial) past."[55] Mayo was not preoccupied with justifying the authority of management, but rather believed that the unparalleled developments in technical skills over social skills led to problems that could only be solved by manipulating personal and social variables instead of technical aspects, like time clocks.[56]

Mayo's advocacy of the human relations movement over scientific management reflected Australia's more "humane orientation" relative to other nations discussed earlier, emboldened by its Irish Catholic population and their greater affinity for the movement's collectivist and egalitarian ideals.

Despite being of nonworking class English-Protestant descent, Mayo's early cultural immersion in a strongly Irish Catholic-infused Australia undoubtedly contributed to his thinking. Coming of age in Adelaide at the turn of the twentieth century, a city where status was dictated by wealth, education, and profession, Mayo later spent many years in Queensland as a young academic. Mayo biographer, Richard Trahair, relates that, though he left South Australia around the time of Federation, Mayo was opposed to the 1904 Australian Labor Party (ALP) formation of the federal government. According to Trahair, Mayo opposed the ALP because their policy benefited only one class, and that their socialism—an ideology which he did not oppose, but objected to their particular approach—placed more emphasis on selfishness and class jealousy. "He loathed socialism because it flourished on mob ignorance, and preferred 'a high ethical Socialism' that developed from 'the voluntary sacrifice of certain advantages by a more cultured class in order to raise the moral and intellectual level of their less enlightened brethren.' "[57]

This Australian cultural immersion may be why Mayo's reactionary position, Guillen maintains, "stimulated the minds of Catholic and

---

[55] Ibid., 60–61.

[56] Ibid., 62.

[57] Richard C.S. Trahair, *The Humanist Temper: The Life and Work of Elton Mayo* (New Brunswick, NJ: Transaction Books, 1984), 42–43.

Christian management intellectuals in Britain, Germany, and Spain, who, unlike their American counterparts, found in religion the initial inspiration to study organizational issues from a human relations perspective."[58] Indeed, the collectivist strand in Australian culture, which saw an assertive emphasis on workers' interests, could be expected to have made Mayo more conscious of the conditions of workers as people and not mere components of a machine, as implied by scientific management. This early cultural exposure in his formative years likely impacted his later views.

Mayo emphasized the importance of human beings—their needs, preoccupations, and interactions within the workplace—to the healthy functioning of organizations. Indeed, in *The Social Problems of an Industrial Civilization*, Mayo stressed the critical importance of people—and limitations of scientific management—to the proper running of organizations. According to Mayo, in the industrial setting where humans interact, the administrator deals with integrated groups of people rather than a mass of individuals. According to Mayo, "Man's desire to be continuously associated in work with his fellows is a strong, if not the strongest, human characteristic. Any disregard of it by management or any ill-advised attempt to defeat this human impulse leads instantly to some form of defeat for management itself."[59]

Mayo's assertion that ignoring or trivializing the importance of the human element leads to managerial failure was a key departure from scientific management thinking. As Mayo writes,

[T]he belief that the behavior of an individual within the factory can be predicted before employment upon the basis of a laborious and minute examination by tests of his technical and other capacities is mainly, if not wholly, mistaken. Examination of his developed social skills and his general adaptability might give better results. The usual situation is that after employment his relation to "the team" will go far to determine the use he makes of such capacities as he has developed.[60]

For Mayo—unlike Taylor and his scientific management colleagues— management should view workers' unique social skills and their relationships with coworkers and superiors as the primary important

---

[58] Guillen, 63.

[59] Elton Mayo, *The Social Problems of an Industrial Civilization* (Boston, MA: Division of Research, Graduate School of Business Administration, Harvard University, 1945), 111.

[60] Ibid.

features for the proper functioning of organizations. Mayo's views certainly reflected dominant Australian cultural values. Not only was a humane orientation a critical feature of the Australian working class and the political activities of the ALP but the Irish aspects that helped foster it were also clearly evident.

As the largest Catholic group in Australia, the Irish were a strong cultural force. Moreover, the ALP, as a labor-focused party, not only featured Catholics prominently among its leadership ranks but also derived a disproportionate percentage of its electoral support from the Australian Catholic community. Prior to the 1955 "Split" that led to the founding of the Democratic Labour Party (DLP), the ALP received the support of about 70 percent of Australian Catholics. Even after the Split, the proportion was still significant at 51–52 percent.[61]

The DLP, established as a radical but noncommunist alternative to the ALP, often received votes from Catholics, Australian historian Chris McConville asserts, "but its strength came from a broader anticommunism which was spread widely across all ranks of Australian society." However, the party's policy retained ideals of Catholic social order. While the DLP was not able to exercise its own power, at its height polling more than 15 percent of the vote in the state of Victoria where it had found its broadest support, representing at least two-thirds of the Catholic electorate, it successfully split the vote and prevented the ALP from achieving electoral success for several decades in federal and some state governments. Their influence reflected a greater influence beyond the working class. McConville observes, "While the Irishness of the First World War survived within a broader working class culture, the Catholicism of the DLP depended on the comfort and wealth of suburban Catholics, most of whom had broken with the inner city worlds of their parents."[62]

Contrary to Australia, Canada's opposition to scientific management and greater interest in human relations appears to have stemmed largely from its British connections and the Social Gospel movement which grew into an influential political force over the course of the first half of the twentieth century. According to American management historian Daniel Wren, the Social Gospel movement "shaped the field of personnel management, formed an antecedent for industrial sociology, and was a social precursor to the politics of progressivism," viewing

---

[61] Hugh V. Emy, *The Politics of Australian Democracy: Fundamentals in Dispute*, 2nd ed. (South Melbourne, VIC: Macmillan, 1978), 632.

[62] Chris McConville, *Croppies, Celts & Catholics: The Irish in Australia* (Caulfield East, VIC: Edward Arnold Publishers, 1987), 131–33.

unions positively as "instruments of social and economic reform."[63] As suggested earlier, such acceptance of a union's role in society is consistent with the view of collectivism held by industrial relations theorists.

The history of Christian social action in Canada was similar to Europe where Catholic and Protestant churches or associations tended to be responsible for social care in health, education, and poverty alleviation. In Canada as well as Australia, the rising social problems during the latter half of the nineteenth century led to the formation of new teachings and new associations. Reflecting Anglo-Celtic differences in each culture, Canada's forceful British Protestant population spread the influence of the Protestant Social Gospel movement,[64] whereas Australia's assertive Irish Catholic population sparked the strong influence of the Catholic Social Action movement.[65] The impact of these movements was particularly evident in each country's labor-oriented parties, the Co-operative Commonwealth Federation (CCF) (later New Democratic Party [NDP]) in Canada, and the ALP in the case of Australia. Regarding the Canadian experience, Canadian historian of religion, Robert Choquette, describes:

> Social Gospel reformers sought a change of perspective, one that moved away from individualism and closer to communalism in Protestant theology. While acknowledging the full importance of modern secular society, Social Gospel reformers wanted to find God in and through it. They were struck by the extent of misery and injustice in society; they wanted to extend the meaning of sin and justice not only to include the social, but to be primarily centred in society.[66]

Social Gospel reformers aimed to create a society, Choquette asserts, "where cooperation replaced competition, where big business and corporations worked hand in hand with workers and consumers in a cooperative effort aimed at the common good."[67] In Canada, Social

---

[63] Daniel A. Wren, *The History of Management Thought*, 5th ed. (Hoboken, NJ: John Wiley, 2005), 269.

[64] Robert Choquette, *Canada's Religions: An Historical Introduction* (Ottawa, ON: University of Ottawa Press, 2004), 332.

[65] Robert Leach, *Political Ideologies: An Australian Introduction* (Melbourne, VIC: MacMillan, 1988), 73–75.

[66] Choquette, 333.

[67] Ibid.

Gospel appealed to many members of the evolving socialist movement, particularly its British strand, considered in detail later within
the context of Canadian egalitarianism. However, it must be noted that,
although the Social Gospel movement was led by various theologians
and church leaders from Great Britain, the United States, and Canada,
foremost among them was American Walter Rauschenbush. In Canada,
leaders of the movement included the Presbyterian William Irvine, and
the Methodists J.S. Woodsworth, William Ivens, and Salem Bland.[68] The
Social Gospel for such Canadian religious leaders, Canadian journalist
Walter Stewart asserts, "was clear in its message" that "it was the duty of
the church to be involved in issues of political and social reform, and if
that led to criticism, even banishment from the pulpit, so be it."[69]

In the Australian context, Australian historian Robert Leach argues,
"A long-term Australian conservative influence has been the intellectual
strand centered around the preservation of conservative cultural values,
such as the family, race, and British links, as evidenced by such symbols
as the flag" and reigning monarch.[70] Perhaps ironic, but a close ideological ally with these pro-British cultural conservatives was what Leach
terms "the historical stream of Catholic Social Doctrine," originating
with the ideological forces that propelled the Catholic Church's reaction
to the liberalism of the French Revolution.[71] The modern influence on
the evolution of Social Doctrine was Pope Leo XIII, who sought to bring
the doctrine to a middle position between capitalism and socialism.
This Christian Socialism was initially outlined in *Rerum Novarum* (1891),
the Papal encyclical that, according to Leach, "enjoined employers and
workers to co-operate in an atmosphere of brotherhood. Class warfare was
unnatural, as it alleged, were the ideologies that taught this belief."[72]

Hence, Considine asserts, "Catholic Social Doctrine elaborated on
'class collaboration', maintained that the first aim of a Catholic worker or
employer should be to fight the individualism of liberalism and the anti-
private property thrust of socialism."[73] Leach maintains, such teachings
fit well in Australia with "the dominant Benthamite liberalism of

---

[68] Ibid., 334.
[69] Walter Stewart, *The Life and Political Times of Tommy Douglas* (Toronto, ON: McArthur & Co., 2003), 56.
[70] Leach, *Political Ideologies*, 73.
[71] Ibid., 73–74.
[72] Ibid., 75.
[73] M. Considine, "The National Civic Council: Politics Inside Out," *Politics* 20, no. 1 (1985): 49. Quoted in Leach, *Political Ideologies*, 74.

state-managed, 'fair' capitalism, and much of the English Chartist tradition of master/man collaboration, along understood legalist principles." Leach asserts that "Catholic Social Doctrine elements were absorbed into this Australian labourist/social democratic melting pot. It was anticommunism and social conservatism that Australian Catholic Social Doctrine made its major impact."[74]

Concerning Benthamite liberalism, it is important to emphasize that Catholic Social Doctrine by the 1930s had become an important aspect of ALP ideology. With the arrival of the Great Depression and the rise in popularity of Marxist socialism among some workers, many Catholics within the ALP had begun organizing themselves into a formal "Movement" in order to fight the rising popularity of Marxist thought and the increasing influence of the Communist Party.[75] The Movement's purpose was to expel communists and their sympathizers from both the trade unions and the ALP in cooperation with the ALP Right Wing.[76]

This conservative wing was where Catholics had a strong base in the ALP. Until the First World War, the leadership of the ALP at both the Commonwealth and State levels tended to emerge from the trade union movement reflecting either Protestant or agnostic backgrounds. A notable Catholic exception was T.J. Ryan, Labor Premier of Queensland. Instead, Catholics tended to fit into an influential middle section of the ALP where their numbers were strongest. Catholics comprised roughly one-third of the Labor members of both Commonwealth and State parliaments, a proportion similar to the number of Catholics in the Australian working class. Hence, their numbers were represented among the masses, and Catholics were few among the leaders of the trade union movement. The radical socialist ideologue section—the "industrialists" and syndicalist promoters of the One Big Union and the Industrial Workers of the World—was secular who, Hogan observes, were "impatient both of moralistic Protestant leaders and politically pragmatic Catholics." The impact of Irish Catholics was increasingly felt in the "machine politics" at the municipal and branch level of the ALP.[77] Machine politics, while dominated by Irish Catholics, was not a religious but cultural phenomenon that revealed the powerful position Irish Catholics had achieved

---

[74] Leach, *Political Ideologies*, 74.
[75] Ibid., 74–75.
[76] Ibid., 75.
[77] Michael Hogan, *Sectarian Strand: Religion in Australian History* (Ringwood, VIC: Penguin, 1987), 177.

in Australian society beyond ecclesiastical circles. It differed from the religious influence that provided a more direct impact on the conservative arm of the ALP.

The Movement led by many Catholics in the ALP was particularly active between 1947 and 1957, and was driven out of the ALP between 1955–1957, notes Leach, "causing a great rupture in that party's membership and electoral support."[78]

Given the central role the ALP held in Australian society, Elton Mayo could not have easily escaped its impact raised in Australian culture. Hence, the cultural impact of socialist, radical, and religious influences on Australia and Canada must be considered for their effect on the working classes and indirect impact on the character of management. First, however, a closer examination of egalitarianism is essential as much of Mayo's beliefs in the importance of worker satisfaction are indicative of an egalitarian impulse traceable to his native Australia. The egalitarianism of Australia contrasts with the egalitarianism of the United States and Canada where it had also emerged as a critical cultural feature, but was displayed in divergent ways.

Egalitarianism, individualism, and the cultural influence of political ideology

Earlier, American society was described as embracing egalitarianism, individualism, liberty, populism and free-market capitalism, a strong set of internalized values that American social theorist Seymour Martin Lipset has labeled the "American Creed."[79] In the United States, it appears that egalitarianism and individualism not only coexist but reflect competing philosophical views that divide liberals and conservatives. The differences are subtle. For instance, many of the inconsistencies in American attitudes to the US domestic policy of "affirmative action" point to a profound contradiction between egalitarianism and individualism.[80] Yet, not unlike Australians, Americans believe strongly in both. In *American Exceptionalism*, Lipset argues that

> One consequence of this dualism is that political debate often takes the form of one consensual value opposing the other. Liberals and

[78] Leach, *Political Ideologies*, 75.
[79] Seymour Martin Lipset, *American Exceptionalism: A Double-Edged Sword* (New York, NY: W.W. Norton, 1996), 19.
[80] Ibid., 128.

conservatives typically do not take "alternative" positions on issues of equality and freedom. Instead, each side appeals to one or the other core value. Liberals stress the primacy of egalitarianism and the social injustice that flows through unfettered individualism. Conservatives enshrine individual freedom and the social need for mobility and achievement as values "endangered" by the collectivism inherent in liberal nostrums. Both sides treat as their natural constituency the entire American public. In this sense, liberals and conservatives are less opponents than they are competitors, like two department stores on the same block trying to draw the same customers by offering different versions of what everyone wants.[81]

Whereas American egalitarianism helped foster the positive consensus in support of the civil rights movement—a series of government programs beginning in the 1960s intended to encourage African Americans and women (regardless of ethnicity) to effectively participate in the job market—individualism contributed to equally strong reservations against the effort. The shifting focus of civil rights "on substantive equality and preferential treatment," Lipset asserts, "has forced the country up against the individualistic, achievement-oriented element in Creed."[82] Thus, American attitudes, while decidedly against discrimination, also tend to oppose efforts that encourage compulsory integration and employment quotas. Many conservatives—most White but some Black—strongly resent these efforts, "not because they oppose racial equality," argues Lipset, "but because they feel these measures violate their individual freedom."[83]

Although liberals are fast to point out the "inegalitarian consequences of the de facto segregation," when it comes to racial matters data indicate that most Whites favor individual freedom over compulsory social egalitarianism.[84] Hence, while Americans generally approve of strong national programs to help the disadvantaged and to fight racial discrimination in society, given a choice between direct government involvement to solve social problems and letting people work out their problems on their own, Lipset says "the [American] public always chooses the latter option."[85] This leaning is evident in the high level

---

[81] Ibid.
[82] Ibid.
[83] Ibid.
[84] Ibid., 128–29.
[85] Ibid., 129.

of "achievement orientation" embraced by American society relative to Australia and Canada, and underscores the significance of the particular type of "achievement-focused" individualism that has evolved in the United States.

In an attempt to simplify the differences when comparing the United States to Canada, contemporary US society is often referred to as "conservative" and Canada as "liberal." According to traditional definitions, however, the reverse is true. Canada has a highly developed social-welfare state, which some might characterize as more collectivist than individualist. While in the United States it is common to refer to attitudes in favor of welfare and public health insurance programs as being liberal, or even "socialist" by its most fierce contemporary conservative critics, the ideological origin of such policies is actually conservative, not liberal. Indeed, what Europeans traditionally refer to as liberalism, suggests Lipset, "Americans refer to as 'conservatism': a deeply anti-statist doctrine emphasizing the virtues of laissez-faire."[86]

According to Canadian political theorist Gad Horowitz, the distinction is fundamental to understanding different categories of egalitarianism:

> Though liberalism and socialism agree that *individuals* ought to be equal, their conceptions of the *society* within which individuals have their being are radically different. Liberalism sees life in society as a competition among individuals; the prize is individual "achievement" or "success"; equality [for liberalism] is essentially equality of *opportunity* in the struggle for success.[87]

According to the American liberal tradition, therefore, equality of opportunity is a key value whereas other societies like Australia—and Canada to a lesser degree—tend to favor equality at the personal level rather than on material concerns, such as securing equal opportunity for those who aspire to the individualistic achievement of economic or social success.

In other words, the unique brand of Australian egalitarianism extends equality beyond the American focus on equality of opportunity. Australians demand from their egalitarianism a "fair and reasonable" standard of living for all, which makes Australians less tolerant

---

[86] Ibid., 36.

[87] Gad Horowitz, *Canadian Labour in Politics* (Toronto, ON: University of Toronto Press, 1968), 5.

of unequal wealth.[88] As will be discussed, this overriding Australian focus underlies the Australian policy of compulsory arbitration and fair wages. Hence, it could be said that Australian society values people according to their equal merit as human beings rather than on an achievement-based hierarchical pecking order. This is because, while Americans place liberty above equality, Australians do the reverse and value equality over liberty, which is why Australians have tolerated radical policies such as compulsory arbitration and compulsory voting. These ideas would not be tolerated in America where personal freedom is paramount. Canada falls in between these two extremes.

While Australian culture has been strongly influenced by liberalism, which the electoral success of the Liberal Party has demonstrated over the twentieth century, to ignore the effect of the Labor Party and the working classes that propelled it to power, ignores an influence of profound cultural importance. Australians were reminded of this in 2005 when a Liberal parliamentarian attempted to forbid the use of the Australian greeting of "mate"—a long-held social equalizer with strong working-class origins. After an internal memo banning parliamentary security staff from publicly addressing visitors to Parliament House as mate became public, Australians protested the order as inherently anti-Australian. Only after Labor MP Roger Price demanded the Speaker to investigate did then Liberal Prime Minister John Howard quickly declare the ban as ridiculously absurd, and quickly overturned the order, allowing security staff to use their judgment on how best to greet members of the public and politicians, including the use of mate as appropriate.[89]

Hence, if "equality of opportunity" is considered liberal, and "equality of condition" is deemed socialist, then Australian egalitarianism could be viewed as "equality of social position," where social hierarchy is not as steep and individual achievement and aspirations for individual distinction are frowned upon. While less prevalent in Canada, Australia's individualist managing class has had to contend with this prevailing cultural norm. There is a strong Irish element in Australia's leveling effect.

---

[88] Boris Kabanoff, Nerina L. Jimmieson, and Malcolm J. Lewis, "Psychological Contracts in Australia: A 'Fair Go' or a 'Not-So-Happy Transition'?" in *Psychological Contracts in Employment: Cross-National Perspectives*, ed. Denise M. Rousseau and Rene Schalk (Thousand Oaks, CA: Sage Publications, 2000), 36.

[89] *See*, for example, Matt Price, "Mate, It's Just Not On," *The Australian* (Sydney), August 19, 2005. http://www.theaustralian.news.com.au/.

If Australian egalitarianism is initially attributable to the British radical working class—whose practice of "mateship," dislike of pretension through cutting down tall poppies, and knocking—then its persistence, at least in part, is attributable to the Irish, for they have always represented a large segment of the Australian working class. Moreover, the Irish felt historically maligned by the British, in Great Britain with regard to Ireland and in Australia during the convict era, and subsequently as a significant component of an underclass directed by a British over class. As Canada's egalitarianism has different origins, Australia's egalitarian roots are first explored.

The Irish impact on Australian egalitarianism

The presence of the Irish in a British Protestant administered Australia appears to have been critical for local egalitarianism to emerge. According to Elaine Thompson in *Fair Enough: Egalitarianism in Australia*, education and politics were two realms that "highlight the extent to which Australians were not 'all the same' and did not share a single, unified culture."[90] Yet, despite this apparent inequality, rights emerged that approach equality.

For example, during the nineteenth century when Catholics expressed dislike and distrust of a Protestant educational system that threatened the continuation of their Catholic community's faith and teachings, Australia's educational system changed to allow for a publicly funded secular public school system and an independent system of Catholic schools supported by the voluntary services of Catholic teaching clergy and donations.[91] Although the Catholic community had to cover their own costs, this educational system provided the means by which Catholics, particularly Irish Catholics who represented the majority of Catholics in Australia in the nineteenth and early twentieth centuries, maintained a cohesive and culturally influential community.

Efforts to ensure cohesion were severe. When the Irish Cardinal Patrick Francis Moran, Archbishop of Sydney (1884–1911), convened the plenary council of 1885, two key decisions were made that affected the daily life of Australian Catholics. First, parents who sent their children to a state school lacking cause or permission, Australian historian Edmund Campion asserts, "were to be denied absolution in the

---

[90] Elaine Thompson, *Fair Enough: Egalitarianism in Australia* (Sydney, NSW: University of New South Wales Press, 1994), 64.
[91] Ibid., 65.

confessional." Second, the council brought the Australian Catholic church in line with the marriage regulations of the Irish dioceses and ended the lenient policy of John Polding—an English Benedictine who served as Bishop of Sydney for forty-two years. The former provision insured the promotion of Catholic schools, while the latter meant that a Catholic who was married before a non-Catholic minister or civil registrar would automatically be excommunicated. Catholic clergy were not permitted to marry non-Catholics except under the most caustic conditions that included, offers Campion, "the non-Catholic promising not to interfere with the Catholic's religious practice and to bring up any children of the marriage as Catholics—and with the barest of ceremonies: no flowers, no candles, no nuptial Mass, in the sacristy."[92] The effect of both provisions was to strengthen the Australian Catholic community, which was achieved through negative reinforcement of "Catholicism as a distinct subculture in the Australian community." Catholics, concludes Campion, "were to be kept separate from surrounding tribes."[93]

A tribe is an inherently collectivist social unit. The "tribal" nature of Australia's Catholic community, therefore, formed an important foundation for egalitarian interests. According to Patrick O'Farrell,

> Ireland and the Catholic Church were, in a real sense, automatic tribal loyalties; they were, in their epic dimensions and grandeur, part of a defence mechanism against the diminishing drudgery of work and the humbling constrictions of low status, and they were one dimension of a set of commitments and organisational expressions which integrated individuals into the local community, which in turn was woven into the wider community.[94]

While causal attributions have yet to be tested, O'Farrell points out how significant the characteristic Irish traits of rebelliousness, lawlessness, and flamboyance were for Australia. Historical research, O'Farrell notes, "has identified a lack of deference towards social superiors in the Ireland of the 1820s, something in sharp contrast with the situation in England: it is tempting to see this, imported, as an Irish basis for

---

[92] Edmund Campion, *Australian Catholics: The Contribution of Catholics to the Development of Australian Society* (Ringwood, VIC: Penguin, 1987), 65.

[93] Ibid.

[94] Patrick O'Farrell, *The Irish in Australia: 1788 to the Present* (Notre Dame, IN: Indiana University Press, 2000), 156–57.

the egalitarianism so noted by observers of the Australian scene."[95] Such transferences appear consistent. In other words, the Irish blended in yet retained distinctive features, and as they blended in, these features were adopted by other Australians, particularly as their influence grew, which was significantly enhanced by the ecclesiastical leadership of Cardinal Moran under whose direction Catholic self-esteem was strengthened in Australia.

Not only did Moran build new Catholic seminaries and found Catholic-subsidized periodicals, but in 1896 released his *History of the Catholic Church in Australasia*, that, according to Campion, was "an enormous compilation that celebrated Australian Catholicism as part of the Irish spiritual world empire."[96] Moran's influence on the Australian Catholic community—and ultimately Australia as a whole—cannot be understated. As Campion relates,

> Its hibernicism did not go unremarked; nor did Moran's revival, also in 1896, of St Patrick's Day as "the national festival," with a cere-mony in the cathedral, athletics at the sports ground, a vice-regal luncheon and a concert at the town hall featuring a half-hour lecture on St Patrick. Like all Irish bishops, Moran deliberately identified Catholicism and Irishism. But the hibernicism of his *History*, which distressed Benedictine circles, should not obscure its other char-acteristic: it proclaimed to its very wide readership that Australian Catholicism was a single entity, one in origin, background, history, discipline and everyday experience. Similarly, Moran initiated national Catholic congresses in 1900, 1904 and 1909 to encourage a unified Catholic mind in Australia.[97]

These steps initiated by Moran not only helped maintain a Catholic identity for Australians of Catholic faith and/or heritage—which was primarily Irish since most Catholics in Australia prior to the Second World War were of Irish origin—but elevated their confidence to enter other areas of Australian life, particularly labor and politics, strongly influencing Australian culture.

Daniel Mannix, Archbishop of Melbourne (1913–1963), articulated an even stronger Irish Catholic voice in Australia, echoing similar senti-ments as his predecessor, Archbishop Thomas Carr. "Mannix personified

---

[95] Ibid., 81–82.
[96] Campion, 66.
[97] Ibid., 66–67.

the assertive Catholic approach," O'Farrell notes, where "assertion replaced amiability as the Catholic mode of social behaviour."[98]

While Catholic membership was strong among Labor ranks, this did not mean their presence helped the Catholic cause. In 1915, J.H. Scullin, a Catholic and future Labor Prime Minister, had refused to support the removal of Labor's policy on secular education in favor of a policy more in line with Catholic aims. According to O'Farrell, Scullin "argued that this would be to introduce divisive religious controversy into party political matters. His colleague Hugh Mahon was of similar mind: sensitive about his Catholicism Mahon was always anxious to avoid any suggestion that he favoured it. Such attitudes were typical of Catholic Labor politicians then and later."[99]

Contrary to Moran's search for a peaceful Catholic presence in Australia, Mannix and other Catholic leaders rigorously substituted Moran's "search for peaceful harmony" with turmoil as Catholics increasingly resented the Labor governments' failure to remedy their various grievances, such as the education issue. Thus, alongside Catholic Labor leaders' conformity to concerns of secular society, an assertively "Catholic mind" developed from 1911 onward symbolized by the "Catholic Federation" formed in Melbourne that same year, which spread to all Australian states attracting about one hundred thousand members within a two-year period. This characteristic "rebelliousness" reflects, notes O'Farrell, that Catholicism embraces "dualistic tendencies, both conservative and revolutionary elements." While there tends to be a natural yearning to conform and integrate with the prevailing environment wherever one is, in Australia, O'Farrell observes, "From 1911 after Moran's death, there was a growing feeling among active Catholics that the policy of integration had failed. Many Catholics felt bitterly disappointed at the failure of Labor governments, first elected in 1910, to make any attempt to remedy their grievances."[100]

Moreover, the location of this change in overt Irish Catholic attitude was significant as it revealed a geographically diverse source of Catholic strength in Australia. O'Farrell describes,

That Melbourne should see the birth of this movement in organised form reflects its distance from Moran's immediate sway, and

---

[98] Patrick O'Farrell, *The Catholic Church and Community: The Catholic Church and Community: An Australian History*, 3rd rev. ed. (Kensington, NSW: New South Wales University Press, 1992), 298.

[99] Ibid., 299.

[100] Ibid.

Archbishop Carr's disenchantment, from the early years of the century, with the Cardinal's social attitudes. Carr had come to believe that Moran's policy of pacifism, enlivened by bursts of moral pressure, was futile, and that only a fighting organisation would yield results. The Melbourne stimulus behind the launching of the Catholic Federation also reflected the greater degree of lay participation in church affairs. . . . It was non-political in any party sense. Its purpose was to achieve organised Catholic unity 'for the purpose of advancing the religious, civil and social interests of Catholics throughout Australia.'[101]

The location of Irish influence was initially rural and farm-based during the mid-nineteenth century. The heaviest wave of Irish immigration came during the agricultural boom of the 1860s and 1870s when close to half of Victoria's Irish lived outside Melbourne, with comparable distributions in other colonies.[102] However, from the 1880s on, the Irish put their mark on Australia's urban centers. Since Australian cities lacked walls as in many European cities, they tended to sprawl outward, blurring the distinction between town and country where the Irish preferred to reside.

Sydney's expansion benefited from the Irish drift toward the cities. "Irishtown," so named because of the rising population of Irish, was situated in Sydney's Bankstown area. However, this was only the beginning of Sydney's Irish settlement. Sydney's growth, along with its suburbs, sped up from the 1860s onward. In 1861, there were 95,789; in 1881, 224,939; in 1901, 480,976—the population multiplied five times over within forty years. Notable Irish communities inevitably developed. Within Sydney, Surry Hills, Redfern, Waterloo, and Paddington, but also in the more respectable suburbs of Hunters Hill, Randwick and Woollahra, revealing the significant percentage of Irish "among the house-and-garden servants of the rich." The number of urban Irish was overrepresented in unskilled occupations, yet showed their desire to dwell near their work places—including the growing railways and docks.[103]

Melbourne was similar to Sydney in its rising trend of urban Irish settlement and, therefore, the large Irish presence among the ranks of labor. By the late nineteenth century, in the northern and western parts, along the

---

[101] Ibid., 299–300.
[102] O'Farrell, *The Irish in Australia*, 154.
[103] Ibid., 155.

Victorian railway system, hundreds of Irishmen tended to work as porters, guards, railway switchmen, and engine drivers, areas that, by necessity, had a bigger Celtic population than southern or eastern Melbourne. This settlement pattern supports the view that Irish workers tended to look for government employment instead of employment with private enterprises. This was the case with laborers as well as clerical workers. The Irish considered government employment as providing more security and greater protection from prejudice.[104] The Irish, therefore, exercised a profound influence on the working class of New South Wales and Victoria.

Highly revealing of radical and Irish influences is the character and career of Australian politician, John T. ("Jack") Lang. As Premier of New South Wales for two terms, Lang was a Labor leader who implemented many radical policies, and earned the unenviable distinction in 1932 of being dismissed from power by a state governor. His policies and tactics demonstrated considerable rebelliousness and gumption.

In J.T. Lang's first term as Premier (1925–1927), his government reduced working hours, improved workers' compensation benefits, introduced several welfare reforms including granting state pensions for widowed mothers with dependent children, abolished student fees in state-run high schools, and established universal suffrage in local government elections. During his second term as Premier at the height of the Depression (1930–1932), not only were his economic policies the cause of the separation of the New South Wales Labor Party from the National Party, but Lang was instrumental in bringing down John Scullin's federal Labor government due to Lang's active resistance to the ALP's agreement to cut government spending and Lang's advocating not paying interest on British loans while reducing interest payments on Australian loans. To assert his views, Lang withdrew state funds from government bank accounts and held them in cash at Trades Hall to prevent the federal government from gaining access to the money. As a result, NSW Governor, Sir Philip Game, dismissed Lang's government in May 1932.[105]

Lang was born in Sydney in 1876 to an Irish Catholic mother and a Scottish Presbyterian father who had converted to Roman Catholicism upon his marriage. "Like many converts," Lang wrote about his father, "he embraced his new faith with extreme zeal, immersed himself in the

---

[104] Ibid.
[105] *See* N.B. Nairn, *The "Big Fella": Jack Lang and the Australian Labor Party 1891–1949* (Melbourne, VIC: Melbourne University Press, 1986), 155–59, 211–12, 255–59.

study of its theology, and was prepared to discuss theological subjects at great length with anyone." Of his mother, Lang wrote, "My mother was an easy-going Irish woman, who never attempted to impose her beliefs on anyone, but remained rigidly loyal to her church."[106] Lang attended a Marist Brothers school, St. Francis, in Sydney.

As a Labor leader, Lang had been attacked as a dictator. Defending himself against the charge, Lang wrote in his first memoir, *I Remember:*

> There were four bodies of people with the power to take away my authority at any time. The electors had given me a mandate. The Legislative Assembly had voted for the legislation I had presented. The Parliamentary Labor Party had made me leader. The Australian Labor Party in conference had confirmed my leadership. Yet they still called me a dictator. I had used no force to seize power, yet they compared me with Lenin and Mussolini, then the best-known examples of dictatorship in action.[107]

As a Labor leader, Lang was legitimately under constant attack from opposition members. In his memoir, Lang concedes that his government's policies were indeed extreme if not revolutionary:

> Our legislation was altogether too radical for our opponents. The Government insurance Office caused much bitterness in the insurance world. The 44-hour week upset the Employers' Federation. Widows' Pensions and Child Endowment made more enemies in the higher strata. . . . But [back then] there was no doubt that I had the support of the rank and file of the Labor Movement. Never had they been more enthusiastic.[108]

Lang's own words show his strong personality, characteristic rebelliousness and brashness that reflected his Australian Irish Catholic upbringing. He also revealed his drive to create a sense of equity in Australian society and "flatten" disparities in wealth, rank, and privilege, consistent with Australian egalitarianism.

Another example of brash Australian Labor leaders of Irish origin is Paul Keating who served as prime minister from 1991 to 1996. Peeters observes that Keating is among the few national politicians depicted by

---

[106] J.T. Lang, *The Turbulent Years* (Sydney, NSW: Alpha Books, 1970), 1.

[107] J.T. Lang, *I Remember* (Sydney, NSW: Invincible Press, 1949), 310.

[108] Ibid., 311.

Australian writers as a *"reluctant* exemplar of the tall poppy species."[109] His ethnocultural background growing up in the working-class Irish enclave of Bankstown in suburban Sydney is a likely reason.

In politics, Keating gained a reputation for arrogance, particularly in the art of verbal aggression against political opponents, and showed less reverence for British parliamentary proprieties, epitomized by his assertion that Australia should become a republic and cut ties to the British monarchy. Keating was among many Australian politicians who excelled at this art, making the American Congress and New Zealand legislature quiet in comparison.[110]

* * *

While Australian individualism is robust and indisputable, the degree of collectivism evident in Australian culture appears traceable to the impact of "Irish tribalism" that permeated Australia in both the rural and urban areas since the mid-nineteenth century. Although contemporary Australia may be characterized among the strongest cultures on measures of individualism—retained by its managerial class—collectivism, arguably at the root of Australian egalitarianism, has proven to be a distinct element of its working culture. The Irish are an important reason, evident in the next chapter's discussion of the Anglo-Celtic aspects of radicalism. Considered in the context of management and influential ideologies, Canada's collective streak—unlike Australia's—points to European conservatism as its primary influence. Before taking into account these ideological origins, however, Canada's egalitarianism, and its sources of difference from Australia, must be considered.

Sources of Canadian egalitarianism

The ideology of conservatism in Europe and Canada was derived from the historic alliance of church and government, and is associated with the emergence of the welfare state.[111] Bismarck and Disraeli, two leaders of the conservatives in their respective nations, reflect this view.

---

[109] Bert Peeters, " 'Thou Shalt Not Be a Tall Poppy': Describing an Australian Communicative (and Behavioral) Norm," *Intercultural Pragmatics* 1, no. 1 (2004): 84.

[110] Ross Terrill, *The Australians: The Way We Live Now* (Sydney, NSW: Doubleday, 2000), 282, quoted in Peeters, 84.

[111] Lipset, *American Exceptionalism*, 35.

They represented the rural and aristocratic elements in Germany and Britain, sectors which despised capitalism, hated the bourgeoisie, and cast off materialistic values, yet whose politics, argues Lipset, "reflected the values of the *noblesse oblige*, the obligation of the leaders of society and the economy to protect the less fortunate."[112] One way to achieve this aim was through social welfare programs which the upper class helps fund.

While Bismarck taxed employers and employees to support the ill and unemployed, Disraeli's "Tory democracy"—giving workers a voice, attending to their needs, and instilling in them a respect for English tradition of monarchy, aristocracy, and the established Church of England—saw an alliance formed between the conservative aristocratic upper class and the potentially revolutionary working class, promoting policies like voting rights and other benefits to contend with the rise of the largely middle-class Liberal Party. Tory democracy became the prevailing form of British conservatism under Disraeli, Churchill, and subsequent British Tory leaders, until the Thatcher era.[113] Nonetheless, a century earlier, Disraeli's influential policies began with the 1867 *Reform Bill*'s legal entitlement to vote for urban working-class males, and legalizing trade unions and recognizing workers' right to strike in the late 1870s.[114]

In the 1860s and 1870s, paternalism, patriotism, and imperialism were the driving forces of Disraeli's Tory democracy. Not only were these views supportive of hierarchy but they were also supportive of collectivism. This view significantly affected Canada. While Australia was strongly influenced by Benthamite utilitarian liberalism, Conservative politicians in Britain, like Disraeli, were opposed to Bentham's utilitarianism.[115]

---

[112] Lipset explains, "The semantic confusion about liberalism in America arises because both early and latter-day Americans never adopted the term to describe the unique American politician. The reason is simple. The American system of government existed long before the word 'liberal' emerged in Napoleonic Spain and was subsequently accepted as referring to a particular party in mid-nineteenth-century England, as distinct from the Tory or Conservative Party." Lipset, *American Exceptionalism*, 35–36.

[113] Terence Ball, Richard Dagger, William Christian, and Colin Campbell, *Political Ideologies and the Democratic Ideal*, Canadian ed. (Toronto, ON: Pearson Longman, 2006), 90, 280.

[114] Ibid., 66, 90.

[115] Robert Leach, *Political Ideology in Britain* (New York, NY: Palgrave, 2002), 53.

Over the course of the nineteenth century, the United States clung strongly to classical liberal thinking which stressed property rights, free trade, individual freedom, and a limited state. In contrast, liberalism in Britain—and by implication the British-ruled colonies of Canada and Australia—saw a division between proponents of "Classical Liberalism" and a new strand of "State Liberalism," embraced by those who believed in the need to control social structure in order for individual freedom to thrive. While this view reflected the growing influence of socialist reformers that government should help the plight of workers, this trend gave rise to the ideology of the liberal Welfare State where state interventionism, and its appeal for government action to promote individual liberty and equality of opportunity, was deemed an accepted creed of the new liberalism.[116] Although Australia and Canada both became, and remain, highly developed welfare states, the guiding ideological strands that influenced them are not identical.

Egalitarianism—the doctrine that interprets human progress as demanding the advancement of society toward both equality of opportunity *and* equality of outcome—is not consistent with conservatism. "It is very much a fundamental tenet of conservatism that equality does not exist in the real world; therefore, that it ought not to be an end sought by public policy," observes Brad Miner.[117] Affirmative action is such a policy of egalitarianism that justifies the preferred treatment—for obtaining jobs, in either the public or private sector, and accessing higher education—of those whose ethnic group were victims of discrimination in the past.[118]

Compared to the American experience, Australia's strong affinity for both egalitarianism and individualism is not inherently contradictory but reflective of liberalism and acceptance of radical socialist ideas, much like in Canada but intensified in the Australian context by the Irish presence. "In dealing with national characteristics it is important to recognize that comparative evaluations are never absolutes, that they always are made in terms of more or less," Lipset cautions. "The statement that the United States is an egalitarian society obviously does not imply that all Americans are equal in any way that can be defined." Such a notion typically means—irrespective of which aspect is being

---

[116] Leach, *Political Ideologies*, 91.
[117] Brad Miner, *The Concise Conservative Encyclopedia* (New York, NY: Free Press, 1996), 76.
[118] Ibid., 10.

considered, whether social relations, status, mobility, and so on—"that the United States is more egalitarian than Europe."[119]

Cultural generalizations depend on the societies being compared. Canada looks different when contrasted with the United States than when compared with Britain. Thus, when Canada is evaluated in reference to the United States, it appears to be more elitist yet deferential to authority, law-abiding, and statist, but when considering the variations between Canada and Britain, Canada looks more anti-statist, violent, and egalitarian.[120] Whereas comparative observations are always relative, they still reveal interesting cultural differences. Compared to the United States, Canada is far less violent. Hence, just as the United States appears more egalitarian than Canada—in the sense of greater opportunity for individual achievement—Australia seems more egalitarian than the United States, in the sense of a greater feeling of equality among people. Irish Catholics appear to have been an important source of this cultural trend. Concerning egalitarianism in Canada, however, local culture submerged its expression.

This Canadian distinction from Australian egalitarianism is evident in Grnak, Hughes and Hunter's *Building the Best: Lessons from Inside Canada's Best Managed Companies*. In their report on organizational design strategies implemented by Canada's PCL Construction Group of Companies between 1987 and 2002, it appears that nonegalitarian vertical organizational structures continue to prevail as a dominant feature of Canadian corporate policy. The various programs implemented for supervisors and managers, such as ongoing career feedback, face-to-face communication, mentoring and coaching proved so popular that they were made available to salaried, nonsupervisory staff as well.[121]

Although these programs were certainly important for employee and managerial morale, given their positive effect on promoting and maintaining employee appreciation throughout the organization, Canadian egalitarianism is hardly comparable to Australian practices described earlier. According to PCL, "We believe that the employee-supervisor relationship is the single most important factor in employee retention and development. . . . We also believe that successful growth

---

[119] Lipset, *American Exceptionalism*, 32.

[120] Ibid., 32–33.

[121] Anthony Grnak, John Hughes, and Douglas Hunter, *Building the Best: Lessons from Inside Canada's Best Managed Companies* (Toronto, ON: Penguin, 2006), 175.

can only come from a strong organization, and competent supervisors/ management is the core of that strength."[122] The PCL training process is intended to identify managerial talent to serve as an endless supply of new leaders from within the organization.[123] In other words, vertical hierarchy is upheld as the ideal form with competent managerial talent supervising workers in a top-down fashion.

Hence, while Canada accepts freedom of rights and shares its democratic principles with other Western democracies, differences among them—between Canada and the United States in particular—are distinctive. Canadian sociologist Kaspar Naegele asserts, "There is *less* emphasis in Canada on equality than there is in the United States. . . . In Canada there seems to be a greater acceptance of *limitation*, of hierarchical patterns. There seems to be less optimism, less faith in the future, less willingness to risk capital or reputation. In contrast to America, Canada is a country of greater caution, reserve, and restraint."[124]

Naegele's description of the Canadian temperament—perhaps more bleak than deserved—reflects the British Tory tradition from which Canada's elites stemmed. Given Australia and English-speaking Canada's early immersion in British political and administrative structures, both share a political philosophical tradition that differs from the United States. This shared experience helps account for certain political, social, and philosophical features of culture that unite Australia and Canada—including managerial temperament—as well as reveal cultural distinctions that appear linked to key dominant Anglo-Celtic groups in each society.

* * *

How did these different notions of egalitarianism find their place in Australia, Canada, and the United States? A number of influential theorists have suggested how this cultural evolution occurred and, as a result, a few key theories of Anglo-cultural disparity are worth noting. Seymour Lipset relied on a value typology proposed by Talcott Parsons, while Gad Horowitz subsequently advocated an argument concerning Canada's uniqueness that relied on Louis Hartz's theory of the significance of

---

[122] Quoted in Ibid.

[123] Ibid., 176.

[124] Kaspar Naegele, "Canadian Society: Some Reflections," in *Canadian Society*, ed. B.R. Blishen, F.E. Jones, K.D. Naegele, and John Porter (Toronto, ON: Macmillan, 1961), 27.

dominant cultural fragments. Given prior discussion of power distance and individualism/collectivism, Lipset and Horowitz's insights can be discussed in more depth as both are useful to help understand the origins of Australian and Canadian cultural differences and how they might apply to managerial style.

Lipset's value typology

In Lipset's comparative historical analysis of the United States in *The First New Nation*, he argues that Australia and Canada "resemble the United States in stressing equalitarianism [that is, egalitarianism], achievement, universalism, and specificity," but there are also "differences which sharply illustrate the way in which even relatively slight variations in value patterns help account for important differences among the stable and highly developed democracies."[125]

Inspired by American sociologist Talcott Parsons' value typology, Lipset asserts that Canadian and Australian values fall in between the following pairs of discernible, contrasting extremes occupied by British and American values (see Table 5.1): (1) elitism–equalitarianism; (2) ascription–achievement; (3) particularism–universalism; (4) diffuseness–specificity; and (5) collectivity–self orientation.[126] Lipset ranks (according to the first

Table 5.1   Lipset's Value Rankings of Four English-Speaking Democracies[127]

	US	Australia	Canada	Great Britain
Elitism–Equalitarianism	3	4	2	1
Ascription–Achievement	4	2.5	2.5	1
Particularism–Universalism	4	2	3	1
Diffuseness–Specificity	4	2.5	2.5	1
Collectivity–Self-orientation	4	1	3	1

Source: Robert J. Brym and Bonnie Fox. *From Culture to Power: The Sociology of English Canada* (Toronto, ON: Oxford University Press, 1989), 28.

---

[125] Seymour Martin Lipset, *The First New Nation: The United States in Historical Perspective* (New York, NY: Basic Books, 1963), 248–49.

[126] Ibid., 249, 270.

[127] The first four items are presented in Table V of Lipset, *The First New Nation*, 249, whereas the fifth was added by Robert J. Brym and Bonnie Fox, *From Culture to Power: The Sociology of English Canada* (Toronto, ON: Oxford University Press, 1989), 28, derived from the discussion in Lipset, *The First New Nation*, 270.

term in polarity) what he interprets to be the core values of the United States, Australia, Canada, and Great Britain.

Lipset describes the United States as being an egalitarian, achievement, universalistic, and self-oriented society while Great Britain is characterized by elitist, ascriptive, particularist, and collective traits. Lipset infers that Canada and Australia occupy the middle ground between the traditional elitism of Great Britain and the revolutionary democratic and equality-infused principles of the United States, an observation supported by Canada's greater acceptance of elitism and Australia's favoring of egalitarianism. Likewise, Australia appears to embrace more collective values than English-speaking Canada, which is almost as "self-oriented" as is the United States.[128] In other words, Lipset stresses the relative strength in Canada of such Tory values as ascription and elitism (deference) and the relative weakness of the liberal values of achievement and egalitarianism.[129]

Although Lipset's value ranking has not escaped criticism—primarily centered on his choice of methodology and relative inattention to economic influences[130]—Lipset's assertions remain a useful way to view Australian, Canadian, and American cultural differences and their origins. After all, liberals reacted strongly against *ascribed* status. This means a person's social standing is ascribed, or fixed, at birth, without much that the person can do to change this status. The opposite is a society based on *achieved* status, where each individual is theoretically given the equal opportunity to move to the highest (or lowest) levels of society.[131] Ascribed status was the norm in feudal societies where one's status and prospects were essentially solidified by one's social rank, order or estate. The ascribed view was consistent with religious conformity, particularly in hierarchical churches such as Roman Catholicism and the Church of England where, as mentioned, the "Great Chain of Being" was the prevailing outlook. The modern evocation of ascription is deference as reflected by high tolerance for power distance, a characteristic that differentiates Canada from Australia and the United States, touched upon earlier in the context of key dimensions of culture.

---

[128] *See* table of value rankings of the English-speaking democracies, in Brym and Fox, *From Culture to Power*, 28.

[129] Horowitz, *Canadian Labour in Politics*, 10.

[130] Brym and Fox, *From Culture to Power*, 29–32, and Encel, *Equality and Authority*, 189–90.

[131] Terence Ball and Richard Dagger, *Political Ideologies and the Democratic Ideal*, 2nd ed. (New York, NY: HarperCollins, 1995), 54.

Besides Lipset's value ranking scheme, another, perhaps even more convincing way to view Australian, Canadian, and American cultural differences and their origins—particularly in light of the interaction between managerial style and worker temperament—is through Louis Hartz's "fragment theory" and the subsequent analysis of Canadian social theorist Gad Horowitz.

Hartzian "fragment theory" and the Horowitz thesis

In his influential study on *Canadian Labour in Politics*, Gad Horowitz argues that Canada's distinctiveness cannot be properly understood without reference to the United States.[132] Indeed, contrasting Canada with the United States is critical not only because it helps discern subtle differences between Canada and the United States but by identifying where they differ helps clarify often subtle distinctions between Canada and Australia. This is especially true in the analysis of ideology on national culture.

According to Horowitz, the relative strength of socialism in Canada compared to the United States is linked to the historical impact of Toryism on the Canadian personality, as well as liberalism's distinctive character in each nation.[133] The "Horowitz thesis,"[134] which stresses the uniqueness of Canada, is an adaptation of American social theorist Louis Hartz's fragment theory. The latter argues that Australia, English Canada, French Canada, Latin America, and Dutch South Africa were established by fragments of European culture that arrived to these new societies by their founders whose views and interests reflected fragments of culture prominent in Europe at the time they left.[135] Indeed, the fragments reflected an array of cultural conditions, asserts Australian political theorist Ian Cook, "including ideological conditions that changed slowly, if they changed at all."[136]

Hartz asserts that Australia reflects the influence of nineteenth-century European radicalism,[137] while American society reflects liberal

---

[132] Horowitz, *Canadian Labour in Politics*, 3.

[133] Ibid.

[134] Outlined in chapter 1 of Horowitz, *Canadian Labour in Politics*.

[135] Louis Hartz, *The Founding of New Societies: Studies in the History of the United States, Latin America, South Africa, Canada, and Australia* (New York, NY, and London, UK: Harcourt Brace Jovanovich, 1964), 3–48.

[136] Ian Cook, *Liberalism in Australia* (South Melbourne, VIC: Oxford University Press, 1999), 6–7.

[137] Hartz, *The Founding of New Societies*, 40–44.

individualism in the classic Lockean sense—John Locke's articulation of the inalienable "natural rights" to life, liberty, and property, which Hartz characterizes as individual liberty, equal opportunity, and capitalist economy.[138] Similarly, Kenneth McRae characterizes English Canadian society as a liberal fragment comparable to the United States.[139] In contrast, Horowitz emphasizes the uniqueness of Canada by arguing against McRae's contention that English Canada was merely a liberal fragment identical with the United States. Horowitz asserts that a significant preliberal or "Tory remnant" in Canada was an essential differentiator, the existence of which is part of the reason that English Canada developed a strong and accepted socialist tradition, unlike the United States where socialism has traditionally been viewed with considerable disdain.[140] This was likewise the case in Australia where a comparable socialist conscience has never fully developed. According to this perspective, socialist ideas, while dependent on liberalism, were nurtured by Canada's Tory conservatism's support of collectivism.

Australia, Ireland, Britain, and Canada have tended to stress collectivity obligations to a greater degree than the United States. The rise of

---

[138] Louis Hartz, *The Liberal Tradition in America: An Interpretation of American Political Thought Since the Revolution* (New York, NY: Harcourt Brace & Company, 1955), 3–5, 111.

[139] McRae outlines Hartz's views of Canada's two fragments, that is, how French Canada differs from English Canada by pointing to Quebec's origins as a fragment of French feudal society characteristic of the pre-French Revolutionary *Ancien Régime*, as opposed to the Lockean liberal fragment that Hartz and McRae assert as having assumed prominence in both the United States and English Canada. The latter is disputed by Horowitz who argues for the Tory fragment's influence on English Canada that differentiates Canada from the Lockean liberalism of the United States. McRae notes, "In France feudalism merely supported a privileged order that had lost its social function; in New France seigneurialism, not unlike the European feudalism of an earlier age, regained some of its primitive rationale in providing elements of security, order, and social cohesion in an environment ringed about with potential dangers. . . . The essence of Canadian feudalism is its mildness, its relaxation, its absence of systematic harshness or oppression." K.D. McRae, "The Structure of Canadian History," in Louis Hartz, *The Founding of New Societies*, 224, 234–47. *See also* K.D. McRae, "Louis Hartz's Concept of the Fragment Society and its Application to Canada," *Etudes Canadiennes/Canadian Studies* 5 (1978): 17–30.

[140] Campbell, Colin. "On Intellectual Life, Politics, and Psychoanalysis: A Conversation with Gad Horowitz." Ed. Arthur Kroker and Marilouise Kroker, *CTheory*, a135 (2003). http://www.ctheory.net/articles.aspx?id=397 (accessed May 26, 2014).

socialist and welfare-state concepts have, therefore, proven less contrary to their values than for American values. Canada, with its greater stress on elitism and particularism, is more collectivity oriented than the United States. As Lipset observed in the early 1960s, "Although modern industrial society, including the United States, appears to be moving generally toward a greater acceptance of collectivity orientations, the American values' emphasis on self-orientation results in a stronger resistance to accepting the new community welfare concepts than occurs elsewhere."[141] Lipset's forecast proved true for Canada between the mid-1960s and 1980s when a host of collectivist policies were initiated, including national healthcare (largely during Liberal minority governments supported by the socialist CCF-NDP).

The reason Canada would be more open to collectivist measures compared to the United States reflects underlying ideological differences inherent in the original cultural fragments. The complete spectrum of these sources spans, both chronologically and ideologically, from right to left, from feudal or Tory through liberal Whig to liberal democrat to socialist. According to Horowitz,

> French Canada and Latin America are "feudal fragments." They were founded by bearers of the feudal or tory values of the organic, corporate, hierarchical community; their point of departure from Europe is before the liberal revolution. The United States, English Canada, and Dutch South Africa are "bourgeois fragments," founded by bearers of liberal individualism who have left the tory end of the spectrum behind them. Australia is the one "radical fragment," founded by bearers of the working class ideologies of mid-nineteenth-century Britain.[142]

Thus, besides the fervent liberalism that marked both countries, there were also important strands of conservatism and socialism which separated Australia from Canada. The notable features of Canadian society, including the greater acceptance of social stratification and hierarchy; deference to authority figures; tolerance of economic inequality; general absence of the historic lawless individualism and egalitarianism of the American frontier; and the general preference of Britain as a social model despite closer proximity to the United States, all point to the

---

[141] Lipset, *The First New Nation*, 270.
[142] Horowitz, *Canadian Labour in Politics*, 4.

Tory influence on the Canadian personality.[143] This appears particularly true for the Canadian manager's disposition.

The Tory influence on the Canadian manager

Tory conservatism's belief in tradition, hierarchy, deference, and paternalism shaped the Canadian manager whose ethnocultural and class position encouraged the emulation of these Canadian cultural features. Considering the political implications of Disraeli's "Tory paternalism," this ideology did not imply that state action was required to provide social relief. Disraeli recognized that the poor who needed help would expect assistance from the traditional aristocracy or the church, which is part and parcel of paternalism. In their absence, however, the state becomes an important vehicle for alleviating social problems. Hence, Tory collectivism—which suggests state interventionism—was born. This sentiment transferred onto the Canadian social and political landscape.

Indeed, as Canadian journalist Charles Taylor observes in his history of Canada's Tory influence, *Radical Tories*, "Canada had evolved as a conservative alternative to the liberal individualism of the United States."[144] While Canadian Liberals rightly believe themselves to be, in Taylor's words, "individualists, rationalists and internationalists," but also "generous, magnanimous and humane," influential Canadian historian William L. Morton strongly argued that Canadian conservatives had emerged as the protectors of true liberalism because conservatism, as opposed to liberalism or socialism, was not constrained by dogma.[145] Morton asserts that conservatives—representing the party of tradition rather than the party of ideology—"can keep going. They can pick up anything, including traditional liberalism. There's no countervailing ideology."[146]

Although Morton's assertion sounds extreme, there is evidence to support it. By the middle of the twentieth century, the Liberals had appeared to become more concerned with the cultivation of state power and technological progress over individual freedom, leaving Conservatives, mostly sitting in the loyal opposition in the House of

---

[143] Ibid., 10.
[144] Charles Taylor, *Radical Tories: The Conservative Tradition in Canada* (Toronto, ON: Anansi Press, 1982), 71.
[145] Ibid., 73.
[146] Quoted in Ibid.

Commons, with the challenge of protecting people from bureaucratic tyranny. This did not require accepting laissez-faire economics and rugged individualism, as neither was a principle of conservative thought. Instead, Morton urged acceptance of the welfare state, in order to keep it humanely administered for the benefit of all. Thus, Morton advocated strong support of education, support of the arts, strengthening of the rule of law and courts, while reducing the power of the Prime Minister's Office by encouraging parliamentary and ministerial independence. Morton believed that in these approaches, conservatives would be able to preserve the liberal spirit in Canada.[147]

Whether Canada's Conservative Party (known as the Progressive Conservative Party between 1942 and 2003) deserves credit, or if these developments were a natural outgrowth of the Canadian personality's early immersion in Toryism that transcends contemporary political party allegiance, it is apparent that Canadians have tended to be less persistent than Americans in asserting their individual rights. For example, the formal "Canadian Charter of Rights and Freedoms" did not become part of the Canadian constitution until 1982 compared to the US Bill of Rights, which became law in 1791 as part of the first ten amendments to the US Constitution. Taylor suggests this is a negative result of Canada's conservative emphasis on the maintenance of "peace, order and good government."[148] This trend helps confirm the underlying Tory character of Canada.

Canada's British heritage was a natural fit for Toryism. Although the modern political entity of Canada traces back to Confederation of 1867 and the creation of a compact between two charter—yet unequal—groups of British and French origin, British cultural influence predominated due to circumstances a century earlier. This inequality arose on the 1759 Quebec battlefield of the Plains of Abraham when the British defeated the French and imposed the rules of governing their mutual existence. In the decades that followed, contrary to America's British migrants in the sixteenth and seventeenth centuries, those who came to Canada reflected a powerful Tory conservative strand in British political culture. Since a majority was steeped in hierarchical churches as Anglicans and Highland Catholic Scots, many immigrants bore a faith fundamentally opposed to the strong individualism inherent in traditional liberalism. This is particularly

---

[147] Ibid., 74.
[148] Taylor, *Radical Tories*, 173.

true for Catholicism, which appears to have shaped socialist parties in numerous twentieth-century capitalist societies. Arguing why Socialism failed as a movement in the United States, Lipset and Marks assert that "Catholicism retained into the modern era [feudal] values formed in medieval times, including disdain for materialism, profits, and usury (interest)" by emphasizing conservative or "Tory communitarian values and the responsibility of the well-to-do, the state, and the church for the underprivileged." As they effectively argue, "While Protestantism has been more individualistic, Catholicism has been more group-oriented or collectivistic."[149] As argued earlier, collectivism is not a strong feature of the United States.

In Australia, Irish Catholics, occupying a significant place within the Australian Labor Party's conservative arm, exercised a "conservative" effect on the ALP. In the Canadian context, the Catholic retention of feudal values was particularly evident among the French population of Quebec—at least until the Quiet Revolution of the 1960s saw the rise of secularization, welfare state principles, and nationalism.[150] This was in stark contrast with English Canada where individualist values were emphasized among the upper echelons of society from which John Porter showed that Canada's cadre of managers was historically drawn. However, besides the presence of liberalism in their political thought, their close attachment to Toryism was strong because of the United Empire Loyalists' ideological affinity for Tory conservatism. After all, many immigrants to English Canada not only identified with Disraeli's Victorian conservatism but also its earlier precursor, the Second Tory Party of the eighteenth century.[151]

Canadian historian Norman Penner argues that, first, the conservative Toryism of British colonial authorities was strengthened by the *Quebec Act* of 1775 through which their latest North American acquisition was ruled in cooperation with the remnants of the ruling elite of New France and the clerical absolutism of the *ancien régime*—a develop-

---

[149] Seymour Martin Lipset and Gary Marks, *It Didn't Happen Here: Why Socialism Failed in the United States* (New York, NY: W.W. Norton & Company, 2000), 148.

[150] James Struthers and Ronald E. Mendelsohn, "Federalism and the Evolution of Social Policy and the Welfare State," in *Federalism in Canada and Australia: Historical Perspectives, 1920–1988*, ed. Bruce W. Hodgins, John J. Eddy, Shelagh D. Grant, and James Struthers (Peterborough, ON: The Frost Centre for Canadian Heritage and Development Studies, Trent University, 1989), 234–36.

[151] William Christian and Colin Campbell, *Political Parties and Ideologies in Canada*, 3rd ed. (Toronto, ON: McGraw-Hill Ryerson Ltd., 1990), 282.

ment that alienated both English-speaking merchants who had wanted an elective assembly, and the French who had hoped to be freed from the burden of Church tithes and payments of feudal rents to the seigneurs. Second, the ruling Tory conservative ideology was further reinforced by waves of United Empire Loyalist immigrants to Canada following the American Revolution, War of 1812, and the defeat of the 1837 and 1838 Rebellions.[152]

The outlook of the Loyalists made them strongly inclined to support and reinforce the Tory ideology of British rule in Canada. As Canadian sociologist, S.D. Clark contends, "The War gave to the Loyalists a new self-consciousness and a new sense of their importance, which quickly made them a powerful conservative force in Upper Canadian politics in a way that they had never been before." Clark asserts, "Through their influence Toryism became a much more distinctive creed of the ruling class, in politics, religion, and social life generally."[153] However, these forces of Canadian conservatism not only drew strength from the local colonial administrators but from its British source. During this period, Clark observes, "Toryism was very much in the ascendancy . . . [and] the political conservatism of the mother country offered direct support to the political conservatism of the colonial population."[154]

Of critical importance to the course of Canadian cultural development, therefore, was the change in roles that occurred following the collapse of Tory power in Britain due to the success of the reform movement. Penner asserts,

> Instead of the local Tory elements acting at the behest of the governors appointed by the British government, these governors began more and more to act as creatures of the local entrenched interest. And when the local Tory power collapsed in the face of the growing popular support for the reform movement in Upper and Lower Canada [Ontario and Quebec], the British army had to step in on behalf of local conservatism, which it regarded as the only reliable bastion of British colonial rule.[155]

---

[152] Norman Penner, *The Canadian Left: A Critical Analysis* (Scarborough, ON: Prentice-Hall, 1977), 7–8.

[153] S.D. Clark, *Movements of Political Protest in Canada, 1640–1840* (Toronto, ON: University of Toronto Press, 1959), 247. Quoted in Penner, 8–9.

[154] Ibid., 251. Quoted in Penner, 9.

[155] Penner, 9.

In other words, Tory conservatism thrived in Canada even when it was on the decline in Britain. Hence, although radical and democratic ideas would find significant channels of support in the twentieth century, these nineteenth-century developments were of vital importance to the cultivation and maintenance of a dominant Canadian ideological view. This description of Tory influence is more correctly applied to central and Eastern Canada where settlement patterns were older, reflecting a more direct impact of Loyalist immigrants than compared to Western Canada's settlement of later waves of British, eastern European, and American migrants. More will be said about this later, particularly in light of Nelson Wiseman's insights on the influences on Canada's political culture. Hence, central and eastern Canada did represent a fundamental driving force behind the development of Canadian culture. Indeed, Canada is a blend of liberalism and conservatism, or what Horowitz has characterized as "liberal with a tory touch."[156]

Two significant implications flowed from the impact of Tory conservatism's retention in Canada compared to its decline in Britain. First, not only did the evolving political culture of Britain not change the political culture of Canada but Britain—despite a domestic movement toward democratic liberalism—had actually supported the conservative elements that were against democratic liberalism in Canada. From this point on, notes Penner, "Canadian Toryism was to develop as a self-generating ideology, in conflict with the local forces of democracy, and taking on distinctive characteristics in response to local circumstances."[157] Second, Canada's Tory elite was able to benefit from the British colonial connection to help strengthen its hold on the privileged positions of domestic Canadian power. Canada's Tory elite increasingly found it useful, if not essential, to keep the forms together with some of the substance of colonialism as a tool of self-protection. Hence, the elite praised the old British values, adhered to a Burkean emphasis on constituted authority, remained conservative about social change, and strongly supported hierarchical tradition and privilege.[158] As noted earlier, it is from the social and economic elite that Canada's managers were generally drawn.

---

[156] Gad Horowitz, "Conservatism, Liberalism, and Socialism in Canada: An Interpretation," in *Canada's Origins: Liberal, Tory, or Republican?*, ed. Janet Ajzenstat and Peter J. Smith (Ottawa, ON: Carleton University Press, 1995), 148–50.

[157] Penner, 9.

[158] Ibid.

Tory paternalism was indeed a distinctive feature of the Canadian manager. For example, the British Columbia Electric Railway (BCER), a large West coast employer, tended to avoid labor disputes by following a policy of deliberate, enlightened paternalism. As Bliss notes:

> Paternalism often worked, particularly in firms profitable enough to give it a real cash value. In human terms, it often led to a willingness to discuss grievances with committees of men, or, as with the BCER, to get along with a local union, especially a cooperative one. There was much more resistance to negotiating with paid union organizers, outside "agitators" whose income seemed to depend on fomenting conflict between capital and labour and whose organization, employers thought, probably had no real concern for either a company's or its workers' interests. . . . [T]he attitude of most businessmen to the power and the leveling tendencies of unions was nicely summarized in the Canadian Manufacturers' Association's journal, *Industrial Canada*, in 1909: "Unionism undoubtedly is a good thing in some ways, but like strychnine, it must be taken in small doses."[159]

While management's toleration of smaller-scale unions permitted a sense of collectivism to exist in the Canadian workplace, "enlightened paternalism" remained a powerful influence on Canadian managers well into the late twentieth century.[160] By the 1980s, when management was experimenting with various ideas to contend with the downward trend in the economy, paternalism continued to represent an enduring characteristic of Canadian managers. During this challenging period, Bliss writes:

> There were no magic answers in creating good firms to work for. Management might be centralized or decentralized, or a little of both. Performance standards, job descriptions, compensation

---

[159] Bliss, *Northern Enterprise*, 358.

[160] Paternalism is a feature of individualism. As "the corollary of paternalism is the deferential worker," Oxford University's John Purcell observes, the Paternalistic style falls in "between high individualism, with its emphasis on employee development, and low individualism concerned with labour control treating employees as a commodity to be exploited in the pursuit of profit." John Purcell, "Mapping Management Styles in Employee Relations," *Journal of Management Studies* 24, no. 5 (1987): 538.

packages, might be rigidly prescribed or highly flexible, or a little of both. A corporation might be lean and hungry, traveling economy fare, or it might decide its high-performing employees deserved the best of everything. It was often shocking when blue-ribbon companies made their first layoffs in the 1980s, but there was a knack of wielding the knife humanely and cementing the loyalties of those who stayed. . . . The idea of showing wise personal concern for the people you worked with, treating them with near-familial regard or affection, rewarding achievement and offering security and a shared value-system, had deep roots in the enlightened paternalism of the best nineteenth-century employers.[161]

Hence, Canadian managers retained a conservative view about change while supporting their historic tradition of hierarchical rule and privilege within the organization. As in Australia, however, it was the working class that helped modulate Canadian management behavior due to the pervasive impact of an influential socialist political movement that developed, in part, because of the Canadian Tory heritage.

The British character of Canadian socialism

The statist orientation brought to Canada primarily by the Loyalists, combined with the rise of Victorian-era Tory collectivism, provided English Canada with a foundation upon which socialist ideas and policies could be accommodated within the Canadian political culture. While Canadian managers and workers largely accepted traditional hierarchical arrangements that were conservative in origin, Canada was also open to the importation of Western European socialist ideas because of an earlier familiarity with collectivist Toryism that neither Australia nor the United States shared to the same degree as Canada.[162] As a result, Canadians were simultaneously accepting of nonegalitarian hierarchies and certain aspects of liberal individualism—like political freedom, equality of opportunity, limited government—but also certain Tory collectivist trends, such as government-run Crown

---

[161] Bliss, *Northern Enterprise*, 567–68.

[162] Encel asserts that the most effective doctrines for Australia came from the collectivist liberals and Fabian socialists of the late nineteenth century, discounting Chartism which more recent historians such as Hugh Collins, discussed in Chapter 6, convincingly claim was distinctly important in Australian culture. *See* Encel, *Equality and Authority*, 51.

corporations, equality of access to such social programs as health care, education, work opportunities, and deferential behavior as maintained in the Canadian political culture with the reigning British monarch remaining the titular head of state. Thus, Canadian managers enjoyed rank and privilege with the tacit approval of the working class provided that the former adhered to Canadian egalitarian principles outlined earlier.

Canadian egalitarianism relied on an assertive socialist-inspired movement that captured the mood of the masses while not disturbing the hierarchical tradition of Canadian management.

Many Americans would regard Canadian socialism as entirely "un-American" not merely because a significant socialist force has made its mark on the Canadian political landscape when it had not done so in the United States, but, notes Horowitz, because "it does not speak the same language as American socialism. In Canada, socialism is British, non-Marxist, and worldly; in the United States it is German, Marxist, and otherworldly."[163] Horowitz's distinction is useful for understanding the British character of Canadian socialist ideas and their support base in Canada.

Many of the builders of Canadian labor and socialist groups were either British immigrants with prior experience in the British labor movement or the Canadian-born offspring of these same immigrants. In contrast, when socialist ideas made their way to the United States, they found themselves in a thoroughly untenable ideological environment because, Horowitz observes, "Lockean individualism had long since achieved the status of a national religion; the political culture had already congealed, and socialism did not fit. American socialism was alien not only in this ideological sense, but in the ethnic sense as well; it was born by foreigners from Germany and other continental European countries."[164] Indeed, they were handicapped not only because they were continental European socialists but because they had supported the Marxist "brand" of socialism, which had never found broad support in the United States or any other English-speaking country—neither in Britain, Canada, Australia, nor New Zealand.[165]

According to Horowitz, "The socialism of the United States, the socialism of De Leon, Berger, Hillquit, and Debs, is predominantly

---

[163] Horowitz, *Canadian Labour in Politics*, 24.
[164] Ibid.
[165] Ibid., 24–25.

Marxist and doctrinaire, because it is European. The socialism of English Canada, the socialism of Simpson, Woodsworth, and Coldwell is predominantly Protestant, labourist, and Fabian, because it is British."[166] Thus, for European socialists in America, many left their socialist ideals behind at the start of the integration process of becoming Americans. Socialism—whether Marxist or Fabian—was not an ideologically acceptable ingredient in the American melting pot.

In contrast to the American socialist experience, the situation was entirely different for a British immigrant to Canada. As Horowitz describes,

> The British immigrant was not an "alien." Canada was British North America, under the British crown and the British flag. The English-Canadian culture not only granted legitimacy to his political ideas and absorbed them into its wholeness; it absorbed him as a person into the English-Canadian community, with relatively little strain, without demanding that he change his entire way of life before being granted full citizenship. He was acceptable to begin with, by virtue of being British. It is impossible to understand the differences between American and Canadian socialism without taking into account this immense difference between the ethnic contexts of socialism in the two countries.[167]

In Canada, the socialist ideas that received the greatest support in the early twentieth century were those associated with labor leaders of British—primarily English and Scottish origin—and a religious tone contrary to Marxist labor rhetoric in Europe and Russia. For example, The Fabian Society, a British socialist intellectual movement founded in 1884 to advance the socialist cause by means of reform rather than revolution, was one of the intellectual pillars that led to the establishment of the British Labour Party in 1900.[168] It tempered British socialism and attracted a strong following in Britain and in Canada.

---

[166] Ibid., 26. *See also*, Horowitz, "Conservatism, Liberalism, and Socialism in Canada," 34.

[167] Horowitz, *Canadian Labour in Politics*, 25.

[168] The British Labour Party, founded in 1900 as a result of the ferment of socialist ideas taking place since 1880, was a federation of various trade unions and several socialist groups featuring the ideas of Labor Marxism of the Social Democratic Federation (SDF), Fabianism of the Fabian Society, and the Ethical Socialism of the Independent Labour Party (ILP). An explicit ideology was not acknowledged until the party's constitution of 1918, but emerged as "a distinctive brand of British socialism which has fed the party's basic ideals and ethics

Contrary to many continental European socialists, Fabian Socialism stood against Marxism and strived to demonstrate that socialism was entirely compatible with British political institutions. Consequently, the Fabians proved to be strict constitutionalists who considered Parliament and the Civil Service as perfectly adequate means of achieving socialism since this British brand of socialism emphasized the peaceful, gradual transition from a capitalist to a socialist society. As British historian Geoffrey Foote observes, contrary to the Marxist call for the replacement of the machinery of the state with a new type of state, "the Fabians identified socialism with the extension of the existing British state— with its monarch, parliament, courts and military."[169] They rejected violence and unconstitutional activities as a means of promoting change because they believed that elections were the most effective means of replacing the state control by the "leisured classes" with members of the industrial classes.[170]

The Fabians were ardent imperialists because they believed in the positive nature of the British Empire. Ironically, they were not particularly supportive of the leadership of the working class which they viewed as largely inept and narrow minded. For this reason they tended to infuse the Liberal and Conservative Parties with their presence, both municipally and nationally.[171] Therefore, despite being one of the founders of the British Labour Party, they were indifferent to its success.

Nonetheless, these early Fabians provided the British Labour Party with an intellectual background that suited its laborist structure. According to Foote:

They made a major contribution to the emerging ideology of British socialism with their doctrines of gradual progress towards a collectivised economy and the necessity of constitutional action, as well as a new theory of the economic surplus which could counter the Marxists. Not all their views were acceptable to British Socialism— their pro-imperial strain offended the liberal element in most socialists—but they succeeded in giving socialism a distinct British form, distancing it from subverting European trappings. They gave the

---

to the present day." Geoffrey Foote, *The Labour Party's Political Thought: A History*, 3rd ed. (New York, NY: St. Martin's Press, 1997), 18.

[169] Ibid., 29.
[170] Ibid., 29–30.
[171] Ibid., 32.

Labour Party a credibility which [served to] *supplement,* not *replace,* its labourism.[172]

The emergence of British socialism as a popular force among the working classes did not depend on the Fabians but the Ethical Socialists.[173] Yet, for the Fabians of England, just like the mainstream labor politicians who emerged in Canada, electoral achievement was deemed the primary means for societal change, not revolutionary Marxist socialism which was so feared by Americans who tended to equate socialism with Marxism. As for mainstream socialism in Canada, Marxism was not a popular trend and did not receive substantial public support. Canadian social democracy, notes Canadian sociologist Lynn McDonald, was shaped

> by the Labour Party (especially Keir Hardie), Fabianism, and Christian socialism (notably F.D. Maurice and Charles Kingsley) in Britain. It was also influenced by the social gospel movement in the United States (especially Walter Rauschenbusch and Reinhold Niebuhr). Most of all, it was influenced by the social gospel movement in Canada itself. . . . [T]his movement drew on all of these sources to arrive at its own distinctive analysis of problems, and to fashion its own response to them.[174]

Without a doubt, in Canada many of the key democratic socialist leaders were closely associated with the Protestant reformist Social Gospel movement. J.S. Woodsworth and Tommy Douglas are two of the most significant given their influential roles in bringing the socialist concerns of the masses into mainstream politics. Woodsworth, a Methodist minister, was the first leader of the CCF and Douglas, a former Baptist minister, the first CCF leader to form a government (as premier of the province of Saskatchewan in 1944).

The influx of large numbers of British immigrants near the turn of the twentieth century to the Canadian West reflected the thriving labor-socialist interests of Britain's working class. They had followed an earlier wave of Canadian migrants from Ontario to the Prairies whose "Tory-touched Canadian liberalism" was at the ideological core of nineteenth-century Ontario and its Prairie derivative. British socialists thrived in

---

[172] Ibid., 33.

[173] Ibid., 33–34.

[174] Lynn McDonald, *The Party That Changed Canada: The New Democratic Party, Then and Now* (Toronto, ON: Macmillan, 1987), 5.

this environment as Tory collectivism was far more compatible than was American liberal individualism.[175]

According to Canadian historian Nelson Wiseman, four waves of immigrants to the Prairie Provinces illustrate this phenomenon. They were, respectively, a Canadian rural Ontarian population infused by Tory-nuanced Canadian liberalism which was at the ideological center of nineteenth-century Ontario and the Prairies; a British working class that held to the British labor-socialist tradition which germinated due to Canada's earlier Toryism; Americans who represented a radical "populist" liberalism devoid of Toryism more prominent in Alberta; and continental central and eastern Europeans who were largely deferential to the ideologies and political parties of Canada's two Charter groups.[176]

Likewise, a later wave of immigrants, continental Europeans, had a strong impact on urban Winnipeg and rural Saskatchewan where they tended to be deferential to dominant Canadian ideologies, wanting to prove their loyalty to their new nation voting Liberal and Conservative, never leading a major party but solidifying the support of those established by other waves. Later, they helped elect socialist governments in Manitoba and Saskatchewan that were built primarily by British immigrants.[177]

Without the new-British impact, however, a Canadian socialist party would never have attained the stature that it did, and may not have even been created at all. According to Wiseman, the impact of "transplanted ideas"—like socialism—was greater in Canada's west than in the United States because the physical impact of immigrants was greater. The British arrived from a highly urbanized industrial society and benefited from a century of evolving working-class consciousness that this new-British group of immigrants to Canada possessed.[178]

The religious background of many leaders among British labor-socialists proved highly influential. Wiseman maintains that "Methodists and other social gospellers had their greatest impact in places like Winnipeg where the British-born laborist wave was particularly strong. Catholicism, brought over by many continental Europeans, was strongest in Saskatchewan and contributed to the Liberals' long hold

---

[175] Nelson Wiseman, "The Pattern of Prairie Politics," *Queen's Quarterly* 88, no. 2 (1981): 299.
[176] Ibid.
[177] Ibid., 300–1.
[178] Ibid., 301.

on power there. Anglicans, with roots in both Ontario and Britain, reinforced Conservative tendencies in all three provinces."[179]

The result of this influx of British immigrants made Winnipeg the central location of labor parties and trade unions. The Winnipeg General Strike of 1919—one in a long series of violent confrontations, and certainly among the most influential in Canadian history with its massive showing of labor defiance by nearly 30,000 workers—took three levels of government combined to defeat the protest. The decision to take this action was made by the Federal Government, which was still the wartime Unionist coalition that had brought the Conservatives together with a majority of Liberals.[180]

Not only was every imprisoned strike leader (with just one exception) originally from Britain—having immigrated to Winnipeg between 1896 and 1912—but the majority of the most influential political representatives of this radical ideology, including Woodsworth and Tommy Douglas, were also not born in the Prairies.[181] Woodsworth was born in Ontario while Douglas hailed from Scotland. Not only did this underscore the immense influence of the immigration of British radicals to Canada, but it shows an important strain of socialism that reflected strong religious overtones. While Marxism tended to be popularized by radical unionists from the US or central Europe, the Canadian Socialist League and CCF believed in and expressed socialism's inherent religious basis.

Woodsworth—descended from United Empire Loyalists through his mother—reflected domestic Tory collectivism but also believed in classless egalitarianism and the Social Gospel movement's goal to educate people and improve their social conditions, not through revolution but through principles of socialism espoused by the British Labour Party, and the associated religious, ethical, and Fabian streams.[182] Hence, after Woodsworth's entry into the political arena in 1921, Manitoba became, like Britain, a hotbed of laborism rather than Marxism or syndicalism, which spread beyond Winnipeg as far west as Vancouver, accounting for the later strength of the CCF-NDP in these cities.[183] Regarding the

---

[179] Ibid., 302.

[180] Penner, *The Canadian Left*, 28.

[181] Wiseman, "The Pattern of Prairie Politics," 299, 305.

[182] Christian and Campbell, *Political Parties and Ideologies in Canada*, 180–83.

[183] Wiseman, "The Pattern of Prairie Politics," 305. The NDP is considered a democratic socialist party as it does not practice the same type of socialism as the CCF. While the CCF wanted to completely rid Canada of capitalism, which

western province of British Columbia where Vancouver remains the largest and most populous city, Canadian historian Gordon Hak observes that, while the intellectual world of socialism includes Marxism, "In BC during the first decades of the twentieth century some socialists were radical, even revolutionary, while others were more moderate in their ideas and behaviours."[184] Socialist thought in British Columbia was considered wide ranging and permitted a variety of views and actions to be deemed socialist.

As significant as the socialist movement was to Canada, it would not have progressed without the earlier acceptance of the Tory collectivist strand. Hence, as Horowitz asserts, "Socialists disagree with liberals about the essential meaning of equality because socialists have a tory conception of society."[185] As pointed out, this Toryism is that part of the Canadian national character that accepts social hierarchy, monarchy, and hierarchical churches. It reflects the Great Chain of Being, the basis of social interaction that held British society together for centuries, and also the Tory collectivist developments of the nineteenth century as represented by Disraeli in Great Britain.

Unlike the later twentieth century variant, traditional conservatism of the nineteenth century was not a strong proponent of individualism and free market, *laissez-faire* economics. From a historical view, just as British liberalism grew out of seventeenth-century Whiggism, British conservatism stemmed from the Tory tradition which was also a product of the seventeenth century.[186] Whereas the Whigs were led by landowning aristocrats in favor of religious dissent and associated with developing manufacturing and commercial interests, the Tories were led by landed gentry who supported the Church of England and who stood for social hierarchy and traditional authority. Tory ideals largely carried into modern conservatism as it evolved in early nineteenth-century Britain.[187]

According to Leach, "For modern Conservatives collectivism has acquired strong negative connotations, becoming closely associated

---

permits Canadians to invest their own money to build their own wealth, the NDP only tries to control capitalism to promote social justice and equality. Hence, the NDP is a strong supporter of such social services as Medicare, pensions, daycare, and unemployment insurance.

[184] Gordon Hak, *The Left in British Columbia: A History of Struggle* (Vancouver, BC: Ronsdale Press, 2013), 35.

[185] Horowitz, *Canadian Labour in Politics*, 6.

[186] Leach, *Political Ideology in Britain*, 48.

[187] Ibid., 49.

with socialism, but it was not always so."[188] This was not the case for Canada as Red Tories were open to collectivist ideas akin to Disraeli's programs in the nineteenth century. As Taylor asserts, Red Tories "are conservatives with a conscience. Respecting tradition and order they are also concerned with social justice and are willing to use public power to curtail private greed."[189]

Given Canada's Tory past, and the significance of welfare liberalism in Canadian political culture, Horowitz coined the term "Red Tory," unique to Canadian parlance, to describe the views of many Canadian conservatives who believe in state intervention to address social policy issues. In contrast with the more fiscally conservative business liberalism of "Blue Tories," Red Tories reflect three key elements: First, they are sympathetic to the British traditions embedded in Canada's heritage, while resisting and resenting American political, economic and cultural intrusion to the extent that they prefer integration with Europe rather than North America. Second, they support using the state to help achieve nation building, and accordingly it was conservative governments that built the first transcontinental railway, established the Canadian Broadcasting Corporation (CBC), and founded the Bank of Canada. Third, they question the power of unregulated capitalism to serve Canada's best interests.[190] Thus, welfare liberalism was not only promoted by proponents within the Liberal Party of Canada but also embraced by socialists and by Red Tory conservatives.[191]

Among Canada's original Red Tories was John A. Macdonald, the nation's first prime minister and Conservative Party leader. Macdonald was born in Glasgow, Scotland to Highland parents, yet thoroughly British in attitude and outlook, and strongly influenced by Victorian-era British conservatism. In 1820, he settled with his parents in Kingston, Ontario, a small city largely populated by recent British immigrants and descendants of American-born United Empire Loyalists.[192] Kingston, notes Gordon Donaldson, had "a well-established Scottish community, close, clannish and canny [where] the Scots tribal password: 'We're all Jock Tamson's bairns' applied. This meant each Scot would help the

---

[188] Ibid., 63.
[189] Taylor, *Radical Tories*, 115.
[190] Ball, Dagger, Christian, and Campbell, *Political Ideologies*, 104.
[191] Ibid., 67.
[192] Michael Bliss, *Right Honourable Men: The Descent of Canadian Politics from Macdonald to Mulroney* (Toronto, ON: HarperCollins, 1994), 8–9.

other up to a certain point—at which he either stood on his own feet or got out from under foot."[193]

In modern-day Ontario where Scots dominated politics, Macdonald, notes Donaldson, "retained as his Scottish birthright a healthy distrust of the English—particularly the chinless aristocrats who ran the North American colonies before the colonies achieved a measure of popular representation and responsible government," but he was also not a fan of the United States. "The Kingston Scots had no time for the Anglican snobs in Toronto," Donaldson notes, "but the town was loyal to the Crown in a way that only a town threatened by repeated Yankee raids from across Lake Ontario could be."[194] Indeed, loyalty to the British Crown ensured a separation from postrevolutionary America.

About this pervasive Scottish atmosphere in central Canada, influential Canadian-born American economist John Kenneth Galbraith wrote in his early memoir, *The Scotch*, of his own experiences growing up in Scottish Canadian Elgin County in southern Ontario.[195]

Macdonald joined the Tories and began a political career about the same time as Benjamin Disraeli began his in England. As Bliss observes, "Macdonald was an avid reader of British history, British fiction, British magazines, and British political writing . . . , met most of the leading British politicians of his time . . . and, in fact, was often mistaken for Benjamin Disraeli, to whom he had a strong physical resemblance."[196] With the British North America Act that created Canada in 1867, Macdonald together with the other Fathers of Confederation created a largely British political structure where provinces were subordinate to the federal government, and where authority flowed from the British monarch through Canada's central government and then to provincial and local governments.

Consistent with the Tory tradition, this was a hierarchical system that allowed for central authority much like in England while also drawing on the American experience. Although the central government, the House of Commons, was based on representation by population, the Senate was to be appointed rather than elected to help protect the minorities from the masses—just as the House of Lords in Britain—and therefore

---

[193] Gordon Donaldson, *The Prime Ministers of Canada* (Toronto, ON: Doubleday Canada, 1994), 3–4.

[194] Ibid., 5.

[195] See John Kenneth Galbraith, *The Scotch* (Boston, MA: Houghton Mifflin, 1964).

[196] Bliss, *Right Honourable Men*, 8–9.

protect local and regional interests by ensuring equal representation from the three large regions of the new Canada—Ontario, Quebec, and the Maritimes along the Atlantic coast. Bliss notes, "This protection of territorial distinctiveness vaguely mimicked the United States Senate, in which each state had equal representation."[197] Despite such American influences, Macdonald, notes Donaldson, "would set no melting pots aboiling; that way disaster lay." Instead, Macdonald worked to cultivate a Canada that would remain a British nation that contained a proud and, he hoped, conciliatory French minority.[198]

In Canada, as politically minded individuals began to align with Tory and Reform parties, and their subsequent variants—the Conservatives and Liberals—Scots initially found themselves in both camps. However, Macdonald's Highland Scottish origin, not unlike those among the ranks of the English gentry, gave him a natural affinity for conservatism. Other Scots followed suit. In the late eighteenth century, a Scot from Edinburgh, Dr. Adam Mabane, had been an early proponent of Toryism in Canada whose warnings of the dangers of American democracy and of the necessity for resistance to political change were later amplified in Toryism.[199] As Margaret MacLaren Evens argues, "It was clear even in the late eighteenth century that the Scots' experience with the English at home would affect their thinking on what should be done about practical questions arising in Canada."[200]

* * *

Since the privileged occupation of management in Australia and Canada was historically comprised of those of British origin, this social stratum retained a strong element of individualism. As a result, there was tension between a more individualist management layer versus a workforce and assertive labor parties more accepting of collectivism. Although collectivism is less evident among the ranks of Australian and Canadian managers—traditionally males with similar ethnic, socioeconomic, and cultural origins—their managerial approaches were compelled to accommodate, at least to some extent, the dispositions of

---

[197] Ibid., 13–14.
[198] Donaldson, *The Prime Ministers of Canada*, 12.
[199] A. Margaret MacLaren Evans, "The Scot as Politician," in *The Scottish Tradition in Canada*, ed. W. Stanford Reid (Toronto, ON: McClelland & Stewart, 1976), 273–74.
[200] Ibid., 274.

their respective working classes. This reflected a general societal trend. At the turn of the nineteenth century, Lloyd Cox observes, "most liberal and radical observers had concluded that although Liberal parties generally ruled in Australasia, the progressive character of its social arrangements was at least in part due to the influence of organized Labour."[201] In Canada, this influence emerged later.

The successful introduction to Australian industry of what John Mathews termed the "new production methods" suggested a cultural fit between these approaches and the Australian worker's temperament. Consistent with Mathews' findings, workplace problems seem to have been more common when Australian firms emphasized what Christopher Wright termed "the low trust model," with Australian managers adopting a "dictatorial and authoritarian approach to the employment and training of workers, providing minimal job security, seeking to sub-divide and dilute work, and exhibiting an explicit hostility to trade unionism."[202] The "low trust" management model reflects the more individualist scientific management trend that, consistent with the Australian character, was not widely accepted by Australian workers; nor were Canadian workers drawn to it.

Accounting for the lesser tolerance of scientific management and greater appeal of the human relations approach is collectivism because of its differential effect on the cultivation of local egalitarianism. Despite their greater affinity for individualism, therefore, managers had to contend with a strong collectivist impulse among the working class. Firms that implemented policies accommodating worker preferences appear to have experienced positive results compared to those that have not.[203] Hence, Australian and Canadian managerial styles, while generally more sympathetic to the ideals of individualism and its derivative of paternalism, often modulated in response to the culturally

---

[201] Lloyd Cox, "The Antipodean Social Laboratory, Labour and the Transformation of the Welfare State," *Journal of Sociology* 42, no. 2 (2006): 108.

[202] Wright, *The Management of Labour*, 215.

[203] Examples were discussed earlier in this chapter, particularly through John Mathews' description of "new production systems," a reform of work structures which were generally well-received by Australian labor. The implementation of team-based performance pay, gainsharing policies, and self-managing shop floor teams proved to be positive workplace motivators, which seemed to accommodate a largely collectivist labor mentality. Indeed, the apparently successful implementation of these policies in such Australian firms as Ford Plastics, Bendix Mintex, and Colonial Mutual, suggests a high degree of Australian cultural acceptance. *See* Mathews, *Catching the Wave*, 10–11, 216–17, 220, 227–28.

dominant values of the respective working classes. Canada's cadre of managers, while emulating the Tory character that helped inspire Canadian socialism, could therefore accept pro-social organizational policies that preserved the dignity of workers, while not feeling under threat of attack on the perceived legitimacy of vertical hierarchy.

The underlying ideological influences on managers and workers are further explored next to contrast the cultural effect of Toryism and socialism in the Canadian context with the more radical and Irish-infused cultural impact in Australia. In both countries, workers wielded considerable power and, as a direct consequence, asserted their values.

6
Labor Power

From colonial times through the mid-twentieth century, as Australia and Canada developed their respective economies, political movements, and national personalities, the ruling British Protestant elite assumed key leadership positions in public administration, commerce, and politics. However, the impact on local culture was not identical because the composition of the dominant populations differed. Unlike Canada, the Australian working class was marked by a strong Irish Catholic presence. Hence, their influence grew as Australia's working class rose to prominence through the establishment of the Australian Labor Party (ALP).

Since electoral success is a strong hint of popular support and common values, Labor's triumphant penetration of the Australian political party system—not matched in Canada to the same degree—confirms Irish influence given the significant Irish Catholic population among the rank and file of Australian workers. Therefore, even more important than the values and attitudes of governing elites to the evolving shape of Australia's national culture were those of the working class. The values, attitudes, and prevailing cultural norms of labor exerted a profound effect on the general culture. For Canada, in contrast, the values of the elite were widely shared by key segments of the working class largely due to complementary ideological support from a broad ethnic cross section of Canadian immigrants.[1]

Class distinctions not only reveal particular Anglo-Celtic origins—strengthened by the culturally empowering and collectively binding force of religious identity—but also the impact of significant ideological

---

[1] *See* Nelson Wiseman, "The Pattern of Prairie Politics," *Queen's Quarterly* 88, no. 2 (1981): 298–315.

204

strands of thought that appealed to these influential populations. Beyond a common thread of liberal individualism that flows through the Anglo cluster of nations, there are also reflections of collectivism derived largely from the evolving ideologies of conservatism and socialism. In the present chapter, therefore, Australia and Canada's state systems of conciliation and arbitration are considered to discern their impact on local culture and to further explore their ideological and ethnocultural attributes. The influence of labor in this process proved vital.

The rise of labor in Australian and Canadian political culture

Over the course of its history, Canada has proven to be a more strongly hierarchical society compared to the United States.[2] The same appears true for Canada over Australia. While the acceptance of hierarchy is less overt in the early twenty-first century compared to the 1950s and 1960s when Canadian sociologist John Porter made his major analysis of Canadian social structure, it remains, as pointed out in the earlier discussion of cultural dimensions research, a strong feature of Canadian culture. Likewise, hierarchy has permeated Canadian society to a far greater extent than in Australia. Not only has it reflected obvious economic differences between wealthy and working class but has become salient during key moments in Canada's history. Examples include the historic political domination of English Canadians over French Canadians, of White British colonial administrators over Aboriginals, of central Canadian power concentrated in Ontario over the rest of the provinces, and of foreign powers like the United Kingdom and the United States over Canadian perceptions of national sovereignty. Similarly, the employer–employee relationship, as considered in the prior chapter, also evokes social hierarchy.

Given the rapid growth and development of trade unionism since the nineteenth century, similar patterns of union membership across the Western industrialized democracies might be expected. However, union densities in industrialized nations reveal widely varying levels of worker participation. Substantial differences in union density are evident when comparing, for example, Scandinavian countries to former British colonies over the second half of the twentieth century. Such a comparison reveals far greater density in Sweden and Denmark than in Canada, Australia, or the United States, as Table 6.1 shows:

---

[2] John Porter, *Vertical Mosaic: An Analysis of Social Class and Power in Canada* (Toronto, ON: University of Toronto Press, 1965), 6.

Table 6.1   Union Density in Developed Nations, 1950–1995 (Ranked by 1995 Estimates)[3]

Country	1950[a]	1960	1970	1980	1990	1995
Sweden	67.3	70.7	66.6	78.2	82.4	87.5
Denmark	53.2	60.2	62.1	77.5	74.5	78.1
Ireland	38.9	45.8	54.2	57.4	48.2	44.4
Canada	n.a.	28.3	29.8	36.0	36.0	37.0[b]
Australia	n.a.	49.1	44.4	48.0	41.0	35.2
United Kingdom	44.1	44.3	48.6	52.8	40.1	32.2
United States	n.a.	28.9	25.9	22.0	16.0	14.2

[a] n.a., not available.
[b] For 1994.

Source: Adapted from Seymour Martin Lipset and Noah M. Meltz, *The Paradox of American Unionism: Why Americans Like Unions More Than Canadians Do But Join Much Less* (Ithaca, NY: ILR Press, 2004), 12, Table 2.2.

Contrary to Scandinavia where trade union membership has been extremely high with figures well above 50 percent, the table suggests that union membership in Australia and Canada—both in excess of 35 percent—is in closer proximity to the general union membership trends in the United Kingdom and Ireland. Among Anglo cultures, however, the rate of union membership in the United States has been substantially lower, particularly in relation to Australia but also in comparison with neighboring Canada.[4] Similarly, among all English-speaking countries, collective-bargaining coverage—another measure of union strength besides union membership—has been low relative to Scandinavian, German-speaking, and southern European countries. It is worth noting that these countries each score lower on levels of individualism compared to the Anglo group of cultures, emphasizing their greater collectivism.[5]

But the notable exceptions among the English-speaking countries are Australia and Ireland, where rates have been significantly higher than in Canada, the United Kingdom, and the United States. By the mid-1990s, rates of collective bargaining coverage were 90 percent for Ireland and

---

[3] Adapted from Seymour Martin Lipset and Noah M. Meltz, *The Paradox of American Unionism: Why Americans Like Unions More Than Canadians Do But Join Much Less* (Ithaca, NY: ILR Press, 2004), 12, *see* Table 2.2.

[4] Ibid.

[5] Geert Hofstede, *Cultures and Organizations: Intercultural Cooperation and its Importance for Survival* (London, UK: McGraw-Hill, 1991), 53, *see* Table 3.1.

65 percent for Australia compared to Canada's 40 percent, the United Kingdom's 47 percent, and the United States' paltry 16.7 percent.[6]

Studying the connection between union density and national culture, Gangaram Singh performed a statistical analysis comparing union density data with Hofstede's cultural dimensions data for 33 countries used in Hofstede's original scales. Singh found strong correlations between union density and power distance and masculinity. His results support the observation that greater union density occurs in societies lower in tolerance of power distance. While the comparison is more noticeable when cultures with very high union density (such as Denmark or Sweden) are compared with those very low (such as Thailand or the Philippines), the trend appears consistent with Australia and Canada.

Denmark and Sweden show union densities of 67.8 and 78.3, respectively, which corresponds to relatively low tolerance for power distance measured at 18 and 31. This contrasts with Thailand's union density of 3.2, the Philippines' 20.6, and their respective higher tolerance of power distance at 64 and 94. Falling in between but still showing an inverse relationship is Australia's average union density versus power distance measure of 34.6 versus 36, in contrast with Canada's 31.0 versus 39.[7]

Considering the earlier discussion of cultural dimensions, Australia's touch of collectivism is consistent with Australia's lesser tolerance of power distance. Just as Australia's lower tolerance of power distance relative to Canada seems strongly influenced by historic Irish sentiment, the corresponding higher union density could underscore this Celtic collectivist influence. The significant relationship evident between union density and power distance and masculinity, Singh argues, confirms that "culture should be regarded as equally important as political or economic explanations of union density."[8]

In the last two decades of the twentieth century, trade union membership declined due to rising internationalization of the global economy.[9]

---

[6] Seymour Martin Lipset and Noah M. Meltz, *The Paradox of American Unionism: Why Americans Like Unions More Than Canadians Do But Join Much Less* (Ithaca, NY: ILR Press, 2004),11–13, *see* Table 2.1.

[7] *See* Table 1 of Gangaram Singh, "National Culture and Union Density," *The Journal of Industrial Relations* 43, no. 3 (2001): 334.

[8] Ibid., 337.

[9] J.W. Shaw asserts that a large portion of the decline can be explained by the reduction in compulsory unionism ("closed shops") that has occurred throughout the economy. Shaw cites the work of David Peetz estimating that the rate of union membership among employees not working in compulsorily unionized jobs has remained steady between 23 percent and 26 percent over the

Strike levels and national government influence over labor standards also declined in many industrialized countries,[10] including Australia and the United Kingdom as revealed in the above urban density data. Until these recent developments, why has Australia shown stronger rates of union membership than many other Anglo cluster countries? And why has Canada, despite close geographical proximity, shown higher rates than the United States?

One reason for union strength that distinguishes Australia and Canada from America is each society's relative acceptance of collectivist ideas, reflecting local trends in ideology. As discussed in connection with political ideologies in the prior chapter, Americans embraced a radical populist form of classical liberalism that stressed the importance of the individual rather than the community or state. This was expressed by less enthusiastic support among American workers for trade unionism, which is inherently collectivist. In contrast with the United States, Canada possessed a Tory-nuanced liberalism that stressed community and state interests, allowing for greater acceptance of socialism and, in relative terms, a greater participation rate in trade unionism. Given these tendencies, it is no surprise that American unionists did not establish a distinctive labor party. This major point of difference in America compared to Australian and Canadian political developments reflects deeply ingrained and divergent ideological trends.

At the same time, there has been a stronger and more successful radical movement in both Australia and Canada, but with different sources of strength and support. The Irish helps account for Australia's higher participation rates in trade unionism compared to both Canada and the United States because their substantial presence in Australia—and the Irish Catholic collectivist concern for the general welfare of working-class peers—fit well with the prevailing radical ideology of the era.

Australian expert in social work and community welfare, Anthony McMahon, emphasizes the considerable contribution Australian Catholics—a substantial percentage of whom with Irish heritage—have made to the development of Australia's professional social services. He says that these contributions have not been well documented because historians like O'Farrell and Campion have written on the "broad sweep

---

same period that overall membership rates have appeared to decline. Quoted in J.W. Shaw, "In Defence of the Collective: New South Wales Industrial Relations in the 21st Century," *Journal of Industrial Relations* 39, no. 3 (1997): 390.

[10] William Brown, "Third Party Intervention Reconsidered: An International Perspective," *The Journal of Industrial Relations* 46, no. 4 (2004): 451.

of political issues that detail the long history of Catholic minority status in Australia" rather than focus specifically on Catholic social services. Likewise, while there exist numerous histories of individual Catholic orders that have provided such social services, these tend to be "vertical" histories that describe the work of their own members rather than "horizontal" histories "to show the breadth of and connections between the work of the different orders." Moreover, McMahon observes that social welfare history in Australia tends to ignore religious involvement over all, which he finds "surprising given that a history of education in Australia is defined by the 'state aid' debate and the role of Catholic schools is central to understanding the development of the Australian education system."[11]

Canada also saw an assertion of power linked to labor interests, but it came later, was strongly influenced by English and Scots steeped in British socialist and religious movements, and was less tied to a majority government in power compared to the situation in Australia. Analyzing the origins and development of the different state approaches to industrial dispute resolution adopted in Australia and Canada further reveals these influences.

State approaches to conciliation and arbitration

Australia and Canada were just two of many advanced economies—including Britain, Sweden, Denmark, Belgium, Italy, Russia, and the United States—that responded to organized workers' paralyzing strikes of the late nineteenth/early twentieth centuries with official state policies. Countries differed considerably as to how much they provided for third party intervention when dealing with the problem of strikes. Describing the diversity of methods, British industrial relations historian William Brown observes, "Some left disputes for the courts to sort out; some created, in effect, special courts; some effectively took them out of the reach of the courts altogether; and some offered third party neutrals as an optional aid." But, Brown asserts, "for none was the third party neutral role more central than for the Australian Commonwealth.[12]

Third-party involvement covers a wide assortment of neutral interventions in dispute resolution, and includes a range of procedures and

---

[11] Anthony McMahon, "Australian Catholics and the Development of Professional Social Services in Australia," in *Proceedings of the 400 Years of Charity Conference*, September 11–13, 2001, University of Liverpool, UK, 2–3. http://www.vahs.org.uk/vahs/papers/mcmahon.pdf (accessed May 14, 2014).

[12] William Brown, "Third Party Intervention Reconsidered: An International Perspective," *The Journal of Industrial Relations* 46, no. 4 (2004): 448.

practices wherein outside parties are used to solve deadlocks and arrive at settlements between employers and either organized labor or individual employees. Compared with other countries, Australia's state system has proven among the most enduring. However, before Australia's innovations first emerged in the early 1900s, the legal position of Australian trade unions had developed almost in parallel with England.[13]

In Britain during the nineteenth century, legally enforced industrial arbitration endeavors flourished. It is no surprise, therefore, that the earliest statutory approaches of conciliation and arbitration in Australia and Canada—which had provisions for *voluntary* councils (with no capacity for dispute settlement without the consent of both parties)—were strongly influenced in shape and content by the British systems. The 1867 Councils of Conciliation Act is a clear example of this trend. Canada's 1873 Trades Arbitration Act (Ontario), and Australia's 1884 and 1890 Councils of Conciliation Bills (Victoria) were based on this British precedent.[14] However, these early attempts were not successful.

The Trades Arbitration Act of Ontario failed because it lacked any practical effect on settlement of Canadian labor disputes. Motivated primarily by political expediency to attract labor support for an imminent election, Ontario's Premier Sir Oliver Mowat and his Attorney General had justified the Canadian Act on British conciliation and arbitration board successes when these boards had not been a product of the 1867 Councils of Conciliation Act but were instead the outgrowth of voluntary and private arrangements. According to Australian labor historian Richard Mitchell, the Canadian legislators "overlooked the fact that these non-statutory schemes, which provided for a mixture of collective negotiation, mediation, conciliation and arbitration were, generally speaking, the only successful devices introduced in Britain during the nineteenth century."[15] The legislation therefore made it impossible to secure any award on future wages, which led to trade union disassociation with the initiative. Hence, these and later Canadian efforts reflected a reluctance to implement any radical labor conciliation

---

[13] Ibid., 449.

[14] Richard J. Mitchell, "Solving the Great Social Problem of the Age: A Comparison of the Development of State Systems of Conciliation and Arbitration in Australia and Canada," in *Canadian and Australian Labour History: Towards a Comparative Perspective*, ed. G.S. Kealey and G. Patmore (Sydney, NSW: Australian Society for the Study of Labour History; St John's, NF: Committee on Canadian Labour History, in association with *Australian Canadian Studies*, 1990), 50–51.

[15] Ibid., 51.

and arbitration legislation, in stark contrast with the approach Australia would take.

After unsuccessful experimentation with voluntary systems of conciliation and arbitration patterned on earlier European models, between 1870 and 1910 Australia and Canada each considered implementing *compulsory* state arbitration to deal with the drawbacks inherent in the voluntary approach to resolving industrial disputes.[16] However, by the first decade of the twentieth century they had reached different conclusions. Despite their common welfare state interventionist policies, relatively week unions, lack of formal labor relations procedures, and sporadic pressure to lower wages due to structural economic weaknesses, only Australia implemented a state policy of *compulsory arbitration* while Canada adopted a state policy of *compulsory investigation*.[17] But what was the underlying basis for the adoption of such radically different approaches?

On the surface it appears that Australia showed far greater interest in the diverse conciliation and arbitration systems in use throughout the industrialized world. While the Canadian provincial parliament of Nova Scotia did pass an arbitration Act in 1888, it covered only mining disputes over new wage levels rather than existing contracts, and ultimately proved unsuccessful as it was used on only two occasions.[18] The situation in Australia was quite different. Such influential politicians as Carruthers and Dibbs of New South Wales, and Richardson of Victoria had developed what Mitchell characterizes as "a personal enthusiasm bordering on the evangelical for the principles of conciliation and arbitration."[19]

Unlike Britain, Australia had no legislation covering conciliation and arbitration before 1890. As early as 1882, however, future premier George Dibbs had introduced a bill into the New South Wales (NSW) Legislative Assembly providing for conciliation patterned on the French *Conseils de Prud'hommes* (Councils of Conciliation Board), but dropped the initiative after it failed to win support of the NSW Trades and Labour Council. The *Conseils de Prud'hommes* was perhaps the best-known early-nineteenth-century European example of dispute settlement practices. The Conseils, similar to British justices of the peace prior to the

---

[16] Ibid., 73.
[17] Ibid.
[18] Greg Patmore, *Australian Labour History* (Melbourne, VIC: Longman Cheshire, 1991), 105.
[19] Mitchell, "Solving the Great Social Problem of the Age," 51.

nineteenth century, dealt with minor industrial disputes on existing contracts, whose decisions were binding and enforceable.[20]

Similarly, Joseph Carruthers, a future Australian Liberal premier, introduced a bill to the NSW Legislative Assembly in 1887, without success, based on the British Councils of Conciliation Act of 1867. Likewise, Richard Richardson called for legislation on conciliation and arbitration in the Victorian Legislative Assembly from 1884 onward until he succeeded following the 1890 maritime strike in persuading the Victoria parliament to pass a statute for voluntary rather than compulsory arbitration based on the unsuccessful 1867 British legislation.[21]

It was not until December 1890 when the South Australian parliament introduced a bill by the Liberal member Charles Cameron Kingston recognizing, observes Greg Patmore, "that disputes arose between collectivities rather than individuals," which provided for "the registration of trade unions and employers" and enabled the Minister of Industry or the parties to refer the dispute to compulsory settlement. The South Australian parliament later passed a considerably modified version of the Bill in 1894, which did not succeed because it failed to force the parties to register under the legislation. Nonetheless, Kingston's legislation emerged as the Australasian model for compulsory arbitration legislation.[22]

A decade prior to Australia's official adoption of compulsory arbitration in 1904,[23] New Zealand introduced a radical state compulsory arbitration system in 1894. While Australia and New Zealand are the only two countries to have adopted compulsory conciliation and arbitration as national policies, a comparison of their early developments, Barry and Wailes note, "reinforces the view that arbitration did not alone shape patterns of industrial relations."[24] Their observation is underscored by the difference in the timing of each country's adoption of

---

[20] Richard Mitchell, "State Systems of Conciliation and Arbitration: The Legal Origins of the Australasian Model," in *Foundations of Arbitration: The Origins and Effects of State Compulsory Arbitration, 1890–1914*, ed. Stuart Macintyre and Richard Mitchell (Melbourne, VIC: Oxford University Press, 1989), 81.

[21] Patmore, *Australian Labour History*, 105–6. *See also* Mitchell, "State Systems of Conciliation and Arbitration," 82–84.

[22] Patmore, 106–7. For a detailed breakdown of the Bill's ten parts, *see* Mitchell, "State Systems of Conciliation and Arbitration," 85–87.

[23] A system of compulsory state arbitration was introduced in 1901 in NSW, and in 1904 at the Federal (that is, Commonwealth) level.

[24] Michael Barry and Nick Wailes, "Contrasting Systems? 100 Years of Arbitration in Australia and New Zealand," *The Journal of Industrial Relations* 46, no. 4 (2004): 432.

arbitration, the differences in wage policies that evolved, and differences in the labor movements' reaction to arbitration in the era prior to the First World War. While Australia and New Zealand adopted very similar systems, dissimilar economic and political interests shaped opposite outcomes.[25]

Compulsory arbitration became more deeply rooted in Australian industrial relations, whereas arbitration was ultimately abolished in New Zealand rather than merely weakened as in Australia. Comparing the results, Barry and Wailes conclude that "because arbitration was less embedded in New Zealand, other regulatory mechanisms—such as statutory wage intervention—served to complement the functions of the arbitral framework."[26]

The introduction of compulsory arbitration not only reflected the impact of "new liberalism" but also the resulting policy choices in response to the political and economic crises of the late nineteenth century, spawned by a decline in wool prices since the mid-1880s that had threatened Australia's and New Zealand's export trade and corresponding economic development.[27] This accounts for similarities in the models of compulsory arbitration pioneered by Kingston in South Australia, William Pember Reeves in New Zealand, and Alfred Deakin in the Australian Commonwealth,[28] and their similar mechanisms of tribunals, registration of industrial associations of employers and employees, and administrative functions.

Reeves used identical or similar concepts as those used by Kingston, including similar definitions of terms, requirements for the registration of unions, associations, industrial agreements, boards of conciliation, courts of arbitration, compulsory arbitration, and enforcement of awards and agreements. The primary differences that separate the two measures, notes Mitchell, were "in Reeves's construction of the types of boards and courts which would exercise jurisdiction over industrial disputes, but even here there were many similarities with Kingston's ideas."[29]

Mitchell emphasizes that, while a modified version of Kingston's Bill was enacted in South Australia in 1894, the original 1890 Bill remains

[25] Ibid.
[26] Ibid., 443.
[27] Ibid., 432–33.
[28] The Australian "Commonwealth" is the term Australia's constitution provides for the federal government of Australia.
[29] Mitchell, "State Systems of Conciliation and Arbitration," 87.

"the earliest version of the classical form of Australasian compulsory arbitration presented to any parliament. The Bill, in form and content, was the forerunner of the New Zealand Act of 1894, which in turn influenced the form and content of the systems established in New South Wales in 1901 and in the Australian Commonwealth in 1904."[30] This set of influences indicates an Australasian trend spearheaded in Australia rather than New Zealand. While their similarities are important, there were also important differences that separated Australia's situation from New Zealand's, particularly surrounding the question of wage policy.

Since union leaders in New Zealand considered arbitration as standing in the way of wage increases, they preferred direct bargaining to avoid this aspect embedded within New Zealand's arbitration system. Hence, assert Barry and Wailes,

> The stronger "anti-arbitrationist" tendencies of New Zealand unions reflected material differences in the benefits that workers derived under the two systems since their inception rather than a more radical ideology.... After 1908, New Zealand witnessed a widespread increase in industrial conflict and the formation of a strongly anti-arbitration trade union federation—the "Red" Federation of Labor.[31]

Although the Red Feds had articulated a revolutionary doctrine, compelling arguments have been advanced linking the decline in economic growth following 1907 and the lack of change in award wages that gave rise to New Zealand's antiarbitration movement. In contrast during the same period, Australia saw an economy continue to rapidly expand with a wage policy not nearly as restrictive due to economic growth and resulting increases in higher wages awarded by arbitration boards.[32] While the Australian Court raised wages through adjustments to cost of living indices, before 1919 there were no equivalent provisions for wage adjustments in New Zealand during the period covered by binding agreements.[33]

---

[30] Ibid.

[31] Barry and Wailes, "Contrasting Systems?," 434.

[32] Ibid., 434–35.

[33] N. Woods, *Industrial Conciliation and Arbitration in New Zealand* (Wellington, NZ: Government Printer, 1963), 98. Quoted in Barry and Wailes, "Contrasting Systems?" 434.

Besides wage issues, agricultural interests posed significant constraints on the New Zealand arbitration system. According to Barry and Wailes,

> In 1908, the [New Zealand] Court of Arbitration refused to make an award for rural labourers while across the Tasman, the Australian Workers Union obtained a federal award for shedhands as early as 1907. Because of the restrictions placed on the scope of operation of arbitration in New Zealand, the relationship of agricultural export capital to the arbitration system was largely indirect. As a result, high levels of state intervention were required to ensure that developments within the arbitration system remained consistent with the demands of the export sector. In Australia, domestic manufacturing capital was directly involved in the workers of the arbitration system. In these circumstances, there was far less need for the state to intervene on behalf of business interests. Differences in state intervention in the operation of the respective arbitration systems reflected more than just the often-cited lack of constitutional impediments to such involvements in New Zealand.[34]

Indeed, given the election of the first majority Labor government in 1910, as opposed to 1935 in New Zealand, there was greater leeway for Australian unions to seek wage increases via the existing arbitration system, while arbitration was not compelled to play the identical role in limiting domestic wage costs as occurred in New Zealand.[35] Thus, different circumstances in Australia and New Zealand gave rise to divergent responses to arbitration and wage disputes.

As the New Zealand Arbitration Court refused to grant an increase in award wages despite appeals by the unions, significant industrial conflicts and direct bargaining arose as workers tried to improve their wage levels. Even after employers joined their cause in demanding a 5 percent wage increase, Barry and Wailes note, "The result was a long-term shift in government policy away from relying on arbitration to ensure economic stabilization toward direct government intervention in the setting of wages and conditions."[36] In contrast, the successes of Australian arbitration, asserts Braham Dabscheck, "has been due to arbitrators being flexible and adaptable in fulfilling the diverse and

---

[34] Barry and Wailes, 434.
[35] Ibid., 435.
[36] Ibid., 436.

changing needs of the parties."[37] Hence, compulsory arbitration in New Zealand's private sector disputes was abolished in 1984 after the election of New Zealand's fourth Labour government.

Since arbitration was adopted in New Zealand a decade earlier than Australia, the time lag reflects a more complicated Australian political process. Macintyre notes, "In New Zealand the farmers matched the influence of the urban bourgeoisie, whereas in Australia they formed a resentful minority."[38] In other words, there appears to have been greater ideological congruence between urban and rural in New Zealand, which suggests more shared values despite class differences that could point to a more common ethnocultural background.

In Australia, there was a strong Irish composition among those in rural regions that strengthened respective ethnocultural value retention, particularly as the ALP expanded its base of support beyond the English and Scots who brought to Australia a strong sense of British radicalism to the Irish who comprised a large share of Australia's working class and therefore stood to benefit from radical changes to labor policy. This Irish influence has not been adequately recognized or given sufficient scholarly attention. For instance, Australian community development specialist, Paul Chantrill, outlines various reasons for the advance of distinct social policies in Australia and Canada, including class and party differences, democratic reforms, the actions of federal politicians, and the influence of the civil service, but in his analysis seemed to avoid identifying underlying ethnic elements.[39] Although he cites H.S. Albinski in connection with "radicalism amongst rural-based workers,"[40] Chantrill's arguments did not allude to significant ethnic aspects.

While Albinski links the Australian tradition of male egalitarianism to the appearance of the ALP and the strength of labor politics, Chantrill's description limits the underlying impetus to a highly homogenized urban population (reflecting a lack of major religious/linguistic divisions as exists in the Canadian context of English and French Canada)

---

[37] Braham Dabscheck, "Arbitration and Relations Between the Parties," *The Journal of Industrial Relations* 46, no. 4 (2004): 397.

[38] S. Macintyre, "Holt and the Establishment of Arbitration: An Australian Perspective," *New Zealand Journal of Industrial Relations* 12, no. 3 (1987), 152. Quoted in Barry and Wailes, 433.

[39] Paul Chantrill, "Social Policy Development in Australia and Canada: Historical and Comparative Approaches," *Australian Canadian Studies* 17, no.1 (1999): 41–58.

[40] Ibid., 50.

alongside the presence of radicalism among rural-based workers, particularly the shearers.[41] Chantrill's narrative of Albinski's link between egalitarianism and the power of labor politics in the Australian setting seems to end prematurely, before probing the religious/cultural elements among the radical population. Having gone this extra step should have revealed the Irish because a closer reading of Albinski indicates his recognition of an Irish connection. According to Albinski, "A large proportion of Australian Catholics were working-class Irish, and the clergy themselves were almost entirely Irish." Albinski notes, "By the First World War, the ALP was the greatest single Australian party. Much of its electoral clientele as well as a goodly number of its leading figures were by then Irish Catholic."[42] While Albinski does not provide a detailed historical examination of the Irish influence in Australia's radical culture, he does allude to their cultural influence in Australian political culture.

Although Australia's radical labor did not see an overwhelming number of Catholic leaders among the upper levels, this does not imply that radical ideas did not appeal to Catholic—primarily Irish—workers. Indeed, they did. At the start of the 1890s, Australian historian Bede Nairm observes, the Shearers' Union had succeeded in making the southwest region of the NSW colony from Goulburn to Wagga Wagga a center of powerful radicalism. The long and bitter shearers' strike in Queensland and New South Wales in 1891 had agitated all the Shearers' Union leaders, as well as most of the country's working class, including farmers.[43] This was exactly the region of densest Catholic rural concentration.

In Australia's pre-Federation years, while many Catholic politicians remained closely connected to the Protectionists' cause, the workers in the workshops and shearing sheds were enthusiastic recruits to the new labor movement.[44] The 1880s had seen a two-party system grow to prominence in the Australian colonies. The Free Trade Party led by Sir Henry Parkes and the Protectionists led by Sir George Dibbs. Most

---

[41] H.S. Albinski, *Canadian and Australian Politics in Comparative Perspective* (New York, NY: Oxford University Press, 1973), 174–75, cited in Paul Chantrill, "Social Policy Development in Australia and Canada: Historical and Comparative Approaches," *Australian Canadian Studies* 17, no.1 (1999): 50.

[42] Albinski, *Canadian and Australian Politics*, 215.

[43] N.B. Nairn, *Civilising Capitalism: The Beginnings of the Australian Labor Party* (Melbourne, VIC: Melbourne University Press, 1989), 53.

[44] Michael Hogan, *The Sectarian Strand: Religion in Australian History* (Ringwood, VIC: Penguin, 1987), 142.

Table 6.2   Catholic Representation in the NSW Labor Party, 1891–1911

Year	No. of Labor Members in NSW Legislative Assembly	No. of Catholic Labor Members	Labor members of Catholic Faith (%)
1891	35	3	8.3
1901	24	7	29.1
1910–1911	46	16 or 17	34.7 or 36.9

Source: Celia Hamilton, "Irish Catholics of New South Wales and the Labor Party," *Historical Studies of Australia and New Zealand* 8, no. 31 (1958): 265.

Irish Catholics favored the Protectionists who tended to oppose free trade because of its deleterious effects in Ireland and also its antagonism toward the colony's free trade fiscal policy, which was more favorable to land-holders.[45]

Hence, the 1890s represented a critical juncture in Australian political and cultural development. Not only did this decade witness severe labor strife that influenced subsequent industrial relations but also was a period of considerable political transformation evidenced by growing nationalism and the rise of a labor-centered political party which, unlike similar movements in Europe and elsewhere, would soon win power in state and federal parliaments following Australia's 1901 Federation that united six British colonies into a single nation. Irish Catholic influence grew alongside these developments.

Providing evidence for the rise of Irish Catholic identification with Australian Labor politics—particularly prominent in New South Wales, but also evident in most of the other colonies—Hogan cites Australian historian Celia Hamilton for her research documenting the accelerating trend and its impact on Australian society in general.[46] It is persuasive.

As evident in Table 6.2, on a state level evidence for the alignment between Catholics and the Labor Party grew significantly over the first twenty years since the ALP's founding.[47]

The rise in the number of Labor seats won in parliament between 1891 and 1911 saw a corresponding rise in the number of Catholic Labor members elected to parliament, particularly in electoral districts where

---

[45] Celia Hamilton, "Irish Catholics of New South Wales and the Labor Party, 1890–1910," *Historical Studies of Australia and New Zealand* 8, no. 31 (1958): 256.

[46] Hogan, 144.

[47] Celia Hamilton, "Irish Catholics of New South Wales and the Labor Party," *Historical Studies of Australia and New Zealand*, 265.

the concentration of Catholic population was high.[48] Given Australia's
Catholic demography, the source of this increase in Labor Party representation was invariably Irish, which supports their continual rise to
prominence in Australian culture.

As for why and how Irish Catholics in Australia became so influential in Australian society, particularly via the Labor Party in the first
half of the twentieth century, Hamilton convincingly asserts that "the
Irish-Catholics were susceptible to the egalitarian economic doctrines
propounded by the Labor Party" as, she maintains, "the great majority
of the Irish immigrants to the colony had little stake in business or the
land. In industrial employment they had entered the ranks of Labor,
and their natural economic interest lay with a working class party."
Moreover, Hamilton notes, the national background of Irish Catholics
served to strongly reinforce their economic preference to support the
Labor Party. According to Hamilton, "Labor offered the greatest promise
of successfully opposing British dominance in Australian affairs.
Labor—anti-Imperialist, sometimes Republican, always sympathetic to
Irish Home Rule—appealed to the older nationalistic tendencies of the
Irish-Australians."[49]

Although the ethnic influences are compelling, Barry and Wailes
instead cite economic differences between the two burgeoning countries as reasons for the divergence in their arbitration systems. While
New Zealand experienced a quick return to positive economic grown
in the late 1890s, Australia did not experience similar growth until
later in the first decade of the twentieth century leading up to the First
World War.[50] Moreover, as described, the pattern of development in
their respective compulsory arbitration polices differed. Though less
pronounced in New Zealand, the efforts of the Australian politicians
reflected a radical liberal view brewing in Australia that was not identical in Canada for reasons steeped in the prevailing ideological trends
of the era.

Before exploring Australia and Canada's state approaches to conciliation and arbitration in more detail, their radicalism requires greater
understanding because Australia's system—whereby state agencies have
been granted authority to settle disputes and create binding agreements
("awards") over prescribed wages and working conditions—suggests a
more radical cultural tradition in Australia compared to Canada.

---

[48] Ibid., 264–65.
[49] Ibid., 266.
[50] Barry and Wailes, 433.

Labor radicalism in Australia and Canada

Just as Canada was shaped by significant European cultural forces, so was Australia. According to Hartz's fragment theory, Australia was built upon a "radical culture" most closely associated with settlement during the first 60 years of the nineteenth century by a particular fragment of British society—first convicts and then free immigrants who experienced the British social and industrial system, and who could not make their way to the less distant shores of North America. Consequently, Australia was never a true representation of Britain.[51] Indeed, this signified a decisive source of Australia's uniqueness. According to Richard Rosecrance,

> The British aristocracy did not touch Australia, and even the substantial middle class did not find an important place in Australian development. At one extreme Australia was bourgeois; at the other, it was unrelievedly proletarian. Laboring classes have had a prominent role in Australian history, and the divisions in Australian society, important as they have been, have taken place within an overarching working context. Australia was and is a land of toilers, and even the graziers have been notable exceptions to this rule.[52]

The early population of Australia arrived during an era of significant social agitation in Britain brought about by a rapid process of industrialization, which attracted to England, and later Australia, a large population of Irish immigrants. Yet, whether English, Scottish or Irish, notes Rosecrance, "herding men, women, and children together to work in the filth and degradation of the factories and mines... sapped personal independence and created powerful discontents. The regimen of manufacturing probably made the British working classes less amenable to other social controls."[53] As a dominant element of the working class, therefore, the rebellious Irish represent a critical source of Australia's uniqueness.

When it came to feelings of oppression and overwork, the Irish were no different from the British working classes. However, Irish

---

[51] Richard N. Rosecrance, "The Radical Culture of Australia," in Louis Hartz, *The Founding of New Societies* (New York, NY, and London, UK: Harcourt Brace Jovanovich, 1964), 281.
[52] Ibid., 276.
[53] Ibid., 277.

influence was disproportionate particularly when the labor movement emerged. As Horowitz interprets Hartz's fragment theory,
"Australia was a radical fragment, because Australia, being founded
at the turn of the twentieth century, by English and other British
working-class people, [was] privileged, as we might say, a very left-
wing, close-to-socialist or social-democratic fragment in Australia."[54]
Hence, just as Canada is more than merely a reflection of Lockean
Liberalism—characterized by Horowitz as Tory conservatism derived
from the Loyalists which contributed to the toleration of later
socialist ideas—Australia was likewise influenced by a greater diversity of influences than just the radical liberal culture brought by
the British working class. In its focus on British fragments of influence, however, Hartzian theory appears to neglect the substantial
Irish population's impact on Australia. Yet an Irish cultural effect is
apparent when the comparison is made to English Canada which did
not share the same Irish experience. In Canada, there was no comparable Australian Irish Catholic cultural factor.

The Irish factor in Australian radicalism

Whereas America was decisively influenced by eighteenth-century
Lockean Liberalism, and Canada by eighteenth- and nineteenth-century Tory collectivism, Australia was profoundly influenced by a radical
culture rooted in nineteenth-century Britain. The "radical tradition"—
so-called because such radicals as politicians, thinkers, and their
followers, sought fundamental reform—had a strong effect on British
liberalism and, later, socialism.[55] According to Horowitz, the radical
political culture of Australia, reflecting "a theoretically underdevel-
oped, nonmilitant quasi-socialisms of Chartists and trade unionists,"
did not evolve "into the more doctrinaire, more militant, more socialist
socialism of twentieth-century Britain" because this type of socialism
required for its evolution "a continuing confrontation with the ideologies the Australians left behind."[56]

---

[54] Colin Campbell, "On Intellectual Life, Politics, and Psychoanalysis: A
Conversation with Gad Horowitz." *CTheory*, a135 (2003). http://www.ctheory.
net/articles.aspx?id=397 (accessed May 26, 2014).
[55] Robert Leach, *Political Ideology in Britain* (New York, NY: Palgrave,
2002), 30.
[56] Gad Horowitz, *Canadian Labour in Politics* (Toronto, ON: University of
Toronto Press, 1968), 5, fn 5.

Indeed, confirming the power of its strand of radicalism, the ALP quickly rose to prominence not only as the first organized political party in Australia but, even more significantly, the first "working class" party in the modern world to form a government,[57] an achievement it won at national and state levels within the first decade after Federation. A politically ambitious Australian labor movement had emerged in the mid-1880s when the working class organized itself into Trades & Labour Councils (TLC). Intensified by a sense of class consciousness and characterized by ever increasing militancy, the power of the Australian working class was epitomized by a strong union role in the 1890 maritime strike and the TLC's later formation of the Labor Party with massive worker support. That the Labor Party's founders saw the party as a "class party" is demonstrated, observes Australian historian Raymond Markey, "by their emphasis on representation of workers by workers in parliament, and by the social democratic nature of the party's 1891 platform, which represented a strategy of class politics."[58] Australia's active union support for the creation of a labor-focused political party was not paralleled in Canada.

The early leadership of the Australian Labor Party was distinctly British, not Irish. Most were of English or Scottish heritage, which was consistent with labor leadership in Great Britain at the time. "The move of Australian trade unions into formal political activity also followed closely the model of the British Trade Union Congress," notes Ian Turner.[59] In 1900, while there were only 100,000 trade union members out of a total workforce of 1.5 million in Australia, within ten years the number of trade unionists increased five times.[60] Consequently the ethnocultural composition of the leadership and membership ranks was still evolving. However, at this early stage, it was British rather than Irish influence that was more discernible. Yet Irish influence grew quickly.

While the Australian working class had a large number of Catholics, they did not provide labor leadership in proportion to their membership.

---

[57] Graham Maddox, "The Australian Labor Party," in *Political Parties in Australia*, ed. Graeme Starr, Keith Richmond, and Graham Maddox (Richmond, VIC: Heinemann Educational Australia, 1978), 160, 168.

[58] Raymond Markey, *The Making of the Labor Party in New South Wales, 1890–1900* (Kensington, NSW: New South Wales University Press, 1988), 5.

[59] Ian Turner, *In Union is Strength: A History of Trade Unions in Australia, 1788–1983*, 3rd ed., revised and updated by Leonie Sandercock (Melbourne, VIC: Thomas Nelson, 1983), 38.

[60] Brian McKinlay, *The ALP: A Short History of the Australian Labor Party* (Richmond, VIC: Heinemann Publishers, 1981), 22.

Not only were there few Catholic trade union leaders in the older craft unions and few among the organizers of newer industrial trade unions, few Irish Catholics had arrived to Australia with the required skills. Hogan asserts, "A list of executive officers and delegates to conferences of the Australian Workers' Union between 1887 and 1911 contains only a few obviously Irish names and accurately reflects the English and Scottish origins of labour radicalism in Australia." But Hogan concedes that "there were a few well-known Catholics in the New South Wales Trades and Labor Council of the 1880s and 1890s (for example, P.J. Brennan, J.D. Fitzgerald and E.W. O'Sullivan), and many of them subsequently had a role in the Labor Party."[61]

Hence, from Hogan's description, it is possible to see that a common ideological perspective, combined with legitimate Irish Catholic self-interest, made this alignment between Irish Catholics and the ALP a natural development. Hamilton asserts that "Religious reasons undoubtedly carried most weight with the Catholic clergy and influenced, in turn, the laity."[62] It was this laity within politics and the trade union movement that proved most influential in the ALP.

Considering the religious connection, however, an alignment between Catholic voters and Labor was not surprising in light of recurrent harassment by assertive Protestant Orangemen. They represented a strong anti-Catholic element in NSW that was historically aligned with the Free Trade Party and later with other non-Labor political groups against those of the Catholic faith—invariably, the Irish—which made any formal Catholic links with these non-Labor Party groups unappealing. Labor's stress on "non-sectarianism" was of fundamental importance to Catholics since it helped keep out of its political program contentious religious elements. This point is emphasized by Patrick O'Farrell, who notes that under the ecclesiastical leadership of Cardinal Moran, "Catholics had no seriously considered leadership in social affairs" because, O'Farrell stresses, "the Cardinal did not provide it; the laity was incapable of exercising it, or even of concluding that serious thought was necessary," resulting in a "natural drift" in the direction of the Australian Labor Party. O'Farrell asserts, "it was natural in the sense that the non-Labor parties had become increasingly identified with Protestantism, even militant Protestantism: Catholics were not only being pulled

---

[61] Hogan, 142.
[62] Hamilton, "Irish Catholics of New South Wales and the Labor Party," 266.

towards Labor by their self-interest as workers, but pushed towards it by the anti-Catholicism of non-Labor." No matter how normal this appeared to be as "a practical political process in Australia, it was far less natural in regard to wider principle: the natural disposition of nineteenth-century Catholic social thought was conservative and anti-socialist."[63]

Given the lack of non-Labor support for specific Catholic interests, particularly financial assistance for Catholic schools, even a Labor-sponsored secular educational program was deemed beneficial by Catholic leaders since it would at least prevent Protestant dominance over public education. All of the above made support for Labor a calculated risk by Australia's Catholics, but also an advantageous one.[64] Hence, the antisocialist conservatism that characterized Australian Catholics in the nineteenth century would prove significant in the twentieth-century course and development of the Australian Labor Party.

The ALP's ideological difference from similar European models was paramount in attracting Irish Catholic support for Labor. The Australian variant, as revealed by its political platform, encouraged them since, Hamilton argues, Australian labor would not "be dominated by the Continental brand of atheistic socialism which the Catholic Church stood bound to oppose," so comforted on this issue, Australian Catholic clerics could give their approval for lay Catholics to participate in the affairs of Labor politics.[65]

There is a fundamental reason for Catholic opposition to socialism, particularly the nonreligious type that proved more popular in Australia than Canada. Marxist socialism, or communism, has no place for religious views. Hence, while Marxism and Christianity share a common opposition to social and economic injustice, their reasons for opposition stems from different outlooks. In the words of British journalist and conservative political commentator, John O'Sullivan, "Christianity is a religion of love, Marxism a doctrine of power."[66] Religious Catholics and irreligious Marxists share a similar opposition to injustice, but they have different sources and outlooks for their views even if they share a mutual cause.

[63] Patrick O'Farrell, *The Catholic Church and Community: An Australian History*, 3rd rev. ed. (Kensington, NSW: New South Wales University Press, 1992), 288.
[64] Hamilton, 266–67.
[65] Ibid., 267.
[66] John O'Sullivan, *The President, The Pope, and The Prime Minister* (Washington, DC: Regnery, 2006), 13.

For example, in the non-Communist world—such as Australia and Canada—while Marxists and Christians might encourage a capitalist employer to raise worker salaries, or even support strike action if the employer resists, the objective of the Marxist would be to reduce the capitalist's strength in order to lead the enterprise into bankruptcy or toward acquisition by a monopoly, or to compel its owners to hand over control to the workers. From an ideological perspective, the ultimate Marxist aim would be the eventual collapse of the capitalist system and the transfer of power to the Proletariat, or working class. Strikes were a useful tool in achieving such results. In contrast, Christians would strive for higher salaries in the quest of justice. Once higher wages were secured, they would try to bring the workers and employer together and foster a harmonious economic system between various social classes on the premise of such ideas as the "living wage."[67]

In part, this distinction helped separate the mentality of the Irish Catholic "conservative" wing of the ALP from the ALP's secular left wing in Australia, as well as separate the Canadian Co-operative Commonwealth Federation (CCF) and its successer, the New Democratic Party (NDP), from more radical communist supporters in Canada.

Catholicism proved, therefore, to be a key element underlying the Irish factor and its effect on Australia's lower power distance and greater collectivism relative to Canada. A significant reason for their pervasive impact on the Australian national character is because Irish Catholics spread throughout Australia. While Irish Catholics did not disperse across Canada in similar numbers, the French—who represent the largest community of Catholics in Canada—tended to remain, for the most part, geographically confined to Quebec. Therefore, Irish Catholics were in a position to influence Australian national culture more pervasively than the French Catholics in Canadian national culture. Nonetheless, since the latter half of the nineteenth century, Catholicism was critical due to the Catholic opposition to socialism and communism.

These fragments of culture underscore the ideological diversity still evident among Anglo nations today. A salient factor that hindered the American union movement compared with other advanced industrialized Western countries like Great Britain, Australia, and Canada is that American unions have neither established a labor or social democratic party nor ever vigorously supported one.[68] Because of the impact

---

[67] Ibid., 13–14.
[68] Lipset and Meltz, *The Paradox of American Unionism*, 174.

of radicalism, Australia was among the first to see the rapid rise of a powerful labor party—the ALP.

British-Australian political scientist James Jupp speculates that Australia's innate spirit of radicalism, surfacing in the second half of the nineteenth century and evident in franchise reforms and State interventions to ameliorate pervasive economic and social problems, was a conscious reflection of "Australia as a new society, freed from the bonds of landlordism, established religion and the industrial slums of England."[69] According to Jupp, "Colonial radicalism had no intellectual basis such as Mill or Green gave to English Liberalism, or Marx, Kautsky or the Fabians to socialism. Australia was, however, studied with great interest in foreign socialist and radical movements, and visited by British leaders of some distinction."[70] Though all of the modern Australian parties inherited aspects of this colonial radical tradition, suggests Jupp, ALP members' "refusal to grant initiative or prestige to any but their most distinguished politicians is but one facet of their egalitarianism."[71]

The radical militancy of Australian workers was renowned. During the First World War, historian Jeremy Mouat observes, "the tactics of underground workers to win reduced hours led them to break with their own union." Mouat relates, militant Australian workers adopted the slogan, "'If you want a 44-hour week, TAKE it', they simply quit work early each week to the dismay of both companies and the federal Arbitration court. Although the Court subsequently gave belated approval to the forty-four hour week underground, the miners' successful defiance illustrated the value of industrial action over legal proceedings."[72]

Though Australian trade unions proved quite confrontational and Australian politics similarly radical over much of the twentieth century, the underlying sense of rebelliousness, at times bordering on belligerence, reflected a profound Irish influence. This is apparent in key Labor Party leaders such as J.T. Lang, mentioned earlier, and his "Lang Labor Party" that dominated New South Wales politics for over a decade after

---

[69] James Jupp, *Australian Party Politics*, 2nd ed. (Carlton, VIC: Melbourne University Press; London, UK, and New York, NY: Cambridge University Press, 1968), 2.

[70] Ibid.

[71] Ibid., 2–3.

[72] George Dale, *The Industrial History of Broken Hill* (Melbourne, VIC: Fraser & Jenkinson, 1918), 185. Quoted in Jeremy Mouat, "The Miners of Broken Hill, Waihi and Rossland: A Comparative Investigation," *Australian Canadian Studies* 8, no. 1 (1990): 53.

the NSW Labor Party split from the national ALP, to the breakaway Democratic Labor Party (DLP) that emerged in the 1950s, and, perhaps above all, the labor strife witnessed in the waterfront union leaders who asserted themselves in a confrontational manner against management.

Legendary waterfront union leader, Paddy Troy, best exemplifies this trend. Between 1948 and 1972, Troy, proud Australian of paternal Irish descent and a staunch communist, served various terms of office as Secretary of the Coastal Dock Rivers and Harbour Works' Union (CDRHWU), the Ship Painters and Dockers' Union of Western Australia (SPDU), and the Maritime Services Union. He experienced serious factional fighting, including red baiting, and went to jail for his beliefs. Troy ran extremely militant unions.[73]

Yet radical policies in all Australian states had their origins in the ALP, especially the industrial groups through which the ALP tried to counter a rising Communist influence within the trade unions. The driving force, Judd asserts, originated with B.A. Santamaria's "Movement," "though most of its leaders had long records in the labour and trade union movement. Thus it was in the same tradition as the 'Lang Labor Party' especially in Victoria, where the State branch of the ALP came into conflict with the Federal Executive in much the same way as Lang's branch at an earlier date."[74]

During the 1930s, Santamaria was closely connected to the Campion Society for whose cause he established the monthly periodical *The Catholic Worker*. Named for Edmund Campion, the English Jesuit who became a martyr during the reign of Elizabeth I, the organization chose his name, notes Santamaria, "to indicate a definite break in the Irish monopoly within Australian Catholic life."[75] Despite these ties to non-Irish Catholicism, and despite Santamaria's personal Italian heritage, as a fervent Catholic he was certainly exposed to, and influenced by, Australian Irish Catholicism. In his autobiography, *Against the Tide*, Santamaria wrote about the Irish-born Daniel Mannix, Archbishop of Melbourne (1913–1963):

The tall, spare figure who seemed to treat my request to establish a new Catholic paper so lightly was by this time deeply established

---

[73] Stuart Macintyre, *Militant: The Life and Times of Paddy Troy* (Sydney, NSW: George Allen & Unwin, 1984), 1, 61–2, 106–26.

[74] Ibid., 81.

[75] B.A. Santamaria, *Against The Tide* (Melbourne, VIC: Oxford University Press, 1981), 15.

in the affection of the mass of Australian Catholics as their one authentic leader. A considerable section of the non-Catholic community regarded him as a mischievous, malicious prelate, who confused religion and politics, and whose politics, to make it worse, favoured the rebellious Irish and attacked the British Crown and Empire. Since he was to exercise so profound an influence on my own thought in relation to public affairs, it is not irrelevant to attempt to understand Daniel Mannix the man, his background, and his perceived mission.[76]

Santamaria's focus on Mannix is appropriate since the Archbishop was a pivotal figure in the assertion of a Catholic—particularly Irish-Catholic—voice in Australia. Born in Ireland, Mannix came to Melbourne in 1913 as coadjutor, and became archbishop in 1917. In this leadership role, he campaigned fiercely for state aid for Catholic schools, opposed conscription during the First World War, and passionately supported the Irish rebels of the 1916 Easter Rebellion. His strong opposition to communism and criticism of capitalism not only brought him closely involved in Australian politics and the founding of the National Secretariat of Catholic Action in 1937, but, in particular, the Catholic Social Studies Movement of which Santamaria served as president. Mannix's support of the anticommunist Movement was unyielding. The Movement's opposition to suspected communist influences in the ALP and trade unions led to a split in the party and the formation of the socially conservative DLP in 1955.

The expulsion from the ALP of Santamaria's parliamentary followers in 1955, resulting in the "Split" that brought down the Labor governments in Victoria and Queensland, led to the formation by Santamaria of a new organization, the National Civic Council (NCC), whose followers continued to control a number of influential unions. Those expelled from the Australian Labor Party formed the DLP, dedicated to opposing both Communism and the ALP, which they believed was controlled by Communist sympathizers. Although Santamaria was unofficial leader and the guiding influence over the DLP, he never joined the party. As there was no strong indication that Australians wanted a religious political party, and because the Vatican was opposed to official political activity, there could be no formal alliance between the NCC and DLP. Yet, Australian historian Niall Brennan observes, "After the split, the

---

[76] Ibid., 20.

Santamaria organisation was still the most active, and united; and it was not long before it began to manage the affairs of the DLP." However, Brennan chastises, "Almost every member of the Catholic intellectual movement of the 1930s, the Campion Society, parted company with the 'Movement' and with the NCC in the 1950s, leaving Santamaria with a team of amiable yes-men—intellectual nonentities, who had earned a clerical pat on the head for doing what they were told without questioning anything." By the end of the 1960s, therefore, the NCC had influenced the Australian Catholic Church and the DLP with a set of radical attitudes that some would label as "reactionary."[77]

In the decades following the establishment of the DLP, the divide between the ALP and Catholic Church over the ALP's tolerance of communist causes, and its staunchly anti-Catholic members who formed industrial groups to gain control over unions they suspected were being infiltrated by communist sympathizers, remains a painful memory. Australian priest and lecturer in history and social ethics, Bruce Duncan, concludes, "the Santamaria Movement has left a distinctive impression on Australia's religious and political culture."[78] While neither a theologian nor economist, Santamaria, the intellectual leader of the DLP, was an effective and charismatic political activist whose influence was enhanced by the support of Australia's bishops, particularly by Melbourne's Archbishop Mannix.[79] According to Duncan, the Movement Santamaria spearheaded, emerged in 1941–1942 "as a militant, defensive mobilization based on religious allegiance, but not against all aspects of modernity.... The powerful sectarian currents in Australian culture helped keep Catholics united with a clear sense of identity, particularly in relation to the grievance over State Aid. Catholic thought and culture were essentially reactive to aspects of political, and especially European, versions of liberalism, though Catholics were grateful for the liberties they enjoyed in Australia."[80]

Hence, while the ALP had its roots in the nineteenth century British socialist movement (particularly Chartism) shared by the British Labour Party, it benefited from significant Australian Irish influences that emanated from the conservative arm of the Labor Party. This was

---

[77] Niall Brennan, *The Politics of Catholics* (Melbourne, VIC: Hill Publishing, 1972), 46–48.
[78] Bruce Duncan, "Santamaria and the Legacy of the Split: Fifty Years On," *The Australasian Catholic Record* 83 (April 2006): 140.
[79] Ibid., 143.
[80] Ibid., 144.

not a contradiction despite Labor's affinity for socialism, particularly in light of the communist elements that caused the split in the 1950s. As Australian political historian Robert Leach points out, "conservatives can appear even inside radical politics usually as the 'right wing' or 'pragmatist' section of the movement, or as the proponents of the correct traditional methods."[81] Such was the case in Australia.

The appearance of a conservative arm within radical politics is a phenomenon particularly evident in post-revolutionary societies, suggests Leach, "where the old culture has been destroyed or degraded by colonialism or the revolutionary act itself" because there is no "old cultural/political tradition to preserve." Leach compares the phenomenon to Maoist China where, following a brief, unstable era of quick change when radicals ruled over the revolutionary process, "the conservative mentality reasserts itself within the revolutionary movement as the guardian of the correct ideological line. The conservative searches eternally for the security of habit which becomes tradition and later prescription."[82]

If the labor upheaval of the 1890s was essentially Australia's revolution, with the 1901 proclamation of Australian Federation as its victorious conclusion, then an important segment of Australian Irish Catholics appears to have helped fill a conservative role within the ALP against a secular left wing from Federation until the 1950s when the third major break occurred within the ALP that led to the formation of the DLP.

Demonstrating characteristic Irish rebelliousness, Irish Catholic considerations were responsible for three devastating splits in the ALP that impeded its achievement of consistent electoral success. The first split emerged in 1916 over fierce opposition within the party among Irish Catholic leaders to the Hughes Labor Government's pro-conscription policies. This kept the ALP out of office until 1929 after Hughes and many of his colleagues left the party to form a New Nationalist Party. Scullin's Labor Government which came to power in 1929 fell apart by 1932 due to failure to respond to the crisis of the Depression. After this, again some Federal ALP parliamentarians, with help from the Opposition, formed a new anti-Labor group known as the United Australia Party, while another group that expressed loyalty to NSW Labor Premier J.T. Lang, formed a separate party. The ALP returned to office from 1941 to 1949 under Prime Ministers Curtin and Chifley,

---

[81] Robert Leach, *Political Ideologies: An Australian Introduction* (Melbourne, VIC: MacMillan, 1988), 46.
[82] Ibid.

introducing various innovative legislation initiatives, until its defeat in 1949 as a result of the assertion of Liberal Party strength. However, as mentioned, in 1955–1957 a predominantly Catholic anti-Communist group left the ALP to establish the DLP, which, for nearly two decades, succeeded in drawing enough votes to keep the ALP in the Opposition. Labor returned to national office under Prime Minister Whitlam's 1972–1975 government.[83] "In the three great splits in the Labor Party—in the Great War, in the Depression, and in the 1950s—the role of Catholics was crucial," Hogan asserts, "It is impossible to understand the Labor Party of today without understanding something of the sectarian dimension."[84]

Even the DLP split, the last great split in the Labor Party, echoes this sentiment. While the ALP owes its origins to trade unions established along British lines and, to a large number of British immigrants who arrived to Australia in the great immigration wave of the 1880s, the ALP attracted a major Irish Catholic component early in the twentieth century and was viewed by many as an "Irish" party until the split of 1955–1957. Nonetheless, the ALP was not particularly receptive to immigrants as it followed, until 1965, an essentially racist "White Australia" platform.[85]

This platform reflected Australian trade unions' general opposition to immigration. However, after abolishing White Australia and accepting multiculturalism as a national policy under Whitlam, the ALP appears to have benefited from an increased ethnic presence, particularly by immigrants from non-English speaking backgrounds. Between 1983 and 1996, Prime Ministers Hawke and Keating, along with their ministers, frequently articulated their concern for the ethnic communities.[86] This apparent tolerance attracted many immigrants to join or show electoral support for the ALP. Ironically, suggests Jupp, it is the ALP's "radical voice in Australian politics" that has made the party a natural home for new Australian immigrants, especially after its "White" preference ceased as guiding policy.[87] This radical voice was strongly articulated by the Irish.

[83] Andrew Parkin, "Party Organisation and Machine Politics: The ALP in Perspective," in *Machine Politics in the Australian Labor Party*, ed. Andrew Parkin and John Warhurst (Sydney, NSW: George Allen & Unwin, 1983), 15–16.

[84] Hogan, 165.

[85] James Jupp, "The ALP and the Ethnic Communities," in *The Machine: Labor Confronts the Future*, ed. John Warhurst and Andrew Parkin (Sydney, NSW: Allen & Unwin, 2000), 250–51.

[86] Ibid.

[87] Ibid., 257.

Whereas Australia was particularly affected by Catholic Social Action, Canada was especially influenced by Protestant Social Gospel. Established on the premise that helping change the environment of workers would help evangelize the populace, "Catholic Action"—an organized movement that began in Brussels, Belgium in 1924—came to Canada in the late 1920s. Because of Quebec's dominant French Catholic population, this is the province where it achieved its greatest impact in Canada. Between the 1930s and 1960s, Catholic Action had a major impact on Catholicism and society, particularly in French Canada. This had an indirect effect on English Canada through the education and training of French–Canadian politicians on the national stage, such as Gérard Pelletier, Jean Marchand, Jeanne Sauvé, and Claude Ryan. As Choquette observes, "The movement taught them to observe a situation dispassionately, to research an issue thoroughly, to accept responsibility for effecting change in society, and to work tirelessly to achieve their objectives in full confidence that the Lord helped those who helped others." Yet, due to the large Protestant population in English Canada, Social Gospel and its many social service agencies established during the first half of the twentieth century proved more influential. In contrast, Australia's Irish Catholic community was substantial, which helped give a significant voice to Catholic Action in Australia.[88]

While the trend of "inheritors of any Irish culture in Australia were slaphappy operators in municipal politics," observes McConville, like the Larrikin mayor of Collingwood, Robert "Sugar" Roberts, who depended on Irish Catholic voters to remain in power and therefore manipulated occupations with the Collingwood Council to keep them pacified, did very little to advance the interests of the Catholic social action movement in Australia. Catholics educated in religious colleges viewed individuals like Roberts difficult to tolerate, and therefore rather than focus their efforts on localized issues like keeping pubs open after hours or monitoring illegal gambling and local corruption, those who took on the call to Catholic Action focused on the larger issues. In Australia they turned their focus to wage war inside branches of the ALP and trade unions. Proponents of Catholic Action attempted to redress the problematic issues of the "urban-industrial world" by building various social institutions to compete against the institutions of secular culture and the political left. McConville notes, "The

---

[88] Robert Choquette, *Canada's Religions: An Historical Introduction* (Ottawa, ON: University of Ottawa Press, 2004), 348–50.

old battle against Protestantism and imperialism was dead; a new war against godless communism now beckoned." Hence, the most dramatic political achievement of the Catholic Activists was the 1950s split from the ALP, which they felt had become too sympathetic to the spread of communism in the trade unions. [89]

Social Gospel's influence in Canada reflected a comparatively less radical culture than Australia, revealing a more moderate level of Canadian radicalism that reflected the clear impact of the British— particularly the English but also the Scots—whose influence on Canadian egalitarianism deserves attention. The underlying ideological aspects impacted working culture and managerial style.

Moderate origins of Canada's political culture

In Canada, although the Trades and Labor Congress (TLC) passed a resolution favoring the formation of an independent labor party in 1900—the same year that the Trades Union Congress (TUC) did so in Britain which led to the rapid formation of the British Labour Party—it took thirty years before the Canadian equivalent, the socialist Co-operative Commonwealth Federation (CCF), was actually formed.

Unlike Australia and Britain, there was no massive trade union support for a Canadian labor party. This appears largely due to strong American influence over Canadian unions. Many union organizers in Canadian industrial relations were actually American, a situation that stemmed from the 1890s decision of American unions— particularly the American Federation of Labor (AFL)—to send paid union organizers into Canada to help increase control of the North American labor market.[90] Not having established a labor party in the United States, the Americans had no interest in advocating one in Canada. They preferred to assert their interests from the platform of a powerful trade union. Hence, in many Canadian cities and towns skilled workers attached themselves to the AFL's brand of international unionism.

The AFL unions focused their efforts on securing collective-bargaining arrangements with employers in formal, mutually binding, written contracts, supported by union strength rather than law, and

[89] Chris McConville, *Croppies, Celts & Catholics: The Irish in Australia* (Caulfield East, VIC: Edward Arnold Publishers, 1987), 131–33.

[90] Michael Bliss, *A Living Profit A Living Profit: Studies in the Social History of Canadian Business, 1883–1911* (Toronto, ON: McClelland & Stewart, 1974), 81–2.

sometimes supported by a union label on consumer goods.[91] This implied less strike activity since "industrial legality," characterized by voluntary agreements throughout industry as opposed to political agitation for state intervention, was believed to spread "fair" work practices and living standards throughout North America.[92] Union leaders therefore perceived no pressing need to assert a labor voice from within a formal political party. This view changed, however, as clashes occurred between locals of international unions. Each local reflected a distinctive character due to the region's particular mix of industries, relations with local employers, links with middle-class allies, and from the personalities and politics of local labor leaders.[93] Few Canadian employers wished to deal with this volatile labor movement. However, compared to other nations, labor radicalism tended to be less prevalent in Canada. In the Canadian industrial setting, there appears to have only been sporadic outbursts rather than extended periods of conflict.

While strike involvement would suggest a radicalizing effect on workers' political consciousness, this does not seem to have been the case for Canada. According to Krahn and Lowe, although strikes might have briefly sparked a degree of class consciousness among Canadian strikers, "their overall political impact within the Canadian working class appears small."[94] If radicalism had proven a pervasive force in Canada, the workplace would have been far more volatile than the historical record suggests.

Regarding Canadian labor history, Krahn and Lowe assert four discernible eras when strike activity was more widespread and common. First, strikes in the early twentieth century revolved around the loss of control of the production process. While skilled artisans had been able to retain control of the production process during the nineteenth century—and, therefore, their economic security and pride—the privileges that accompanied their craft status declined after 1900 due to industrialization. As mentioned, scientific management and new technology eroded craft workers' autonomy. Hence, craft worker resistance gave rise to many of the 421 strikes and lockouts that broke out between 1901 and 1914 in the manufacturing cities of southwestern Ontario.[95]

---

[91] Craig Heron, *The Canadian Labour Movement*, 2nd ed. (Toronto, ON: James Lorimer & Company, 1996), 32.

[92] Ibid.

[93] Ibid., 34.

[94] Harvey J. Krahn and Graham S. Lowe, *Work, Industry & Canadian Society*, 4th ed. (Scarborough, ON: Nelson, 2002), 395.

[95] Ibid., 385.

Second, between the two world wars, many Canadian strikes broke out because of employer refusals to recognize the legitimacy of unions. In such cases, bargaining was not even a possibility. It was not until the end of the Second World War that union recognition and compulsory collective bargaining was enacted into Canadian law. Hence, despite this legislation eliminating the most pressing causes of worker militancy, the historic peak in Canadian labor militancy had actually already occurred in the immediate years following the First World War. According to Krahn and Lowe:

> Workers across the country were agitating against oppressive working conditions, low wages, and declining living standards due to soaring wartime inflation. Most of all, they wanted recognition of their unions. Western Canadian unions were far more militant and inclined toward radical politics than those in the rest of the country. Thus, in 1919 when Winnipeg building and metal trades employers refused to recognize and negotiate with unions over wage increases, the Winnipeg Trades and Labour Council called a *general strike.*[96]

Occurring nearly thirty years after Australia's paralyzing strikes of the 1890s, Canada's "Winnipeg General Strike" of 1919—a massive showing of Canadian working-class solidarity—brought the Canadian economy to a sudden stop, with sympathy strikes erupting across Canada's cities and even across the border into the United States. This gave rise to a massive response by a combined force of police and employer-sponsored armed vigilantes, which represented one of the few cases in Canadian history when class warfare was so open. Fear of revolution led Winnipeg's upper class, aided by several levels of government, to join forces in the fight to defeat the strike.[97]

The third period of substantial Canadian worker radicalism did not occur until the mid-1960s. The 1945 Ford strike that led to the 1946 implementation of the Rand Formula in defense of union security, and the subsequent introduction of collective agreements, set the tone of Canadian labor relations. The Rand Formula is part of the Canada Labour Code and labor relations laws of most provinces that make payment of trade union dues mandatory regardless of a worker's union

---

[96] Ibid.
[97] Ibid., 387.

status.[98] The legitimization of unions, while ensuring orderly collective bargaining, proved to be a successful formula in the stabilization of Canadian industrial relations that lasted for two decades.[99] In the mid-1960s, however, rampant inflation agitated the Canadian workforce and a series of strikes broke out. About a third of them featured wildcat strikes over wage levels which increased confrontation between labor and management.

The fourth period of major strike activity, assert Krahn and Lowe, reached a climax in 1976, a year after the Trudeau Liberal government imposed wage and price controls to combat inflation. This measure made strikes over higher wages a pointless exercise. Significantly, between 1976 and 1996, time lost because of work stoppages due to strike or lockout declined to levels similar to the low levels immediately following the Second World War. The period of deep recession that characterized the 1980s and 1990s tended to reduce strike activity and labor radicalism in Canada.[100]

But what role did socialism play in the radicalization—to the extent it existed—of Canadian labor? There was significant socialist impact on the unions. Dissatisfied with craft unionism, Canadian socialists, supported by union leaders who arrived from Britain and Eastern Europe, had helped popularize the new model of "industrial unionism" marked by its desire to unite all workers within the same organization. The enthusiasm for industrial unionism, which peaked in the early 1900s, was most active in the resource industries, particularly among miners whose radical Western Federation of Miners (WFM) had endorsed socialism, and the new American Labor Union, to compete against the craft unionism of the AFL. Industrial unionism became particularly popular in western Canada among the unskilled or semiskilled workers

[98] According to Gérard Dion, "The original formula was based on the assumption that the union is essential for all workers and must be responsible for them." In provinces where the Rand Formula has legal force, an employer deducts from salary an amount from employers, whether or not union members, and sends these amounts to the governing union. In provinces where it does not apply, the automatic payment of union dues can become part of the collective bargaining agreement between employers and the trade unions if both parties agree. As part of collective agreements, this kind of modified Rand Formula has spread throughout Canada. Gérard Dion, "Rand Formula," in *The Canadian Encyclopedia: Year 2000 Edition*, ed. James H. Marsh (Toronto, ON: McClelland & Stewart, 1999), 1,974.

[99] Krahn and Lowe, *Work, Industry & Canadian Society*, 387.

[100] Ibid., 387–88.

who tended to be poorly paid, recent immigrants whose knowledge of English was limited.[101] This experiment in radicalism led to the 1905 expansion of the ALU into the Industrial Workers of the World (IWW) which, notes Heron, "envisioned the new society as being run by workers and built around the industrial organizations workers had created in their struggles against capitalists."[102] As noted by Krahn and Lowe, strike activity in Canada rose as a result.

Although coal miners chose to remain within the craft-union movement, they espoused an aggressive resistance to monopoly capitalism's new managerial style, particularly under the influence of such militant immigrants as Nova Scotia's James B. McLachlan. They also supported the US coal union leadership of the United Mine Workers of America for assistance in organizing and asserting their interests in lengthy strikes, primarily in the coastal extremes of Nova Scotia and British Columbia.[103] Canadian labor, therefore, had grown more assertive in the early twentieth century, particularly in the realm of politics.

Whereas only one union representative attended the 1932 meeting in Calgary that led to the formation of the CCF, there were no trade union representatives in attendance at the 1933 Regina Convention. Even after the CCF's founding there was no trade union affiliation for six years. A Nova Scotia local of the United Mineworkers union became the first to affiliate in 1938.[104] Rather than trade union leaders, it was Canadian labor parliamentarians who were instrumental in forming the CCF party. During the 1940s, the CCF had become the official opposition party in several Canadian provinces spanning the Pacific to the Atlantic coasts—British Columbia, Ontario, and Nova Scotia—and in 1944, after being elected as the government in Saskatchewan, it emerged as the first socialist government democratically elected in North America.

The CCF, a political coalition of progressive, socialist and labor forces intended to reform the economy and help people who were suffering during the Depression, went on to form provincial governments in Saskatchewan and—following the CCF's reorganization as the NDP in 1961—in British Columbia, Manitoba, and Ontario. However, unlike the Australian and British experience with their socialist parties, neither the CCF nor the NDP that replaced it has ever led the federal government. As

---

[101] Heron, *The Canadian Labour Movement*, 36–38.

[102] Ibid., 28.

[103] Ibid., 39–40.

[104] Lynn McDonald, *The Party That Changed Canada: The New Democratic Party, Then and Now* (Toronto, ON: Macmillan, 1987), 131.

238 *The Development of Managerial Culture*

a democratic socialist party (and member of the Socialist International), the closest the NDP has come to power in Canadian federal politics was its election as Her Majesty's Loyal Opposition in 2011, a defining year for the NDP in federal politics.[105]

Trade union support of this pro-labor political party did not emerge until the NDP was formed. Although the 1940 merger of the Canadian section of the US-based Committee for Industrial Organizing (CIO) unions into the Canadian Congress of Labour (CCL)[106] led to a Political Action Committee that endorsed the CCF, such passive participation remained the trend for nearly two decades. It was not until after the 1958 election, and the substantial setback the CCF sustained, that a true working alliance was forged, which led the unions to take up a prominent role in the organization of the NDP's founding convention, sending about a third of the total delegates.[107]

While the CLC helped found the NDP in 1961 and remained closely affiliated with it, if every Canadian union member had voted for the NDP—either then or since—the party would have actually formed the federal government. Yet the NDP has not succeeded in over five decades of its existence.[108] Hence, while the influence of labor was very important in helping found a political party focused on the interests of Canadian workers, the relative lack of radicalism among the ranks of Canadian labor compared to Australia is clear. The Canadian conservative voice has effectively prevented the NDP from winning enough votes to dominate the federal parliament.

In contrast with the different levels of worker radicalism in Australia and Canada, a similarly proactive approach by labor did not develop in the United States. As previously mentioned, the reasons for this

---

[105] The NDP, comprised of a unification of the CCF, affiliated unions of the Canadian Labour Congress (CLC), and New Party clubs, is a democratic socialist party and member of the Socialist International. The NDP formed provincial governments in British Columbia (1972–1975; 1991–1996; 1996–1999; 1999–2000; 2000–2001, Saskatchewan (1944–1964; 1971–1982; 1991–2001; 2001–2007), Manitoba (1969–1977; 1981–1988; 199–present), Ontario (1990–1995), and the Yukon Territory (1985–1992, 1996–2000), and has served as the Official Opposition in Alberta and Nova Scotia.

[106] The CCL, from an initial membership of about 77,000, expanded to 360,000 workers by 1956 when it joined with the TLC of Canada to form the CLC. *See* Irving Abella, "Canadian Congress of Labour," in *The Canadian Encyclopedia: Year 2000 Edition*, ed. James H. Marsh (Toronto, ON: McClelland & Stewart, 1999), 369. *See also* Horowitz, *Canadian Labour in Politics*, 70–71.

[107] McDonald, *The Party That Changed Canada*, 131–32.

[108] Krahn and Lowe, 395.

disparity involve Australia's particular ethnocultural composition, Canada's greater ideological affinity with Europe, and the United States' origins from a liberal revolution that had misgivings about the concept of "interventionist politics."[109] Regarding Australia's ethnocultural composition, the Irish factor proved most salient.

While Australia had the influential Irish, Canada had its influential, though comparatively more pro-British and assimilating Scottish population. The Scots—arguably English Canada's most influential ethnic group given their power in the evolving administrative and political landscape—were politically assertive.

Between the era of Sir John A. Macdonald and the Second World War, Scottish representation in Canada's House of Commons was an astounding 25 percent, making the Scots the largest ethnic group in the House. Moreover, those of Scottish ancestry were considerably over-represented as cabinet ministers. According to a study by Richard Van Loon, 20 percent of Prime Minister Wilfred Laurier's appointees were Scots, 13.3 percent of PM Robert Borden's, nearly 27 percent of PM Arthur Meighen's, 23.9 percent of PM William Lyon Mackenzie King's, and 28.6 percent of PM R.B. Bennett's.[110]

But what factors determined their ideological and party allegiance? Although many nineteenth-century emigrants from the British Isles left in possession of liberal political ideas formed by local events, they did not necessarily retain the same mind-set in the new environment of North America. As Evens argues, "For many Scots, as for English and Irish, migration had a conservatizing effect," particularly as Scots attained political office and greater prosperity and therefore lacked much reason to be political reformist since, in nineteenth-century Canada, they had assumed some of the most senior government positions in both Upper Canada (Ontario) and Lower Canada (Quebec).[111]

A tendency favoring family tradition as a form of hereditary party identification was important to determining party orientation, but religious affiliation was particularly critical due to the alignment of ideology and religious outlook. In the nineteenth and early twentieth centuries, Scots who belonged to either the Church of Scotland or the Church of England tended to be Tories due to the Churches'

[109] Lipset and Meltz, 175.
[110] Matthew Shaw, *Great Scots!: How the Scots Created Canada* (Winnipeg, MB: Heartland Associates, 2003), 95–96.
[111] Margaret MacLaren Evans, "The Scot as Politician," in *The Scottish Tradition in Canada*, ed. Reid, 276.

social respectability and inherent conservatism, whereas Scots who were inspired by liberal movements in Britain, Europe, and the United States, leaning toward reformism and radicalism, were aligned with the Dissenting churches.[112] A tendency against a vertically oriented church and lack of an extensive English-style class hierarchy also fostered a strong sense of egalitarianism among the Scots that made its way to Canada, but of a type that fit the Canadian context, which was different from Australia and the United States.

The banking industry in Canada is a case in point. The Bank of Montreal (1817) and the Bank of Nova Scotia (1832), two of Canada's largest national banks, were founded by immigrant Scots. From early on Scottish immigrants to Canada dominated the upper ranks of early Canadian banking, not only serving as presidents and directors but also making up a majority of managers and clerks. During the pre-Confederation years of the 1820s, Canadian banks aggressively recruited Scots because Lowlanders, in particular, were generally better educated in accounting and finance compared to most of the colonial workforce and had an unparalleled work ethic.[113] During the global financial crisis of 2008, and the subsequent collapse of numerous banks around the world—including many in the United States—no bank failed in Canada. "Indeed, the World Economic Forum declared the Canadian banking system the soundest in the world," notes Ken McCoogan, a system that "was built by nineteenth-century Scots." The Canadian banking system flourished, he maintains, "because the fathers of Confederation, the majority of them Scots, insisted that banking was a national concern, not a provincial one—a judgment that encouraged the emergence of large banks with many branches."[114]

Similarly, the life insurance industry in Canada was dominated by Scottish directors, managers and clerks, many of whom were recruited in Scotland during the last half of the nineteenth century. For example, Canada Life Assurance Company—founded in 1847 in Hamilton, Ontario by Hugh Baker, a branch manager of the Bank of Montreal—recruited Thomas Macaulay as chief accountant and Alexander Gillespie as general manager in the 1850s. Canada Life was just one of a myriad of insurance companies run mostly by Scots, including Sun Life, Mutual Life, Confederation Life, London Life, Manufacturers Life, and

[112] Ibid., 276–77.
[113] Shaw, *Great Scots!*, 151.
[114] Ken McGoogan, *How the Scots Invented Canada* (Toronto, ON: HarperCollins, 2010), 183–84.

Great West Life. Just like the Irish Celts, the Scots shared a tribal nature. According to Matthew Shaw, "Scots in the insurance industry tended to stick together in Canada and draw on talent from back home. They were also inclined to invest in one another's enterprises." He asserts, "This sort of clannishness, coupled with their unparalleled actuarial, accounting and managerial expertise, kept them in firm control of the Canadian life insurance industry well into the twentieth century," to the point that an obvious majority of Canadian insurance officials from the mid-1800s to today have Scottish names.[115]

This strand of English and Scottish radicalism would later be evident in the early twentieth-century socialist movements in Canada's Prairie Provinces where men like J.S. Woodsworth and Tommy Douglas, inspired by the Social Gospel movement—ascending during the nineteenth century in English Canada's Protestant churches to achieve social change and create a "heaven on earth" only to decline following the First World War (though, Gordon Hak asserts, "socially conscious Christians still were evident in the left in the 1930s"[116])—merged their interests with the trade unions and working class to assert their ideology into the political realm. This was quite similar to what the Irish Catholics had accomplished in Australia.

The impact of the strongwilled industrious Scots on Canada transcended political affiliation. From Sir John A. Macdonald's progressive conservatism—his Tory opposition to radical social reform combined with genuine concern for social justice and liberal ideas—to Liberal and reform-minded Mackenzie King's longest period of service as prime minister, to the socialist Scottish Baptist minister Tommy Douglas, who took Mackenzie King's social reforms to new levels and emerged as the father of socialized medicine in Canada. In turn, Douglas inspired Trudeau (of maternal Scottish descent) to expand social democracy and Canadian sovereignty through his repatriation of the Constitution and introduction of the Canadian Charter of Rights and Freedoms in 1982.[117]

Canada's adoption of the Charter appears to have been a departure from Canada's parliamentary tradition in favor of an individualist and rights based system. However, unlike the US Bill of Rights, the change was not completely based on the attainment of total freedom. For instance,

---

[115] Shaw, *Great Scots!*, 155–56.
[116] Gordon Hak, *The Left in British Columbia: A History of Struggle* (Vancouver, BC: Ronsdale Press, 2013), 81.
[117] Shaw, *Great Scots!*, 83, 96, 100, and 103.

besides limitations on free speech known as "hate speech"—that is, hateful speech against identifiable groups—Canada added Section 33 to the *Canadian Charter of Rights and Freedoms*. It is a "notwithstanding clause" enabling the federal Parliament or provincial legislatures to override certain portions of the Charter if specified rights are deemed to go against provincial interests. Always controversial, this clause nonetheless preserves parliamentary authority over the judiciary.

The Canadian Charter, therefore, appears to preserve the British tradition of parliamentary supremacy alongside an American-style system of written constitutional rights. In comparison, note Alexander and Galligan, "Australia lacks the Charter component and the strong tradition of group accommodation, and in their absence it remains an open question how well individual rights are protected by its federal parliamentary system."[118] Because of this Australian ambiguity there have been recent developments at the state level toward enacting a Charter.

The "Override by Parliament" provision in Section 31 of Australia's *Victoria Charter of Rights and Responsibilities Act, 2006*, appears to serve the same function as Canada's notwithstanding clause. Victoria is the first state in Australia to enact a charter of rights. Although former Prime Minister John Howard had ruled out making a similar move, Charter advocates have suggested that Victoria's bill would lead to other states, and eventually the Federal Government passing similar legislation.[119] Whether or not Australia ultimately gets such a document, Australia remains the only democratic nation in the world lacking a national charter or bill of rights. In a counterintuitive way, this certainly makes Australia radical.

* * *

Canadian radicalism had its origins in the English and Scottish personality, combining both the earlier Tory collectivist and later British socialist strands. There were also American influences due to close proximity and regionally significant American immigration to Canada since the late nineteenth century. Comparing Australian and Canadian radicalism,

---

[118] Malcolm Alexander and Brian Galligan, "Australian and Canadian Comparative Political Studies," in *Comparative Political Studies: Australia and Canada*, ed. Malcolm Alexander and Brian Galligan (Melbourne, VIC: Pitman, 1992), 7.

[119] Nick McKenzie, "Victoria to Introduce New Human Rights Charter," December 21, 2005. http://www.abc.net.au/am/content/2005/s1535533.htm (accessed May 15, 2014).

however, indicates that Canada's approach—especially before the Second World War—was inherently more conservative than Australia's choice of compulsory arbitration. Considering these policies is essential to help reveal Australian and Canadian cultural differences, and for subsequent clarification of the Irish factor's effect on Australian society.

Canadian compulsory investigation

Canada's nineteenth-century industrial elites showed a strong sense of conservatism in their fervent belief in the legitimacy of class entitlement, social hierarchy, and worker deference. Scrutinizing their writings in *A Living Profit: Studies in the Social History of Canadian Business,* Michael Bliss observes that Canadian businessmen's objections to the trade-union movement—rather than relying on arguments over difficulties in maintaining economic competitiveness—focused primarily on their "direct and personal objections to the effects of unions on the worker and his employer."[120] Hence, relations between the upper class elite and working class unions were tense. Bliss notes, "the trade-union movement was too powerful, too disruptive of established ways of doing things, too erratic in its early days, its strikes too expensive, and its activities far too close to home for businessmen to preserve a particularly detached position on the labour question. Almost all business comment on unions was critical."[121]

Elite resistance to organized labor activity relied on liberalism's view of individual differences. For example, in response to union demands for fixed hours of work and standard pay scales, employers had strongly objected at first due to their view that such demands relied on the false premise that every worker possessed equal ability and motivation.[122] In other words, employers feared that by accepting union demands for equality, overall standards would be lowered to suit the interests of the least capable workers, thereby reducing quality to a mediocre level. Inspired by the prevailing liberalism of the era, therefore, a popular approach to eradicate the trade union movement was to suggest that organized labor represented an attack on "natural law." In this case, the particular natural law was supply and demand, which trade unions were accused of wanting radically modified to suit their interests.[123]

---

[120] Bliss, *A Living Profit*, 77–78.
[121] Ibid., 76.
[122] Ibid., 78.
[123] Ibid., 77.

Given the privileged views of Canada's mostly British elites, not only were employer–union relations in Canada strained but in the extreme they were nonexistent. For instance, in 1872, just one year after the first Canadian trade alliance, the Toronto Trades Assembly, was formed, a strike broke out against Canadian journalist and politician George Brown's *Globe* newspaper. Brown's fervent belief in liberal individualism led him to forcefully reject the collectivist nature of trade unions, and he attempted to break the strike by referring to the *English Combination Acts* of 1792 and 1800, abolished in England but still law in Canada.[124]

The consequences of Brown's action was the complete opposite of what employers had hoped for as public rallies in Toronto were organized by working men's associations while the Conservatives, who were not willing to let such an opportunity escape, started to court workers. The egalitarian component of trade unions was not a pleasant reality for Victorian Canadian Conservatism, but collectivism was among the Tory inheritance. Prime Minister John A. Macdonald brought in legislation to improve laws that related to Trades Combinations in Canada, in accordance with the British *Trade Union Act* of 1871. The workers' response was to look upon the Conservatives as their allies and provide them with their political support. What was learned from this? Primarily, that labor could not only be politically influential but could obtain important gains for union members through such political alliances. Macdonald's astute political tactic temporarily reduced the agitation of the trade-union movement as a political force.[125]

These early unionists welcomed Macdonald's Conservative government's actions on their behalf. Through his shrewdness, Macdonald achieved what Bismarck and Disraeli had accomplished in Europe—pacifying labor and, at least temporarily, minimizing the rise of organized political socialism.

Bismarck and Disraeli, staunch conservatives who believed strongly in the maintenance of tradition, recognized that the welfare state represented the best way to oppose the growth of socialism.[126] In their own ways, Bismarck and Disraeli believed that an effective means to achieve this aim was through government-sponsored social welfare programs

[124] William Christian and Colin Campbell, *Political Parties and Ideologies in Canada*, 3rd ed. (Toronto, ON: McGraw-Hill Ryerson Ltd., 1990), 178.

[125] Ibid.

[126] Terence Ball, Richard Dagger, William Christian, and Colin Campbell, *Political Ideologies and the Democratic Ideal*, Canadian ed. (Toronto, ON: Pearson Longman, 2006), 64.

which upper class aristocrats helped fund through their taxes. This was a modern evocation of traditional conservative paternalism where the monarchy and aristocrats were expected to look after their subjects. Tory paternalism, notes Leach, reflected "an organic whole, necessarily involving ties of mutual dependence which in turn suggested social duties and responsibilities as well as individual rights."[127] Thus, such a policy maintained the individualist status quo of deference to higher links in the chain.

By implementing welfare-state principles, Disraeli's Tory conservatism effectively undercut the rising liberal/labor partnership that was to emerge as the significant radical force in industrializing countries like Australia.[128] Disraeli's views recognized that the upper and middle classes were not alone in their desire for "order and respectability" and that a new "social contract" was necessary to attract the conservative-minded constituents among the working class. However, Leach maintains, "Conservative approaches to this national progress varied according to cultural heritages."[129]

While British Tory conservatism was amenable to the Canadian environment, it was not easily accepted in the United States due to the earlier adoption of the Whig mentality of classical liberalism and its focus on individual liberty. Likewise, Australia, strongly imbued in radical and liberal ideas, lacked the appropriate ideological ground in which British Tory political conservatism could take root and blossom.[130] Despite their common origins as colonies of the British crown, therefore, Australia and Canada evolved according to a combination of influential ideologies and local ethnocultural circumstances, evident in the emergence of divergent state systems of industrial conciliation and arbitration. Notwithstanding the Tory collectivist success, employer–union relations in Canada remained strained.

Bliss cites the example of James Dunsmuir, a premier of British Columbia and wealthy coal and timber magnate. When speaking before the 1903 federal *Royal Commission on Industrial Disputes in British Columbia* investigating why labor relations had gone so bad since the latter part of the nineteenth century—when strikes occurred in the railway, construction, cigar-making, and mining industries—that he refused to recognize the unions, Dunsmuir responded: "I want the

---

127 Leach, *Political Ideology in Britain*, 60.
128 Leach, *Political Ideologies*, 54.
129 Ibid.
130 Ibid., 69.

management of my own works, and if I recognize the union, I cannot have that. Then we are dictated to by a committee of the union as to what should be done and what should not be done."[131] This response only succeeded in encouraging the Canadian union movement to assert itself politically in subsequent decades. Rather than continue allying with previously existing political parties as had been the preference of most early Canadian trade-union leaders and would remain the American trend well into the twentieth century, Canadian unions would eventually help found a political movement of their own to promote their interests.[132]

Although James Dunsmuir represented an ideal stereotype of the reactionary employer, his brand of imperial pride was not to remain so open in Canada. Without a satisfactory alternative to end hostilities between capital and labor, asserts Bliss, employers would neither be able to keep the "freedom of action and the authority that almost all" employers believed was threatened by unionism nor would they be able to "prevent the industrial violence endemic in the United States from spilling into Canada."[133] A solution arrived in Canada's system of compulsory investigation, which was largely the outcome of the efforts of Canadian Liberal parliamentarian William Lyon Mackenzie King, who, during the first decade of the twentieth century, stood almost alone as a leading figure of labor reform.

As Deputy Minister of Labour, Mackenzie King—grandson of radical reformer William Lyon Mackenzie, the Scottish-born rebel leader of the Upper Canada Rebellion in 1837—recognized the need for change in Canada to solve the industrial relations problem. This was decades prior to King becoming the longest serving prime minister in Canadian history, an era in which he would introduce various social welfare programs, including an old age pension (1926), unemployment insurance (1940), and a family allowance system (1944) to improve Canadian

---

[131] Quoted in Bliss, *A Living Profit*, 87–8. For additional discussion of Dunsmuir's testimony, *see* Bliss, *Northern Enterprise*, 357–58.

[132] Forging alliances between trade unions and existing political parties became known as "Gomperism," named for the American trade-union leader Samuel Gompers who successfully imposed this doctrine on the American trade-union movement. While Canadian unionists preferred this form of laborism's pursuit of economic ends within the framework of the prevailing economy and society, the founding of labor parties in Britain and Australia led to a more active interest in the pursuit of a more active socialism. *See* Christian and Campbell, 179.

[133] Bliss, *A Living Profit*, 89.

living standards. As a young man, King had studied political economy at Chicago and Harvard, and then served as the Canadian labor department's chief conciliator and royal commission secretary. Hence, King's solution as Deputy Minister of Labour emerged in 1907 in the form of the Industrial Disputes Investigation Act (IDIA), which featured compulsory conciliation, a "cooling off" period, a tripartite board, and special treatment of disputes in the public interest. It largely grew out of developments of the railway disputes legislation of 1902–1903 that threatened the nation with a national strike.[134]

While the government had introduced legislation for compulsory arbitration of railway strikes and lockouts in 1902, the TLC had successfully opposed this provision, leading to the 1903 Railway Labour Disputes Act that lacked this approach. Instead it included all of the features that would come with the IDIA a few years later, including the appeal to public opinion, the *ad hoc* tripartite board consisting of one representative nominated by each of the employer and union with a chairman chosen by them (or, if lack of unanimity, the government), ministerial initiative, and the unenforceable award. The IDIA added only two new elements—the larger scope of "public utilities,"[135] and, even more significantly, the postponement of work stoppages.[136] No strike or lockout could occur before the board's report was delivered. If the report were not ultimately accepted by both parties, however, it would be published to bring on the weight of public opinion. Thus, the board was equipped with "quasi-judicial power of inquiry," and was authorized to make every possible suggestion to help induce the parties to arrive at a fair and amicable settlement.[137]

King's opposition to compulsory arbitration existed long before the Canadian Pacific Railway strike. In January 1901, King had recorded

---

[134] Paul Craven, *"An Impartial Umpire": Industrial Relations and the Canadian State, 1900–1911* (Toronto, ON: University of Toronto Press, 1980), 271–73.

[135] While the term "public utilities" was not explicitly defined within the document it was incorporated in the definition of "employer" as "any person, company or corporation employing ten or more persons and owning or operating any mining property, agency of transportation or communication, or public service utility, including, except as hereinafter provided, railways, whether operated by steam, electricity or other motive power, steamships, telegraph and telephone lines, gas, electric light, water and power works." Quoted in Craven, *"An Impartial Umpire,"* 288.

[136] Ibid., 279.

[137] Ibid., 287–88.

in his personal diary his response to Smith Curtis, BC Mines Minister, who was a strong proponent of compulsory arbitration. King wrote:

> I do not favour this tendency, & was inclined to feel that it were better to leave industry more alone, save in laying down rules & restrictions against unfair play, & also subjecting it to the influence of public opinion where this could be focused thro' a Department or other means as e.g. in Conciliation…I think tho' that [Curtis] is mistaken in regarding compulsory arbit'n as a great panacea. Most men who consider & advise it see only the seeming immediate effect upon stoppage of strikes, they fail to see that a strike may after all bring greater good than its prevention. I cannot believe [in] the compulsory adjustment of wages schedules. No judge unless he be an economic divinity could regulate rightly wages in any trade of importance for 1 year.[138]

Contrary to Australia's *compulsory arbitration* of disputes, therefore, Canada's was a system of *compulsory investigation* wherein all employers and workers in resource, transportation, and utilities industries were compelled to submit their disputes to a board of conciliation prior to embarking on a strike or lockout. Under King's IDIA, strikes and lockouts were banned during a mandatory cooling off period until the full procedure of compulsory conciliation, investigation and reporting was carried out. The key difference from Australia was the lack of pressure on either party in the dispute to recognize the other or to bargain in good faith, nor any legal force to accept the terms of the report issued under the legislation.[139] According to Canadian labor historian Craig Heron, "The act provided no guiding principles for these boards, leaving them to work out their own solutions without clear precedents."[140]

Although most unionists initially believed that this measure would foster collective bargaining, they soon found that it gave no protection from the employer's countermoves of importing strikebreakers, firing organizers, or stockpiling goods in order to weaken the momentum of a strike. Even though the TLC believed by 1911 that this legislation should be repealed due to the legislation's limited ability to curb

---

[138] Quoted in Craven, *"An Impartial Umpire"*, 274.

[139] Mitchell, "Solving the Great Social Problem of the Age," 69.

[140] Craig Heron, *The Canadian Labor Movement*, 2nd ed. (Toronto, ON: James Lorimer & Company, 1996), 42.

strikes,[141] the IDIA, though amended over time, remained the fundamental labor relations policy of Canadian governments until the Second World War. A key amendment was the wartime Order-in-Council, PC 1003, introduced in 1944, incorporating the principle of compulsory collective bargaining, which led to the 1948 Industrial Relations and Disputes Investigation Act (IRDIA). This legislation retained King's IDIA provisions for compulsory investigation—complete with its conciliation boards and obligatory cooling off periods before lockouts or strikes could occur—along with compulsory collective bargaining.[142]

Of course, the postwar Canadian model was strongly influenced by American legislation as about two-thirds of unionized Canadian workers were then in "international" or American-based unions. Indeed, Canada's labor legislation incorporated the basic ideas of the 1935 *Wagner Act*, including the provision for majority rule whereby a representative designated by the majority of employees within a plant unit had the exclusive authority to bargain with the employer—who recognized the representative's authority to bargain—over work conditions on behalf of all of the unit's employees. As both parties—at the request of either party—were now also obliged to engage in good faith collective bargaining, strikes for union recognition were therefore deemed illegal while "union pluralism," common particularly in Quebec, was discarded due to collective representation within particular work sites.[143]

Hence, this new postwar Canadian model merged American ideas, which focused on building a rapport for collective bargaining, with an already ingrained Canadian tradition of third-party intervention and compulsory cooling-off periods in labor conflicts. As Canadian legal specialist Pierre Verge observes,

This reliance of the state on parties to determine their own collective work regime certainly went a step further than its previous more abstentionist attitude, which had been confined to the acceptance and basic protection of freedom of association. Although already in

---

[141] As Craven notes, the TLC's demand "arose not so much out of opposition to the principles of the legislation, as in reaction to that old bugbear of the union movement, unfavourable judicial interpretation." Craven, *"An Impartial Umpire,"* 273.

[142] Ibid., 319.

[143] Pierre Verge, "How Does Canadian Labour Law Fare in a Global Economy?" *The Journal of Industrial Relations* 42, no. 2 (2000): 277.

place in the main jurisdictions at the end of the war, this new legislative framework could be seen as part of the *Zeitgeist* favourable to
collective bargaining in the immediate post-war period, as reflected
by the International Labour Organisation's adoption of its two main
conventions concerning freedom of association in, respectively, 1948
and 1949 (although Canada only ratified Convention 87 in 1972 and
has not yet seen fit to ratify Convention 98).[144]

While the legislation guaranteed that the process of bargaining could
occur, there was no assurance of the outcome. Unions could still be
broken up in strikes over first contracts. Yet by taking advantage of the
new legislation, unions throughout Canada successfully agreed on first
contracts with employers. In this way, Heron asserts, "The state had
thus intervened decisively in the face of considerable resistance from
many capitalists, to keep industrial conflict from overflowing into
more serious industrial and political challenges to the existing social
order."[145] Strikes for union recognition were no longer necessary or even
legal as the legislation provided for legal certification—thus requiring
employers to sit down at the bargaining table—as long as employee
representatives could prove that they were supported by the majority of
workers in a particular workplace.

Australian compulsory arbitration

Union recognition was one of the causes for the massive strikes in
Australia during the volatile 1890s. The Maritime Strike of 1890
followed by the Shearers' Strikes in Queensland in 1891 and 1894 represented momentous conflicts in Australian history, bordering on civil
war. Although they were essentially fighting for the recognition of
unionism and freedom of contract, the unions' defeats encouraged the
trade unions to form the ALP even before the British Labour Party itself
was formed.

Reasons were not difficult to comprehend. During the pivotal 1890s,
the unions realized that most politicians in the colonial parliaments
were hostile to the unions and more than willing to support legislation giving exceptionally harsh powers to governments that sought
to end the strikes.[146] Governments had sided with employers, and in

---

[144] Ibid.
[145] Heron, *The Canadian Labor Movement*, 72.
[146] McKinlay, *The ALP*, 6.

Queensland and New South Wales trials occurred which led to the jailing of unionists and union leaders. This systematic repression of unions which spread throughout all the colonies saw police and military forces used to break up strike demonstrations and to enable non-union workers to take jobs and help break up strikes. Union defeats, combined with an earlier call in 1889 by the Inter-Colonial Trade Union Congress in Brisbane to endorse candidates for election, led a reorganized labor movement to enter the political arena in order to transform trade unions from the role of spectators in parliaments to that of participants in the creation of social policy legislation.[147]

Despite the ascent of Labor into the Australian political realm, Alfred Deakin, leader of the Protectionist Party, became prime minister of Australia in 1903, after the second federal election following Australian Federation. Born in Melbourne to English immigrants, Alfred Deakin had been a strong supporter of an "All White" Australian immigration policy that strove for an Australia with a singular British heritage, which was the Protectionist Party's aim. As prime minister (1903–1904, 1905–1908, 1909–1910), initially with the support of the recently founded Labor Party, Deakin helped launch many welfare state reforms including old age pensions, laws to control business practices, tariffs to protect Australian industry, and the first serious attempts at conciliation and arbitration between management and labor. Deakin's governments established the site of Canberra as the national capital, began work on the Transcontinental Railway, established several Commonwealth departments, and built the foundations for the Australian Army and Navy. His foreign policy encouraged closer ties between Australia and the rest of the British Empire.[148]

Although Deakin and his fellow Protectionists formed the government in 1903, the Labor Party had quickly emerged as a truly national party with equal standing alongside the Protectionist and Free Trade (later Reform) parties, winning more seats in total than ever before, in all six states, and had a greater share of the popular vote. This resulted in the ALP claiming a larger share of power in parliament where it would soon gain control over government in 1904 before losing again to Deakin's Protectionists, but demonstrating ever greater influence in each new parliament. Hence, policies that

---

[147] Ibid., 6–7.
[148] Michael Page, *The Prime Ministers of Australia* (Sydney, NSW: Robertsbridge, 1988), 33.

Labor had campaigned for during the 1903 election ultimately came into force the following year, particularly relating to compulsory arbitration.

By embracing economic protection as a key element of his national policy, Deakin initially introduced tariff duties to raise revenue and protect domestic industry. He then required employers who wished to benefit from the protectionist policy to provide "fair and reasonable" wages as determined by the Commonwealth Arbitration Court. In 1907, while adjudicating a case involving Harvester, a large manufacturer of agricultural machinery, Henry Bournes Higgins, president of the Arbitration Court, determined fair and reasonable to mean "sufficient to maintain a man as a 'human being in a civilized community'" and to meet the needs of a family. Despite a successful court challenge and subsequent changes to the concept of "sufficient wage" becoming known as the "basic wage" to be adjusted for changes in the cost of living, Higgins' ruling became an underlying characteristic of Australian national life.[149]

Protected employment at a legally prescribed wage was deemed sufficient to enable the majority of Australians to meet their needs. In this way, a national standard was born with wages determined by an independent arbitrator rather than bargaining, based on human need as the yardstick rather than profits or productivity. According to Peter Beilharz, while retrogressive in the sense that it was fixed on *male* wage rates, the judgment "was radical in that it elevated the criterion of proletarian need over that of the capacity of industry to pay as a wage-fixing principle."[150]

The 1907 Harvester Award was the first clear sign of how the new arbitration process would work in Australia. Not only did it recognize that workers and their families deserved minimal levels of income to afford basic sustenance but the basic living wage concept further implied the exercise of wage justice compared to owners and the upper classes. Australian labor relations specialist J.D. Hill asserts that the basic wage could be considered "the industrial expression of the Australian notion

---

[149] Stuart Macintyre, "Alfred Deakin," in *Australian Prime Ministers*, ed. Michelle Grattan (Sydney, NSW: New Holland, 2000), 49–50.

[150] Peter Beilharz, "The Labourist Tradition and the Reforming Imagination," in *Australian Welfare: Historical Sociology*, ed. Richard Kennedy (South Melbourne, VIC: Macmillan, 1989), 139.

of fair play and egalitarianism."[151] However, as its guiding notion of "fairness," the judgment tended to institutionalize the values of *equity* rather than *equality* because, according to Beilharz, "Higgins's values, widely shared among the labour movement, were based upon the notion of equity between the unequal."[152]

Besides being a highly influential liberal-radical Australian politician and judge, Ireland-born Higgins was also a staunch proponent of the cause of Irish nationalism. Higgins' views drew upon significant Catholic themes, such as Pope Leo XIII's *Rerum Novarum*, that "reasonable and frugal comfort" was every working man's right.[153] As a means of achieving harmony in society, Beilharz maintains, "the Harvester Judgment embodied the interventionist but masculinist principles of new liberalism, while protection itself (along with White Australia) maintained the racist current of labourism. The market was to be regulated; substantial alternatives in state or society, however, were foreclosed."[154]

Rather than developing a stronger propensity for socialism, therefore, Australia was more enamored by a radical affinity for "laborism," which, Beilharz describes, "identified its political subject as the organised, male working class, and developed a strategy directed towards the defence and protection of the interests of that 'class.'"[155] Hence, as an ideology, laborism was cultivated by colonial liberalism, suggests Beilharz, "by the progressive ideology forged in the alliance between local manufacturers and workers."[156] Progressive legislation was an effect of this laborist ideology, for "Labourism in Australia, even more so than in Britain, has long enjoyed a special relationship with the state, yet one which has maintained a sense that the market held primary responsibility for the delivery of social goods."[157] Australia was to be a capitalist state, but the government was to intervene on behalf of the people. This was a view held by the Labor Party, which was supported by large numbers of Australian Irish. Whether due to an interest in achieving equity, equality or both, egalitarianism was among the pedestals on

---

[151] J.D. Hill, "Australian Industrial Relations and the 'National Character'," in *Australian Labour Relations: Readings*, ed. G.W. Ford, J.M. Hearn, and R.D. Lansbury, 4th ed. (Melbourne, VIC: Macmillan, 1987), 181.

[152] Beilharz, "The Labourist Tradition and the Reforming Imagination," 139.

[153] John Rickard, *H.B. Higgins: The Rebel as Judge* (Sydney, NSW: Allen and Unwin, 1984), 173, quoted in Beilharz, "The Labourist Tradition and the Reforming Imagination," 139.

[154] Beilharz, 139.

[155] Ibid., 137.

[156] Ibid., 138.

[157] Ibid., 137.

which this outlook, and policies such as the basic wage and compulsory arbitration, took shape.

* * *

Egalitarianism, mateship, the legendary unwillingness among Australian workers to defer to employers compared to the United Kingdom or Canada, the nonacceptance of elitism demonstrated by the Australian enthusiasm to "cut down tall poppies" are all Australian core values that impacted Australian industrial relations. These core values reflected the desire, argues Hill,

> to create a new society free of the 'old world's' class, caste and racial divisions. Liberal ideas were accepted not only by the emergent Labor Party but also by the colonial Liberals. The legislation establishing the Arbitration Court was initiated by Deakin's Protectionist Party, with strong support from particular interest groups. Mateship and equality were Labor Party variants of these values which became more important as the Labor Party subsequently developed as a powerful institution. During the first decade of the twentieth century there was in Australia a strong belief that Australia was a working man's country in which the common man could look forward to a secure, dignified life.[158]

Compulsory arbitration was more than egalitarian. The policy reflected a strong sense of liberal utilitarianism that proved strong in Australia. Because their initiative had prevailed in parliament, it appeared to be a victory for Irish and non-Irish Australian workers alike. Thus, the more conservative Canadian solution was quite distinct from Australia's more radical compulsory arbitration, which, unlike New Zealand, remains a prominent feature of Australian labor relations system. However, while the Irish benefited from, and contributed to, the rise of Australian radicalism, the legislation that created these laws was not entirely Celtic. In this instance, the legalism underpinning the introduction of such radical policies as compulsory arbitration was more reflective of Australia's British heritage than its Irish constituency.

Legalism and the Australian utilitarian tradition

British liberalism was characterized by individualism in the areas of civil and political rights, politics, parliamentary government, limited

---

[158] Hill, "Australian Industrial Relations and the 'National Character,'" 180–81.

state intervention, moderate reform, and the endorsement of private enterprise. Another core assumption of liberalism is "rationalism," which means that no other person—neither a ruler, priest nor bureaucrat—should determine the individual's own interest.[159] Yet "freedom" is perhaps the pre-eminent value of liberalism as a classic liberal view. However, freedom was defined in different ways according to the individual societies in which it made its mark.

In the nineteenth century, while the United States clung strongly to classical liberal thinking that stressed property rights, free trade, individual freedom, and a limited state, in Britain—and by implication the British-ruled colonies of Canada and Australia—liberalism, under the growing influence of socialist reformers that government should help the plight of workers led to a division between proponents of "classical liberalism" and a new strand of "state liberalism" that believed in the need to control the social structure in order for individual freedom to thrive. This trend gave rise to the ideology of the liberal Welfare State, where state interventionism, and its appeal for government action to promote individual liberty and equality of opportunity, was deemed an accepted creed of the new liberalism.[160] Welfare liberalism became a dominant characteristic of both Australia and Canada in different ways. While it thrived during Tory conservative influence in Canada, it appears to have risen to prominence in Australia via liberal Benthamite utilitarianism.[161]

Whereas America embraced the eighteenth-century ideas of Lockean liberalism and its emphasis on individual freedom, Australia deemed of greater importance the nineteenth-century "Philosophic Radicals" like Jeremy Bentham whose utilitarianism left a profound mark on Australia's cultural and political development. Historian Hugh Collins cites the influence of Benthamite utilitarian values that accompanied many early settlers to Australia—notably the emphasis on pragmatism and desire for a strong legal framework—on building the ideological foundation upon which later developments depended.[162]

Bentham's utilitarian philosophy reconciled liberalism's pursuit of individual interests with sovereign concerns by emphasizing legislation as an effective means of achieving public good while maximizing

---

[159] Leach, *Political Ideology in Britain*, 25–27.
[160] Leach, *Political Ideologies*, 91.
[161] Hugh Collins, "Political Ideology in Australia: The Distinctiveness of a Benthamite Society," *Daedalus* 114 (1985): 151.
[162] Ian McAllister, *Political Behaviour: Citizens, Parties and Elites in Australia* (Melbourne, VIC: Longman Cheshire, 1992," 24–25.

private interest. In a sense, this form of individualism makes utilitarianism seem almost anticollectivist because, asserts Collins, while "the agenda of Bentham's utilitarian state includes issues that are now associated with a collectivist age, such as education, health, and welfare, in Bentham's system these tasks are firmly secured to individualist interests."[163] Hence, Bentham's utilitarianism emphasized legalism over unregulated individual freedom since legislation was for Bentham a key means of ensuring the greater good for individuals and society as a whole.

Nineteenth-century utilitarians were fervent believers in the benefits of representative democracy because if every man were able to vote for government representatives he could protect his interests. (Male suffrage was extended to females in the twentieth-century in the United Kingdom, Ireland, Australia, Canada and the United States, among other nations.) According to Bentham, "The business of government is to promote the happiness of society, by punishing and rewarding."[164] Therefore, utilitarians held the view that laws should be reformed to bring the greatest good and the greatest happiness to the greatest number of people.

Australian political thought was strongly influenced by British thought. According to Noel Ebbels, the first working class political agitation in Australia during 1840–1860 had been "obviously influenced by English radicalism" and Victorian Chartist ideas.[165] Chartism was a British working-class movement prominent in the 1830s and 1840s that called for sweeping changes to the British political system according to a Six-Point Charter in order to achieve parliamentary democracy as a step toward social and economic reform. An emotional reaction to the workers' feelings of an unjust economy and social conditions marked by relentless change brought by the industrial revolution, Chartism was Utopian in its belief in quick socio-economic improvements as a result of constitutional reform.[166]

Chartism became prominent in Australia after British chartists, having left England after the collapse of the movement in 1848,

---

[163] Collins, "Political Ideology in Australia," 148–49.

[164] Jeremy Bentham, *Introduction to the Principles of Morals and Legislation* (New York, NY: Hafner, 1948), 70.

[165] R.N. Ebbels, *The Australian Labor Movement, 1850–1907: Historical Documents* (Sydney, NSW: Hale & Iremonger, 1983), 4–5.

[166] Marjie Bloy, "Chartism: An Introduction," *The Victorian Web*, http://www.victorianweb.org/history/chartism.html (accessed November 15, 2005).

came to Australia where the ideas continued to ferment not only among the working class, the base of support in England, but also among the middle class united against the "landowning squattocracy." Chartism grew particularly strong in New South Wales and Victoria between 1840 and 1860, reaching its height in the political agitations in Victoria between 1852 and 1857, such as Ovens, Bendigo, the Ballarat Reform League, Eureka, and the July 1857 Land Convention.[167]

Those who succeeded in imprinting upon Australia the Benthamite ideology during the nineteenth century arrived with these ideas. For instance, Chartism had a direct connection to Benthamic thought via Henry Parkes, a free-trader and proponent of radical politics who, as head of the New South Wales Government, was influential in the cause for Australian federation. As Jack Lang recalled in his memoir, *The Turbulent Years*, Parkes' radicalism led Parkes to advise disaffected workers following the disastrous 1890 Maritime Workers' Union and Shearers' Union strikes to "consider sending their own representatives into Parliament."[168] Parkes had been a member of the Birmingham Political Union during local tensions that occurred prior to the Reform Bill of 1832; he was present at the 1838 meeting when Birmingham accepted the movement's Charter; and in 1839, in London for the Chartist Convention, left for Australia just before the alliance between the middle and working classes collapsed.[169]

The justification for the Chartist movement—reform based on suffrage rather than revolution as the primary path for social change, and the combined effort of disaffected lower classes and reformist middle classes to achieve a common interest—was fundamentally Bentham's achievement because Bentham not only articulated these interests but linked them with radical reform.[170] "That Chartism should have succeeded so completely in Australia by the 1860s, while failing so bitterly in Britain, is doubly significant in any appreciation of the distinctiveness of Australia's political culture," asserts Collins, "for, as well as marking the point of departure of Australia's political culture from its British background, it also marks the essentially Benthamite character of this antipodean offshoot."[171]

---

167 Ebbels, *The Australian Labor Movement, 1850–1907*, 5.
168 J.T. Lang, *The Turbulent Years* (Sydney, NSW: Alpha Books, 1970), 11.
169 Collins, "Political Ideology in Australia," 150.
170 Ibid., 150.
171 Ibid., 151.

The legacy of utilitarianism for Australia is political pragmatism and a robust legalistic emphasis on how groups of people should behave. The state is expected to rectify the problems that arise swiftly and effectively, in addition to adopting a strong moral stance on what it regards as the proper conduct of society. Among the best examples of Australia's application of utilitarian values to politics is the system of compulsory voting, by which voters are forced under the threat of financial penalties to appear at a polling place to collect a ballot form. Australia is among only a few democratic countries to require its citizens to vote in this manner.[172] Since one of the attributes of a democracy is to ensure that all citizens have a role in decision making, the utilitarian method of achieving this goal in Australia is through compulsion and legal enforcement of casting ballots.

Besides compulsory voting, another example of Australian legalism is the compulsory arbitration system. The origins of Australian compulsory arbitration can be found in widespread strikes of the late nineteenth century, as discussed, reflecting a strand of radicalism in Australian culture that the Irish shared to achieve their political interests while respecting their cultural heritage. Although liberal values had also infused Canada, they were modified by a strong conservative strand linked to Toryism.

According to Ian McAllister, "Utilitarian values have been a constant theme in Australian society since the nineteenth century and reflect the desire to see everyday problems resolved quickly and efficiently by the use of practical, positive methods. In turn, there is agreement that the goal should be achieved by whatever means are available

---

[172] McAllister, *Political Behaviour*, 24–25. First advocated by Deakin at the turn of the twentieth century, compulsory voting was voluntary during the first nine federal elections. In 1915, under Digby Denham's Liberal Government, Queensland was the first place in the British Empire to introduce compulsory voting. Implemented as a means of leveling the playing field, Denham believed that ALP shop stewards were more effective in getting people to vote. Despite the new measure, Denham lost the 1915 election. Compulsory voting was introduced to Victoria in 1926, NSW and Tasmania in 1928, Western Australia in 1936, South Australia in 1942, and federally in 1924. By 2006, there were 32 countries with compulsory voting, of which 19 nations, including Australia, Belgium, Greece, and Turkey, employ a system of enforcement. The remaining 13, including Italy and the Netherlands, do not enforce the practice. Tim Evans, *Compulsory Voting in Australia* (Australian Electoral Commission, 2006), http://www.aec.gov.au/pdf/voting/compulsory_voting.pdf (accessed January 30, 2007), 5–7.

and at whatever cost."[173] Instead of appearing solely individualist, the cultural effect also featured an overlap of utilitarianism and collectivism because, as McAllister asserts, the idea of "collectivism implies group action as the best means of achieving goals," and is, therefore, "inextricably linked with the role of the state, which is seen as the most effective means of attaining collectivist goals."[174] Hence, agreements on employment conditions and minimum wages provided a means of acquiring material gains via collective action. Such achievements represented an important motivation for the nineteenth-century battles of the trade unions, which led to the formation of a robust union movement that was closely supportive of the Labor Party.[175]

Expediency and novelty were guiding principles in the radical political culture of the emerging Australian nation. The adoption of compulsory arbitration was a strong example of novel and expedient policies that did not emerge in Canada during the same period given a political culture more closely aligned with British conservatism via a strong Tory association among Loyalist and later British immigrants. Hence, in the Australian political culture, a utilitarian view prevailed which saw the state as existing first and foremost to settle problems and disputes, not to defend individual liberty. McAllister asserts, such "instrumentalism has manifested itself in a desire to see the state and the government deliver certain goods and values to citizens, largely independent of the costs of the exercise in terms of individual liberty or freedom."[176] For Australia, among these "goods and values" was compulsory arbitration.

Collective bargaining and Australian and Canadian labor relations

Contrary to voluntary arbitration where both parties in a dispute agree to involve an arbitrator and further agree to accept the decision, compulsory arbitration is comprised of four unique elements.[177] Both parties in a dispute are compelled to appear before a tribunal; the tribunal determines a settlement without a prior agreement from the parties to accept

[173] McAllister, *Political Behaviour*, 24.
[174] Ibid., 26.
[175] Ibid.
[176] Ibid., 24.
[177] John Niland, *Collective Bargaining and Compulsory Arbitration in Australia* (Kensington, NSW: University of New South Wales Press, 1978), 19–20.

and abide by the decision; noncompliance with the tribunal's decision generates penalties; fines are collected if penalties are imposed. Not only does Australian compulsory arbitration include a requirement to refer disputes to courts and tribunals, but also to have compulsory awards, limitations on strikes and lockouts, the registration and regulation of trade unions all function under the jurisdiction of the arbitration and tribunal process.[178] Canada's approach to dispute settlement differed, favoring a process of compulsory investigation, and adding a structure during the Second World War to encourage collective bargaining based upon the American system.[179]

Though compulsory arbitration of labor disputes had been advocated in Canada during the 1880s by local members of the US Knights of Labor,[180] Canadian labor historian Paul Craven observes that there was initial uncertainty whether they meant arbitration in the contemporary sense of a third party drawing up a binding settlement, or collective bargaining. Analyzing the cases brought before the Royal Commission on the Relations of Labour and Capital in the 1880s, Craven asserts that "arbitration seems to have meant collective bargaining between appointed representatives of the two principals."[181] Hence, the TLC's 1886 resolution advocating binding arbitration in every case where a dispute arises was clarified by the 1892 recommendation that the government establish a Board of Conciliation and Arbitration, and the TLC's 1894 endorsement of the voluntary board established through Ontario legislation.[182]

The post–Second World War Canadian legislation only applied to nonmanagerial employees, therefore establishing a significant division between managerial personnel and other employees. It was not intended

---

[178] Mitchell, "Solving the Great Social Problem of the Age," 47.

[179] Ibid.

[180] American dominance of Canadian labor during this early period was substantial. For instance, the powerful "Noble and Holy Order of the Knights of Labor," a secret society founded in Philadelphia in 1869, came to Canada in 1881 when a group of Hamilton painters launched the first local. For a time, the Knights had emerged as a force among workers throughout the United States and Canada among other countries, boasting a membership of more than a million around the world by 1886, and over two hundred local assemblies in Canada with at least 14,000 members, over 75 percent in Ontario. The Knights of Labor became popular because of their ideology of protecting and building the nobility of labour, and their effectiveness in dealing with employers. Their power faded quickly in Canada after 1887. Heron, *The Canadian Labour Movement*, 20–3.

[181] Craven, *"An Impartial Umpire,"* 142.

[182] Ibid., 143.

to cover professional employees, civil servants, or farm workers. Hence, it had limited coverage and only applied to workplaces where a majority of employees were in favor of collective representation.[183] The state system still retains most of the original characteristics, but with some refinements. For instance, professional employees were later included, as were public and "quasi-public" sectors such as health and education. Moreover, legislation banning the use of replacement workers during lockouts or legal strikes came into force in many jurisdictions, including Quebec (1977), followed by Ontario and, partly, in British Columbia. Hence, about 34 percent of the Canadian working population (40 percent of Quebec) is covered by this system, which does not coexist with other forms of employee representation as in some European countries.[184]

Collective bargaining refers to a process of dispute resolution that is now common in the western industrialized nations, including Australia where it has always coexisted alongside the operation of arbitration tribunals as a form of pre-arbitral negotiations and in the areas of "above award bargaining,"[185] award payments, collective negotiations of certified agreements and consent awards, award variations, and in problems surrounding contract interpretation.[186] As J.E. Isaac observes, "the founders and early practitioners of compulsory arbitration saw this process not as displacing collective bargaining but as supplementing it whenever negotiations broke down."[187] However, since it takes place within an environment dominated by arbitration tribunals, and is therefore always subject to arbitration in the event negotiations fail, the char-

---

[183] Verge, "How Does Canadian Labour Law Fare in a Global Economy?" 277–78.

[184] Ibid., 278.

[185] In Australia, "above award bargaining" refers to further bargaining that occurs following an agreement. Since wage rates and work rules stipulated in Australian awards represent *minimum* terms and conditions, the Australian system allows the parties who are bound by such awards the freedom to bargain for wage rates and work rules above these rates. Ronald Clive McCallum, "Deregulating Australian Labour Relations: Collective Bargaining Reforms within Australia's System of Compulsory Conciliation and Arbitration," *Queen's Papers in Industrial Relations* (Kingston, ON: Queen's University IR Centre, 1990), 2.

[186] Stephen J. Deery and David H. Plowman, *Australian Industrial Relations*, 3rd ed. (Sydney, NSW: McGraw-Hill, 1991), 274.

[187] J.E. Isaac, "Equity and Wage Discrimination," paper presented to 51st ANZAAS Congress, May 12, 1981, 11. Quoted in Deery and Plowman, *Australian Industrial Relations*, 274.

acter of Australian collective bargaining is different from Canada and other countries. Nonetheless, at its essence bargaining involves seeking a resolution through direct negotiation between equally powerful parties when, at the outset of negotiations, there is considerable uncertainty of the end result, both parties negotiate in good faith, and, in the event of disagreement over terms of settlement, parties determine how to resolve the matter.[188]

Indeed, by the late twentieth century, many Australian workers and employers preferred noncompulsory arbitration procedures, and collective bargaining is just one of the options favored. Analyzing 1970s survey data, Australian economist John Niland observes that 42 percent of respondents favored "negotiation between both sides, followed if need be by binding arbitration at the initiative of *both* sides," whereas 45 percent favored "negotiation between both sides, without recourse to binding arbitration."[189]

Niland cites influence from other countries on Australia's rising interest in more direct negotiation, since numerous Australian trade union leaders traveled overseas where they witnessed alternative dispute resolution procedures for themselves.[190] Hence, more global interaction combined with higher education among workers indicates, Niland asserts, that "direct negotiation is increasing and will continue to increase, not because of a specific policy decision favoring its adoption, but because it caters better to the heightened taste for self-determination than does compulsory arbitration."[191] Even though collective bargaining has risen in prominence to at least equal footing with compulsory arbitration, the latter remains a distinctive feature of Australia's labor relations process.[192]

While collective bargaining permits the use of strikes as a tactic in the overall process of dispute resolution, compulsory arbitration was intended to reduce, if not completely prevent, the outbreak of strikes. In this respect, collective bargaining has not been successful. Prior to the rise of unions and the use of the strike tactic, Palmer notes that riots represented a popular form of worker protest in nineteenth-century Canada, particularly among workers in major construction projects involving railway employees, canal laborers, raftsmen, mechanics,

---

[188] Niland, *Collective Bargaining and Compulsory Arbitration in Australia*, 17.
[189] Ibid., 85.
[190] Ibid., 86.
[191] Ibid., 89.
[192] Ibid., 82.

seamen, soldiers, and other laborers.[193] While Irish Catholics in Canada were neither as large nor influential as the Australian Irish community, they did play a role in the development of the Canadian working class.

Mid-nineteenth century discourse linked Irish immigrants—particularly Irish Catholics—to crime, violence, and urban poverty. While they were overrepresented among the urban poor and, according to jail registers, as fighters in riots, many Irish Catholic workers found their niche, in the case of women, in domestic service, and, in the case of men, manual labor jobs like dock work, carting, and heavy construction.[194] Whether due to English Canadian anti-Catholicism or Orange-Green disputes between Irish Protestants and Irish Catholics, there was significant Irish Catholic rebelliousness evident. Citing a number of studies, Iacovetta *et al.* observes that

> Irish Catholic men gained the greatest notoriety for their collective violence when massed as navvies on large-scale construction projects, particularly during the great canal-building era of the 1840s in central Canada. Driven by wretched working conditions, acute economic hardship, and unscrupulous contractors, the Irish navvies drew on their cultural resources—secret societies and fierce, if temporary, ethnic cohesion—to mount the biggest strikes of the decade. This rowdy industrial proletarian was sharply repressed by the state, which created mounted police forces for the purpose. The ethnic identities of the Irish could cut both ways, at times fuelling bitter internecine battles among workers, while at other times forging class solidarities and a broadly based labour movement.[195]

Evidence from the Australian colonies in the same era suggests little equivalent rioting among workers since capitalism took a somewhat different path during Australia's early development. As Quinlan and Gardner note, convicts had formed the majority of the labor force between 1788 and 1830 and were still significant until the 1850s in

---

[193] Bryan Palmer, "Labour Protest and Organization in Nineteenth Century Canada, 1820–1890," *Labour/Le Travail* 20 (Fall 1987): 62–65.

[194] Franca Iacovetta, Michael Quinlan, and Ian Radforth, "Immigration and Labour: Australia and Canada Compared," *Labour/Le Travail* 38 (Spring 1995): 92–93.

[195] Ibid., 93.

some colonies. They worked on the kinds of civil construction projects that were common in Canada.[196] According to Atkinson, while convicts occasionally rioted they tended to engage in more covert work protest such as slowdowns or even arson.[197] Convicts arriving to Australia's shores had a substantial proportion of Irish among them, making work protest no surprise. After all, the historic Irish fighting terms of "boycott"[198] and "donnybrook"[199] point to native Irish rebelliousness.

Strikes only reveal part of the total picture of industrial labor protest. In Australia between 1815 and 1900, industrial disputes that did not involve strikes occurred twice as frequently as strikes, and the ability to participate in nonstrike collective action, such as bans or collective demands, was more noticeably influenced by formal union organization than active strikes.[200] After 1860, the rise in union organization provided the possibility of workers to pursue their objectives by means other than strikes. For instance, in the 1880s, Australian unions increasingly relied on "bans and secondary boycotts" that were feasible tactics only after the development of union organization and interunion collaboration. Just as riots were replaced by strikes, increased labor organization gave rise to greater opportunities to engage in other types of collective action.[201]

---

[196] Michael Quinlan and Margaret Gardner, "Strikes, Worker Protest, and Union Growth in Canada and Australia, 1815–1900: A Comparative Analysis," *Labour/Le Travail* 36 (Fall 1995): 179.

[197] Alan Atkinson, "Four Patterns of Convict Protest," *Labour History* 37 (November 1979): 28–51. Quoted in Quinlan and Gardner, "Strikes, Worker Protest, and Union Growth," 179.

[198] "Boycott" is defined as a "concerted economic or social ostracism of an individual, group, or nation to express disapproval or coerce change. The practice was named (1880) after Capt. Charles Cunningham Boycott, an English land agent in Ireland whose ruthlessness in evicting tenants led his employees to refuse all cooperation with him and his family." Boycott. Reference.com. The Columbia Electronic Encyclopedia. Columbia University Press. http://www.reference.com/browse/boycott?s=t (accessed August 25, 2014).

[199] "Donnybrook, parish and suburb of Dublin...was famous for its annual fair, licensed by King John of England in 1204 and suppressed in 1855 because of its disorderliness. The disorder gave rise to the term "donnybrook," meaning an uproarious brawl." Donnybrook. Reference.com. The Columbia Electronic Encyclopedia. http://www.reference.com/browse/Donnybrook?s=ts (accessed August 25, 2014).

[200] Quinlan and Gardner, "Strikes, Worker Protest, and Union Growth," 191.

[201] Ibid., 193.

Although focusing exclusively on strike activity risks distorting the total picture of industrial action, strikes provide a useful lens through which to discern the general temperament of the laboring class. But in the Australian setting where the population of convicts—with their significantly Irish composition—was so high, various nonstrike methods of demonstrating displeasure were common. Unlike in Canada, the Irish who reached the Australian colonies had no easy access to alternative immigration destination like the United States, and, therefore, Irish convicts as well as Irish free immigrants played a conspicuous role in both industrial struggle and political conflict from the earliest era. The Irish not only represented a large proportion of transported convicts but also constituted a significant proportion of assisted free immigrants during and after the 1830s.[202] Hence, unlike the free workers, convicts were purposely spread out in order to lower the potential for mass rebellion. Any rioting gave rise to a quick and severe response from the colonial authorities. Consequently, prior to the mid-1850s, Australia lacked large groups of free seasonal or transient workers able to participate in rioting against employers.[203]

After the convict system ended in Australia, strike activity rose substantially until the massive protests of the early 1890s brought about compulsory arbitration to contend with the crises. The Irish played a strong role because, unlike Canada where Irish Catholics tended to occupy certain occupational niches, in Australia they were not only found among unskilled occupations but also in skilled trades. Confining Irish immigrants to a constricted group of occupations was never a viable option, and the same was true within the union movement. The Irish took on leadership positions within many unions during the nineteenth century, particularly those of shearers, construction workers, and numerous categories of laborers, a pattern that continued within the ALP.[204]

Although the original intention of Australia's compulsory arbitration was to diminish—if not actually eliminate—strikes from occurring, the evidence shows that the system was not entirely successful. Strikes continued to occur in Australia. Table 6.3 shows that, in the decade between 1965 and 1974, Australia logged more strike time than many other developed nations.

---

[202] Iacovetta, Quinlan, and Radforth, "Immigration and Labour: Australia and Canada Compared," 93.
[203] Quinlan and Gardner, "Strikes, Worker Protest, and Union Growth," 179–80.
[204] Iacovetta, Quinlan, and Radforth, "Immigration and Labour," 95.

Table 6.3   Strike Days Lost Per 1,000 People Employed[205]

Country	Average 1965–1969	Average 1970–1974	Average 1965–1974
Australia	482	1344	913
Belgium	156	512	334
Canada	1556	1732	1644
Denmark	110	912	511
Finland	206	1414	810
France	242[a]	300	271(a)
West Germany	10	90	50
Ireland	1348	688	1018
Italy	1584	1746	1665
Japan	198	288	243
Netherlands	12	118	65
New Zealand	242	402	322
Norway	4	116	60
Sweden	28	64	46
Switzerland	–	2	1
United Kingdom	300	1186	743
United States	1230	1380	1305

Notes: (a) 1968 excluded from averages.

Source: Used with permission from John Niland, *Collective Bargaining and Compulsory Arbitration in Australia* (Kensington, NSW: University of New South Wales Press, 1978), 43, Table 1.

Australia is among the group of Western nations, including Britain, Canada, Finland, Ireland, Italy, and the United States, most prone to strikes.[206] While Australia's work days lost to strikes are far less than Canada's experience—Canada's average is second highest after Italy during the same period—one can only speculate what the number would be if arbitrated settlements were not compulsory. It is possible that Australia could rank higher than Canada and the United States or even Italy. Strikes are simply far too effective to be ignored in helping workers bring employment grievances to the attention of unions, management,

---

[205] Niland, *Collective Bargaining and Complsory Arbitration in Australia*, 43, See Table 1.

[206] Clifford B. Donn, "How Much Do Strikes Cost?" *The Australian* (Sydney), January 18, 1977, cited in Niland, *Collective Bargaining and Compulsory Arbitration in Australia*, 42.

and tribunals.[207] However, evidence shows that strike activity tended to occur more often in Australia than Canada, particularly between 1880 and 1890, with a substantial decline in Australia between 1891 and 1900 due to the unions' major defeats and the economic depression of the early part of that decade.[208]

Despite widespread opposition to the maritime, mining, and pastoral strikes of the 1890s that brought about compulsory arbitration, Australia's radical culture accepts strike action within its compulsory conciliation and arbitration system. In the more conservative Canadian culture, however, private sector employees have traditionally been free to strike as long as they complied with the rather strict rules of their provincial or federal labor relations statute. In the expanding public sector, however, strikes have tended to be quite limited. Half of Canada's provinces ban strikes in their public sectors.[209] Even within federal jurisdiction, when public sector employees elect to participate in collective bargaining the issues over which they may legally strike are narrow.[210]

Contrary to Canada, the Australian position is quite different. According to Australian industrial relations specialist, Ronald Clive McCallum:

> The handing down of an Australian federal award does not mean by itself that strike activity is expressly forbidden. It is possible for the Industrial Relations Commission, on the application of an employer, to insert a clause (known as a "bans clause") into an award prohibiting strikes. This procedure is still infrequently utilised. This is because many strikes are of short duration. They are, in many instances, a symbolic show of force during negotiations. . . . The forbidding of all strikes would prevent employees from negotiating wages and work rules above award minima. When strikes occur, however, employers are of course free to take retaliatory action in the courts. They can

---

[207] Deery and Plowman, *Australian Industrial Relations*, 59.

[208] Quinlan and Gardner, "Strikes, Worker Protest, and Union Growth," 180–81.

[209] The Canadian provinces of Alberta, Manitoba, Nova Scotia, Ontario, and Prince Edward Island, all forbid public sector strikes. J. Sack and T. Lee, "The Role of the State in Canadian Labour Relations," *Relations Industrielles* 44 (1989): 195, 201–2. Cited in Ronald Clive McCallum, "Deregulating Australian Labour Relations: Collective Bargaining Reforms Within Australia's System of Compulsory Conciliation and Arbitration," *Queen's Papers in Industrial Relations* (December 1990): 2, fn 5.

[210] McCallum, "Deregulating Australian Labour Relations," 2.

assert either that the industrial action contravenes Australia's competition statute, or that the trade union's conduct is tortious.[211]

* * *

Just as strikes were not avoided within Australia's system of compulsory arbitration, they were not prevented in Canada's system of compulsory investigation. Although Canadian businessmen did not see a simple substitute for strikes as a method of resolving labor disputes, compulsory arbitration was believed to cause more problems than could be solved. While Canadian employers had no particular objection to submitting industrial disputes to nonbinding arbitration and conciliation, compulsory arbitration was seen by Canadian employers, observes Bliss, as a means of encouraging "unions to escalate demands in the hope that arbitrators would split the difference, add the already untrustworthy force of public opinion to industrial disputes, and ultimately involve governments in attempts at wage-fixing on one hand and coercion of disputants on the other."[212] Indeed, compulsory arbitration is not without inherent limitations.

While compulsory arbitration may serve the public interest by minimizing the occurrence of strikes, this does not imply that the decisions of tribunals are necessarily fair or that disputes actually get fully resolved. Compulsory arbitration always guarantees a settlement but whether or not the dispute is resolved is another matter. With collective bargaining, initially extreme positions can be resolved through compromise that can transform them into more realistic positions acceptable to both sides. In compulsory arbitration, argues Niland, "the parties follow their opening posture throughout, until at the very end they are still presenting evidence in support of that initial position," potentially leading to an artificial final settlement that gives rise to wide points of difference between the parties' respective positions.[213] The important point, however, is that compulsory arbitration was successfully introduced in Australia, an environment that favored its adoption. This suggests an amenable political ideology and distinct ethnocultural influences.

In the late nineteenth and early twentieth centuries, employers in Australia and Canada were generally united in their opposition to any

---

[211] Ibid., 2–3.
[212] Bliss, *A Living Profit,* 91.
[213] Niland, 36.

form of state intervention in labor disputes.[214] A key difference between Canada and Australia, however, was in the parliamentarians during the first five years of the twentieth century when industrial dispute legislation came into force. While their actions reflected the mood of the workers in both countries, this was especially true for Australia. Australian colonial parliaments appear to have had a much larger proportion of their members from among the ranks of unions and union supporters both through the rising Labor Party and independently. Therefore, as Mitchell rightly asserts, there was "a critical connection in Australia between union policy and parliamentary policy which was largely absent in Canada."[215]

Given that prior British arbitration laws were not models used for Australian arbitral legislation, the adoption of compulsory arbitration in Australia was a sign of domestic Australian conditions that coalesced during the formative period at the turn of the twentieth century. As suggested in this chapter, first, the new formal regulations reflected a British utilitarian influence in early Australia that gave vigor to Australian radical culture. Second, the rise of a pro-compulsory arbitration movement happened to coincide with a rise in Irish assertion of influence in the Labor Party and in union leadership. Irish collectivism and innate rebelliousness helped foster a collectivist mood where compulsory arbitration was seen as radical—thereby fitting the British radical ideological fragment that had come to Australia—and in the best interests of workers, many of whom were of Irish descent. The Australian Irish community was, therefore, not a minor player in the implementation of radical policy.

While Australia and Canada were both influenced by radicals among nineteenth-century British immigrants, the character and effect of their radicalism differed. Nonetheless, unlike the United States, both share a tolerance for social democratic movements. This history reveals underlying cultural distinctions, especially between Canada and the United States. According to Horowitz, "the relative strength of socialism in Canada is related to the relative strength of toryism, and to the different position and character of liberalism in the two countries."[216] Thus, given general cultural trends, it is no surprise that these effects would also be evident in management culture, and the underlying personal values that help shape it.

---

[214] Mitchell, "Solving the Great Social Problem of the Age," 69.
[215] Ibid., 69–70.
[216] Horowitz, *Canadian Labour in Politics*, 3.

7
Australian and Canadian Managerial Culture: A Summary

While adherence to British values predominated in English Canada across the spectrum of socioeconomic class, Australia, being far removed from the United States but with British colonial rule on its doorstep, tended to be less accepting largely because of the presence of a significant and assertive working class that, from early on, included a strong Irish component. Although the Australian elite tended to embrace British identity and heritage, the working class was less enamored, particularly when it came to the inherent inequality associated with British rank and privilege. In the words of Australian historian Geoffrey Blainey, "Australian life suffers at times from an inadequate respect for enterprise, originality, and talent. On the other hand, it also gains from the democratic and communal sense that 'Jack is as good as his master'—if not better."[1] This sentiment evokes the Australian preference for flatter hierarchies.

As these pages have asserted, the contribution of an Irish sensibility to Australian irreverence, rebelliousness, and egalitarianism—or desire for flatter hierarchies—is evident in such Australian practices as "knocking," "cutting down tall poppies," and the social phenomenon of "mateship." These and other Australian cultural features distinguish Australia from Canada and point to a historically significant "Irish factor" that Canada does not share. Therefore, underlying values were explored to help point Australia and Canada's salient cultural characteristics to particular regions of Anglo-Celtic origin.

---

[1] Geoffrey Blainey, "Australia: A Bird's-Eye View," in *Australia: The Daedalus Symposium*, ed. Stephen R. Graubard (North Ryde, NSW: Angus & Robertson, 1985), 23.

Values and national culture in perspective

Australians and Canadians are not identical. Research supports the view that Australians are more assertive and individualistic than their English-speaking Canadian counterparts.[2] Likewise, Canadians are not identical with Americans. As Tom Atkinson and Michael Murray, psychologists at York University's Institute for Behavioural Research in Toronto, conclude, "The greater value of social relationships in Canada and of achievement in the United States reflects long-standing societal differences which will persist in the future."[3] The persistence of difference is a result of enduring cultural features traced, in large part, to the influx of significant populations at critical junctures in each nation's history. By taking up residence in Australia and Canada, these populations succeeded in perpetuating their cultural values to the broader culture around them. Subsequent immigrants, therefore, emulated many of the prevailing views, norms, and values. They brought them into their homes and passed them onto their children, whose descendants acquired them through a continuous process of socialization. These tendencies are not only apparent in society at large but also in management behavior.

As managerial culture is a reflection of general culture, this comparison of Australian and Canadian managerial culture has made an effort to reveal subtle differences between broad cultural values as a means to account for existing cultural variation. Differences prove more revealing than a superficial focus on cultural similarities. After all, similarities are more obvious, from common use of the English language and British colonial heritage to their shared political traditions and legal systems. From a managerial point of view, however, identifying differences in national character, temperament, dominant values, and management models, as well as the underlying influences that shaped them, not only enhances awareness of individual culture but helps promote more effective cross-cultural communication. This is important to ensure cooperation and mutual understanding.

Two people possessing fundamental similarities tend to make their differences stand out. Instead of appearing interesting, their differences

---

[2] Neal M. Ashkanasy, "Studies of Cognition and Emotion in Organisations: Attribution, Affective Events, Emotional Intelligence and Perception of Emotion," *Australian Journal of Management* 27 (Special Issue, September 2002): 4.

[3] Tom Atkinson and Michael A. Murray, *Values, Domains and the Perceived Quality of Life: Canada and the United States* (Toronto, ON: Institute for Behavioural Research, York University, 1982), 29.

can be frustrating.[4] Expectations play a large role in how people react to these differences. When two cultural groups expect to encounter differences in the other—such as Americans and Japanese—their discovery of a point in common is both reassuring and exciting. However, when two similar cultural groups—like Australians and Canadians—expect the other to be much like themselves but instead discern a conspicuous difference, considerable confusion is likely to occur. When difference then follows upon unexpected difference, encounters easily become more challenging. As Renwick suggests, "Chronic aggravation results when the disruptive differences are felt but not specifically located, labeled and dealt with."[5]

Culture is a powerful force as it shapes managerial attitudes, values and assumptions, which in turn determine behaviors, or how organizations function. While cross-cultural misinterpretations may not be as significant to a manager's ability to perform within the country of acculturation, they can be a serious obstacle to managing effectively in other cultures and countries. Neglecting cultural considerations, therefore, evokes a powerful cycle that can be detrimental to an organization's overall performance. According to the vast cross-cultural literature, O'Grady and Lane summarize, "Culture affects an executive's attitudes and values. These attitudes and values, in turn, affect the executive's business behaviors and practices, including his or her strategic decisions. The strategic decisions made, in turn, affect the performance of the organization..."[6] While cross-cultural manuals exist to help smooth intercultural communication and business relationships,[7] this book has discerned the origins of dominant values and help account for their underlying differences in order to bring about greater cultural harmony for managerial interactions both within each culture and in cross-cultural interaction.

Australian cynicism toward individual power and rebelliousness among large segments of the population appears linked to the

[4] George W. Renwick, *InterAct: Guidelines for Australians and North Americans* (Yarmouth, ME: Intercultural Press, 1980), 1.

[5] Ibid., 2.

[6] Shawna O'Grady and Henry W. Lane, "Culture: An Unnoticed Barrier to Canadian Retail Performance in the USA," *Journal of Retailing and Consumer Services* 4, no. 3 (1997): 161.

[7] For example, Philip R. Harris, Robert T. Moran, and Sarah V. Moran, *Managing Cultural Differences: Global Leadership Strategies for the Twenty-First Century*, 6th ed. (Amsterdam, The Netherlands: Elsevier/Butterworth-Heinemann, 2004); and Terry Morrison, Wayne A. Conway, and George A. Borden, *Kiss, Bow, Shake Hands: How to Do Business in Sixty Countries* (Holbrook, MA: B. Adams, 1994).

substantial nineteenth-century Irish Catholic presence in Australia. In contrast, English-speaking Canada was largely shaped by waves of English, Scottish, and Irish Protestant immigrants—a process that began in earnest with the arrival of the Loyalists in the late eighteenth century—which made subsequent immigrants of varied backgrounds who chose to settle in Canada instead of the United States more readily embracing of British colonial values. A strong emotional attachment to Great Britain on the part of Canadians of British origin was essential for Canada to remain separate from the United States.[8] Given that Canada (apart from the French population of Quebec) was overwhelmingly "British," it is not surprising that British values would predominate and their prevailing outlook, strengthened by successive waves of British immigrants, would influence other ethnic groups in Canada toward a similar point of view. A greater tolerance of power distance appears to reflect Canada's closer emotional ties to Britain compared to Australia.

The sectarian conflict within the Australian Irish community during the second half of the nineteenth century intensified an already wide Protestant–Catholic divide. Consequently, the top-down power structure which saw a mostly Protestant power elite in charge led a predominantly Irish Catholic Australian working class to view vertical power structures with far greater cynicism than in English-speaking Canada where the British Protestant elite and large segments of the working class were of similar ethnic and religious affiliation. Interestingly, this was in contrast to the administration of the Catholic Church, which is highly hierarchical. Nonetheless, this working-class cynicism of vertical hierarchy where elites effectively ruled over the masses—ostensibly rooted in economic and political disparity but also reflective of opposing religious-cultural identities—subsequently became a widespread Australian cultural norm.

Contrary to Australia, Canada's working classes either resembled a similar ethnocultural affiliation as the elites or showed a greater propensity or willingness to accept their cultural views in a highly charged geopolitical environment where the choice between national values was either "Canadian"—implying a strong British connection—or American. In Australia the sizeable Irish Catholic community seemed to exert a profound influence on Australian society that is still evident

---

[8] S.D. Clark, "The Canadian Community," in *Canada*, ed. G.W. Brown (Berkeley, CA: University of California Press, 1950), 307.

in the contemporary culture. What began as a grassroots movement to assert Catholic rights in early Australia—seen particularly in the leadership of the Irish Catholic religious community—soon spread into organized labor and politics.

Australia's Irish factor is an important source of Australian cultural differences that has not been considered in cross-cultural communication manuals. One popular cross-cultural manual, *Culture Shock! Australia*, outlines a range of stereotypes that depict the 'typical Australian.' Continental Europeans are reported as seeing "the Aussie as barbaric, loud-mouthed, ignorant and uncultured, hopelessly provincial," while the British are described as viewing their "Antipodean cousin as a rather alarming, alien being bereft of the (hypocritical) courtesies of the mother country..." Despite these generalizations, the author notes that the Australian accent "is execrable by British standards and unfortunately slots the Australian firmly into 'the lower classes,' since it best resembles working-class Cockney from East End London, or Irish-dialect English."[9] Other than a general warning to resist telling Australian hosts of uncertain family origins any Irish jokes, that is the extent of the Irish analysis.

Yet Australia's Irish factor becomes evident in comparison with Canada where no equivalent Irish factor is discernible. Moreover, despite the significant impact of the Scots on Canada, there was no comparable "Scottish factor" that could equate with the Australian Irish factor. While the Irish represented a distinctive, noncompliant element that helped influence the national Australian culture, the Scots of Canada fostered acceptance of the prevailing British culture. Hence, Scottish membership in the Canadian elite was more closely connected to Scottish regard and connection to British Protestant rule than class differences. Even those Scots attracted to Canada's radicalism and socialist movement did not tend to advocate anti-British sentiments. The result of these various influences on each national culture—and the managerial culture that evolved—broadly points to a cultural phenomenon of Australian irreverence versus Canadian deference.

Assessing the extent of Australia's Irish factor

Explored through comparison of Australia and Canada's ethnic composition, socio-economic class, and influence of dominant ideological

---

[9] Ilsa Sharp, *Culture Shock! Australia: A Guide to Customs and Etiquette* (Portland, OR: Graphic Arts Center Publishing Company, 2000), 10–11, 49.

movements, the impact and source of the Irish factor becomes clear. The role of management and the ideological and Anglo-Celtic distinctions in managerial style that helped account for labor's reaction to dominant management models showed important distinctions. The religious, ideological, and working-class aspects of radicalism and socialism in Australia and English Canada did the same for their direct and indirect effect on local managerial culture.

Scientific management, reflecting a strong sense of individualism, was not embraced by the working classes in Australia or Canada. Labor was partial to the more collectivist-oriented outlook of the human relations movement. Although managers in both countries favored individualism—showing a cultural preference for vertical hierarchy which provided a sense of supervisory authority, or superiority, over those they managed—and a dislike for trade unions that contested for power in the workplace, they could not function in a vacuum. Their ability to manage often depended on their willingness to accommodate the collective mood of labor.

In other words, despite Australian and Canadian managers' preference for individualism—fostered by their common British heritage and class membership—their managerial practices modulated to some degree in response to a working class more attuned to collectivism. In Australia, however, this collectivist mood reflected British radicalism and Irish sensibilities, whereas in English Canada it stemmed primarily from Toryism, which encouraged acceptance of aspects of collectivism that later enabled socialism—the British variety derived from Fabian, radical, and religious influences—to spread across the political and cultural terrain. French Canada's collectivist impulse had different origins.[10]

Alongside the strong British labor ethos that infused Australia and Canada, both experienced the conservatizing effect of significant population groups. Although the effect in Australia stemmed primarily from Irish Catholics, in Canada it was largely expressed by the French of

---

[10] See, for example, Nelson Wiseman, "A Note on 'Hartz-Horowitz and Twenty,'" *Canadian Journal of Political Science* 21, no. 4 (1988): 804–05; Carolyn P. Egri, David A. Ralson, Cheryl S. Murray, and Joel D. Nicholson, "Managers in the NAFTA Countries: A Cross-Cultural Comparison of Attitudes Toward Upward Influence Strategies," *Journal of International Management* 6, no. 2 (2000): 154–55; Douglas E. Baer and James E. Curtis, "French Canadian-English Canadian Differences in Values: National Survey Findings," *The Canadian Journal of Sociology* 9, no. 4 (1984); and Chanlat and Bedard, "Managing in the Quebec Style: Originality and Vulnerability," *International Studies of Management and Organization* 21, no. 3 (1991): 10–37.

Quebec with the Scots playing a similar but less decisive role in English Canada. Given Australia's broad Irish Catholic geographical dispersion relative to Canada's more concentrated French Catholic settlement pattern, the Irish arguably impacted Australian national mores and attitudes to a greater degree than the French in Canada's national culture. Hence, this pervasive Irish Catholic conservatizing effect helps explain why Australia never developed the same socialist conscience as Canada. Other reasons include the dominant Australian cultural values of egalitarianism, mateship and antiauthoritarianism that British radicals, and especially the Irish, helped foster.

Irish collectivism is very strong relative to other Anglo nations.[11] This provides an explanation for the strong sense of collectivism that permeated Australian culture since the settlement of the Irish. Moreover, collectivism and the historic rebelliousness of the Irish can be reconciled with the seemingly antithetical placidity in Ireland that emerged following 1922's achievement of the Irish Free State. This euphoric moment was of immense psychological importance for both the Irish in Ireland and abroad. After being a subjected people for so long, their collective focus necessarily shifted from active rebellion to nation building, requiring skills of conciliation and diplomacy. However, active rebellion did not cease as the turmoil in Northern Ireland proved during the balance of the twentieth century. In contrast with the Irish Republic, Northern Ireland emerged as a place of considerable agitation as the traditional Irish antagonism between Protestant and Catholic became increasingly violent. For the larger numbers of Irish in an independent Ireland, some degree of rebelliousness was understandably placated by other important features of an emerging sovereign nation. The shift of focus occurred because of political and economic uncertainty.[12]

With the achievement of Irish independence, therefore, rebelliousness was joined by a strong sense of purpose and responsibility. This new situation enhanced the Irish collective impulse that had served to build Irish Catholic solidarity over the centuries, a sentiment that continued among the Irish of Australia. Like other newly independent states that

---

[11] Mary A. Keating and Gillian S. Martin, "Leadership and Culture in the Republic of Ireland," in *Culture and Leadership Across the World: The GLOBE Book of In-Depth Studies of 25 Societies*, ed. J.S. Chhokar, F.C. Brodbeck, and R.J. House, 361–396 (New York, NY: Lawrence Erlbaum, 2008).

[12] Thomas E. Hachey, "From Free State to Republic, 1922–1996," in Thomas E. Hachey, Joseph M. Hernon, Jr., and Lawrence J. McCaffrey, *The Irish Experience: A Concise History*, rev. ed. (Armonk, NY: M.E. Sharpe, 1996), 178.

emerged in continental Europe following the First World War, Ireland now had to prove that it had not won its self-determination in vain. In the Republic of Ireland, a sense of relative placidity grew alongside the characteristic rebelliousness that had been a distinctive Irish trait for centuries, but it did not eradicate rebellion as demonstrated by subsequent decades of tragic violence in Northern Ireland—and, without the brutality, in Australian politics and labor.

Yet it is the emphasis on the Irish in eastern Australia that has led some scholars to question Patrick O'Farrell's view of the Irish as "a constant liberalising creative irritant" in national Australian culture.[13] Critical of the relative lack of attention paid to the Irish impact on western regions of the country, Australian historian Anne Partlon has objected to the two dominant approaches to assessing the Irish influence in eastern Australia—Chris McConville's search for archetypal figures such as Ned Kelly and Peter Lalor in order to define a model Irish character, and Patrick O'Farrell's belief that the Irish "exerted a greater, if more subtle, influence on Australian society by assimilating with it."[14]

Ned Kelly and, in an earlier era, the Irish rebels at Castle Hill and the Eureka Stockade rebellion—especially Peter Lalor, the Irish-born leader at Eureka, the violent and controversial birthplace of Australian democracy—"were in their time seen as outlaws and criminals not only causing civil disruption but threatening to tear the fabric of colonial society," argues Simon Caterson, "nowadays they are generally viewed as being on the heroic side of the argument."[15]

In Partlon's view, McConville's approach suffers from the problem that such high-profile Irish Catholic figures like Kelly, Lalor, and Mannix were "hardly typical of the behaviour of the majority of their countrymen," while, she claims, O'Farrell's theory is limited by the difficulty in measuring "subtle influences" of an Irish population large enough to attract attention, "but too small and disorganized to bring about immediate social and political change."[16] Despite Partlon's criticisms, however, she accepts that Irish Catholics presented an important source of general influence on the country as a whole. Partlon concedes, "McConville has

[13] Quoted in Anne Partlon, "'Singers Standing On The Outer Rim': Writing About the Irish in WA," *Studies in Western Australian History* 20 (2000): 190.

[14] Partlon, "Singers Standing On The Outer Rim," 189.

[15] Simon Caterson, "Irish-Australian Attitudes," *Quadrant* 48, no. 11 (2004): 12, 15.

[16] Ibid.

warned of the dangers of using 'Catholic' and 'Irish' as interchangeable terms, and yet it is true to say that, until the 1960s, the Catholic Church in Australia was chiefly run by, and for, Irish men and women."[17] While there may not have been as much assisted immigration of Catholic Irish from Ireland, nor were they significantly represented in the convict population, Partlon notes that a significant "influx of Irish was not from Ireland but via the eastern colonies during the gold rushes of the 1890s."[18] Hence, even though the impact of the Irish was felt primarily in the eastern Australian states of New South Wales and Victoria where their populations were largest, they affected the nation as a whole since the bulk of Australia's population has, for much of Australia's history, been situated in the east, and populations affected by their presence took these influences with them as they spread across the continent. In the words of Australian historian John Gascoigne, O'Farrell "regarded the Irish in Australia as being like the grit in the oyster preventing Australia accepting too readily a prepackaged imperial culture and producing a distinctive culture of its own."[19] Thus, considering individuals of Irish descent and the community's collective, often subtle, influences on Australian culture as a whole, significant Irish patterns are indeed evident. This helps explain the intriguing patterns noted in the cultural dimensions of power distance and individualism/collectivism.

In a revisionist interpretation, Judith Brett, argues that Catholics' preference for Labor was not merely due to their predominant working-class membership. Rather than referring to the widely accepted class-based explanation that the majority of working-class Catholics became aligned with the Australian Labor Party (ALP), Brett asserts that it was Protestantism that caused this situation in Australia. Brett argues that "the identification of Catholics with Labor is in good part the result of the Protestantism of the non-labour parties which made them inhospitable places for Australian Catholics."[20] While Brett makes an interesting observation, it does not negate the impact the Australian Irish had on the general culture. Moreover, contrary to Australia's relative

---

[17] Ibid., 192.

[18] Ibid., 190.

[19] John Gascoigne, "Catholicism, Australia and a Wider World: The Historiographical Legacy of Patrick O'Farrell and Tony Cahill," *The Australasian Catholic Record* 83, no. 2 (2006): 139.

[20] Judith Brett, "Class, Religion and the Foundation of the Australian Party System: A Revisionist Interpretation," *Australian Journal of Political Science* 37, no. 1 (2002): 40.

collectivism/individualism, which points to Ireland as a strong influence given Australia's historic, large, and influential community of Irish, Canada's individualism appears to stem from its significantly British—strongly Scottish-nuanced—heritage.

Interestingly, studying the differences in English and Scottish church governance, Alistair Mutch argues the case for the existence of an orderly approach to authority in Scotland in contrast with a personal approach in England. He asserts that "the forms of governance of the Presbyterian church as established in Scotland placed considerable emphasis on individual accountability within an overall system supported by detailed record keeping." In contrast with the Scottish model, Mutch suggests that "it was the English model of gentlemanly individualism that continued to dominate." However, it is plausible that the immigration of the Scots to Canada infused an element of their individualism on the Canadian landscape. For instance, Andrew Wedderburn, a Scottish member of the Governing Committee of the Hudson Bay Company in 1810, introduced innovations that "were designed to ensure the detailed accountability of every trading post."[21]

These views underscore the significance of Louis Hartz's fragment theory, and its subsequent local refinements by Richard Rosecrance (Australia) and Gad Horowitz (Canada), which postulate that Australia, Canada, and the United States were influenced by differing colonial fragments of European culture, particularly of prevailing British values and beliefs of the time. In other words, although Australia, English Canada and the United States are all members of the Anglo cluster of world cultures, they are not identical. Ideology represented another means of cultural value transmission.

The cultural effect of ideological fragments

Ideology played an important role in transferring cultural values because Canadian leaders—the political and business elites—shaped by the Tory character that combined liberal individualism with an acceptance of a certain degree of collectivism, enabled socialism to grow. Australia's elite was more closely aligned with the liberalism characteristic of the mid-nineteenth century. However, radicalism proved a stronger and more pervasive factor among Australian labor than Canadian workers due to

---

[21] Alistair Mutch, "The Institutional Shaping of Management: In the Tracks of English Individualism," *Management & Organizational History* 1, no. 3 (2006): 262, 264–65.

dominant populations and subtle ideological differences. Except for a few years in between the two world wars, militancy was less prevalent in Canada. Yet there is an important exception: Militancy was more frequent in Canada's western province of British Columbia in comparison with central or eastern Canada. This hints of an American influence. A regional affinity for radicalism among Canadian labor led Nelson Wiseman to refer to British Columbia as "Canada's Australia" because:

> Both were radical offshoots of Europe: Australian settlement came earlier in the nineteenth century and inherited the then radical liberal ideology of Bentham's utilitarianism; BC's settlement came later, inheriting the ideology of labour-socialism. Both developed left-right, urban-rural, and class-driven political cleavages with parties offering the rhetoric of class conflict. Both represent upstart parvenu societies offering rags-to-riches success, liberation, and class mobility. Radicals in both societies saw them as a potential 'working-man's paradise'....Like Australia, BC offered [its immigrants] indolence, opportunity, and a new beginning.[22]

Wiseman suggests that the underlying cultural reasons for these similarities reflect different sources of migratory influences. Australia received an earlier formative wave of British immigrants imbued by the radical liberal views of Benthamite utilitarianism. Western Canada, in contrast, absorbed a subsequent, though equally formative, wave of British immigrants who were shaped by turn-of-the-century labor-socialism that was characteristic of the era in Great Britain. However, the analysis of Canadian historian Jean Barman suggests an urban/rural distinction. Rural areas seem to have attracted a population possessing American-style assertiveness compared to the urban areas influenced more by British settlers.

Barman hypothesizes that many settlers beyond the large urban centers of Vancouver and Victoria can trace their origins to the United States via Alberta, a phenomenon that provides a plausible explanation for regional support for the Reform Party in BC, unlike Saskatchewan to the east of Alberta.[23] The Reform Party was a right-wing populist federal

---

[22] Nelson Wiseman, "Provincial Political Cultures," in *Provinces: Canadian Provincial* Politics, ed. Christopher Dunn, 2nd ed. (Peterborough, ON: Broadview Press, 2006), 51.

[23] Jean Barman, "The West Beyond the West: The Demography of Settlement in British Columbia," *Journal of Canadian Studies* 25, no. 4 (1990): 5–18.

political party, founded in 1987 in Alberta that merged in 2000 with the Canadian Alliance, only to subsequently merge with the Progressive Conservative Party in 2003 to become the modern Conservative Party of Canada, the national governing party in Canada since 2006.

Migrants moved from the United States to Alberta with the establishment of the railway, and from there moved west to British Columbia's rural regions. Despite the religious orientation of the assertive Social Credit Party and Reform Party,[24] which both originated in Alberta, their temperament seemed more in tune with American authoritarian values. This influence is plausible as a large proportion of Alberta's settlers in the nineteenth century had come from the western United States where they experienced their formative years.[25] Indeed, the success of the Social Credit party in BC provincial elections during the 1950s—particularly in such provincial ridings as the Fraser Valley, Kamloops, Okanagan, Penticton and Cariboo that would subsequently support the Reform (and later Canadian Alliance) Party in federal politics—reflects the cultural predisposition of the same Albertan migrants who had earlier established the United Farmers of Alberta.[26] Social Credit led provincial governments in BC and Alberta for decades until support ultimately waned.

However, the success of the Social Credit and Reform parties was achieved in the rural regions of both British Columbia and Alberta as opposed to urban areas. Hence, while many of British Columbia's settlers had their formative experience in Scotland, particularly Edinburgh and Glasgow's Clyde, their descendants tended to settle in the larger urban population centers of Vancouver and Victoria. In light of their British heritage, their

[24] The Reform Party of Canada (1987–2000) held a political platform that emphasized traditional Prairie reform ideas, including free trade, direct democracy in the form of referendums, and an elected senate. It also called for a reduction in the size, scope, and spending of government, particularly cuts to social welfare and cultural support programs, like multiculturalism. In 2000, the party ceased to exist after it became part of the Canadian Alliance Party to oppose the governing Liberal Party. In 2003, the Canadian Alliance Party ceased to exist after consolidating with the Progressive Conservative Party to become the new Canadian Conservative Party of Canada, which won a minority government in 2006. *See* Trevor W. Harrison, "Reform Party of Canada," *The Canadian Encyclopedia*, http://www.thecanadianencyclopedia.ca/en/article/reform-party-of-canada/, and Trevor W. Harrison, "Canadian Alliance," *The Canadian Encyclopedia*, http://www.thecanadianencyclopedia.ca/en/article/canadian-alliance/ (accessed May 18, 2014).

[25] Paul F. Sharp, *Whoop-Up Country: The Canadian-American West, 1865–1885* (Minneapolis, MN: University of Minnesota Press, 1955), 310–16.

[26] Christian Leuprecht, "The Tory Fragment in Canada: Endangered Species?" *Canadian Journal of Political Science* 36 (2003): 403.

values were more in sync with central Canada's urban and rural populations. In other words, Canada's large urban centers featured relatively consistent personal values that helped solidify Canada's national culture. Fragment analysis holds up well in accounting for patterns in Canada's political culture. While a distinctive influential migration from the United States to Alberta occurred largely in the late nineteenth century, the earlier northward migration from the United States to eastern Canada had different origins. As described, the American Revolution led many Loyalists to relocate in British territory—especially in the present-day Maritime Provinces of Nova Scotia and New Brunswick, as well as Ontario, leading to relatively stable voting patterns in favor of conservative parties.[27]

Despite these pockets of rebellious, American-style assertiveness that found a voice in parts of Alberta and rural areas of British Columbia, the British influence on British Columbia, as in much of English Canada, is clear. Fragment analysis is particularly helpful in identifying which fragments proved most influential and when. According to Gordon S. Galbraith,

> In the case of Lower Canada, Quebec, the early founding population was drawn predominantly from the minor gentry and peasantry of pre-revolutionary France. Upper Canada drew its early population, around and about the time of the point of congealment, from early 19th-century Britain—after the wars against Bonaparte, but before the massive industrialization and urbanization of the latter part of the 19th century. British Columbia also drew its founding population from the United Kingdom, but at a time when the social and economic conditions of the United Kingdom had changed greatly....There can be no doubt that, at the time of its founding in the early 1900s, British Columbia was a *fragment of Edwardian Britain*. The immigrant manual and clerical workers brought with them their hopes, aspirations, expectations, anxieties, and quarrels. The atmosphere of strife and striving they established has remained until today.[28]

Galbraith separates the impact of a number of influential waves of immigrants to BC. The first wave, which he terms the Edwardian fragment,

---

[27] Ibid., 404–5.
[28] Gordon S. Galbraith, "British Columbia," in *The Provincial Political Systems: Comparative Essays*, ed. David J. Bellamy, Jon H. Pammett, and Donald C. Rowat (Toronto, ON: Methuen, 1976), 68–69.

arrived to British Columbia from "a hierarchical society in a status-conscious frame of mind, in a situation of status anxiety, of uncertainty about their place in the scheme of things."[29] Subsequent immigrants from other parts of Canada, particularly the Prairie Provinces, arrived with their own uncertainties but blended into the prevailing community. Galbraith asserts, however, that many British Columbians came to terms with their "status anxiety" by either "vigorously asserting their membership in the working class and their trade unionism, or by equally vigorously asserting the opposite, their bourgeois and middle class status."[30]

These divergent sets of attitudes go beyond mere differences of political opinion. They are strong beliefs closely bound with individual self-conception. They reflect what Galbraith characterizes as BC's "bipolar political culture," a polarization between two sets of attitudes:

One set of attitudes, one pole, emphasizes individual achievement and economic growth. It finds its social centre of gravity among white-collar workers, professionals, and businessmen. Its political vehicles have been the Conservative Party, the Liberal Party, the Social Credit League, and at times all three. The second set of political attitudes emphasizes distribution of existing wealth and social egalitarianism. It finds its centre of gravity among trade unionists, and blue-collar workers generally. It has found its political expression first in the Co-operative Commonwealth Federation (CCF), then in the New Democratic Party (NDP).[31]

United Farmers, Social Credit, Reform, and Canadian Alliance were strong populist parties peculiar to the regions in which they originated. The success of these regionally assertive parties reinforces the significance of fragment analysis. Given Canada's proximity to the United States, it is not surprising that American values would make their way across the border via migrants. Nonetheless, it appears that the dominant set of values in English Canada are more closely aligned with British influences, reflecting immigrants and their descendants of both English and Scottish heritage. In other words, despite pockets of Canadian behavior that appear American in origin—particularly in rural BC as opposed to the urban centers and in largely rural Alberta—the Prairies, with their British influence, served as Canada's source of an assertive collectivist

[29] Ibid., 69.
[30] Ibid.
[31] Ibid.

284 The Development of Managerial Culture

impulse that fueled labor interests and helped found a labor-oriented political party, the CCF, which later became the NDP. Their values infused Canadian culture. Hence, these values entered the workplace through managers who shared an ethnocultural British heritage, retained or acquired through the process of socialization, and through the rank and file of the Canadian working class who were imbued with these same values.

Hence, given the formative impact of Australia and Canada's culturally defining British populations, and the conservative role of sizable minority cultures, socialist and radical influences were not identical in each society. Australia, defined by greater radicalism derived from the liberalism characteristic of the early nineteenth century, also experienced the conservatizing effect of the Irish who were radical but less inclined to embrace socialism because of religious reasons, such as outlined in the Papal encyclical, *Rerum Novarum*. Canada's early immersion in Tory collectivism appears to have helped absorb a later wave of migrants sympathetic to socialist views, but this did not come at the expense of the traditional respect for hierarchy and British rule, which Scottish conservative forces helped retain.

Australia's radical tradition, rooted in collectivist origins and embraced by both the British working class and the Irish, remains a strong cultural force. But it has moved beyond these origins. In the late 1990s, many Australians increasingly looked toward the United States for inspiration. As Jupp observes,

> While America, too, inherits a radical tradition, it is individualist rather than collectivist. Personal advancement rather than group solidarity seems more attractive to Australians today and this attraction pulls them towards the Liberals, rather than to the Australian Labor Party. Both of these major parties inherit something of the radical tradition. What there is of a conservative inheritance to Australia has passed down to the Liberals, leaving the ALP to repeat phrases and strike attitudes which are sometimes reminiscent of the "golden days" from 1891 to 1916.[32]

Since the turn of the twenty-first century, the Australian workplace appears to have moved closer toward an American individualist model,

---

[32] James Jupp, *Australian Party Politics*, 2nd ed. (Carlton, VIC: Melbourne University Press; London and New York, NY: Cambridge University Press, 1968), 2.

at least for the moment. Although the overall changes reflect a domestic political agenda led by non-Labor parties, this development also reflects the current trend toward individualism shared with Britain among other nations. This phenomenon, suggests John Purcell, is "seen in the shift to human resource management, the growth in merit pay, assessment systems and greater attention paid to recruitment, selection and internal training schemes linked to flexibility."[33] It also reflects a move toward centralizing the labor relations system in the hands of the federal government rather than at state levels. This new and revolutionary approach currently being pursued by the Commonwealth government of Australia happens to be the American trend.

Unlike the United States, observes Pierre Verge, the Canadian "provincial systems normally govern labor relations, while federal labor laws only prevail throughout the country with respect to 'federal undertakings' (such as banks, interprovincial and international transportation and broadcasting)."[34] In Canada, collective labor relations law prevails and does not seem to have been destabilized by the forces of globalization,[35] but could still evolve in response to a change of government policy as occurred in Australia. As Verge asserts, the "relative stability of the Canadian system of labor law faces the challenge of maintaining its significance and of adapting to the transformation of work already in progress in contemporary industrialised societies."[36]

From the start of the twentieth century, the Australian industrial relations system assisted and encouraged collective industrial relations; however, by the beginning of the twenty-first century John Howard's Liberal–National Coalition Government had pursued an equally radical path in the other direction by moving away from the collective approach. Whereas NSW's *Industrial Relations Act 1996* preserved collective industrial relations at the state level, the Commonwealth's *Workplace Relations Act 1996* reflected individual industrial relations. The difference between the two underscores inherent differences between collectivism and individualism.

A collective approach to industrial relations encourages workers to act together during bargaining over an award or enterprise agreement

---

[33] John Purcell, "Mapping Management Styles in Employee Relations," *Journal of Management Studies* 24, no. 5 (1987): 547.
[34] Pierre Verge, "How Does Canadian Labour Law Fare in a Global Economy?" *The Journal of Industrial Relations* 42, no. 2 (2000): 276.
[35] Ibid., 285.
[36] Ibid., 291–92.

that serves to govern the industrial relationship between employees and employers. Individual contracts are between individual employees and employers, which are characterized by an imbalance in power between them.[37] Thus, the rise in individual contracts in Australia since the 1990s was indicative of this trend. Australian "Workplace Agreements" are individual contracts that must be signed by individual workers (even though they may be collectively negotiated). Individualism is clearly the underlying philosophy that the government chose to enforce through its legislation. Shaw observes, a desire to exclude third parties is evident in object 3(b) of the *Workplace Relations Act 1996 (Commonwealth)*. It provides that the " . . . primary responsibility for determining matters affecting the relationship between employers and employees rests with the employer and employees at the workplace or enterprise level."[38] In other words, responsibility should not require third-party intervention as had been the practice under the Australian Conciliation and Arbitration Commission (or, after being renamed in 1989, the Australian Industrial Relations Commission (AIRC)).[39]

Acceleration toward an individualist-based industrial relations system was embraced by Howard's Coalition Government as part of a grand plan of radical reforms. Despite massive worker-led protests across the country objecting to the federal government's industrial relations reforms,[40] the amended legislation—*Workplace Relations Amendment (Work Choices) Act 2005* (known as "WorkChoices")—came into effect in 2006 after an unsuccessful challenge in the High Court by Australia's state governments and trade unions. Key features of the new law included the encouragement of direct bargaining between employees and employers to form individual workplace agreements, the reduction in strength of the AIRC by eliminating its former general powers of compulsory conciliation and arbitration, and the restriction of unfair dismissal actions to

---

[37] J.W. Shaw, "In Defence of the Collective: New South Wales Industrial Relations in the 21st Century," *Journal of Industrial Relations* 39, no. 3 (1997): 390.

[38] Quoted in Ibid., 401.

[39] The decline in the role of the Commission is outlined in Braham Dabscheck, "The Slow and Agonising Death of the Australian Experiment with Conciliation and Arbitration," *The Journal of Industrial Relations* 43, no. 3 (2001): 277–93.

[40] For example, *see* Australian Associated Press, "Workplace Rally Attracts Thousands," *The Age* (Melbourne), November 30, 2006. http://www.theage.com.au/news/National/Workplace-rally-attracts-thousands/2006/11/30/11647776896 57.html# (accessed May 18, 2014).

enterprises with more than one hundred employees.[41] As these labor reforms are a complex mix of short-term politics and long-term cultural change, it is too early to determine what long-term effect these trends may ultimately have on Australian and Canadian culture.[42]

* * *

Despite the various splits that have occurred within the ALP, whose significant Irish Catholic segment in the early part of the twentieth century began to diminish by the late 1950s, Labor's core support among Catholics remained strong well into the 1990s. A clear majority of Australian Catholic voters supported the ALP in the 1993 election. However, the impact of Australian Catholics proved as powerful as ever when just three years later during the 1996 election, Catholic support of Labor fell by a significant 12 percent in favor of the Coalition, which benefited from the sudden change of alliance. Rather than a wholesale abandonment of Australian Catholics from the Labor party, the situation appeared to reflect lack of confidence in the ALP among the electorate as a whole.

The ALP's 1996 defeat was not the first time the ALP had been compelled to reinvent itself, to broaden its appeal and reinvigorate the party. In the 1977 federal election, the ALP followed its devastating defeat with a National Committee of Inquiry in 1978 that concluded that the "ALP's blue collar, male Anglo-Irish image increasingly handicaps its ability to appeal to emerging forces in contemporary Australia."[43]

---

[41] Shani Hartley, "Work Choices?" *Businessdate* 14, no. 1 (2006): 1.

[42] Former Australian Liberal Prime Minister John Howard—who led from 1996 until 2007 when his center-right Liberal–National Coalition government lost to the center-left ALP in the 2007 Australian federal election—and Canadian Conservative Prime Minister Stephen Harper, shared similar pro-corporate, anti-labor economic views that are consistent with their common ideological and ethnocultural backgrounds. In anticipation of Howard's first official visit to Canada following Harper's election, the *Australian* newspaper succinctly reported the fundamental Australian and Canadian differences: "Harper believes in a society that combines US enterprise and individualism with British traditions of order and co-operation. Howard believes the same, with a splash of Australian egalitarianism." David Nason, "Howard's New Best Friend," *The Australian* (Sydney), May 18, 2006. http://www.theaustralian.news.com.au. The different implications for Australia and Canada is that Howard used his majority government to reduce some of the most significant labor reforms ever achieved by Australian workers, while Harper's then-minority government prevented him from implementing similar legislation.

[43] Australian Labor Party, *National Committee of Inquiry Discussion Papers*, Australasian Political Studies Association Monograph, no. 23 (Adelaide, SA:

Clive Bean notes, "Since Labor also lost ground among members of the major Protestant denominations, the traditional differential remained, although slimmer, in terms of the stronger likelihood of Catholics, than Protestants, of voting Labor."[44]

In Australia, there is still a crucial role for third-party intervention even though its nature may have changed. According to William Brown, in Europe and elsewhere, a shift of emphasis has occurred from judicial to voluntary methods of dispute resolution, a trend which has seen the concurrent rise of an advisory function for third-party agencies that aims to prevent disputes.[45] For example, not only does Canada's Federal Mediation and Conciliation Service (FMCS) offer a "labor management partnership program," recent legislation has moved the New Zealand system toward an advisory and facilitative approach. Even the Irish Labour Relations Commission and the Northern Ireland Labour Relations Agency have each cultivated advisory services to promote best practices in dispute resolution and also in employment practice.[46] Thus, when the Australian electorate chose to bring back the ALP—as it did in 2007 with a triumphant victory—the pendulum swung back and reversed the trend because of perceived inconsistency with Australian cultural values.

In its 2007 campaign, the ALP, under the leadership of Prime Minister Kevin Rudd, had vowed to abolish the WorkChoices legislation, which it did after Rudd assumed power. The pendulum may continue swinging for a while, however, as the ALP was defeated in the 2013 federal election to Tony Abbott, the new leader of the Liberal Party, who became prime minister of another Australian Liberal–National Coalition.

Notwithstanding the current political climate in Australia, it should not be forgotten that fierce Irish influence was perpetuated by their socioeconomic status in the nineteenth and early twentieth centuries. As O'Farrell keenly observes,

> That Catholics were over-represented among Australia's poor is a historical truism, but it is usually related to an image of pious docility.

Flinders University of South Australia, 1979), 7. Quoted in Marian Sawer, "Women and Labor: A Question of Heartland?" in *The Machine: Labor Confronts the Future*, ed. John Warhurst and Andrew Parkin (Sydney, NSW: Allen & Unwin), 265.

[44] Clive Bean, "Who Now Votes Labor?" in *The Machine: Labor Confronts the Future*, ed. John Warhurst and Andrew Parkin (Sydney, NSW: Allen & Unwin), 81.

[45] William Brown, "Third Party Intervention Reconsidered: An International Perspective," *The Journal of Industrial Relations* 46, no. 4 (2004): 453.

[46] Ibid.

In fact, Catholic—and ex-Catholic—poverty at its most intense had a much harsher, uglier face contorted with resentment, even hatred, of all those who had wealth, security and status—their own clergy included. The venom and violence of these elements which had been repressed and denied by the more affluent seldom surfaced in attacks on the Catholic church, for the Protestant establishment offered better targets. But it existed, sometimes volatile, usually sullen, as a mood at the bottom of the fringes of Catholic society, where religious practice tailed off into apathy or hostility. It could be fiercely anti-clerical. Archbishop Kelly was to feel its scorching blast in 1918. Much of Archbishop Mannix's popularity derived from the burning sense of injustice and deprivation that dwelt in Melbourne's Catholic slums.[47]

The sense of inequality that fueled Australia's working class's antagonism toward the British Protestant leadership also helped push Australian Irish Catholics beyond the confines of their Irish Catholic communities. Labor unions and politics were the most logical and attainable areas to maximize their greatest impact for themselves and, in turn, the nation as a whole. In this way, their cultural influence spread throughout Australia.

Australian managers, therefore, must be able to recognize and contend with Australia's consequent lesser tolerance of power distance and the corollary impact on the relatively greater tolerance of labor's collective impulse. This is particularly true as the Australian manager becomes increasingly global having more interactions with superficially similar cultures like Canada. Likewise, Canadian managers may have less to be concerned about within the confines of Canadian industry. However, with the rise of globalization, which makes intercultural management an ever-present reality and concern, they too need to understand how the Canadian workforce's relatively greater toleration of power distance may have its limits when Canadian managerial talent, and their inevitable assumptions, move into other cultures like Australia.

*   *   *

Focusing on managerial culture, the underlying ethnocultural and socioeconomic influences that impacted on the behavior of managers

---

[47] Patrick O'Farrell, *The Catholic Church and Community: An Australian History*, 3rd rev. ed. (Kensington, NSW: New South Wales University Press, 1992), 263.

and workers in Australia and Canada have necessarily been explored. The approach being historical meant the populations considered were largely comprised of those of Anglo-Celtic origin, reflecting the largest contingent of migrant ancestry in each nation. These populations were substantial in both Australia and English Canada. In the period following the Second World War, however, increasing numbers from other ethnic populations came to both countries, ultimately giving rise to official policies of multiculturalism to reflect the evolving mosaics. Canada's official policy emerged first, while Australia was influenced by Canada's example and initiated its own policy some years later.[48] Indeed, the postwar period saw in both nations a greater respect for human rights in general, and minority rights in particular. Hence, political awareness of the greater ethnic diversity among the Australian and Canadian peoples was evident in progressive immigration and refugee programs and strategies. According to Canadian historian Freda Hawkins,

> Multiculturalism as a national policy is also an inevitable outcome of the broadening base of immigrant recruitment by Canada and Australia during this period, as well as of the adoption of universal, non-discriminatory immigration policies by Canada in 1962 and by Australia in 1973. Canada's 1981 census showed that 43.5 percent of her population was of British origin, 28.9 percent of French origin, and 27.6 percent of all other origins combined. In Australia, of course, the percentage of the population which is of British origin is far higher—about 77 percent.[49]

Immigrants, though continuing to preserve their ethnic heritages, have tended to accept prevailing cultural values of the countries where they settled—especially among subsequent generations of ethnic immigrants born and raised in Australia and Canada—their relative percentage among the general population, by the dawn of the twenty-first century, has undoubtedly risen. In light of the changing composition of the Australian and Canadian populations, therefore, future research should explore more recent developments in the cultural composition of the managerial populations of both nations in order to determine if any—or

---

[48] Peter Kivisto, *Multiculturalism in a Global Society* (Malden, MA: Blackwell Publishers, 2002), 110.
[49] Freda Hawkins, *Critical Years in Immigration: Canada and Australia Compared*, 2nd ed. (Montreal, QC & Kingston, ON: McGill-Queen's University Press, 1991), 214.

rather to what magnitude—subtle changes have occurred in each culture's dominant values.

Returning to a historical focus, however, these pages also provide a basis upon which further research can be conducted in order to investigate the prevalence of the Irish factor in industry, industrial disputes, trade union activity, and the general Australian culture. Likewise, though there does not appear to be a "Scottish factor" (or other ethnic factors) as uniquely or powerfully equivalent to Australia's Irish factor, further investigation would be useful to determine the full ramifications of Scottish influence on Canadian industry, politics, and general culture. As Canada and Australia are increasingly more culturally diverse, with strong contributions from, and influences by, several other ethnic groups (especially in the private sector, as the public sector management style was largely influenced by a colonial WASP elite), the influence of other significant communities—including, but not limited to, various Asian, Germanic, Jewish, and Slavic cultures—should also be explored. Perhaps in doing so, more specific "management styles" that link to ethnocultural background might be found.

Bibliography

Abella, Irving. "Canadian Congress of Labour." In *The Canadian Encyclopedia: Year 2000 Edition*, ed. James H. Marsh. Toronto, ON: McClelland & Stewart, 1999.

Adams, Michael. *Fire and Ice: The United States, Canada and the Myth of Converging Values*. Toronto, ON: Penguin, 2003.

Adler, N.J., and J.L. Graham. "Business Negotiations: Canadians are Not Just Like Americans." *Canadian Journal of Administrative Sciences* 4, no. 3 (1987): 211–38.

Ahmed, S.A. "Impact of Social Change on Job Values: A Longitudinal Study of Quebec Business Students." *Canadian Journal of Administrative Science* 7, no. 2 (1990): 12–24.

Ahmed, S.A., and J. Jabes. "A Comparative Study of Job Values of Business Students in France and English Canada." *Canadian Journal of Administrative Sciences* 5, no. 2 (1988): 51–62.

Ajzen, I., and M. Fishbein. *Understanding Attitudes and Predicting Social Behavior*. Englewood Cliffs, NJ: Prentice-Hall, 1980.

Akenson, Donald Harman. "Data: What is Known about the Irish in North America?" In *Ireland and Irish-Australia: Studies in Cultural and Political History*, ed. Oliver MacDonagh and W.F. Mandle, 1–17. London, UK: Croom Helm, 1986.

———. "Immigration and Ethnicity in New Zealand and the USA—the Irish Example." In *New Worlds? The Comparative History of New Zealand and the United States*, ed. Jock Phillips, 28–58. Wellington, NZ: Stout Research Centre, 1989.

———. "Irish Migration to North America, 1800–1920." In *The Irish Diaspora*, ed. Andy Bielenberg. New York, NY: Longman, 2000.

———. "Ontario: Whatever Happened to the Irish?" In *Immigration in Canada: Historical Perspectives*, ed. Gerald Tulchinsky, 86–134. Toronto, ON: Copp Clark Longman, 1994.

———. *Small Differences: Irish Catholics and Irish Protestants, 1815–1922*. Montreal, QC & Kingston, ON: McGill-Queen's University Press, 1988.

———. *The Irish in Ontario: A Study in Rural History*, 2nd ed. Montreal, QC & Kingston, ON: McGill-Queen's University Press, 1999.

Albinski, Henry S. "Australia and the United States." In *Australia: The Daedalus Symposium*, ed. Stephen R. Graubard, 395–420. North Ryde, NSW: Angus & Robertson, 1985.

———. *Canadian and Australian Politics in Comparative Perspective*. New York, NY: Oxford University Press, 1973. Cited in Chantrill.

Alexander, Malcolm, and Brian Galligan. "Australian and Canadian Comparative Political Studies." In *Comparative Political Studies: Australia and Canada*, ed. Alexander and Galligan, 1–11.

———, ed. *Comparative Political Studies: Australia and Canada*. Melbourne, VIC: Pitman, 1992.

Angus, H.F. "British Columbia." In Angus, *Canada and Her Great Neighbor*, 55–58.

——, ed. *Canada and Her Great Neighbor: Sociological Surveys of Opinions and Attitudes in Canada Concerning the United States*. New Haven, CT: Yale University Press, 1938.

——. "Canadian Nationalism." In Angus, *Canada and Her Great Neighbor*, 3–7.

Ashkanasy, Neal M. "A Cross-National Comparison of Australian and Canadian Supervisors' Attributional and Evaluative Responses to Subordinate Performance." *Australian Psychologist* 32, no. 1 (1997): 29–36.

——. "Studies of Cognition and Emotion in Organisations: Attribution, Affective Events, Emotional Intelligence and Perception of Emotion." *Australian Journal of Management* 27 (Special Issue, September 2002): 11–20.

Ashkanasy, Neal M., Edwin Trevor-Roberts, and Louise Earnshaw. "The Anglo Cluster: Legacy of the British Empire." *Journal of World Business* 37, no. 1 (2002): 28–39.

Atkinson, Alan. "Four Patterns of Convict Protest." *Labour History* 37 (November 1979): 28–51. Quoted in Quinlan and Gardner.

Atkinson, Tom, and Michael A. Murray. *Values, Domains and the Perceived Quality of Life: Canada and the United States*. Toronto, ON: Institute for Behavioural Research, York University, 1982.

Australian Associated Press. "Workplace Rally Attracts Thousands." *The Age* (Melbourne), November 30, 2006. http://www.theage.com.au/news/National/Workplace-rally-attracts-thousands/2006/11/30/1164777689657.html# (accessed May 18, 2014).

Australian Labor Party, *National Committee of Inquiry Discussion Papers*, Australasian Political Studies Association Monograph, no. 23 (Adelaide, SA: Flinders University, 1979). Quoted in Marian Sawer, "Women and Labor: A Question of Heartland?" In *The Machine: Labor Confronts the Future*, ed. John Warhurst and Andrew Parkin, 264–80. Sydney, NSW: Allen & Unwin, 2000.

Baer, Douglas E., and James E. Curtis. "French Canadian-English Canadian Differences in Values: National Survey Findings." *The Canadian Journal of Sociology* 9, no. 4 (1984): 405–27.

Ball, Terence, and Richard Dagger. *Political Ideologies and the Democratic Ideal*, 2nd ed. New York, NY: HarperCollins, 1995.

Ball, Terence, Richard Dagger, William Christian, and Colin Campbell. *Political Ideologies and the Democratic Ideal*, Canadian ed. Toronto, ON: Pearson Longman, 2006.

Barman, Jean. "The West Beyond the West: The Demography of Settlement in British Columbia." *Journal of Canadian Studies* 25, no. 4 (1990): 5–18.

Barry, Michael, and Nick Wailes. "Contrasting Systems? 100 Years of Arbitration in Australia and New Zealand." *The Journal of Industrial Relations* 46, no. 4 (2004): 403–47.

Bean, Clive. "Who Now Votes Labor?" In *The Machine: Labor Confronts the Future*, ed. John Warhurst and Andrew Parkin, 73–88. Sydney, NSW: Allen & Unwin, 2000.

Beilharz, Peter. "The Labourist Tradition and the Reforming Imagination." In *Australian Welfare: Historical Sociology*, ed. Richard Kennedy, 132–53. South Melbourne, VIC: Macmillan, 1989.

Bentham, Jeremy. *Introduction to the Principles of Morals and Legislation*. New York, NY: Hafner, 1948.

Berger, Carl. "An Introduction." In Goldwin Smith, *Canada and the Canadian Question*. Toronto, ON: University of Toronto Press, 1971.

Berton, Pierre. "The War of 1812." In *The Canadian Encyclopedia: Year 2000 Edition*, ed. James H. Marsh. Toronto, ON: McClelland & Stewart, 1999.

———. *Why We Act Like Canadians*. Toronto, ON: McClelland & Stewart, 1982.

Black, Conrad. *A Life in Progress*. Toronto, ON: Key Porter Books, 1993.

———. *A Matter of Principle*. Toronto, ON: McClelland & Stewart, 2011.

Blainey, Geoffrey. "Australia: A Bird's-Eye View." In *Australia: The Daedalus Symposium*, ed. Stephen R. Graubard, 1–28. North Ryde, NSW: Angus & Robertson, 1985.

Bliss, Michael. *A Living Profit: Studies in the Social History of Canadian Business, 1883–1911*. Toronto, ON: McClelland & Stewart, 1974.

———. *Northern Enterprise: Five Centuries of Canadian Business*. Toronto, ON: McClelland & Stewart, 1987.

———. *Right Honourable Men: The Descent of Canadian Politics from Macdonald to Mulroney*. Toronto, ON: HarperCollins, 1994.

Blockson, Charles L. *The Underground Railroad*. New York, NY: Prentice-Hall, 1987.

Blount, Frank, Bob Joss, and David Mair. *Managing in Australia*. Sydney, NSW: Landsdowne Publishing, 1999.

Bloy, Marjie. "Chartism: An Introduction." *The Victorian Web*. http://www.victorianweb.org/history/chartism.html (accessed November 15, 2005).

Bolton, Geoffrey. "The Irish in Australian Historiography." In *Australia and Ireland, 1788–1988: Bicentenary Essays*, ed. Colm Kiernan, 5–19. Dublin, Ireland: Gill and Macmillan, 1986.

Bothwell, Robert. "Lester Bowles Pearson." In *The Canadian Encyclopedia: Year 2000 Edition*, ed. James H. Marsh. Toronto, ON: McClelland & Stewart, 1999.

Brady, A. "The Province of Ontario." In Angus, *Canada and Her Great Neighbor*, 41–49.

Brennan, Niall. *The Politics of Catholics*. Melbourne, VIC: Hill Publishing, 1972.

Brett, Judith. "Class, Religion and the Foundation of the Australian Party System: A Revisionist Interpretation." *Australian Journal of Political Science* 37, no. 1 (2002): 39–56.

Brown, William. "Third Party Intervention Reconsidered: An International Perspective." *The Journal of Industrial Relations* 46, no. 4 (2004): 448–58.

Brym, Robert J., and Bonnie Fox. *From Culture to Power: The Sociology of English Canada*. Toronto, ON: Oxford University Press, 1989.

Bumsted, J.M. "Scots." In *The Canadian Encyclopedia: Year 2000 Edition*, ed. James H. Marsh. Toronto, ON: McClelland & Stewart, 1999.

Burke, Collean Z., and Vincent Woods, ed. *The Turning Point: Poems and Songs of Irish Australia*. Armidale, NSW: Kardoorair Press, 2001.

Cahill, A.E. "Cardinal Moran's Politics." *The Journal of Religious History* 15, no. 4 (1989): 525–31. Quoted in Smyth, "Reclaiming Community? From Welfare Society to Welfare State in Australian Catholic Social Thought."

Calder, Jenni. *Scots in Canada*. Edinburgh, UK: Luath Press, 2003.

Campbell, Colin. "On Intellectual Life, Politics, and Psychoanalysis: A Conversation with Gad Horowitz." Ed. Arthur Kroker and Marilouise Kroker, *CTheory*, a135 (2003). http://www.ctheory.net/articles.aspx?id=397 (accessed May 26, 2014).

Campion, Edmund. *Australian Catholics: The Contribution of Catholics to the Development of Australian Society.* Ringwood, VIC: Penguin, 1987.

Canadian Broadcasting Corporation. "The Loyalists." *Ideas.* Montreal, QC: CBC Enterprises and CBC Transcripts, 1983.

Cannadine, David. *Ornamentalism: How the British Saw Their Empire.* Oxford, UK: Oxford University Press, 2001.

Caterson, Simon. "Irish-Australian Attitudes." *Quadrant* 48, no. 11 (2004): 11–18.

Chanlat, A., and R. Bedard. "Managing in the Quebec Style: Originality and Vulnerability." *International Studies of Management and Organization* 21, no. 3 (1991): 10–37.

Chantrill, Paul. "Social Policy Development in Australia and Canada: Historical and Comparative Approaches." *Australian Canadian Studies* 17, no.1 (1999): 41–58.

Choquette, Robert. *Canada's Religions: An Historical Introduction.* Ottawa, ON: University of Ottawa Press, 2004.

Christian, William, and Colin Campbell. *Political Parties and Ideologies in Canada,* 3rd ed. Toronto, ON: McGraw-Hill Ryerson Ltd., 1990.

Clark, Andrew. *Stand and Deliver: Inside Canadian Comedy.* Toronto, ON: Doubleday, 1997.

Clark, Joe. *How We Lead: Canada in a Century of Change.* Toronto, ON: Random House Canada, 2013.

Clark, S.D. *Movements of Political Protest in Canada, 1640–1840.* Toronto, ON: University of Toronto Press, 1959. Quoted in Penner.

———. "The Canadian Community." In *Canada,* ed. G.W. Brown. Berkeley, CA: University of California Press, 1950.

Clement, Wallace. "Elites." In *The Canadian Encyclopedia: Year 2000 Edition,* ed. James H. Marsh. Toronto, ON: McClelland & Stewart, 1999.

———. "John Porter and the Development of Sociology in Canada." *Canadian Review of Sociology and Anthropology* 18, no. 5 (1981): 583–94.

Collins, Hugh. "Political Ideology in Australia: The Distinctiveness of a Benthamite Society." *Daedalus* 114 (1985): 147–69.

Conner, Patrick E., Boris W. Becker, Takashi Kakuyama, and Larry F. Moore. "A Cross-National Comparative Study of Managerial Values: United States, Canada and Japan." In *Advances in International Comparative Management,* ed. S. Benjamin Prasad and Richard B. Peterson, Vol. 8, 3–29. Greenwich, CT: JAI Press, 1993.

Considine, M. "The National Civic Council: Politics Inside Out." *Politics* 20, no. 1 (1985): 48–58. Quoted in Leach, *Political Ideologies: An Australian Introduction.*

Cook, Ian. *Liberalism in Australia.* South Melbourne, VIC: Oxford University Press, 1999.

Cox, Lloyd. "The Antipodean Social Laboratory, Labour and the Transformation of the Welfare State." *Journal of Sociology* 42, no. 2 (2006): 107–24.

Craven, Paul. *"An Impartial Umpire": Industrial Relations and the Canadian State, 1900–1911.* Toronto, ON: University of Toronto Press, 1980.

Dabscheck, Braham. "Arbitration and Relations Between the Parties." *The Journal of Industrial Relations* 46, no. 4 (2004): 385–99.

———. "The Slow and Agonising Death of the Australian Experiment with Conciliation and Arbitration." *The Journal of Industrial Relations* 43, no. 3 (2001): 277–93.

Dale, George. *The Industrial History of Broken Hill*. Melbourne, VIC: Fraser & Jenkinson, 1918. Quoted in Jeremy Mouat, "The Miners of Broken Hill, Waihi and Rossland: A Comparative Investigation." *Australian Canadian Studies* 8, no. 1 (1990): 47–73.

Davey, Gwenda Beed, and Graham Seal. *A Guide to Australian Folklore*. Sydney, NSW: Simon & Schuster, 2003.

Davidson, Alastair. *From Subject to Citizen: Australian Citizenship in the Twentieth Century*. Cambridge, UK: Cambridge University Press, 1997.

Davis, J.G. "Australian Managers: Cultural Myths and Strategic Challenges." In *Australia Can Compete: Towards a Flexible Adaptable Society*, ed. Ian C. Marsh, 103–19. Melbourne, VIC: Longman Cheshire, 1988.

Davis, Richard. "Irish and Australian Nationalism: The Sporting Connection: Football & Cricket." *Centre for Tasmanian Historical Studies Bulletin* 3, no. 2 (1991–1992): 47–59.

Deery, Stephen J., and David H. Plowman, *Australian Industrial Relations*, 3rd ed. Sydney, NSW: McGraw-Hill, 1991.

Deery, Stephen, David Plowman, and Janet Walsh. *Industrial Relations: A Contemporary Analysis*. Sydney, NSW: McGraw-Hill, 1997.

Dengate, John. "The Answer's Ireland." In Burke and Woods.

Devine, T.M. *Scotland's Empire: 1600–1815*. London, UK: Penguin, 2003.

Dion, Gérard. "Rand Formula." In *The Canadian Encyclopedia: Year 2000 Edition*, ed. James H. Marsh. Toronto, ON: McClelland & Stewart, 1999.

Dixson, Miriam. *The Imaginary Australian: Anglo-Celts and Identity—1788 to the Present*. Sydney, NSW: University of New South Wales Press, 1999.

Dodek, Adam. *The Canadian Constitution*. Toronto, ON: Dundurn, 2013.

Donaldson, Gordon. *The Prime Ministers of Canada*. Toronto, ON: Doubleday Canada, 1994.

Donn, Clifford B. "How Much Do Strikes Cost?" *The Australian* (Sydney), January 18, 1977. Cited in Niland.

Drucker, Peter F. *The Essential Drucker: The Best of Sixty Years of Peter Drucker's Essential Writings on Management*. New York, NY: HarperCollins, 2001.

Duncan, Bruce. "Santamaria and the Legacy of the Split: Fifty Years On." *The Australasian Catholic Record* 83 (April 2006): 140–53.

Dwivedi, O.P., and James Iain Gow. *From Bureaucracy to Public Management: The Administrative Culture of the Government of Canada*. Peterborough, ON: Broadview Press, 1999.

Eagleton, Terry. *The Truth About The Irish*. New York, NY: St. Martin's, 1999.

Eaton, Jack. *Comparative Employment Relations*. Cambridge, UK: Polity Press, 2000.

Ebbels, R.N. *The Australian Labor Movement, 1850–1907: Historical Documents*. Sydney, NSW: Hale & Iremonger, 1983.

Egri, Carolyn P., David A. Ralson, Cheryl S. Murray, and Joel D. Nicholson. "Managers in the NAFTA Countries: A Cross-Cultural Comparison of Attitudes Toward Upward Influence Strategies." *Journal of International Management* 6, no. 2 (2000): 149–71.

Elliott, Bruce S. *Irish Migrants in the Canadas: A New Approach*. Montreal, QC & Kingston, ON: McGill-Queen's University Press, 1988.

Emy, Hugh V. *The Politics of Australian Democracy: Fundamentals in Dispute*, 2nd ed. South Melbourne, VIC: Macmillan, 1978.

Encel, S. *Equality and Authority: A Study of Class, Status and Power in Australia*. Melbourne, VIC: Cheshire, 1970.

England, George W. "Managers and Their Value Systems: A Five-Country Comparative Study." *Columbia Journal of World Business* 13, no. 2 (1978): 33–44.

———. "Personal Value Systems of American Managers." *Academy of Management Journal* 10, no. 1 (1967): 53–68.

———. *The Manager and His Values: An International Perspective from The United States, Japan, Korea, India, and Australia*. Cambridge, MA: Ballinger Publishing Company, 1975.

Evans, A. Margaret MacLaren. "The Scot as Politician." In *The Scottish Tradition in Canada*, ed. Reid, 273–301.

Evans, Tim. *Compulsory Voting in Australia*. Australian Electoral Commission, 2006. http://www.aec.gov.au/pdf/voting/compulsory_voting.pdf (accessed January 30, 2007).

Fazio, R.H. "How Do Attitudes Guide Behavior?" In *Handbook of Motivation and Cognition: Foundation of Social Behavior*, ed. R.M. Sorrentino and E.T. Higgens. New York, NY: Guilford, 1986.

Feather, N.T. "Attitudes Toward High Achievers and Reactions to Their Fall: Theory and Research Concerning Tall Poppies." In *Advances in Experimental Social Psychology*, Vol. 26, ed. Mark Zanna, 1–73. New York, NY: Academic Press, 1993.

———. "Attitudes Toward High Achievers, Self-Esteem, and Value Priorities for Australian, American, and Canadian Students." *Journal of Cross-Cultural Psychology* 29, no. 6 (1998): 749–59.

———. "Authoritarianism and Attitudes towards High Achievers." *Journal of Personality and Social Psychology* 65 (1993): 152–64.

———. "Devaluing Achievement Within a Culture: Measuring the Cultural Cringe." *Australian Journal of Psychology* 45, no. 3 (1993): 182–88.

———. "Values and National Identification: Australian Evidence." *Australian Journal of Psychology* 46, no. 1 (1994): 35–40.

———. *Values in Education and Society*. New York, NY: Free Press, 1975.

Feather, N.T., and I.R. McKee. "Global Self-Esteem and Attitudes Toward the High Achiever for Australian and Japanese Students." *Social Psychology Quarterly* 56, no. 1 (1993): 65–76.

Feather, Norman T., and John G. Adair. "National Identity, National Favoritism, Global Self-Esteem, Tall Poppy Attitudes, and Value Priorities in Australian and Canadian Samples." In *Latest Contributions to Cross-Cultural Psychology*, ed. J.-C. Lasry, J. Adair, and K. Dion, 42–61. Lisse, The Netherlands: Swets & Zeitlinger, 1999.

Finlayson, Iain. *The Scots*. London, UK: Constable, 1987.

Foote, Geoffrey. *The Labour Party's Political Thought: A History*, 3rd ed. New York, NY: St. Martin's Press, 1997.

Ford, Patrick. *Cardinal Moran and the A.L.P.* Melbourne, VIC: Melbourne University Press, 1966.

Francis, Diane. *Merger of the Century: Why Canada and America Should Become One Country*. Toronto, ON: HarperCollins, 2013.

Galbraith, Gordon S. "British Columbia." In *The Provincial Political Systems: Comparative Essays*, ed. David J. Bellamy, Jon H. Pammett, and Donald C. Rowat, 62–75. Toronto, ON: Methuen, 1976.

Galbraith, John Kenneth. *The Scotch*. Boston, MA: Houghton Mifflin, 1964.

Gascoigne, John. "Catholicism, Australia and a Wider World: The Historiographical Legacy of Patrick O'Farrell and Tony Cahill." *The Australasian Catholic Record* 83, no. 2 (2006): 131–39.

Gavin, Bea. "A Sense of Irishness." *Psychodynamic Counselling* 7, no. 1 (2001): 83–102.

Gibson, Sarah Katherine. "Self-Reflection in the Consolidation of Scottish Identity: A Case Study in Family Correspondence 1805–50." In *Canada and the British World: Culture, Migration, and Identity*, ed. Phillip Buckner and R. Douglas Francis, 29–44. Vancouver, BC: UBC Press, 2006.

Gill, Stewart D. " 'The Sword in the Bishop's Hand': Father William Peter MacDonald, A Scottish Defender of the Catholic Faith in Upper Canada." *Canadian Catholic Historical Association, Study Sessions* 50 (1983): 437–452.

Grnak, Anthony, John Hughes, and Douglas Hunter. *Building the Best: Lessons from Inside Canada's Best Managed Companies*. Toronto, ON: Penguin, 2006.

Guillen, Mauro F. *Models of Management: Work, Authority, and Organization in a Comparative Perspective*. London, UK, and Chicago, IL: The University of Chicago Press, 1994.

Hachey, Thomas E. "From Free State to Republic, 1922–1996." In Thomas E. Hachey, Joseph M. Hernon, Jr., and Lawrence J. McCaffrey, *The Irish Experience: A Concise History*, rev. ed., 167–267. Armonk, NY: M.E. Sharpe, 1996.

Hak, Gordon. *The Left in British Columbia: A History of Struggle*. Vancouver, BC: Ronsdale Press, 2013.

Hamilton, Celia. "Irish Catholics of New South Wales and the Labor Party, 1890–1910." *Historical Studies of Australia and New Zealand* 8, no. 31 (1958): 254–67.

Hampden-Turner, Charles, and Fons Trompenaars. *The Seven Cultures of Capitalism*. London, UK: Judy Piatkus, 1993.

Harper, Stephen J. *A Great Game: The Forgotten Leafs & the Rise of Professional Hockey*. Toronto, ON: Simon & Schuster Canada, 2013.

Harris, Philip R., Robert T. Moran, and Sarah V. Moran. *Managing Cultural Differences: Global Leadership Strategies for the Twenty-First Century*, 6th ed. Amsterdam, The Netherlands: Elsevier/Butterworth-Heinemann, 2004.

Harrison, Trevor W. "Canadian Alliance," *The Canadian Encyclopedia*, http://www.thecanadianencyclopedia.ca/en/article/canadian-alliance/ (accessed May 18, 2014).

———. "Reform Party of Canada," *The Canadian Encyclopedia* http://www.thecanadianencyclopedia.ca/en/article/reform-party-of-canada/ (accessed May 18, 2014).

Hartley, Shani. "Work Choices?" *Businessdate* 14, no. 1 (2006): 1–4.

Hartz, Louis. *The Founding of New Societies: Studies in the History of the United States, Latin America, South Africa, Canada, and Australia*. New York, NY, and London, UK: Harcourt Brace Jovanovich, 1964.

———. *The Liberal Tradition in America: An Interpretation of American Political Thought since the Revolution*. New York, NY: Harcourt Brace & Company, 1955.

Hawkins, Freda. *Critical Years in Immigration: Canada and Australia Compared*, 2nd ed. Montreal, QC & Kingston, ON: McGill-Queen's University Press, 1991.

Heap, James L. "Conceptual and Theoretical Problems in the Vertical Mosaic." *Canadian Review of Sociology & Anthropology* 9, no. 2 (1972): 176–87.

Henderson, R. *Ninety Years in the Master's Service.* Edinburgh, UK: Andrew Elliott, 1911. Quoted in Hans Mol, *The Faith of Australians.*

Heron, Craig. "Punching the Clock." *Canadian Dimension* 14, no. 3 (1979): 26–29.

———. *The Canadian Labour Movement*, 2nd ed. Toronto, ON: James Lorimer & Company, 1996.

Higley, John, Desley Deacon, and Don Smart. *Elites in Australia.* London, UK: Routledge, 1979.

Hill, J.D. "Australian Industrial Relations and the 'National Character.' " In *Australian Labour Relations: Readings*, ed. G.W. Ford, J.M. Hearn, and R.D. Lansbury, 4th ed., 179–201. Melbourne, VIC: Macmillan, 1987.

Hirst, John. "Egalitarianism." In *Australian Cultural History*, ed. S.L. Goldberg and F.B. Smith, 58–77. Cambridge, UK: Cambridge University Press, 1988.

Hofstede, Geert. *Cultures and Organizations: Intercultural Cooperation and its Importance for Survival.* London, UK: McGraw-Hill, 1991.

———. *Culture's Consequences: Comparing Values, Behaviors, Institutions, and Organizations Across Nations*, 2nd ed. Thousand Oaks, CA: Sage, 2001.

Hogan, Michael. *The Sectarian Strand. Religion in Australian History.* Ringwood, VIC: Penguin, 1987.

Horowitz, Gad. *Canadian Labour in Politics.* Toronto, ON: University of Toronto Press, 1968.

———. "Conservatism, Liberalism, and Socialism in Canada: An Interpretation." In *Canada's Origins: Liberal, Tory, or Republican?* ed. Janet Ajzenstat and Peter J. Smith. Ottawa, ON: Carleton University Press, 1995.

House, Robert, Mansour Javidan, Paul Hanges, and Peter Dorfman. "Understanding Cultures and Implicit Leadership Theories Across the Globe: An Introduction to Project GLOBE." *Journal of World Business* 37, no. 1 (2002): 3–10.

Iacovetta, Franca. "The Irish in Nineteenth-Century Canada: Class, Culture, and Conflict." In *A Nation of Immigrants: Women, Workers, and Communities in Canadian History, 1840s–1860s*, ed. Franca Iacovetta, Paula Draper, and Robert Ventresca. Toronto, ON: University of Toronto Press, 1998.

Iacovetta, Franca, Michael Quinlan, and Ian Radforth. "Immigration and Labour: Australia and Canada Compared." *Labour/Le Travail* 38 (Spring 1995): 90–115.

Inglis, K.S. "Multiculturalism and National Identity." In *Australian National Identity*, ed. Charles A. Price, 13–32. Canberra, ACT: The Academy of the Social Sciences in Australia, 1991.

———. "Religious Behaviour." In *Australian Society: A Sociological Introduction*, ed. A.F. Davies and S. Encel, 2nd ed. Melbourne, VIC: F.W. Cheshire, 1970.

Inkeles, Alex. *National Character.* New Brunswick, NJ: Transaction Publishers, 1997.

Isaac, J.E. "Equity and Wage Discrimination." Paper presented to 51st ANZAAS Congress, May 12, 1981. Quoted in Deery and Plowman, *Australian Industrial Relations.*

Jackson, Steven J., and Pam Ponic. "Pride and Prejudice: Reflecting on Sport Heroes, National Identity, and Crisis in Canada." *Culture, Sport, Society* 4, no. 2 (2001): 43–62.

Jupp, James. *Australian Party Politics*, 2nd ed. Carlton, VIC: Melbourne University Press; London, UK, and New York, NY: Cambridge University Press, 1968.

————. "The ALP and the Ethnic Communities." In *The Machine: Labor Confronts the Future*, ed. John Warhurst and Andrew Parkin, 250–63. Sydney, NSW: Allen & Unwin, 2000.

Kabanoff, Boris, Nerina L. Jimmieson, and Malcolm J. Lewis. "Psychological Contracts in Australia: A 'Fair Go' or a 'Not-So-Happy Transition'?" In *Psychological Contracts in Employment: Cross-National Perspectives*, ed. Denise M. Rousseau and Rene Schalk, 29–46. Thousand Oaks, CA: Sage Publications, 2000.

Kalbach, Warren E. "Ethnic Diversity: Canada's Changing Cultural Mosaic." In Kalbach and Kalbach, *Perspectives on Ethnicity in Canada*, 59–72.

Kalbach, Madeline A., and Warren E. Kalbach, ed. *Perspectives on Ethnicity in Canada: A Reader*. Toronto, ON: Harcourt Canada, 2000.

Kalin, Rudolf, and John W. Berry. "Ethnic and Civic Self-Identity in Canada." In Kalbach and Kalbach, *Perspectives on Ethnicity in Canada*, 88–105.

Kanji, Mebs, and Neil Nevitte. "Who are the Most Deferential—Canadians or Americans?" In *Canada and the United States: Differences that Count*, ed. David M. Thomas, 2nd ed., 121–41. Orchard Park, NY: Broadview Press, 2000.

Kay, F. George. *The British: From Pre-History to the Present Day*. London, UK: Frederick Muller, 1969.

Kealey, G.S., and G. Patmore, ed. *Canadian and Australian Labour History: Towards a Comparative Perspective*. Sydney, NSW: Australian Society for the Study of Labour History; St John's, NF: Committee on Canadian Labour History, in association with *Australian Canadian Studies*, 1990.

Keating Mary A., and Gillian S. Martin. "Leadership and Culture in the Republic of Ireland." In *Culture and Leadership Across the World: The GLOBE Book of In-Depth Studies of 25 Societies*, ed. J.S. Chhokar, F.C. Brodbeck, and R.J. House, 361–396. New York, NY: Lawrence Erlbaum, 2008.

Keenleyside, Hugh. *Canada and the United States: Some Aspects of the History of the Republic and the Dominion*. Port Washington, NY: Kennikat Press, 1929.

Kiernan, Colm. "Introduction." In *Ireland and Australia*, ed. Colm Kiernan, 5–11. Dublin, Ireland: Mercier Press, 1984.

Kivisto, Peter. *Multiculturalism in a Global Society*. Malden, MA: Blackwell Publishers, 2002.

Kluckhohn, C. *Values and Value Orientations in the Theory of Action*. Cambridge, MA: Harvard University Press, 1951.

Krahn, Harvey J., and Graham S. Lowe. *Work, Industry & Canadian Society*, 4th ed. Scarborough, ON: Nelson, 2002.

Lang, J.T. *I Remember*. Sydney, NSW: Invincible Press, 1949.

————. *The Turbulent Years*. Sydney, NSW: Alpha Books, 1970.

Lansbury, Russell D., and Robert Spillane. *Organisational Behaviour: The Australian Context*, 2nd ed. Melbourne, VIC: Longman Cheshire, 1991.

Leach, Robert. *Political Ideologies: An Australian Introduction*. Melbourne, VIC: MacMillan, 1988.

————. *Political Ideology in Britain*. New York, NY: Palgrave, 2002.

Leitch, Gillian I. "Scottish Identity and British Loyalty in Early-Nineteenth-Century Montreal." In *A Kingdom of the Mind: How the Scots Helped Make Canada*, ed. Peter E. Rider and Heather McNabb, 211–226. Montreal, QC & Kingston, ON: McGill-Queen's University Press, 2006.

Leuprecht, Christian. "The Tory Fragment in Canada: Endangered Species?" *Canadian Journal of Political Science* 36 (2003): 401–16.

Lipset, Seymour Martin. *American Exceptionalism: A Double-Edged Sword.* New York, NY: W.W. Norton & Company, 1996.

———. *Continental Divide: The Values and Institutions of the United States and Canada.* New York, NY: Routledge, 1990.

———. "Social Class." In *Social Stratification: Canada,* ed. James E. Curtis and William G. Scott, 19–43. Scarborough, ON: Prentice-Hall, 1973.

———. *The First New Nation: The United States in Historical Perspective.* New York, NY: Basic Books, 1963.

Lipset, Seymour Martin, and Gary Marks. *It Didn't Happen Here: Why Socialism Failed in the United States.* New York, NY: W.W. Norton & Company, 2000.

Lipset, Seymour Martin, and Noah M. Meltz. *The Paradox of American Unionism: Why Americans Like Unions More Than Canadians Do But Join Much Less.* Ithaca, NY: ILR Press, 2004.

Lovejoy, Arthur O. *The Great Chain of Being,* new ed. Cambridge, MA: Harvard University Press, 2005.

Lowe, Graham S. "The Rise of Modern Management in Canada." *Canadian Dimension* 14 (December 1979): 32–38.

Lyons, Mark. "Sectarianism." In *The Oxford Companion to Australian History,* rev. ed., ed. Graeme Davison, John Hirst, and Stuart Macintyre, 583–84. South Melbourne, VIC: Oxford University Press, 2001.

MacGinley, M.E.R. "The Irish in Queensland: An Overview." In *The Irish Emigrant Experience in Australia,* ed. John O'Brien and Pauric Travers, 103–19. Dublin, Ireland: Poolbeg Press, 1991.

Macintyre, Stuart. "Alfred Deakin." In *Australian Prime Ministers,* ed. Michelle Grattan, 36–53. Sydney, NSW: New Holland, 2000.

———. "Holt and the Establishment of Arbitration: An Australian Perspective." *New Zealand Journal of Industrial Relations* 12, no. 3 (1987): 151–9. Quoted in Barry and Wailes.

———. *Militant: The Life and Times of Paddy Troy.* Sydney, NSW: George Allen & Unwin, 1984.

Mackay, Donald. *Flight from Famine.* Toronto, ON: McClelland & Stewart, 1990.

MacLean, R. "The Highland Catholic Tradition in Canada." In Angus, *Canada and Her Great Neighbor,* 93–117.

Maddox, Graham. "The Australian Labor Party." In *Political Parties in Australia,* ed. Graeme Starr, Keith Richmond, and Graham Maddox, 159–316. Richmond, VIC: Heinemann Educational Australia, 1978.

Madgwick, R.B. *Immigration into Eastern Australia, 1788–1851.* Sydney, NSW: Sydney University Press, 1969.

Mandle, W.F. *Winners Can Laugh: Sport and Society.* Ringwood, VIC: Penguin, 1974. Quoted in Richard Davis, "Irish and Australian Nationalism."

Markey, Raymond. *The Making of the Labor Party in New South Wales, 1890–1900.* Kensington, NSW: New South Wales University Press, 1988.

Mathews, John. *Catching the Wave: Workplace Reform in Australia.* Ithaca, NY: ILR Press, 1994.

Mayo, Elton. *The Social Problems of an Industrial Civilization.* Boston, MA: Division of Research, Graduate School of Business Administration, Harvard University, 1945.

McAllister, Ian. *Political Behaviour: Citizens, Parties and Elites in Australia.* Melbourne, VIC: Longman Cheshire, 1992.

McCallum, Ronald Clive. "Deregulating Australian Labour Relations: Collective Bargaining Reforms within Australia's System of Compulsory Conciliation and Arbitration." *Queen's Papers in Industrial Relations*. Kingston, ON: Queen's University IR Centre, 1990.

McCarrey, M.W., S. Ahmed, Y. Gasse, G. Conrad, S. Seguin, M. Major, and P. Mercier. "The Subjective Culture of Public Sector Women and Men Managers: A Common Instrumental/Expressive Value Orientation, or Two Different Worlds?" *Canadian Journal of Administrative Sciences* 6, no. 2 (1989): 54–61.

McConville, Chris. *Croppies, Celts & Catholics: The Irish in Australia*. Caulfield East, VIC: Edward Arnold Publishers, 1987.

McCrae, Robert R., and Oliver P. John. "An Introduction to the Five-Factor Model and Its Applications." *Journal of Personality* 60, no. 2 (1992): 175–215.

McCrae, Robert R., Michelle S.M. Yik, Paul D. Trapnell, Michael Bond, and Delroy Paulhus. "Interpreting Personality Profiles Across Cultures: Bilingual, Acculturation, and Peer Rating Studies of Chinese Undergraduates." *Journal of Personality and Social Psychology* 74, no. 4 (1998): 1041–55.

McDonald, Lynn. *The Party That Changed Canada: The New Democratic Party, Then and Now*. Toronto, ON: Macmillan, 1987.

McDonald, Robert A.J. *Making Vancouver: Class, Status, and Social Boundaries, 1863–1913*. Vancouver, BC: UBC Press, 1996.

McGoogan, Ken. *How the Scots Invented Canada*. Toronto, ON: HarperCollins, 2010.

McKenzie, Nick. "Victoria to Introduce New Human Rights Charter." December 21, 2005. http://www.abc.net.au/am/content/2005/s1535533.htm (accessed May 18, 2007).

McKinlay, Brian. *The ALP: A Short History of the Australian Labor Party*. Richmond, VIC: Heinemann Publishers, 1981.

McLean, Marianne. "Peopling Glengarry County: The Scottish Origins of a Canadian Community." In *Immigration in Canada: Historical Perspectives*, ed. Gerald Tulchinsky. Toronto, ON: Copp Clark Longman, 1994.

———. *The People of Glengarry: Highlanders in Transition, 1745–1820*. Montreal, QC & Kingston, ON: McGill-Queen's University Press, 1991.

McMahon, Anne, and Nicholas Jans. "Organisation Behavior in Australia." In *Dynamics in Australian Public Management: Selected Essays*, ed. Alexander Kouzmin and Nicholas Scott, 354–66. South Melbourne, VIC: Macmillan, 1990.

McMahon, Anthony. "Australian Catholics and the Development of Professional Social Services in Australia." In *Proceedings of the 400 Years of Charity Conference*, September 11–13, 2001, University of Liverpool, UK. http://www.vahs.org.uk/vahs/papers/mcmahon.pdf (accessed May 14, 2014).

McRae, K.D. "Louis Hartz's Concept of the Fragment Society and its Application to Canada." *Etudes Canadiennes/Canadian Studies* 5 (1978): 17–30.

———. "The Structure of Canadian History." In Louis Hartz, *The Founding of New Societies*, 219–62. New York, NY, and London, UK: Harcourt Brace Jovanovich, 1964.

Miner, Brad. *The Concise Conservative Encyclopedia*. New York, NY: Free Press, 1996.

Mitchell, Richard J. "Solving the Great Social Problem of the Age: A Comparison of the Development of State Systems of Conciliation and Arbitration in Australia and Canada." In *Canadian and Australian Labour History: Towards a Comparative Perspective*, ed. Kealey and Patmore, 47–80.

———. "State Systems of Conciliation and Arbitration: The Legal Origins of the Australasian Model." In *Foundations of Arbitration: The Origins and Effects of State Compulsory Arbitration, 1890–1914*, ed. Stuart Macintyre and Richard Mitchell, 74–103. Melbourne, VIC: Oxford University Press, 1989.

Mol, Hans. *The Faith of Australians*. Sydney, NSW: Allen & Unwin, 1985.

Moore, Christopher. *The Loyalists: Revolution, Exile, Settlement*. Toronto, ON: McClelland & Stewart, 1994.

Morrison, Terry, Wayne A. Conway, and George A. Borden. *Kiss, Bow, Shake Hands: How to Do Business in Sixty Countries*. Holbrook, MA: B. Adams, 1994.

Morton, Desmond. *A Military History of Canada: From Champlain to Kosovo*, 4th ed. Toronto, ON: McClelland & Stewart, 1999.

Mosler, David. *Australia, The Recreational Society*. Westport, CT: Praeger, 2002.

Mouat, Jeremy. "The Miners of Broken Hill, Waihi and Rossland: A Comparative Investigation." *Australian Canadian Studies* 8, no. 1 (1990): 47–73.

Mutch, Alistair. "The Institutional Shaping of Management: In the Tracks of English Individualism." *Management & Organizational History* 1, no. 3 (2006): 251–71.

Naegele, Kaspar. "Canadian Society: Some Reflections." In *Canadian Society*, ed. B.R. Blishen, F.E. Jones, K.D. Naegele, and John Porter, 1–53. Toronto, ON: Macmillan, 1961.

Nairn, N.B. *The "Big Fella": Jack Lang and the Australian Labor Party 1891–1949*. Melbourne, VIC: Melbourne University Press, 1986.

———. *Civilising Capitalism: The Beginnings of the Australian Labor Party*. Melbourne, VIC: Melbourne University Press, 1989.

Nason, David. "Howard's New Best Friend," *The Australian* (Sydney), May 18, 2006. http://www.theaustralian.news.com.au

Newman, Peter C. "Business Elites." In *The Canadian Encyclopedia: Year 2000 Edition*, ed. James H. Marsh. Toronto, ON: McClelland & Stewart, 1999.

———. *The Canadian Establishment: Volume One*. Toronto, ON: Penguin, 1999.

———. *The Canadian Establishment, Volume Two: The Acquisitors*. Toronto, ON: Penguin, 1999.

———. *The Canadian Revolution: From Deference to Defiance*. Toronto, ON: Penguin, 1995.

Ng, Ignace, and Dennis Maki. "Trade Union Influence on Human Resource Practices," *Industrial Relations* 33, no. 1 (1994): 121–35.

Nichols, T. *Ownership, Control and Ideology: An Enquiry into Certain Aspects of Modern Business Ideology*. London, UK: Allen and Unwin, 1969.

Niland, John. *Collective Bargaining and Compulsory Arbitration in Australia*. Kensington, NSW: University of New South Wales Press, 1978.

O'Farrell, Patrick. *The Catholic Church and Community: An Australian History*, 3rd rev. ed. Kensington, NSW: New South Wales University Press, 1992.

———. *The Irish in Australia: 1788 to the Present*. Notre Dame, IN: Indiana University Press, 2000.

O'Grady, Shawna, and Henry W. Lane. "Culture: An Unnoticed Barrier to Canadian Retail Performance in the USA." *Journal of Retailing and Consumer Services* 4, no. 3 (1997): 159–70.

O'Sullivan, John. *The President, The Pope, and The Prime Minister*. Washington, DC: Regnery, 2006.

Page, Michael. *The Prime Ministers of Australia.* Sydney, NSW: Robertsbridge, 1988.

Palmer, Bryan. "Labour Protest and Organization in Nineteenth Century Canada, 1820–1890." *Labour/Le Travail* 20 (Fall 1987): 61–83.

Parkin, Andrew. "Party Organisation and Machine Politics: The ALP in Perspective." In *Machine Politics in the Australian Labor Party,* ed. Andrew Parkin and John Warhurst. Sydney, NSW: George Allen & Unwin, 1983.

Partington, Geoffrey. *The Australian Nation: Its British and Irish Roots.* New Brunswick, NJ: Transaction Publishers, 1997.

Partlon, Anne. " 'Singers Standing On The Outer Rim': Writing About the Irish in WA." *Studies in Western Australian History* 20 (2000): 188–94.

Patmore, Greg. *Australian Labour History.* Melbourne, VIC: Longman Cheshire, 1991.

Peabody, Dean. "Nationality Characteristics: Dimensions for Comparison." In *Personality and Person Perception Across Cultures,* ed. Yueh-Ting Lee, Clark R. McCauley, and Juris G. Draguns, 65–84. Mahwah, NJ, and London, UK: Lawrence Erlbaum, 1999.

Peeters, Bert. " 'Thou Shalt Not Be a Tall Poppy': Describing an Australian Communicative (and Behavioral) Norm." *Intercultural Pragmatics* 1, no. 1 (2004): 71–92.

Penner, Norman. *The Canadian Left: A Critical Analysis.* Scarborough, ON: Prentice-Hall, 1977.

Pepper, Stephen C. *The Sources of Value.* Berkeley, CA: University of California Press, 1958.

Peters, Helen, and Robert Kabacoff. *Shared Beginnings and Diverse Histories: A Comparison of Leadership Behavior in Five Countries with Anglo-Saxon Based Cultures.* Portland, ME: Management Research Group, 1999.

Phillips, Walter W. *Defending "A Christian Country": Churchmen and Society in New South Wales in the 1880s and After.* St. Lucia, QLD: University of Queensland, 1981. Quoted in Hans Mol, *The Faith of Australians.*

Pike, Douglas. *Paradise of Dissent.* London, UK: Longmans Green, 1957. Quoted in Hans Mol, *The Faith of Australians.*

Porter, John. "Conceptual and Theoretical Problems in the Vertical Mosaic: A Rejoinder," *Canadian Review of Sociology & Anthropology* 9, no. 2 (1972): 188–89.

———. *The Vertical Mosaic: An Analysis of Social Class and Power in Canada.* Toronto, ON: University of Toronto Press, 1965.

Prentis, Malcolm D. *The Scots in Australia: A Study of New South Wales, Victoria and Queensland, 1788 to 1900.* Sydney, NSW: Sydney University Press, 1983.

Price, Matt. "Mate, It's Just Not On." *The Australian* (Sydney), August 19, 2005. http://www.theaustralian.news.com.au/.

Purcell, John. "Mapping Management Styles in Employee Relations." *Journal of Management Studies* 24, no. 5 (1987): 533–48.

Quinlan, Michael, and Margaret Gardner. "Strikes, Worker Protest, and Union Growth in Canada and Australia, 1815–1900: A Comparative Analysis." *Labour/ Le Travail* 36 (Fall 1995): 175–208.

Reid., W. Stanford. "The Scot and Canadian Identity." In *The Scottish Tradition in Canada,* ed. Reid, 302–10.

———. "The Scottish Background." In *The Scottish Tradition in Canada,* ed. Reid, 1–14.

———. "The Scottish Protestant Tradition," in *The Scottish Tradition in Canada*, ed. Reid, 118–36.

———, ed. *The Scottish Tradition in Canada*. Toronto, ON: McClelland & Stewart, 1976.

Reilly, J.T. *Fifty Years in Western Australia*. Perth, WA: Sands and McDougall, 1908. Quoted in Mol, *The Faith of Australians*.

Renwick, George W. *A Fair Go For All: Australian/American Interactions*. Yarmouth, ME: Intercultural Press, 1991.

———. *InterAct: Guidelines for Australians and North Americans*. Yarmouth, ME: Intercultural Press, 1980.

Richards, Eric. "Irish in Australia." In *The Oxford Companion to Australian History*, rev. ed., ed. Graeme Davison, John Hirst, and Stuart Macintyre, 353–54. South Melbourne, VIC: Oxford University Press, 2001.

Rickard, John. *H.B. Higgins: The Rebel as Judge*. Sydney, NSW: Allen and Unwin, 1984. Quoted in Beilharz, "The Labourist Tradition and the Reforming Imagination."

Rokeach, M. *Beliefs, Attitudes and Values*. San Francisco, CA: Jossey-Bass, 1968.

Rosecrance, Richard N. "The Radical Culture of Australia." In *The Founding of New Societies*, ed. Louis Hartz , 275–318. New York, NY, and London, UK: Harcourt Brace Jovanovich, 1964.

Rubenstein, Bill. "The Top Wealth-holders of New South Wales in 1830–44." *The Push from the Bush* 8 (December 1980).

Sack, J., and T. Lee. "The Role of the State in Canadian Labour Relations." *Relations Industrielles* 44 (1989): 195–221. Cited in McCallum.

Saha, Sudhir K., David O'Donnell, Thomas N. Garavan, and Stan Mensik. "An International Comparison of Managerial Values and HR Decision-Making: How are Canadian Managers Different from Irish and Australian Managers?" *Proceedings of the Eastern Academy of Management Conference* (San Jose, Costa Rica, 2001), *"Managing in a Global Economy IX,"* in press.

Santamaria, B.A. *Against The Tide*. Melbourne, VIC: Oxford University Press, 1981.

Savicki, Victor. *Burnout Across Thirteen Cultures: Stress and Coping in Child and Youth Care Workers*. Westport, CT: Praeger, 2002.

Sawer, Marian. "Women and Labor: A Question of Heartland?" In *The Machine: Labor Confronts the Future*, ed. John Warhurst and Andrew Parkin, 264–80. Sydney, NSW: Allen & Unwin, 2000.

Saywell, John. *Canada: Pathways to the Present*. Toronto, ON: Stoddart Publishing, 1999.

Schermerhorn, John R., James G. Hunt, and Richard N. Osborn. *Basic Organizational Behavior*, 2nd ed. New York, NY: John Wiley & Sons, 1998.

Schwartz, S.H. "Beyond Individualism/Collectivism: New Cultural Dimensions of Values." In *Individualism and Collectivism: Theory, Method, and Applications*, ed. U. Kim, H.C. Triandis, C. Kagitcibasi, S.-C. Choi, and G. Yoon, 85–119. Thousand Oaks, CA: Sage, 1994.

Sharp, Ilsa. *Culture Shock! Australia: A Guide to Customs and Etiquette*. Portland, OR: Graphic Arts Center Publishing Company, 2000.

Sharp, Paul F. *Whoop-Up Country: The Canadian-American West, 1865–1885*. Minneapolis, MN: University of Minnesota Press, 1955.

Shaw, J.W. "In Defence of the Collective: New South Wales Industrial Relations in the 21st Century." *Journal of Industrial Relations* 39, no. 3 (1997): 388–404.

Shaw, Matthew. *Great Scots!: How the Scots Created Canada.* Winnipeg, MB: Heartland Associates, 2003.

Singh, Gangaram. "National Culture and Union Density." *The Journal of Industrial Relations* 43, no. 3 (2001): 330–39.

Smart, Russell C., and Mollie S. Smart. "Group Values Shown in Preadolescents' Drawings in Five English-Speaking Countries." *The Journal of Social Psychology* 97, no. 1 (1975): 23–37.

Smith, Adam. *An Inquiry into the Nature and Causes of the Wealth of Nations.* London, UK: W. Strahan and T. Cadell, 1776.

Smith, G.M. "The Prairie Provinces." In Angus, *Canada and Her Great Neighbor,* 50–54.

Smith, Goldwin. *Canada and the Canadian Question.* Toronto, ON: University of Toronto Press, 1971.

Smyth, Paul. "Reclaiming Community? From Welfare Society to Welfare State in Australian Catholic Social Thought." *Australian Journal of Politics and History* 49, no. 1 (2003): 17–30.

Spann, Richard N. "The Catholic Vote in Australia." In *Catholics and the Free Society: An Australian Symposium,* ed. H. Mayer. Melbourne, VIC: Cheshire, 1961. Quoted in Mol, *Faith of Australians.*

Stewart, H.L. "The Maritime Provinces." In Angus, *Canada and Her Great Neighbor,* 27–31.

Stewart, Walter. *The Life and Political Times of Tommy Douglas.* Toronto, ON: McArthur & Co., 2003.

Storey, John, and Nicolas Bacon. "Individualism and Collectivism: Into the 1990s." *The International Journal of Human Resource Management* 4, no. 3 (1993): 665–84.

Strachan, Alex. "And the Winner is . . . Tommy Douglas." *The Vancouver Sun,* November 30, 2004, C6.

Struthers, James, and Ronald E. Mendelsohn. "Federalism and the Evolution of Social Policy and the Welfare State." In *Federalism in Canada and Australia: Historical Perspectives, 1920–1988,* ed. Bruce W. Hodgins, John J. Eddy, Shelagh D. Grant, and James Struthers, 228–260. Peterborough, ON: The Frost Centre for Canadian Heritage and Development Studies, Trent University, 1989.

Sutton-Smith, B. "A Development Structural Account of Riddles." Paper presented to meetings of the Society for Research in Child Development, Philadelphia, PA, March 31, 1973. Cited in Smart and Smart.

Taft, R., and K.F. Walker. "Australia." In *The Institutions of Advanced Societies,* ed. A.M. Rose, 131–91. Minneapolis, MN: University of Minnesota Press, 1958.

Taylor, Charles. *Radical Tories: The Conservative Tradition in Canada.* Toronto, ON: Anansi Press, 1982.

Taylor, F.W. "The Principles of Scientific Management." In *Classics of Organization Theory,* ed. J.M. Sharfritz and J.S. Ott, 2nd ed., 66–81. Chicago, IL: The Dorsey Press, 1987.

Taylor, Graham D., and Peter A. Baskerville. *A Concise History of Business in Canada.* Toronto, ON: Oxford University Press, 1994.

Terrill, Ross. *The Australians: The Way We Live Now.* Sydney, NSW: Doubleday, 2000. Quoted in Peeters.

Thompson, Elaine. *Fair Enough: Egalitarianism in Australia.* Sydney, NSW: University of New South Wales Press, 1994.

Tien, H.Y. *Social Mobility and Controlled Fertility*. New Haven, CT: College and University Press, 1965. Quoted in Mol.

Toner, Peter M. "Irish." In *The Canadian Encyclopedia: Year 2000 Edition*, ed. James H. Marsh. Toronto, ON: McClelland & Stewart, 1999.

Trahair, Richard C.S. *The Humanist Temper: The Life and Work of Elton Mayo*. New Brunswick, NJ: Transaction Books, 1984.

Trainor, Luke. *British Imperialism and Australian Nationalism: Manipulation, Conflict and Compromise in the Late Nineteenth Century*. Cambridge, UK: Cambridge University Press, 1994.

Trevor-Roberts, Edwin, Neal M. Ashkanasy, and Jeffrey C. Kennedy. "The Egalitarian Leader: A Comparison of Leadership in Australia and New Zealand." *Asia Pacific Journal of Management* 20, no. 4 (2003): 517–40.

Triandis, Harry C. *Individualism & Collectivism*. Boulder, CO: Westview, 1995.

Triandis, H.C., and M. Gelfand. "Converging Measurement of Horizontal and Vertical Individualism and Collectivism." *Journal of Personality and Social Psychology* 74, no. 1 (1998): 118–28.

Triandis, H.C., G. Martin, C.H. Hui, J. Lisansky, and V. Ottati. "Role Perceptions of Hispanic Young Adults." *Journal of Cross-Cultural Psychology* 15, no. 3 (1984): 297–320.

Trompenaars, Fons, and Charles Hampden-Turner. *Riding the Waves of Culture: Understanding Cultural Diversity in Global Business*. New York, NY: McGraw-Hill, 1998.

Tulchinsky, Gerald, ed. *Immigration in Canada: Historical Perspectives*. Toronto, ON: Copp Clark Longman, 1994.

Turner, Ian. *In Union is Strength: A History of Trade Unions in Australia, 1788–1983*, 3rd ed., revised and updated by Leonie Sandercock. Melbourne, VIC: Thomas Nelson, 1983.

Twopenny, R.E.N. *Town Life in Australia*. London, UK: Elliott Stock, 1883. Quoted in Mol, *Faith of Australians*.

Verge, Pierre. "How Does Canadian Labour Law Fare in a Global Economy?" *The Journal of Industrial Relations* 42, no. 2 (2000): 275–94.

Vigod, B.L. "Canada First." In *The Canadian Encyclopedia: Year 2000 Edition*, ed. James H. Marsh. Toronto, ON: McClelland & Stewart.

Walker, Franklin A. *Catholic Education and Politics in Upper Canada*. Toronto, ON: Nelson, 1955.

Ward, Russel. *The Australian Legend*. Melbourne, VIC: Oxford University Press, 1958.

Warhurst, John, and Andrew Parkin, ed. *The Machine: Labor Confronts the Future*. Sydney, NSW: Allen & Unwin, 2000.

Weber, Max. *The Protestant Ethic and the Sprit of Capitalism*. London, UK: Allen and Unwin, 1930.

Westwood, Robert I., and Barry Z. Posner. "Managerial Values Across Cultures: Australia, Hong Kong and the United States." *Asia Pacific Journal of Management* 14, no. 1 (1997): 31–66.

Wilson, David A. *The Irish in Canada*. Ottawa, ON: Canadian Historical Association, 1989.

Wiseman, Nelson. "A Note on 'Hartz-Horowitz and Twenty.' " *Canadian Journal of Political Science* 21, no. 4 (1988): 795–806.

———. "Provincial Political Cultures," in *Provinces: Canadian Provincial* Politics, ed. Christopher Dunn, 2nd ed., 21–56. Peterborough, ON: Broadview Press, 2006.

———. "The Pattern of Prairie Politics." *Queen's Quarterly* 88, no. 2 (1981): 298–315.

Wolak, Arthur J. "Australian and Canadian Managerial Values: a Review." *International Journal of Organizational Analysis* 17, no. 2 (2009): 139–59.

———. "Australia's 'Irish Factor' as a Source of Cultural Difference from Canada." *Australasian Canadian Studies* 25, no. 1 (2007): 85–116.

Wood, Greg. "A Cross Cultural Comparison of the Contents of Codes of Ethics: USA, Canada and Australia." *Journal of Business Ethics* 25, no. 4 (2000): 287–98.

Wood, Patricia K. "Defining 'Canadian': Anti-Americanism and Identity in Sir John A. MacDonald's Nationalism." *Journal of Canadian Studies* 36, no. 2 (2001): 49–69.

Woods, N. *Industrial Conciliation and Arbitration in New Zealand.* Wellington, NZ: Government Printer, 1963. Quoted in Barry and Wailes.

Wren, Daniel A. *The History of Management Thought,* 5th ed. Hoboken, NJ: John Wiley, 2005.

Wright, Christopher. *The Management of Labour: A History of Australian Employers.* Melbourne, VIC: Oxford University Press, 1995.

Wright, David. *Australians At Work: Harmony and Conflict in Industrial Relations.* Carlton, VIC: Pitman, 1980.

Index

Abbott, Tony, 288
above award bargaining, 261,
  261n185
Act of Union of 1707 (England and
  Scotland), 81n116
Act of Union of 1840 (Upper and
  Lower Canada), 16
Adams, Michael, 53
affirmative action, 164
Against the Tide (Santamaria), 227
agreeableness, Canada, 49–53
Akenson, Donald, 72, 116
Albinski, H. S., 216
Alger, Horatio, 142
Amalgamated Engineering Union
  (AEU), 154–5, 156
American Creed, 56, 164, 165
American dream, 24
American Exceptionalism (Lipset), 164
American Federation of Labor
  (AFL), 233–4
American Labor Union (ALU), 236,
  237
American liberalism, 152
American Revolution, 81, 82, 133
ancien régime, 187
Anglicans, 12, 105, 106, 108, 110, 136
Anglo-Celtic, 1, 17, 175
  culture, 4, 62, 75, 139, 141,
    144, 161
  distinctions, 127–9, 275
  identity, 58, 91
  origins, 1, 40, 42, 114, 204, 270
Anglo Cluster, 18, 125–6, 127
Angus, Henry, 76
anti-Americanism, Canada, 60–3
Anzac Day, 122
arbitration, state approach to, 209–19
Artificial Fertilisers and Chemical
  Workers Union, 157
ascription-achievement, 180
assimilation, Irish community in
  Canada, 69–70, 72

atheistic socialism, 224
Atkinson, Tom, 271
Australia. *See also* Irish factor
  comparing Irish of, and
    Canada, 74–5
  cultural dimensions, 5t
  ethnoreligious identity of working
    class, 98–106
  identity, 14–15
  Iraq war in 2003, 52
  Irish Catholics, 15–16, 63–9
  jail for convicts, 1, 17, 63, 67–8
  national identification, 43–4
  ruling elites, 92–8
  sport, Irish and irreverence, 46–9
  transmigration of British
    values, 55–60
  values, 22–3, 180–2
Australian Commonwealth, 213, 214
Australian Conciliation and
  Arbitration Commission, 286
Australian Federation, 230, 251, 257
Australian Industrial Relations
  Commission (AIRC), 286
Australian Labor Party (ALP), 14–15,
  47, 59, 93, 111, 112, 158, 163, 167
  leadership, 222–4
  local culture influence, 204
  working-class Catholics, 278
The Australian Legend (Ward), 64, 117
Australian Rules Football, 47
Australian Socialist League, 112
Australian Workers' Union
  (AWU), 157
Australia Post, 148
Australia Post and
  Telecommunications Union, 149
authority, 9
  American, Canadian and
    Australian, 31–2
  deference by Canadians, 28–9, 35,
    45–6, 49–53
  quest for achievement, 27

Industrial Workers of the World, 163, 237
Inglis, Ken, 107
Inkeles, Alex, 41
inner-directedness, 5–6, 39
Institute for Behavioural Research, 271
insurance industry, Canada, 240–1
Inter-Colonial Trade Union Congress, 251
International Labour Organisation, 250
Iraq War, 50, 52
Ireland, 115
  collectivism, 132–3
  cultural dimensions, 5t
  union membership, 206
I Remember (Lang), 174
Irish Catholic
  Australia, 1, 9 10, 15 16, 66–9, 115–16, 217–19, 288–9
  Australian egalitarianism, 168–75
  British Protestant and, 69, 98–106
  Canada, 10–13, 69–73, 100, 117
  comparing Australia vs. Canada, 74–5
  individualism-collectivism, 129
  leadership in group identity, 106–13
  solidarity, 276–7
Irish factor, 8–9, 225
  assessing Australia's, 274–9
  Australian culture, 63–9, 91, 114
  Australian radicalism, 221–33
  Canada, 70, 89
Irish Free State, 132, 276
Irish Home Rule, 219
The Irish in Australia (O'Farrell), 115
Irish Labour Relations Commission, 288
Irish National Readers, 71–2
Irishness, 13
Irish Protestants, assimilation, 13–14
Irish Republican Brotherhood, 73n95
Irishtown, Sydney, 172
Irvine, William, 162
Isaac, J. E., 261
Israel, Canada and, 50–1
Ivens, William, 162

James II (king), 79
Jessop, John, 71
job redesign, 148, 154
Joss, Bob, 124
Judeo-Christian values, 18
Jupp, James, 226
Just-in-Time (JIT), 154

Kalbach, Warren, 75
Kay, F. George, 61–2
Keating, Paul, 47, 174–5, 231
Keenleyside, Hugh, 61
Kelly, Ned, 74, 127, 277
Kiernan, Colm, 14, 69
King, William Lyon Mackenzie, 84, 239, 241, 246
Kingsley, Charles, 195
Kingston, Charles Cameron, 212
Kingston Scots, 200
Knights of Labor, 260n180
knocking, 25, 26, 46, 91, 114, 168, 270
Knox, John, 14

labor factionalism, 15
laborism, 197, 253
labor power
  Australian compulsory arbitration, 250–4
  Australian utilitarian tradition, 254–9
  Canadian compulsory investigation, 243–50
  collective bargaining, 259–68
  conciliation and arbitration, 209–19
  Irish factor in Australian radicalism, 221–33
  labor radicalism, 220–1
  labor relations, 259–68
  legalism, 254–9
  origins of Canada's political culture, 233–43
  rise of labor in political culture, 205–9
  union density in developed nations, 206t
laissez-faire economics, 166, 186, 198
Lalor, Peter, 277
Land Convention, July 1857, 257

Printed and bound in the United States of America